LABYRINTH OF NATIONALISM COMPLEXITIES OF DIPLOMACY

Essays in Honor of Charles and Barbara Jelavich

Edited by

Richard Frucht

Slavica Publishers, Inc.

Slavica publishes a wide variety of scholarly books and textbooks on the languages, peoples, literatures, cultures, folklore, history, etc. of the USSR and Eastern Europe. For a complete catalog of books and journals from Slavica, with prices and ordering information, write to:

Slavica Publishers, Inc.
PO Box 14388
Columbus, Ohio 43214

ISBN: 0-89357-233-0.

Printed in the United States of America.

For Charles and Barbara Jelavich:

Teachers, Scholars, Mentors, Colleagues, Friends

TABLE OF CONTENTS

I. Introduction 9

II. Charles and Barbara Jelavich: A Bibliographical Appreciation 13

III. Chronological Bibliography 55

IV. National Economy or Economic Nationalism in the Bohemian Crownlands 1848-1914 69

V. Karel Havlíček in Czech Historiography and the Czech Intellectual Tradition 84

VI. Habsburg Educational Reform, National Consciousness, and the Roots of Loyalism: West-Galicia During the Period of Neo-Absolutism 104

VII. Miklós Horthy and the Jews of Hungary 121

VIII. The Camp of National Unity: A Polish Experiment in "State Nationalism," 1936-1939 143

IX. Tradition and Rite in Transylvania: Historic Tensions Between East and West 161

X. Ceauşescu's Nationalism: Ancient Dacian Translated into Modern Romanian 180

XI. On the Condition of Women in Wartime Slovakia and Croatia 190

XII. The Eastern Question and the European States System: Linkage From a Small Power Perspective 214

XIII. Europeans, Ottoman Reformers, and the *REAYA*: A Question of Historical Focus 234

XIV. The Hotel Lambert and French Foreign Policy in the Balkans 1840-1848 249

XV. The Romanian Dilemma: Russia and the Double Election of Cuza 275

XVI. A Perilous Liaison: Russo-Romanian Relations in 1877 290

XVII. The Ending of Hostilities on the Romanian Front: The Armistice Negotiations at Focşani, December 7-9, 1917 318

XVIII. Evolving Soviet Views of the Nazi-Soviet Pact 331

XIX. Lessons of the East European Revolutions of 1989 361

XX. List of Contributors 375

INTRODUCTION

Teaching presents a unique problem: year-in and year-out the students never appear to age. We face the same age group every semester. That can create the obviously false illusion that despite the fact that we teach new ideas, concepts, and theories, use new books, materials, and methods, and we actively try to pursue our craft from classroom to archive, we also somehow never change. Of course this is nonsense. Where would we historians be without the passage of time? Time allows us the distance to reflect and analyze. Yet, when a few students of Charles and Barbara Jelavich got together at a conference in 1988 at, ironically enough, Indiana University, someone raised the question of the Jelaviches' retirement. Frankly, many of us had never even considered such a notion, that the day might indeed come when their active tenure at Indiana University might end. What seemed implausible when we sat in their seminars now was something we would at least have to contemplate. Fortunately, as of this writing, it is still something that remains for the future (and the Jelaviches themselves) to decide, and even then it would only be from Indiana University itself, never from the pursuit of scholarship to which they have dedicated their lives. But a logical question soon followed: how were we going to honor them?

The answer, of course, was obvious and, for historians, most fitting--a *Festschrift*. Great scholars have long been honored with a volume dedicated to them and their work by their students and/or colleagues. Charles and Barbara Jelavich are certainly deserving of such accolades, for they, along with a few others, were pioneers in modern East European studies, individuals who not only left a significant mark on the field (and, in fact, continue to do so), but, in many cases, showed where the field was in the first place. Eastern Europe was in many respects "discovered" in the 1950s by these scholars for it was they who found meaning and substance in lands often overlooked by others. The field has grown and matured because they not only led, but they inspired others to follow. Those efforts should not go unrecognized.

To produce a *Festschrift* for Charles and Barbara Jelavich, however, was a daunting challenge that also presented a fundamental problem. Who should be asked to contribute? No answer proved to be entirely satisfactory. To invite selected members of the academic community opened the obvious danger of exclusion; someone, no matter how deserving, would be left off "the list," thereby inviting resentment. Furthermore, this would have required asking the Jelaviches to name those they wished to contribute, thus forcing them to make difficult, unenviable, and frankly impossible choices. As such, the decision was made instead to turn to their former students. As Paul and Jean Michelson explain in the conclusion of their "Bibliographical Appreciation," the Jelaviches were more than mere scholars; they were also mentors who opened the field to young graduate students eager to follow in the path they had set. I thus set out to contact those who had obtained their degrees under the guidance of the Jelaviches. While I hope that the lists I obtained were complete and accurate, if anyone was overlooked, it was purely accidental and I sincerely apologize for the oversight. Obviously not all former Jelavich students are represented here. Many regretted not having anything ready. Others felt that their work did not fit the volume's themes. Frankly, had everyone asked submitted an article, this would be but the first volume in a much larger project. But, whether submitting an article or not, everyone asked to be represented in spirit.

There was never a doubt as to the themes of the book: nationalism and diplomacy, pillars of the Jelaviches' scholarly pursuits over the last four decades. Of course, no matter how closely one seeks to ensure strict adherence to a theme, works such as this are always somewhat eclectic. In a field as diverse as "Eastern Europe," which, after all, is a misnomer itself--albeit sometimes convenient--for Central and Southeastern Europe, such a collection will naturally be broad-ranging. But in that diversity, the expansive nature of the Jelaviches' own work is truly reflected--as the Michelsons' essay will show. The interests of the Jelaviches were hardly narrow, and neither are those of their students.

Unfortunately, the realities of publishing in the 1990s means that few publishers are willing to produce such a work. However, I received an enthusiastic response from Charles Gribble at Slavica Publishers. He provided the encouragement to proceed with the project. Therefore, he must be the first to be acknowledged, for without his support this volume might never have appeared.

Thanks must go to each of the contributors for their patience in seeing this project through, as well as their speedy responses to my often frantic correspondence.

I would also be remiss if I did not mention again the countless former Jelavich students who sent along their encouragement and support even if they did not have anything ready to contribute at the moment.

My sincere thanks also go to Tracie Knapp, my secretary for the American Association for the Advancement of Slavic Studies' Public Education Project which I directed the past two years. A computer "whiz," she provided the technical support--that is, coaching--that enabled this project (read: the editor) to join the computer, camera-ready age. In addition, I must express my appreciation to my graduate student Tanya Dunlap who graciously volunteered to help "proof" the text. And then there is my wife, Su, who served not only as an editorial consultant but also as a "shrink" whenever problems arose.

And finally, our profoundest thanks go to Charles and Barbara Jelavich. Without them there certainly would not be this modest tribute, of course. But, more importantly, without their years of dedication to the study of Eastern Europe and to their students, the "field" would have suffered. "We," their students, have been inspired by their knowledge and made richer by their friendship. So to Charles and Barbara this book is dedicated with pride, gratitude, and warmth.

Richard Frucht
Northwest Missouri State University
July 1992

CHARLES AND BARBARA JELAVICH: A BIBLIOGRAPHICAL APPRECIATION

Paul E. and Jean T. Michelson
Huntington College

I.

It might appear unseemly or premature for the students of Charles and Barbara Jelavich to claim that the work of their teachers has not only been formative but decisive in the scholarly development of Russian and East European studies in the United States and as a field of study generally. Unseemly because they were and are our mentors. Premature because they are still in the prime of their academic lives with, we may be permitted to wish, many more scholarly contributions yet to come.

On the other hand, as should be clear from the review which follows of the Jelavich *oeuvre*, such reservations have force only for those burdened with exaggerated sensibilities or professional jealousies. Charles and Barbara Jelavich richly deserve their pre-eminent reputation both in the United States and abroad on the basis of their original research, their considerable scholarly production, their tireless and generous teaching and guidance of students and graduate students over more than four decades, their preoccupation with the life and advancement of Habsburg and East European studies, and their continued support for, encouragement of, and friendship with the majority of those in the field, including the leading scholars in Eastern and Central Europe itself.[1]

However, it is not the intention of this essay, in the main, to focus on the personal element of the contribution of Charles and Barbara Jelavich to their field, students, and scholarship, though sometimes this is unavoidable. Rather, it is to examine here their published work, thematically and chronologically. It is hoped that this will not only illuminate the contribution of the Jelaviches to East European studies in the United States and elsewhere, but will also assist in the urgent task now confronting all of us in assessing and reassessing what such studies have accomplished in the last four decades and where they should go in the immediate future. Charles and Barbara Jelavich certainly deserve recognition for the fine people that they are, but this is a matter perhaps best left for personal reflection and expression. There is no question, however, that their scholarly activity stands on its own as a major part of the very substantial foundations that have been created for and in our field since 1945. This essay, thus, hopes to outline, in a very preliminary way, that activity in its richness and detail. On the other hand, the essay is an expository appreciation, not a critical analysis, that is, it is designed to present the work of Charles and Barbara Jelavich, not to critique it, and to make it more accessible through providing a comprehensive bibliography.[2]

II.

Eastern Europe and Russia, especially the former, are the areas to which Charles and Barbara Jelavich have devoted their scholarly lives. Just how have they conceptualized this once and again chaotic region? And what is its significance--is it worth the study and scholarly effort? Charles Jelavich's preface to the Joint Committee on Slavic Studies survey of East Central and Southeastern European studies is a concise summary:[3]

1) This region deserves attention because it is a fascinating

> historical mosaic influenced by divergent political, social, economic, religious, cultural, and linguistic developments over the centuries...a unique political, social, and economic laboratory whose significance for the contemporary world cannot be overestimated.

2) From a comparative point of view, it is useful because its diversity comprises

> at least a dozen distinct national groups, [that] have been influenced and shaped by the major movements of European civilization: by classical and Christian Rome, Byzantium and the Orthodox church, the Ottoman Turks and Islam, the Renaissance, the Reformation, the Enlightenment, nationalism, socialism, and the industrial revolution.

3) Finally, though greatly affected by their imperial neighbors (Russian, Soviet, Habsburg, Ottoman, and German), the people of this region preserved their identities, made significant contributions to European civilization,[4] and constituted "not only an interesting subject for comparative study, but will be of great influence in the future on the political and economic decisions of other countries."

And yet, "despite the extreme interest and importance of events in Eastern Europe in both the past and present, the area...has not been adequately studied."[5] The reasons for this neglect have been many and varied,[6] but certainly the need and the challenge are clear. To address this problem was a scholarly task assumed by the Jelaviches very early on. This, of course, raises other questions and problems. Do the countries of the region constitute a single "area" of study? What is their relationship to the West? What is their relationship to the peoples further east, of the former Russian Empire and former Soviet Union? Indeed, the relative lack of progress in East European studies, in the Jelaviches' view, is due in part 1) to the fact that the area has always been too greatly subordinated to, and submerged by, Russian and Soviet studies, something which has been especially to the detriment of the non-Slavic peoples, and 2) to the lack of unifying or central factors needed to make this an "area" in the strict sense of the term.[7]

It was the Balkans, rather than Eastern Europe as a whole, that the Jelaviches saw as having an arguable unity, which explains, perhaps, their concentration on Southeastern Europe.[8] Whereas Eastern Europe is just too diverse to form a coherent entity, "the Balkan peninsula does represent a unity in its historical, social, economic, political, and cultural development, especially since the era of liberation from Ottoman control."[9] Particularly this is true of the influence of their common historical heritage (Classical, Byzantine, Ottoman, Habsburg) and their "mutual desire to escape from foreign rule and to achieve the material standards of life enjoyed by the Western nations." All of this contributed to similar characteristics, habits of mind, institutions, and patterns of development and transition sufficient to make this region one that could reasonably be viewed as a whole and from a comparative standpoint.[10]

Put another way, the Jelaviches argue, it is precisely history, with its striking continuities and severe discontinuities, that makes the "seven Balkan peoples--the Albanians, Bulgarians, Croatians, Greeks, Romanians, Serbians, and Slovenes--all of whom have a historical base of equal or greater antiquity than that of the western European states" a unity and a *bona fide* area of study, despite the fact that unlike "the western European medieval states, the historical continuity of Balkan national development was interrupted by a long period of subjugation to outside rule."[11] And even that was crucial since its main manifestation, the Ottoman conquest, was, in the Jelaviches' opinion, "the great event that shaped the future life of all the Balkan people." As they stress:

> this period of almost five centuries marked the submergence but never the complete annihilation of national awareness. The Ottoman government did not attempt to assimilate or destroy the Christian people. Although the Balkan kingdoms disappeared, national identity was preserved through the church, the languages, and popular culture. The memory of the past was never completely erased.[12]

When the age of nationalism and revolution dawned and unfolded in the nineteenth century, it paradoxically also contributed further to making the region an "area;" throughout the peninsula, the epoch saw "not only the revival of national feeling among the Balkan peoples, but also the growth of awareness of their economic, social, and political backwardness and the first attempts to remedy this situation." This led, in turn, to the "demise of the two great imperial powers of central and southeastern Europe [and] marked the final victory of the national principle for the organization of the political life of the area."[13]

At the same time, the Jelaviches underline, all the new states emulated Western models and, despite local variations:

> became constitutional monarchies with highly centralized administrative systems. The concentration of power in the capital city often meant the destruction

> of systems of autonomous local government that had functioned throughout the Turkish period. In practice this shift also created a situation in which politics was in fact in the hands of a small percentage of the population and one that became increasingly separated from the mass of the people.[14]

Other characteristic patterns appeared as well. The Jelaviches summarize:

> Balkan subordination to foreign dictation resulted primarily from geography rather than from choice, and the effects were unfortunate for the new states. The temptation for each Balkan government to cooperate with a great power against a neighbor and the necessity of maintaining a high level of armament were the direct results of the fact that the peninsula was a prime area of world tension. The percentage of national income devoted by each nation to war was extremely high. In fact, these states spent more on arms on a per capita basis that did the great powers.[15]

Even given these commonalities in both the past and the study of Southeast Europe, the difficulties are still myriad since "the Balkans appear to be a puzzle of confusing complexity."[16] And, though the "fascination of the area has always lain in the contradictions and conflicts of its history," we need to remember that "the very conditions which appear romantic or exciting to the student or the casual observer are those which have made unusually difficult the lives of the people directly involved."[17] For this reason, both the semi-humorous stereotypes of "Balkan" and their violent counterpoints also need amendment and modification in popular imagery and scholarly investigation.[18]

In the end, Southeastern Europe "deserves a larger place in modern historical studies" because of its past and present importance, its role in world power competition, and its nature as:

> in a very real sense a testing ground for alternative systems. In the past two centuries the Balkans have been a laboratory in which some of the more elusive aspects of national and liberal forms of political organization and economic development could be observed....[19]

And, as such, it is far from exhausting its importance or utility.

Few people have been so well qualified professionally and personally to work in this laboratory or have made such significant efforts toward helping the region find its larger place in the world of historical scholarship as Charles and Barbara Jelavich. Working as a team, through travel, research, and persistent scholarly effort, they have developed a thorough, intimate, and empathetic acquaintance not only with the histories, lives, and cultures of the principal Balkan countries (Romania, Bulgaria, Yugoslavia, and Greece), but also with the empires which so deeply influenced their histories: the Russian, Austrian, and Turkish. Let us turn now to that work.

III.

The contributions made by Charles and Barbara Jelavich to East European studies are not merely theoretical, pedagogical, or editorial. As even a cursory look at the bibliography which accompanies this study shows, their work has been substantial on every level from the detailed and painstaking study of voluminous unpublished and archival materials, to superb monographic treatises, to exceptionally readable syntheses, to concise popularizations that accurately assist the effort to register the findings of scholarship in the consciousness of audiences larger than the relatively restrained circle of East European specialists. Their work falls into two broad categories: 1) approaches to Balkan studies generally; and 2) their own specialized studies. We begin here with their more general contributions.

In looking at the work of Charles and Barbara Jelavich on the Balkans and their contribution to Southeast European studies, it now seems obvious that the Jelavich-inspired and edited volume on

The Balkans in Transition[20] played a significant and pivotal role--along with Robert Lee Wolff's *The Balkans in Our Times*[21] and L. S. Stavrianos' *The Balkans since 1453*[22]--in the creation and maturation of the second and third generations of American specialists on the Balkans. The volume was the result of the 1960 Berkeley Center for Slavic and East European Studies conference on the Balkans, which, in turn, was partly an outgrowth of Charles' long-term interest in the area and its resources such as library holdings, graduate training, and research needs of the field.[23] In the late 1950s, he had, in fact, been asked by the Joint Committee on Slavic Studies to lead a needs assessment and study of libraries and research centers.[24]

Not only did the conference, the first of its kind in the United States, provide a rich opportunity for dialogue on the progress, problems, and needs of the area, *The Balkans in Transition* became an essential resource work for budding young scholars in the field, then and now, as its reprinting in 1974 testifies. The conference and book's stress on "developments common to the Balkans as a whole and not characteristic only of some individual states"[25] was an important one, while the effort to view the region panoramically both showed what could be done, as well as what needed to be done. Geopolitics, the Ottoman legacy, modernization, religion in Balkan life, the influence of the West, nationalism, and historical continuities were only a few of the themes addressed by this Jelavich-inspired and directed enterprise.

This led in the mid-1960s to an even more ambitious and massive effort. Charles Jelavich had been a driving force behind activities by the Joint Committee on Slavic Studies to assess and further develop the field. He was now asked by the American Council of Learned Societies and the Social Science Research Council to chair a special effort to tackle the problems and needs of East European studies as a whole, "to examine the state of American scholarship on the countries and cultures of East Central and Southeast Europe, and take leadership in planning the stimulation and development of such studies."[26]

This demanding and often thankless task resulted in 1969 in a volume on *Language and Area Studies: East Central Europe and Southeastern Europe. A Survey*, edited by Charles Jelavich, and two collateral bibliographical volumes edited by Paul Horecky.[27] These works unquestionably played a key role in the expansion of research and funding in East European area studies in the 1970s and 1980s. And, not surprisingly, substantial sections in these volumes were from the Jelaviches, including "History" in the former volume and "Yugoslavia: History," in one of the latter.[28] In addition, Charles wrote the extensive study on "Graduate Training and Research Needs," which constituted the report's comprehensive agenda for the future.[29]

It would be interesting and informative, now more than two decades later, to review where we have gone since then, but in any case, it is certain that a lot less would have been done had it not been for this work spearheaded by the Jelaviches.[30] In 1986-1987, when Charles served as president of the American Association for the Advancement of Slavic Studies, he did return to some of these matters. His presidential address, "East European Studies Today,"[31] provided further reflections on developments and problems facing the field. Though many significant accomplishments had been registered since 1945 (expanded exchange programs, new journals, establishment of various research bodies and centers), the continued annexation of East European studies to Soviet studies, in his view, seriously "distorted our understanding of East-Central Europe and Southeastern Europe" and continues to do so to the present. This is illustrated by the usual exclusion of Greece and Austria and the inclusion of East Germany in the field. It also had led to a perverse kind of "current events" focus on these countries as interest waxes and wanes with crisis and tension in one or another of the states in the area, which in turn leads to an obscuring of long-term issues.[32]

Furthermore, the "identity crisis" of the area has been deepened by an increasing compartmentalization as various national studies groups tend to become more ingrown and indifferent to each other. This is compounded by the perennial language issue: language study is vital, but presents inevitable pressures for narrowing scope and concentration. He concluded by stressing that we must make renewed efforts to "establish the importance of maintaining the integrity of our area," to "study it in the light of its own inherent and unique qualities," and to "recognize the critical importance of language study." Otherwise, our field will not "gain the recognition it rightfully deserves."[33]

On another plane, the development of Southeast European studies has been significantly advanced by the efforts of Charles and Barbara Jelavich to deal more generally and comprehensively with the history of the Balkans. In 1965, there appeared the first in a series of works which they produced over the next two decades that not only summarized what we knew about the area, but also cogently organized and reorganized this material while sifting it for insights and integrative characterizations. Space and purpose do not permit here an extended analysis and comparison of these works and ideas, but a brief review should suffice to give the general lines and themes of their thinking and study. The 1965 volume, *The Balkans*, was their initial synthesis.[34] This was followed in 1977 by their joint volume (in the University of Washington History of East Central Europe series) entitled *The Establishment of the Balkan National States, 1804-1920*,[35] and then in 1983 by Barbara's *History of the Balkans*.[36]

In each case, their purposes were different. The 1965 volume was designed to present a thematic epitome of Balkan history focusing on nationalism, great power interference in the area, and the problem of backwardness. The 1977 study, the first of its kind, concentrated on the nationalism theme--obviously a primary emphasis of the Jelaviches' perspective on the area, but this time presented in much greater depth and detail and in a much narrowed time frame--substantially unravelling the working out of the national problem in nineteenth century Southeastern Europe in the interplay of neighboring empires, great power politics, and national self-assertion and self-affirmation.

Finally, there was Barbara's *History*, which was undertaken at the request of the Joint Committee on Eastern Europe of the ACLS and SSRC and returns us to a much larger canvas, beginning with the late seventeenth century and ending with the 1980s. It is both descriptive/factual and analytical/synthetic, much in the style of her diplomatic histories, and written with the same fluency and no nonsense clarity. It is an attempt to bring Stavrianos up to date, a task carried out with verve and skill. Stavrianos wrote his epic treatment of the Balkans just when American study of the area was moving out of its infancy. Barbara's survey not only summarizes the work of the next scholarly era, but also brings us up to the level that a quarter century of maturation in the study of Southeastern Europe had made possible.

In 1965, the Jelaviches wrote:

> The emphasis has been placed on those aspects of the past which, the authors believe, contribute to an understanding of the present. Therefore, the main topic throughout has been Balkan nationalism and the development of each state as a political unit. There is less emphasis on the medieval period and on certain economic, social, political, and diplomatic problems, which--while predominant in their own epoch--have lost much of their significance today.[37]

Though their aim was to downplay the "Balkan" element as somehow inevitably comical, explosive, violent, or chaotic, and instead "to describe the conditions that led to these events [of an extreme nature] and gained for the Balkans their sad reputation," the Jelaviches recognized "that the Balkan peninsula is indeed a land of conflict and contrast, of instability and change...of division and disunity," of astonishing diversity.[38]

From the Jelaviches' 1965 study, three themes emerged: "the national sentiments of the Balkan peoples and the conflicts among them; the interference of the great powers in Balkan affairs; and the economic backwardness of the area compared with other sections of Europe....Of the three, the influence of nationalism has certainly been the greatest" and the most divisive, with "the emphasis on the attainment of national unity and, later, on economic reform" leaving, unfortunately, "little room for the development or the understanding of Western conceptions of personal freedom."[39]

Geography, they affirmed, was the bane of the region: the "first and perhaps the major cause for this diversity" was due to the Balkans' nature as an accessible crossroads region, a tempting strategic and economic target for foreign powers, an area whose mountains isolate and divide peoples while allowing easy penetration from outside via land and sea--all of which make it an area often dependent on others.[40] At the same time, competitive nationalism made these peoples politically weak and blocked cooperation, almost inviting outside domination.[41]

The Jelaviches' analysis was much more concentrated in their 1977 study of the establishment of the Balkan national states. The first extended treatment of this crucial era in the history of Southeastern Europe, it also set forth clearly where we needed to go in future studies. The narrative concentrated on the modern emergence of the major Balkan peoples as distinct and conscious national groups. Some of the difficulties of this task were underlined at the outset as the Jelaviches noted that these peoples, despite their rather late emergence as nations in the modern sense, were, at the same time, the heirs to histories as ancient as any on the continent.[42] Their abrupt appearance on the European stage was, thus, not exactly from a *tabula rasa*--with all the attendant traditions, influences, and complications that such a historical base brings with it.

The Jelaviches further emphasized the impact of nearly half a millenium of Ottoman rule in the area, a domination that not only had a homogenizing influence on the area, but also "shaped the future life of all the Balkan people." National awareness was submerged, but not destroyed. Indeed the Ottoman millet system helped preserve national identity "through the church, the languages, and popular culture. The memory of the past was never completely erased."[43] This became unmistakable in the story of the nineteenth century as set forth by the Jelaviches. In the end, most:

> national programs, as enunciated by intellectuals and politicians, emphasized the historical arguments and referred back to the medieval kingdoms, or for the Greeks, the Byzantine Empire. The right of self-determination played a lesser, although significant role, in particular as a weapon to influence public opinion among the great powers. In practice each state concentrated on asserting its prerogatives and not in forwarding the national idea in general.[44]

Unhappily, after:

> national liberation no state felt comfortable with its minorities; in the post war period all resisted laws guaranteeing the civil rights of these people, who were uniformly regarded as a source of national weakness and subversion, which indeed they often were. Despite centuries of humiliation and debasement at the hands of an alien conquering power, the victorious nationalities too often found no better way to treat those under their control than simply to apply the same methods to which they themselves had been subjected in their period of weakness.[45]

This was to continue to plague their development and does so today.

Another unfortunate outcome of the way in which the Balkan states emerged in the nineteenth century, in the Jelaviches' view, was the adoption of centralized, bureaucratic state systems controlled down to the most minor detail from their capitals. The result of this mimicry of Napoleonic French centralism was two-fold: new political power was the domain of very, very small elites, which in turn became increasingly distant from average people, particularly the peasantry, who "played no significant political role in the actual functioning of the new state apparatuses."[46] In both the short and long run this plagued and continues to plague Balkan political development.

Finally, the Jelaviches came to feel that "the major problem of the new Balkan nations was economic, not political, a fact that was neither clearly defined nor even recognized. From their establishment the states were not truly economically viable units on a modern level." This "was, of course, simply a reflection of the poverty of the people" and led to further excuses, pretexts, or opportunities for "intervention on the part of the great powers...." In addition, these matters were exacerbated by the preoccupation of Balkan regimes and elites with alleged national issues over domestic concerns. The result was that much of their meager resources were squandered on military expenditures.[47] Need it be said that these problems also seem perennial ones for the region?

Though no one was more aware of the role of external influences on the Balkan peninsula than the Jelaviches, they were also at pains to stress the decisiveness of local conditions. Thus, although political and revolutionary ideology in Southeast Europe was much the same as in Western or Central Europe, the "national idea obviously worked differently in a nation such as Britain, with her vast colonial empire, and France and Germany, with their extensive territories and adequate resources for an industrial economy, than in a state such as Greece or Albania."[48] These local distinctives mean that even as common characteristics are examined, we must be alert to differences not only with other parts of Europe, but also within the Balkans themselves.

The Jelaviches' evaluation of the great century?

> In studying the history of any country, no matter how powerful or fortunate, hindsight and a wide historical perspective make it easy to point out the errors and failures in national development. In regard to the Balkan states the great accomplishments of the century and the positive gains from national unification should, in the final analysis, take precedence over any reservations or negative judgments. Criticism has been made of the results of applying the national solution to the peninsula, but it must be strongly emphasized that no other practical alternative existed at the time. From a purely theoretical standpoint it can be regretted that no political evolution was possible that would have allowed an adoption of a system by which different nationalities could live peacefully under the same government, but the fact is that in modern times no such organization has been developed. All advanced states are national in character....The economic and political weaknesses of the new states have also received much emphasis in this study. Here too, however, it must be emphasized that despite their extreme backwardness and

> the increasing economic burdens, the individual states did achieve a great deal....Much remained to be done, but a beginning had been made.[49]

This is where the Balkans were in 1920. Interestingly enough, it appears to be where they are in 1992 as well. *Plus ça change, plus c'est la même chose.*

In 1983, Barbara Jelavich not only brought this analysis up to date, but also produced an effective and worthy successor to Stavrianos' venerable, but now seriously out-dated classic, with her magisterial two volume *History of the Balkans*. While the increased pace of study on Southeastern Europe, especially in the post-Communist era, will mean that this work, too, will eventually be superseded, there is no doubt that it is an achievement that deserves to stand alongside Stavrianos and will, like Stavrianos, be read with pleasure and utility long into the future.

Most of the characteristic notes of this work have already been heard, but here they find their places in a much wider panorama. She begins with a plea for "study of the area on its own terms."[50] Though she would be among the first to agree that the Balkans are interesting and important as a testing ground for historical theories and theses, she stresses that this should never cause us to subordinate and depersonalize its peoples or to submerge and deny their distinctiveness.[51]

The overall purpose of this concluding (to date) Jelavich version of the Southeast European past is to thoroughly "introduce the reader to the dramatic and fateful history of the Balkan peninsula" from 1699 to the 1980s. Her:

> aim is to present a balanced picture...of the development of this region in the modern era. The major theme will be the process by which the Balkan nationalities broke away from imperial control, both Ottoman and Habsburg, established independent national states, and then embarked on the even more arduous road to economic and social modernization.

In this way "both Balkan developments and the place of the peninsula in history" will be covered, analyzed, and explained.[52]

Various themes, motifs, and counterpoints emerge in the process:

--the nature, impact, and consequences of Ottoman and Habsburg rule, especially on the subsequent appearance and development of Balkan national movements;

--the story of independence and/or autonomy and the organization of the governments and political regimes of the area;

--"the completion of the territorial unification of the modern states; the great wars and their consequences; and in particular, the measures taken to meet the enormous political, social, and economic problems faced by these nations in the modern world";

--"The difficulties caused by constant outside great-power interference and domination, issues that were very important in the previous centuries, [which] also carry over into the recent period";

--the "comparatively little cooperation among the Balkan nationalities";

--the shared common characteristics of the peoples in the area: similar cultural revivals, political and economic vision and goals, pressures from outside;

--the constant external interference and interest in the region, particularly during the life of the vexing Eastern Question; and finally,

--the enormous attraction of Western Europe materially and culturally, of an Eastern Europe drawn by the power and success of modernization and simultaneously repelled by fears of this same West.[53]

Many of these themes have been developed elsewhere in the work of the Jelaviches, but here they appear in their richest, fullest context. Additional stress is given especially to the dilemma of modernization, which is identified as "a constant element in Balkan history." As the effort to modernize proceeded, an:

> ambivalent attitude toward foreign influences was clearly shown. Although the Balkan states, lacking the necessary capital, resources, expertise, and experience, needed assistance, they feared foreign

> exploitation or imperial domination. The theme of the conflicting attraction to and rejection of foreign political, ideological, and economic influence has thus been a constant element in Balkan history. However,...even where foreign institutions and ideas were adopted, they were subsequently molded and changed to fit national traditions and prejudices. Certainly, the major element in Balkan life is that drawn from the long historical experience of the people and their own unique reactions to the outside interferences to which the peninsula has been so vulnerable.[54]

The role and motives of the great powers and the Balkan response are, as one would suppose, also stressed and well integrated into the presentation. The story is not unusual: "Balkan people often asked foreign governments for assistance; they expected this aid to be given freely and without political implications."[55] Or, as the Russian diplomat A.G. Jomini summarized in 1877:

> even if, in one way or another, we finish by achieving our object, it would still be impossible for me to see things through rose-tinted glasses!...Once the gunsmoke and the clouds of glory have faded away the net result will remain; that is to say enormous losses, a deplorable financial situation, and what advantages? Our Slav brothers freed, who will astonish us with their ingratitude....[56]

Finally, the theme of the effects of Western centralism and of superficial constitutionalism is reiterated. There was:

> a strong European influence over the political institutions adopted by the Balkan states. In every case, the governments came to be based on constitutions drawn after Western models. However, the extent of this outside influence can be overstated.

> Certainly the form and language of European liberalism was used, but the Balkan societies did have precedents for representative institutions.

In fact, the combination of European liberalism, local traditions, and the adoption of centralized bureaucratic Western regimes had unfortunate results as:

> representative institutions granted in the constitutions were thus canceled out by the existence of a strong, centralized bureaucracy that, in control of the police and the electoral procedures, could manipulate and dominate the political process.[57]

It proved to be the case that by:

> Adopting Western, principally French, administrative practices, the national leaderships preferred to concentrate political power in the capitals....The new political system, although conforming in its outer aspects to contemporary [i.e., French] liberal ideals, in practice gave the control of each nation to a small minority.[58]

And what did all of this lead to? The nineteenth century upheavals in the Balkans:

> paralleled the rise of nationalism in Western and Central Europe. The liberal and national ideology of the European revolutionaries influenced Balkan leaders so strongly because it was immediately applicable to local conditions....Although these aspects of the national revivals were closely connected with native institutions and traditions, the Balkan leaders accepted certain political institutions from Europe, in particular the constitutional monarchy and the centralized state administrative system. This

> choice, which did in fact reflect Balkan opinion, was also made necessary by the enormous direct influence of the great powers on events in the peninsula.

Unfortunately, the "national liberation movement of all the nationalities were made more complex by the frequent intervention of the European governments." This was because the:

> central strategic position of the peninsula and of the Ottoman Empire itself made the area the focus of the imperial drives of Britain, France, Russia, the Habsburg Empire, and later united Italy and Germany. Although the Balkan leaders were often able to exploit this situation....the new national governments were forced to endure constant interference in their internal affairs by outside powers. The Eastern Question did indeed turn the Balkans into the "powderkeg of Europe," but the responsibility for this situation lay as much with the great powers and the principle of balance of power as with the Balkan states.[59]

Bringing to bear the experiences of the interwar period makes this narrative a bit more pessimistic than its predecessors. It is Barbara Jelavich's conclusion that the World War I peace treaties not only left the "great issues of internal organization and economic development...unresolved....[In addition, all] of the difficulties of the national division of the Balkans became clearly apparent."[60] As the interwar period went on, the national principle in Southeast Europe:

> developed stronger negative than positive features....Competition over [disputed] lands served both to divide the Balkan peoples and to provide excuses for great-power intervention. France, Britain, Italy, Germany and the Soviet Union all played on these mutual animosities to further their own interests.

> This situation was to continue during the war and in the post-war world.[61]

Here again, the past meets the present and the future.

Moving into the era of the Cold War, the Balkans found themselves subjected to even more drastic external influence and control. Patterns that were to remain constant were established early on. Various:

> attempts were made to assert independence from Soviet direction. As in the past, the five Balkan states were unable to join together to resist great-power domination. All went their own ways and sought different means of adjusting to an international situation dominated by the two great military powers, the Soviet Union and the United States.[62]

Internally, the four socialist Balkan States:

> had many attributes in common. All adopted governments based on Marxist-Leninist theory, and with the exception of Albania, which was at first under Yugoslav direction, all were at the outset subject to strong Soviet influence. Each nation had a one-party political system; civil liberties were suspended. The major effort of the government was directed to a total reorganization of the economic life of the country. Stalinist Soviet models [i.e. forced industrialization and planning, collectivization of agriculture] were adopted.[63]

Nevertheless, despite "similar beginnings, differences soon appeared" as each country focused on its own internal development. In the end, however, the:

> real revolution in the Balkans was...not the Communist seizure of political power, but the subsequent

> slow destruction of patterns of life that had held for centuries....These processes, which are continuing, are not easy to characterize, nor can their final results be clearly pictured....By the 1980s the Balkan nations could look back on their record of the past thirty-five years with mixed feelings. Undoubtedly much had been achieved, but the...expectations for the economic future of the people have become less optimistic.[64]

This cautious assessment, made in 1983, has been borne out in the startling events of 1989-1992.

IV.

It is self-evident that the more general and/or comprehensive of the Jelaviches' writings are founded on an extensive base of more specialized studies. It is to these that we now turn, beginning first with those of Barbara Jelavich.

Her initial work was in diplomatic history, with a dissertation on *The German Alliance System, 1939-1941*.[65] This was to establish her major emphases as a scholar, with a lifelong interest in foreign policy, Russia, Eastern Europe, and great power politics in the region. The second decisive factor in shaping the direction of her work was the access that the Jelaviches gained to the papers of the prominent Russian diplomat Nikolai Karlovich Giers (1820-1895) and his family. This rich collection of materials relating to much of the diplomatic and political history of Russia and the Balkans in the nineteenth century provided substantial new insights into the entire period and region and became a cornerstone of the extensive and systematic research of both Jelaviches which we survey here.[66]

Barbara initially collaborated with Charles in the analysis and publication of the Giers materials, including the letters of A.P. Davydov to Giers,[67] the Jomini letters,[68] and some of the miscellaneous correspondence.[69] And it was through the Giers papers that Barbara's connection with Romania began. Giers had been a

Russian agent at Iaşi (1842-1847) and Bucharest (1858-1863) as well as being married to a Romanian.[70] Barbara's first major book, a study of *Russia and the Rumanian National Cause, 1858-1859*[71] made possible by Giers' papers, was one of the pioneer works on Romanian studies in the United States. This book not only began what became a long and fruitful association with Indiana University, but also with Romanian studies, which began to expand in the 1960s as a subject of interest in itself rather than just an adjunct of post-World War II political concerns.[72] Her story of Russian efforts in the Romanian Principalities, like Charles' study of Russian efforts in Bulgaria and Serbia,[73] successfully and illuminatingly blends diplomatic and domestic history to elucidate the complex development of the Balkans in the nineteenth century. And, as in Bulgaria and Serbia, the Russians are shown to have found themselves fruitlessly embroiled in the Eastern Question, serving as the unwitting patrons of Balkan nationalists, and promoting changes which wound up serving neither Russian interests nor desires.[74]

Barbara Jelavich's continued interest in Romania and Romanian diplomacy was reflected after this in a wide range of studies dealing with such matters as the Revolution of 1848,[75] Prince Cuza,[76] Moldovan separatism,[77] the abdication crisis of 1870-1871,[78] Bessarabia,[79] the commercial convention of 1876,[80] the Eastern Crisis of 1876-1880,[81] Romania's geographical position,[82] and the impact of foreign events on Romanian development[83] as well as Great Power interests more generally.[84]

In 1984, she capped these efforts on Russia and Romanian development with a summative account of the relationship between *Russia and the Formation of the Romanian National State, 1821-1878*,[85] a study that will be the primary reference on the subject for a long time to come, as well as an elaboration of the basic themes first identified in her 1959 book on the Romanian national cause. At the same time, it should be mentioned, Barbara Jelavich also solidified her key role in Romanian studies in the United States by serving as the mentor of a substantial proportion of the next generation of American specialists on Romania.

Barbara's next major effort after 1959 was to turn to the parallel subject of Russian involvement in yet another Balkan nation, Greece. *Russia and Greece during the Regency of King Othon, 1832-1835. Russian Documents on the First Years of Greek Independence*,[86] was the result of a productive sojourn in Saloniki at Basil and Louise Laourdas' Balkan Institute and at the Bavarian State Archives in Munich. This was followed by *Russland 1852-1871: Aus den Berichten der bayerischen Gesandtschaft in St. Petersburg*[87] and *Russia and the Greek Revolution of 1843*.[88] All three books reflect the multiplicity of her interests: the Balkans, Russia, Great Power diplomacy, and expounding the insights provided by the Giers Papers. All three told once more the same story of frustrated and frustrating Russian efforts in the Balkans as in the Serbian, Bulgarian, and Romanian cases.[89]

At the same time, she continued to work with the Giers materials. In 1962, she and Charles published *The Education of a Russian Statesman: The Memoirs of Nicholas Karlovich Giers*,[90] covering his life between 1820-1847. The second half deals primarily with Moldova and is a revealing look at life under the Russian Protectorate in Romania prior to 1848 as well as Russian attitudes toward the Balkans. Additional letters in the Giers collection were also published by Barbara Jelavich in various diplomatic studies over the next decade, relating to Romanian affairs[91] and the Bulgarian Crisis of 1885-1886.[92]

Barbara's other major effort in the areas of Russian and Austrian foreign policy in the 1960s and 1970s is also worthy of note: this was to present in survey form the diplomatic history of the two East European empires. Starting from her specialized investigations of numerous aspects of the ticklish, disputed, and significant problems of nineteenth century Tsarist[93] and Habsburg[94] policy and of their activity in the Balkans and elsewhere--such as mentioned above in connection with the Romanian national cause or in Greek affairs--she moved to communicating these findings to a much broader audience through two remarkable books on Russian and Austrian foreign policy: *A Century of Russian Foreign Policy*[95] and *The Habsburg Empire in European Affairs*.[96]

Her purpose in the former was:

> to explain and describe how Russia, who became a European great power in the eighteenth century, was

> able to maintain that position and to extend her borders...although possessing a social, political, and economic system not up to the level reached by her neighbors....[and] to follow major issues and the main lines of development in the policies adopted by Russia toward her neighbors with the hope that this description will provide a clear picture of Russian intentions, which were usually simple and logical in design.[97]

The expanded 1974 edition carried this story forward into an analysis of the Soviet era. The USSR was able, in her view, to succeed in ways that were not possible for the Tsarist regime owing to its revolutionary ideology and a new economic system uniquely designed to support a high level of armaments and military strength.[98] Ironically, the post-1917 regime also "never made the mistake of sacrificing state interests" to its ideals.[99] In the end, both Tsars and commisars were remarkably successful, despite numerous setbacks, as there was "steady progress of Russian national power...[to] win control of and subsequently hold a large section of the earth's surface."[100]

In the Habsburg case, the story was less positive since they did not get a second chance after the debacle of World War I. The Habsburgs' role in European affairs from 1815 to 1914 was as central as its geographical location might lead one to suppose. Yet "unlike its companions on the European scene its way led downward--toward a steady diminution of power in international relations and to eventual political disintegration."[101]

The purpose of the book was to explain how and why this occurred in the context of an analysis of the contest between the "traditional institutions of attraction" of the empire--the dynasty, the bureaucracy, the army, and the Catholic church--and the "natural disintegrating forces that were bound to be at work within a multinational empire in an age of nationalism."[102] At the same time, the study details the unique diplomatic and geographic issues that confronted the empire as it moved through the nineteenth century to the conflagration that eventually proved its doom.

Both of these surveys were enormously successful and useful. Indeed, it might be argued that they more or less preempted the field, combining depth of research and command of the primary materials with a clarity and ease of exposition truly rare in academic writing. Certainly the acid test of these works from a teaching point of view is the good stead in which they have stood generations of graduate students trying to prepare for relevant field exams.

Progressively, Barbara Jelavich expanded the scope of her research and analyses. In 1973, she turned to a comprehensive look at the role of the Ottoman Empire in the Balkans with a study of *The Ottoman Empire, the Great Powers, and the Straits Question, 1870-1887*.[103] Obviously she was no stranger to Ottoman development and Ottoman policy, since this--the essence of the vexing Eastern Question--impinged on Russian, Habsburg, and British policy as well as those of the Balkan peoples themselves. The book is one of the few Western studies to be based on substantial original research in Ottoman diplomatic archives dealing with the pre-World War I era. Though it is concentrated on the eighth and ninth decades of the nineteenth century and the straits question (which the author believes to be "for the Ottoman Empire perhaps the most important single diplomatic issue which arose in the years before the First World War"),[104] its scope is far wider and includes an excellent introduction on "The Great Powers and the Ottoman Empire," as well as a postscript on the Bosnian Crisis of 1908-1909 which brings the story almost up to the war. Later on, she would follow her interests in Ottoman affairs and the Eastern Question by examining contemporary Soviet scholarship on the Eastern Question,[105] sketching the issues involved in the Treaty of San Stefano,[106] and summarizing the role of the Ottoman Empire in the diplomatic history of the region.[107]

All of this work on the diplomacy of the Eastern Question and of Southeast Europe culminated in 1991 with the appearance of *Russia's Balkan Entanglements, 1806-1914*.[108] Barbara Jelavich synthesizes here some forty years of study of Russian diplomacy in the nineteenth century as it relates to the Balkans, particularly the Slavic, Orthodox Balkans. Between 1806 and 1914, the Russian Empire was involved in five wars over and in the Balkans. She shows clearly why they were drawn into these conflicts even when such involvement was contrary to the Empire's overall interests and how this involvement culminated with the First World War.

Russian entanglement in the Balkans is presented in five distinct stages: advance, 1806-1828; defense and extension, 1828-1831; defense of the status quo up to the Crimean fiasco, 1831-1856; further entanglements, 1856-1887; and the Balkan factor in the origins of World War I, 1887-1914. In each of these periods, she outlines the reasons for Russian involvements in the Balkans, the connections and convictions that drew them into the area, the emotional and other commitments that they made, and finally why what happened happened.

Since the Romanian case, which differed in significant ways from that of the Bulgarians, Serbians, and Montenegrins, was covered in her 1984 study, the emphasis here is on the Orthodox Slavic peoples. The story is seen as one of many paradoxes. The Russian Empire was motivated not only by considerations of its general security and strategic situation, but also by those of a religious, cultural, ethnic, and altruistic nature. The story of Russian involvement is also one of a progressive shattering of Tsarist illusions that their efforts would lead to the formation of a grateful group of liberated Balkan states under Russian tutelage. Given the rather different conception of this relationship as seen by Balkan leaders, as well as the decidedly "colonial" coloration of Russian military and cultural action in the region, it is not surprising that constant tension existed between patron and the patronized. Finally, she notes the often drastic and crucial effects on internal Russian development of their Balkan entanglements. At the conclusion, one will find a concise review of the gains and losses incurred by this fatal relationship. Though the book is not a history of the Eastern Question, it does provide what is now the best short overall review of Russian involvement in the region prior to 1914, including the run up to the war.

If we take into account Barbara Jelavich's work discussed in Section II (independently and with her husband), as well as the work just discussed, the appearance in 1987 of her *Modern Austria: Empire and Republic, 1815-1986*[109] comes as a bit of a surprise--but only to those who have neglected to take seriously both her (and Charles') conviction that the history of Eastern Europe is intimately tied to that of the rest of Europe, particularly through the Habsburg Monarchy, and her life-long interest in the Dual Monarchy. We have already seen this manifested in her work on Habsburg diplomacy[110] and in large portions of her *History of the Balkans* dealing with the Habsburg Empire.[111] We should note in addition her collaboration with Charles in 1959 on the brief but suggestive Rinehart Source Problems volume dealing with *The Habsburg Empire: Toward a Multinational Empire or National States?*[112] The comments that one could make on this book begin to sound repetitive: clear organization and presentation, sound integration of external and internal development, and an eye for both the larger context and the significant detail. In short, synthesis without caricature or loss of scholarly depth, the sort of book we have come to expect from Barbara Jelavich, and the kind of book we want to get into the hands of our students once we have benefited from it ourselves.

There should be no question by now that the work of Barbara Jelavich--whether it is on some arcane scholarly topic or for a larger audience--is characterized by lucidity, straightforward presentation, and an ease of exposition and analysis which have been known to provoke not a little collegial and uncollegial envy. That this is not simply the product of native good fortune is attested to by the care with which she worked and works with the writing of her students. Anyone who has taken a Barbara Jelavich seminar will remember with amusement and chagrin, as the case may be, her attention to clarity, insistence that one say what one means and mean what one says, and merciless surgery on the facile or unsupported generalization.

Barbara Jelavich's integration of good scholar with good writer, so often mentioned above, is unfortunately not all that common--which is why we celebrate it here. That this is appreciated not only by her students is attested to, *inter alia*, by the comments of a Romanian scholar of similar gifts, Cornelia Bodea, who notes that the hallmarks of Barbara's work are "clarity, critical insight, and narrative skill," and a pen characterized by "authority, interest, [and] poise."[113] Professor Bodea also concurs with the picture that emerges above, namely the success of Barbara Jelavich's scholarly activity is due to her integration of 1) painstaking archival research; 2) mastery of the primary and secondary sources; 3) long experience as an outstanding teacher; 4) intimate acquaintance with the widely varied pasts and traditions of the diverse peoples of Southeast Europe; and 5) first-hand knowledge of the region's countries and people and their problems and concerns in the present, all of which make Barbara Jelavich "a respected ruler in her territorial waters."[114]

V.

Let us turn now to the works of Charles Jelavich. Charles' writings are less prolific than those of Barbara, but no less important in their subjects and findings and no less readable. He began his professional study of the Balkans with his dissertation at Berkeley in 1949 on *Russian Influence in Serbia and Bulgaria, 1881-1897.*[115] This investigation was subsequently developed into a work whose very title reflects two favorite Jelavich preoccupations: *Tsarist Russia and Balkan Nationalism.*[116] The book also neatly captures the essence of Russian policy in the Balkans in the nineteenth century as well as its basic problems in dealing with the indigenous populations.

The motto for those problems might very well be the 1870 statement from Liuben Karavelov with which Charles begins the study: "If Russia comes to liberate, she will be received with great sympathy; but if she comes to rule, she will find many enemies."[117] Characteristically, as this book graphically shows, even when the Russians wanted peace and maintenance of the status quo, their inconsistent actions and aims, and the often contradictory activities of their military and diplomatic agents, kept creating dangerous and destabilizing situations.

The book is a model of integrating internal and diplomatic history--something essential for doing well the history of Eastern Europe. It also does an excellent job of using the particular to illuminate the more general aspects of development in this area, while presenting its story of turmoil and intrigue in a manner that makes the history of Serbia and Bulgaria in the 1880s sound both interesting and significant.

Finally, the study elaborates what turns out to have been a very critical epoch in Balkan political development; it is here that one can find the roots of inter-Balkan conflict, an understanding of why the issues of Macedonia and Bosnia-Hercegovina became so troublesome, and why both Balkan developmental problems, and those of Russian foreign policy, were so intractable and probably unsolvable. As the events of the post-World War II era have also shown, the Russian solution for dealing with Balkan nationalism--intimidation and military force--could work in the short run, but not indefinitely.[118]

Charles Jelavich's first publication was a study of Greater Serbianism which appeared in 1951.[119] This became a recurring theme in his studies of Southeast European nationalism, particularly that of the South Slavs, of Habsburg policy and actions in the area, of Serbian-Croatian relations, or even South Slavic church history.[120] And, of course, it heavily informed his and Barbara's history of the Balkans in the nineteenth century discussed previously.

In the 1970s, Charles' interest in nationalism, especially the problems of Yugoslavism, took the form of a more concentrated focus on the role of education in shaping nationalist attitudes and ideas.[121] It culminated in 1990 with the publication of his *South Slav Nationalisms: Textbooks and Yugoslav Union before 1914*.[122] Some may wonder why such a massive scholarly effort would be devoted to the topic of textbooks, but to do so is to fall victim to what David Hackett Fischer has called the elitist fallacy, namely the tendency to confuse the history of elites with the history of a whole group.[123] As Eugen Weber has eloquently argued, such history is seriously incomplete:

> The history I thought and taught about went on chiefly in cities; the countryside and the little towns were a mere appendage of that history, following, echoing, or simply standing by to watch what was going on, but scarcely relevant on their own account....[I began] to sense in my work in political and intellectual history...that I was ignoring a vast dimen-

> sion of reality. What happened in the small towns and countryside?[124]

It is precisely this "dimension of reality" that Charles Jelavich attacks in his most recent book.

The premise of the study was enunciated by the noted Serbian historian Slobodan Jovanović in 1948: what the peoples of independent Yugoslavia learned prior to World War I (from, e.g., grammar, geography, history and literature textbooks) goes a long way toward explaining the failure of Yugoslavism--which was always something of a paradox anyway.[125] It is Jelavich's firm conviction that the role Yugoslavism:

> has played in South Slavic affairs during the past 150 years cannot be minimized. To a greater or lesser extent it has influenced all areas of South Slavic activity--political, religious, economic, cultural, linguistic, social, military--and even sporting events....In reality, however, Yugoslavism was a nebulous concept, and lent itself to a number of dissimilar political programs.[126]

The basis for Yugoslavism was in part the impossibly intermixed populations of the South Slav lands, but the separate development of the major groups (especially the Slovenes, Croats, and Serbs) disguised its utopian nature as did the less than candid use of the term and concept by nationalist leaders. The key accomplishment of the book is to elucidate the related problems of Yugoslavism and nationalism in this area by analyzing "the role of education and the textbooks in the development of nationalism and Yugoslavism" through which "it can be seen that broad support for South Slav unity was limited at best. Neither the Serbs nor the Croats nor the Slovenes embraced the concept unreservedly....Indeed, many writers who used Yugoslav terminology were in fact advancing their own nation's interests."[127] In the end, Yugoslavism proved illusory.

It is to be hoped that this book will open the way to similar studies on Romanian, Magyar, Bulgarian, and Greek textbooks, with similar salutary (if not always pleasant) consequences for our understanding of nationalism, opinion formation of people other than those in the elites, and the problems facing these nations in our times. Unhappily, this analysis is no less applicable to the Yugoslavia of the 1980s-1990s than to that of the 1920s. As Yugoslavia disintegrates in the 1990s, Jelavich's study of nineteenth and early twentieth century nationalism has become violently contemporary.[128]

Finally, in addition to these concerns--and the extensive efforts devoted by Charles Jelavich to the concerns of the field and area already discussed above[129]--there is his interest in the resources and tools of our profession. Among these we might mention his consulting editorship on Russia, Eastern Europe, and Europe since 1914 for R.R. Palmer's *Atlas of World History*,[130] for Russia and East Europe on the special map "History of Europe--The Major Turning Points," in the December 1983 issue of *National Geographic*, and his contribution to *The American Historical Association Guide to Literature*.[131]

VI.

Concluding Unscientific Postscript

This review of the work of Charles and Barbara Jelavich cannot be complete without at least a mention of their work with students. This present volume is, of course, testimony to their work. There are many scholars who provided the shoulders on which the next generation can stand. What we would like to stress here is that the Jelaviches' not inconsiderable scholarly work just presented was never done at the expense of their students. They have been involved with hundreds of future specialists in history, in the history of Europe, Eastern Europe, Russia, and Southeastern Europe. They have been involved with dozens of doctoral dissertations and scholarly monographs from the minds, pens, and researches of others. Their work with these generations of graduate students has been characterized by care, consideration, and commitment to the individual and his or her work. And, it is worth stressing, this involvement has never been exploitive or domineering. Whereas it is not at all unusual for graduate students to function as unpaid research assistants and un-named co-authors for senior professors, the Jelaviches, if anything, sacrificed their own work and time for the benefit of their students. That they have been able to do this while producing their own remarkable work is one more tribute to two fine individuals and scholars.

NOTES

[1]Cf. Cornelia Bodea's appreciation in "Barbara Jelavich and East-European Historiography," *Revue Roumaine d'Histoire*, Vol. 24 (1985), pp. 267-276; V.I. Vinogradov, "Rossiia i balkany v trudakh Barbary i Char'za Elavichei," *Sovetskoe Slavianovedenie*, vol. 24 (1989) nr. 3, pp. 27-41; and Nikolai Todorov, "Tsentrove za iztochnoevropeiski i balkanistichni izsledvaniia v SASHT" (Centers for East European and Balkan Research in U.S.A.), *Istoricheski Pregled*, XXIV: 5 (1968), pp. 127-135. This article stresses the prominent role of Indiana University's East European Center and the work of the Jelaviches.

[2]A brief biographical note: Charles Jelavich was born 15 November 1922 in Mountain View, California. He received an A.B. honors degree in Slavic languages from the University of California at Berkeley in 1944, where he also completed the M.A. and Ph.D. degrees in history in 1947 and 1949 respectively. He taught Serbo-Croatian at Berkeley, before being appointed to the faculty of history in 1949, where he served until he accepted an appointment as Professor of History at Indiana University in 1961. He was also chairman of the University of California's Center for Slavic and East European Studies from 1957 to 1960 and a Visiting Fulbright Professor at the University of Munich in 1960-1961. He served as president of the American Association for the Advancement of Slavic Studies in 1986-1987. Barbara Jelavich was born Barbara Brightfield on 12 April 1923 in Belleville, Illinois. She received an A.B. honors degree in history from the University of California at Berkeley in 1943, followed by an M.A. and Ph.D. in history from Berkeley in 1944 and 1948. She taught briefly at

Berkeley and Mills College, then devoted her time to raising their two sons, Mark and Peter, prior to accepting an appointment in the Department of History at Indiana University in 1961. Promoted to Professor of History in 1967, she was named Distinguished Professor of History at Indiana in 1984. She served as chairman of the Conference on Slavic and East European History (1979) and President of the Society for Romanian Studies (1988-1990). In 1992, she was elected an honorary member of the Romanian Academy.

[3]See Charles Jelavich, ed., *Language and Area Studies: East Central Europe and Southeastern Europe. A Survey* (Chicago, 1969), pp. ix-xi.

[4]It should be noted that the Jelaviches, probably because of their lifelong concern with the Habsburg Monarchy, never forgot or ignored the European nature of this area.

[5]C. Jelavich, *Area Studies*, 1969, p. xi.

[6]*Ibid.*, pp. 7-28, for discussion and explanation of this problem.

[7]*Ibid.*, pp. 3ff.

[8]In what follows, "Southeastern Europe" and "the Balkans" will be used more or less interchangeably.

[9]Charles and Barbara Jelavich, "Introduction," in: Charles and Barbara Jelavich, eds., *The Balkans in Transition* (Berkeley, 1963), p. xi.

[10]*Ibid.*, pp. xii-xv. Cp. Charles and Barbara Jelavich, *The Balkans* (Englewood Cliffs, 1965), pp. 13-14, which stresses the same "common characteristics" of this area: predominantly peasant, economically backward, but modernizing, with a history of almost continuous foreign domination.

[11]Charles and Barbara Jelavich, *The Establishment of the Balkan National States, 1804-1920* (Seattle, 1977), pp. ix-x.

[12]*Ibid.*, p. x.

[13]*Ibid.*, pp. x, 320.

[14]*Ibid.*, p. 321.

[15]*Ibid.*, p. 324.

[16]Barbara Jelavich, *History of the Balkans* (Cambridge, 1983), Vol. I, p. ix.

[17]Jelavich and Jelavich, *The Balkans*, 1965, pp. 134-135.

[18]*Ibid.*, p. 1.

[19]B. Jelavich, *History of the Balkans*, 1983, Vol. I, pp. ix-x.

[20]Subtitled "Essays on the Development of Balkan Life and Politics since the Eighteenth Century," (Berkeley, 1963).

[21]Cambridge, 1956.

[22]New York, 1958.

[23]His study of "Bulgarian Incunabula," *Quarterly Journal of Current Acquisitions of the Library of Congress*, Vol. 14 (1957), Nr. 3, pp. 77-94, was one such manifestation; "The Importance of the Leksikografski Zavod to the Scholar," *Slavic Review*, Vol. 21 (1962), pp. 330-335; and his contribution on "Yugoslavia," in: George Frederick Howe, *et al*, eds., *The American Historical Association's Guide to Historical Literature* (New York, 1961), pp. 584-590, were others.

[24]A report on this work was published as "Slavic Studies and Library Acquisitions," *College and Research Libraries*, Vol. 20 (1959), pp. 118-124. Cf. also Melville J. Ruggles, "East European Publications in American Libraries," *Library Quarterly*, Vol. 28 (1958), pp. 337-349, on the same project; and Melville J. Ruggles and Vaclav Mostecky, *Russian and East European Publications in the Libraries of the United States* (New York, 1960).

[25]Jelavich and Jelavich, eds., *Balkans in Transition*, 1963, p. v.

[26]C. Jelavich, *Area Studies*, 1969, p. xii.

[27]Paul L. Horecky, ed., *East Central Europe. A Guide to Basic Publications* (Chicago, 1969), and *Southeastern Europe. A Guide to Basic Publications* (Chicago, 1969).

[28]"History," in: C. Jelavich, *Area Studies*, 1969, pp. 79-128; and "Yugoslavia: History," in: Horecky, *Southeastern Europe*, 1969, pp. 501-515.

[29]C. Jelavich, *Area Studies*, 1969, pp. 1-45. For a preliminary report on this work, see his "East Central and Southeast European Studies," *ACLS Newsletter*, Vol. 19 (1968), Nr. 7, pp. 1-11.

[30]Barbara further contributed to this dialogue in the 1960s with a survey and bibliography of East European and Soviet studies in the United States between 1945-1963: "Die Osteuropastudien in Amerika und der akademische Austausch mit der Sowjetunion," *Österreichische Osthefte*, Vol. 6 (1964), pp. 70-75. That this concern was not a passing phase is evidenced by her "Recent Soviet Publications on the Eastern Question," *Russian Review*, Vol. 37

(1978), pp. 177-187; and "Recent Publications on the Habsburg Empire in the United States," *Études Danubiennes*, Vol. 3 (1987), pp. 45-53.

[31]*Newsletter of the American Association for the Advancement of Slavic Studies*, Vol. 28 (1988), Nr. 1, pp. 1, 3-4.

[32]Cp. his comments on "American Perceptions of the South Slavs, 1975-1941," *RAD. Journal of the Jugoslav Academy of Arts and Sciences*, Zagreb, Vol. 405 (1984), pp. 195-214, which describes American neglect and ignorance of this area alternating with American dismay at recurring crises in the region. The bottom line was that the South Slavs were not a priority for the United States and serious study was generally lacking. Unfortunately, after 1945, what attention there was given to this area often seemed to be motivated by other concerns than merely a desire for "deeper understanding of the peoples of Jugoslavia and Jugoslav affairs."

[33]C. Jelavich, "East European Studies," 1988, pp. 3-4. Mention should also be made here of the extensive contributions of the Jelaviches to the field through long hours of dedicated service on fellowship, study, and other committees.

[34]Jelavich and Jelavich, *The Balkans*, 1965, a volume in the Modern Nations in Historical Perspective series edited by Robin Winks.

[35]Jelavich and Jelavich, *Balkan National States*, 1977, Volume 8 in the series edited by Peter Sugar and Donald Treadgold.

[36]B. Jelavich, *History of the Balkans*, 1983, in two volumes: Volume I--The Eighteenth and Nineteenth Centuries; Vol. II--The Twentieth Century.

[37]Jelavich and Jelavich, *The Balkans*, 1965, p. vii.

[38]*Ibid.*, pp. 1-2.

[39]*Ibid.*, pp. 129-130.

[40]*Ibid.*, pp. 2-4.

[41]*Ibid.*, pp. 131-133.

[42]Jelavich and Jelavich, *Balkan National States*, 1977, p. ix.

[43]*Ibid.*, p. x.

[44]*Ibid.*, p. 320.

[45]*Ibid.*, p. 321.

[46]*Ibid.*, pp. 321-322.

[47]*Ibid.*, pp. 322-324.

[48]*Ibid.*, p. 325.

[49]*Ibid.*, pp. 325-237.

[50]B. Jelavich, *History of the Balkans*, 1983, Vol. I, pp. ix-x.

[51]For the Jelaviches, the question of whether external or internal forces are primary in historical development is a non-issue. The history of a region such as the Balkans demonstrates that this is a false dichotomy and that any history which ignores one or the other is bound to be inadequate.

[52]B. Jelavich, *History of the Balkans*, 1983, Vol. I, pp. x-xii. Cf. Vol. II, pp. 1-2.

[53]On all of this, see *Ibid.*, Vol. I, pp. x-xiii. Cp. Vol. II, pp. ix ff.

[54]*Ibid.*, Vol. I, pp. xi-xii.

[55]*Ibid.*, Vol. I, p. 378.

[56]A.G. Jomini to N.K. Giers, 1/13 September 1877, published in Charles and Barbara Jelavich, eds., *Russia and the East, 1876-1880* (Leiden, 1959), p. 59.

[57]B. Jelavich, *History of the Balkans*, 1983, Vol. I, pp. 379-380.

[58]*Ibid.*, Vol. II, p. 441.

[59]*Ibid.*, pp. 439-440.

[60]*Ibid.*, pp. 441-442.

[61]*Ibid.*, pp. 242-243.

[62]*Ibid.*, pp. 334-335.

[63]*Ibid.*, pp. 404-405.

[64]*Ibid.*, pp. 444, 404-405.

[65]Unpublished doctoral dissertation, University of California at Berkeley, 1948, 348 pp.

[66]The Giers collection was composed of 1) letters to Giers from various Russian political and diplomatic figures; 2) Giers' despatches when he was consul-general in the Romanian Principalities along with letters to Giers from Russian agents at Constantinople and Iaşi in the period 1858-1863; and 3) Giers family papers, including his memoirs up to 1847. Cf. Jelavich and Jelavich, eds., *Russia and the East*, 1959, pp. x-xi.

[67]Charles and Barbara Jelavich, "Russia and Bulgaria, 1879: The Letters of A.P. Davydov to N.K. Giers," *Südost-Forschungen*, Vol. 15 (1956), pp. 427-458.

[68]Charles and Barbara Jelavich, "Jomini and the Revival of the Dreikaiserbund, 1879-1880," *Slavonic and East European Review*, Vol. 35 (1957), pp. 99-107; and Jelavich and Jelavich, eds., *Russia and the East*, 1959.

[69]Charles and Barbara Jelavich, "Bismarck's Proposal for the Revival of the Dreikaiserbund in October 1878," *Journal of Modern History*, Vol. 29 (1957), pp. 99-101.

[70]His wife, Olga Cantacuzino, was also the niece of the powerful long-time Russian foreign minister, A.M. Gorchakov.

[71]Bloomington, 1959, xi + 169 pp.

[72]She was a leader in the founding of the Society for Romanian Studies (1973) and served as the president of the society in 1988-1990. In addition, she has served from the outset on the editorial board of Keith Hitchins' *Rumanian Studies* (1970+). Her contributions to Romanian studies were recognized in 1992 by her election as an honorary member of the Romanian Academy.

[73]See below.

[74]These same themes are found in two additional articles by the Jelaviches: "The Danubian Principalities and Bulgaria under Russian Protectorship," *Jahrbücher für Geschichte Osteuropas*, Vol. 9 (October, 1961), pp. 349-366; and "The Call to Action: Religion, Nationalism, Socialism," *Journal of Central European Affairs*, Vol. 23 (1963), pp. 3-11; as well as their collection of the Jomini-Giers letters, *Russia and the East*, 1959. This line of analysis was subsequently expanded and elaborated by Barbara in other studies and syntheses: "Balkan Nations under European Protectorship," in: N. Todorov and E. Sarafova, eds., *Actes du premier congrés international des études balkaniques et sud-est européennes* (Sofia, 1969), Vol. 4, pp. 397-408; "Negotiating the Treaty of San Stefano," *Southeastern Europe*, Vol. 6 (1979), pp. 171-193; "Russian Balkan Policy in the Era of Revolutions," in: Béla K. Király, ed., *East Central European Society and War in the Era of Revolutions, 1775-1856* (New York, 1984), pp. 627-642; "Tsarist Russia and Balkan National Liberation Movements: a Study in Great-Power Mythology," in: Roland Sussex and J.C. Eade, eds., *Culture and Nationalism in Nineteenth Century Eastern Europe* (Columbus, 1985), pp. 56-66; "Tsarist Russia and the Balkan Slavic Connection," *Canadian Review of Studies in Nationalism*, Vol. 16 (1989), pp. 209-

226; and "Tsarist Russia and the Unification of Bulgaria and Eastern Rumelia, 1856-1864," in: Don Karl Rowney, ed., *Imperial Power and Development: Papers on Pre-Revolutionary Russian History* (Columbus, 1990), pp. 101-115. Her most recent summary study of all of this--*Russia's Balkan Entanglements, 1806-1914*--is discussed below.

[75]"The Aftermath: the effect of the Revolution on the Romanian National Movement until 1878," *Conference on the 1848 Revolutions in the Romanian Principalities* (New York, 1972), 11 pp.; and "The Russian Intervention in Wallachia and Transylvania, September 1848 to March 1849," *Rumanian Studies*, Vol. 4 (1976-1979), pp. 16-74.

[76]"The Ottoman Empire, the Great Powers, and the Legislative and Administrative Union of the Principalities," *Rumanian Studies*, Vol. 2 (1971-1972), pp. 48-83.

[77]"Russia and Moldavian Separatism: The Demonstration of April, 1866," in: Alexander Fischer, Günter Moltmann and Klaus Schwabe, eds., *Russland-Deutschland-Amerika: Festschrift für Fritz T. Epstein* (Wiesbaden, 1978), pp. 73-87.

[78]"The Abdication Crisis of 1870-1871: The International Aspects," *Revue Roumaine d'Histoire*, Vol. 21 (1982), pp. 89-99.

[79]"Russia and the Reacquisition of Southern Bessarabia, 1875-1878," *Südost-Forschungen*, Vol. 28 (1969), pp. 199-237.

[80]"Russia and the Rumanian Commercial Convention of 1876," *Rumanian Studies*, Vol. 3 (1973-1975), pp. 39-60.

[81]"Austria-Hungary, Rumania and the Eastern Crisis, 1876-1878," *Südost-Forschungen*, Vol. 30 (1971), pp. 111-141; "Diplomatic Problems of an Autonomous State: Romanian Decisions on War and Independence, 1877," *Southeastern Europe*, Vol. 5 (1978), pp. 26-35; "Romania at the Congress of Berlin: Problems of Peacemaking" in: Ralph Melville and Hans-Jürgen Schröder, eds., *Der Berliner Kongress von 1878* (Wiesbaden, 1982), pp. 189-204; "British Eastern Policy, 1878-1880: the View from Bucharest; the Letters of William White," *Rumanian Studies*, Vol. 5 (1980-1986), pp. 41-83; and "Mihail Kogălniceanu: Historian as Foreign Minister, 1876-1878," in: Dennis Deletant and Harry Hanak, eds., *Historians as Nation-Builders: Central and South-East Europe* (London, 1988), pp. 87-105.

[82]"Geographic Determinants of Rumanian Foreign Policy," *International Journal of Rumanian Studies*, Vol. 6 (1988), Nr. 1, pp. 7-16.

[83]"The Effects of the Franco-Sardinian-Austrian War, the Austro-Prussian War, and the Polish Insurrection on Romanian Political Development," in: Béla K. Király, ed., *The Crucial Decade: East Central European Society and National Defense, 1859-1870* (New York, 1984), pp. 15-27.

[84]"The Great Power Protectorate and Romanian National Development, 1856-1877," *Revue des Études Sud-Est Européennes*, Vol. 15 (1977), pp. 681-694. See also the additional Giers-based items given below in Notes # 90, 91, 92.

[85]Cambridge, 1984, xii + 356 pp.

[86]Thessaloniki, 1962, 155 pp.

[87]Wiesbaden, 1963, 156 pp.

[88]Munich: Oldenbourg, 1966, 124 pp.

[89]Other studies dealing with Greece by Barbara Jelavich include: "Russia, Bavaria, and the Greek Revolution of 1862-1863," *Balkan Studies*, Vol. 2 (1961), pp. 125-150; "The Philorthodox Conspiracy of 1839," *Balkan Studies*, Vol. 7 (1966), pp. 89-102; and "Tsarist Russia and Greek Independence," in: John T.A. Koumoulides, ed., *Greek Connections: Essays on Culture and Diplomacy* (Notre Dame, 1987), pp. 75-101.

[90]Berkeley, 1962, ix + 241 pp.; reprinted in 1982.

[91]"Russia and the Double Election of Alexander Cuza, 1858-1859. The Letters of S.I. Popov to N.K. Giers," *Südost-Forschungen*, Vol. 24 (1965), pp. 119-137; and "Russia, the Great Powers and the Recognition of the Double Election of Alexander Cuza: The Letters of A.P. Lobanov-Rostovskii to N.K. Giers, 1858-1859," *Rumanian Studies*, Vol. 1 (1970), pp. 3-34.

[92]"A Russian Diplomat's Comments on the Bulgarian Crisis, 1885-1888: The Letters of E.E. Staal to N.K. Giers," *Südost-Forschungen*, Vol. 34 (1975), pp. 247-274.

[93]In addition to items cited both above and below, see: "Russland und die Einigung Deutschlands unter preussischer Führung," *Geschichte in Wissenschaft und Unterricht*, Vol. 19 (1968), pp. 521-538; "Great Britain and the Russian Acquisition of Batum, 1878-1886," *Slavonic and East European Review*, Vol. 48 (1970), pp. 44-

66; "Russia, Britain and the Bulgarian Question, 1885-1888," *Südost-Forschungen*, Vol. 32 (1973), pp. 168-191; "Bulgaria and Batum, 1886," *Southeastern Europe*, Vol. 1 (1974), pp. 72-79; "British Means of Offense against Russia in the Nineteenth Century," *Russian History*, Vol. 1 (1974), pp. 119-135; "Russia and the April Uprising," *Southeastern Europe*, Vol. 4 (1977), pp. 217-232; "Ignatiev u Carigradu 1876 godine," *Spomenik. Srpska Akademija Nauka i Unetnosti* CXXXII. Odeljenje istoriski nauka, Vol. 8 (1991) pp. 87-136. Barbara Jelavich, ed., "L'Ambassade russe à Paris, 1881-1898: Les Mémoires de Nicholas Giers," *Canadian Slavic Studies*, Vol. 1 (1967), pp. 1-23, 212-237, 379-403, 587-617; Vol. 2 (1968), 68-85, 219-238, 368-390, 525-541; and "The Polish Immigration, 1831-1871: The Challenge to Russia," in École française de Rome, *L'emigration politique en Europe aux IX ième--XX ième siècles* (Rome, 1991), pp. 235-245.

[94]For her other related studies, see below Note #110.

[95]Philadelphia: J. B. Lippincott, 1964, vii + 308 pp.; revised and updated in 1974 as *St. Petersburg and Moscow: Tsarist and Soviet Foreign Policy, 1814-1974* (Bloomington, 1974), xii + 480 pp.

[96]Chicago, 1969, viii + 190 pp., reprinted in 1975.

[97]B. Jelavich, *Russian Foreign Policy*, 1964, pp. v-vi.

[98]B. Jelavich, *St. Petersburg and Moscow*, 1974, p. 455.

[99]*Ibid.*, p. 456.

[100]*Ibid.*, 1974, p. 457.

[101]B. Jelavich, *Habsburg Empire*, 1969, pp. 2-3.

[102]*Ibid.*, 1969, p. 8.

[103]Bloomington, 1973, xi + 209 pp.

[104]B. Jelavich, *Ottoman Empire*, 1973, p. vii.

[105]"Recent Soviet Publications on the Eastern Question," *Russian Review*, Vol. 37 (1978), pp. 177-187.

[106]See Note #74 above.

[107]"The Ottoman State and the Study of the Diplomatic History of Southeastern Europe," *International Journal of Turkish Studies*, Vol. 2 (1981), pp. 56-65.

[108]Cambridge, 1991, xi + 291 pp.

[109]Cambridge, 1987, xvii + 346 pp.

[110]Cf. her "Comments" in the *Austrian History Yearbook*, Vols. 4-5 (1968-1969), pp. 259-265, dealing with Habsburg diplomatic and military history between 1854-1911; "Foreign Policy and the National Question in the Habsburg Empire: A Memorandum of Kálnoky," *Austrian History Yearbook*, Vols. 6-7 (1970-1971), pp. 142-159; her "Commentary" in *East Central Europe*, Vol. 7 (1980), pp. 345-348, on the impact of the Dual Alliance of 1879 on the Austro-Hungarian Monarchy; "Recent Publications on the Habsburg Empire in the United States," *Études Danubiennes*, Vol. 3 (1987), pp. 45-53; "What the Habsburg Government Knew about the Black Hand," *Austrian History Yearbook*, Vol. 22 (1991), pp. 131-150; and "Clouded Image: Critical Perceptions of the Habsburg Empire in 1914," *Austrian History Yearbook*, Vol. 23 (1992), pp. 23-35.

[111]B. Jelavich, *History of the Balkans*, 1983, Vols. I-II.

[112]New York, 1959, 57 pp.

[113]Bodea, "Barbara Jelavich," 1985, pp. 267, 276.

[114]*Ibid.*, pp. 269, 276.

[115]Unpublished doctoral dissertation, University of California at Berkeley, 1949, 417 pp.

[116]Subtitled "Russian Influence in the Internal Affairs of Bulgaria and Serbia, 1879-1886" (Berkeley, 1958), x + 304 pp. In addition to the study, use, and publication of the aforementioned Giers papers, other important primary source analysis carried out by the Jelaviches for this work included: "The Occupation Fund Documents: A Diplomatic Forgery," *American Slavic and East European Review*, Vol. 12 (1953), pp. 343-349; and "The Occupation Fund Documents. Additional Evidence," *American Slavic and East European Review*, Vol. 14 (1955), pp. 390-401. Charles also collaborated with Barbara on the publication of the Giers memoirs discussed earlier.

[117]C. Jelavich, *Tsarist Russia*, 1958, p. vii.

[118]Cf. *Ibid.*, pp. 283, viii. For another exploration of Russian-Bulgarian relations, see Charles Jelavich, "Russo-Bulgarian Relations, 1892-1896: With Particular Reference to the Problem of the Bulgarian Succession," *Journal of Modern History*, Vol. 24 (1952), pp. 341-351.

[119]"Nikola P. Pašić, Greater Serbia or Jugoslavia?" *Journal of Central European Affairs*, Vol. 11 (1951), pp. 133-152.

[120]"The Revolt in Bosnia-Hercegovina, 1881-1882," *Slavonic and East European Review*, Vol. 31 (1953), pp. 420-436; "Some Aspects of Serbian Religious Development in the Eighteenth Century," *Church History*, Vol. 23 (1954), pp. 144-152; "Die Habsburger Monarchie und die nationale Frage der Südslawen," *Südosteuropa Jahrbuch*, Vol. 5 (1961), pp. 61-74; "Serbian Nationalism and the Question of Union with Croatia in the Nineteenth Century," *Balkan Studies*, Vol. 3 (1962), pp. 29-42; "The Croatian Problem in the Habsburg Empire in the Nineteenth Century," *Austrian History Yearbook*, Vol. 3 (1967), pt. 2, pp. 83-115; "Garašanins 'Načertanije' und das Grossserbische Programm," *Südost-Forschungen*, Vol. 27 (1968), pp. 131-147; and (with Barbara Jelavich) "The Call to Action: Religion, Nationalism, Socialism," *Journal of Central European Affairs*, Vol. 23 (1963), pp. 3-11.

[121]"Zemljopis Srbije i Srpskih Zemalja: An Episode in Austro-Serbian Relations, 1907-1912," *Historijski Zbornik*, Vol. 29-30 (1976-1977), pp. 419-429; "Serbian Textbooks: Toward Greater Serbia or Jugoslavia?," *Slavic Review*, Vol. 42 (1983), pp. 601-619; "Nationalism as Reflected in the Textbooks of the South Slavs in the Nineteenth Century," *Canadian Review of Studies in Nationalism*, Vol. 16 (1989), pp. 11-29; "Milenko M. Vukičević: From Serbianism to Yugoslavism," in Dennis Deletant and Harry Hanak, eds., *History and Historians in Central and South-Eastern Europe* (London, 1988), pp. 106-123; "The Issue of Serbian Textbooks in the Origins of World War I," *Slavic Review*, Vol. 48 (1989), pp. 214-233; and "Serbian Nationalism and the Croats: Vuk Karadžić's Influence on Serbian Textbooks," *Canadian Review of Studies in Nationalism*, Vol. 17 (1990), pp. 31-42.

[122]Columbus, 1990, xvii + 359 pp. It is worth noting parenthetically, in connection with our comments elsewhere about breadth and depth, that, with this book, the Jelaviches had to their credit at least one major monograph dealing with each of the countries and empires involved in Southeast Europe except for Albania.

[123]David Hackett Fischer, *Historians' Fallacies* (New York, 1968), pp. 230-232.

[124]Eugen Weber, *From Peasants into Frenchmen: The Modernization of Rural France, 1870-1914* (Stanford, 1976), p. xi.

[125]C. Jelavich, *South Slav Nationalism*, 1990, p. xi.

[126]*Ibid.*, pp. xi-xii.

[127]*Ibid.*, pp. 30-31. Cp. pp. 263-277.

[128]Another example of this unfortunate "timeliness" is Charles' 1962 discussion of Serbian policymakers and intellectuals in "Serbian Nationalism and the Question of Union with Croatia in the Nineteenth Century," which is as accurate a description of the present as it is of a century ago.

[129]These time-consuming and often thankless contributions explain why Charles' bibliography is a good deal shorter than it might otherwise be.

[130]Chicago, 1957; and also R.R. Palmer, ed., *Abridged Historical Atlas* (Chicago, 1958). He also advised Rand McNally on its European wall map series.

[131]"Yugoslavia," in George Frederick Howe, *et al*, eds., *The American Historical Association's Guide to Historical Literature* (New York, 1961), pp. 584-590.

CHRONOLOGICAL BIBLIOGRAPHY

I. Works by Barbara Jelavich

A. Doctoral Dissertation

BJ1. *The German Alliance System, 1939-1941* [Unpublished doctoral dissertation, University of California at Berkeley, 1948], 348 pp.

B. Books

BJ2. *Russia and the Rumanian National Cause, 1858-1859* [Bloomington: Indiana University Publications, 1959], xi + 169 pp. Volume 17 in the Indiana Slavic and East European Series. Reprinted with a new bibliographical preface. [Hamden: Archon Books, 1974], xv + 169 pp.

BJ3. *Russia and Greece during the Regency of King Othon, 1832-1835. Russian Documents on the First Years of Greek Independence* [Thessaloniki: Institute of Balkan Studies, 1962], 155 pp. + illustrations.

BJ4. *Russland 1852-1871. Aus den Berichten der Bayerischen Gesandtschaft in St. Petersburg* [Wiesbaden: Otto Harrassowitz, 1963], 156 pp.

BJ5. *A Century of Russian Foreign Policy, 1814-1914* [Philadelphia: J.B. Lippincott, 1964], x + 308 pp.

BJ6. *Russia and the Greek Revolution of 1843* [Munich: Oldenbourg, 1966], 124 pp.

BJ7. *The Habsburg Empire in European Affairs, 1814-1918* [Chicago: Rand McNally, 1969], viii + 190 pp. Reprint edition: [Hamden: Archon Books, 1975], viii + 190 pp.

BJ8. *The Ottoman Empire, the Great Powers, and the Straits Question, 1870-1887* [Bloomington: Indiana University Press, 1973], xi + 209 pp.

BJ9. *St. Petersburg and Moscow: Tsarist and Soviet Foreign Policy, 1814-1974* [Bloomington: Indiana University Press, 1974], xii + 480 pp. The section of this book on Tsarist foreign policy is a moderately updated version of BJ5 above.

BJ10. *History of the Balkans*, two volumes [Cambridge: Cambridge University Press, 1983], xiv + 407 pp., and xi + 476 pp.

BJ11. *Russia and the Formation of the Romanian National State, 1821-1878* [Cambridge: Cambridge University Press, 1984], xii + 356 pp.

BJ12. *Modern Austria: Empire and Republic, 1815-1986* [Cambridge: Cambridge University Press, 1987], xvii + 346 pp. The cover gives the dates as "1800-1986."

BJ13. *Russia's Balkan Entanglements, 1806-1914* [Cambridge: Cambridge University Press, 1991], xi + 291 pp.

C. Articles

BJ14. "The British Traveller in the Balkans: the Abuses of Ottoman Administration in the Slavonic Provinces," *Slavonic and East European Review*, Vol. 33 (1955), pp. 396-413.

BJ15. "Servia in 1897: A Report of Sir Charles Elliot," *Journal of Central European Affairs*, Vol. 18 (1958), pp. 183-189.

BJ16. "Russia, Bavaria, and the Greek Revolution of 1862-1863," *Balkan Studies*, Vol. 2 (1961), pp. 125-150.

BJ17. "Document: The Russian Student Abroad, 1861," *Journal of Central European Affairs*, Vol. 22 (1962), pp. 220-221.

BJ18. "Die Östeuropastudien in Amerika und der akademische Austausch mit der Sowjetunion," *Österreichische Osthefte*, Vol. 6 (1964), pp. 70-75.

BJ19. "Russia and the Double Election of Alexander Cuza, 1858-1859. The Letters of S.I. Popov to N.K. Giers," *Südost-Forschungen*, Vol. 24 (1965), pp. 119-137.

BJ20. "The Philorthodox Conspiracy of 1839," *Balkan Studies*, Vol. 7 (1966), pp. 89-102.

BJ21. "Russland und die Einigung Deutschlands unter preussischer Führung," *Geschichte in Wissenschaft und Unterricht*, Vol. 19 (1968), pp. 521-538.

BJ22. "Comments," *Austrian History Yearbook*, Vol. 4-5 (1968-1969), pp. 259-265. Commentary on articles by Paul Schroeder, Burton Kaufman, Ruth Zerner, and Louis Gebhard, Jr., dealing with Habsburg diplomatic and military history between 1854-1911, with a reply by Schroeder, p. 272.

BJ23. "Balkan Nations under European Protectorship," in: N. Todorov and E. Sarafova, eds., *Actes du premier congrès international des études balkaniques et sudest européennes* [Sofia: Académie Bulgare, 1969], Vol. 4, pp. 397-408.

BJ24. "Russia and the Reacquisition of Southern Bessarabia, 1875-1878," *Südost-Forschungen*, Vol. 28 (1969), pp. 199-237.

BJ25. "Great Britain and the Russian Acquisition of Batum, 1878-1886," *Slavonic and East European Review*, Vol. 48 (1970), pp. 44-66.

BJ26. "Russia, the Great Powers and the Recognition of the Double Election of Alexander Cuza: The Letters of A.P. Lobanov-Rostovskii to N.K. Giers, 1858-1859," *Rumanian Studies*, Vol. 1 (1970), pp. 3-34.

BJ27. "Foreign Policy and the National Question in the Habsburg Empire: A Memorandum of Kálnoky," *Austrian History Yearbook*, Vols. 6-7 (1970-1971), pp. 142-159, with a commentary by Adam Wandruszka, pp. 160-163.

BJ28. "Austria-Hungary, Rumania and the Eastern Crisis, 1876-1878," *Südost-Forschungen*, Vol. 30 (1971), pp. 111-141.

BJ29. "The Ottoman Empire, the Great Powers, and the Legislative and Administrative Union of the Principalities," *Rumanian Studies*, Vol. 2 (1971-1972), pp. 48-83.

BJ30. "The Aftermath: the Effect of the Revolution on the Romanian National Movement until 1878," *Conference on the 1848 Revolutions in the Romanian Principalities* [New York: The Romanian Library, 1972], no pagination, 11 pp. Paper presented at the Romanian Library, 14 May 1972, commemorating the 125th anniversary of the Revolutions of 1848.

BJ31. "Russia, Britain and the Bulgarian Question, 1885-1888," *Südost-Forschungen*, Vol. 32 (1973), pp. 168-191.

BJ32. "British Means of Offense against Russia in the Nineteenth Century," *Russian History*, Vol. 1 (1974), pp. 119-135.

BJ33. "Bulgaria and Batum, 1886," *Southeastern Europe*, Vol. 1 (1974), pp. 72-79.

BJ34. "Russia and the Rumanian Commercial Convention of 1876," *Rumanian Studies*, Vol. 3 (1973-1975), pp. 39-60.

BJ35. "A Russian Diplomat's Comments on the Bulgarian Crisis, 1885-1888: The Letters of E.E. Staal to N.K. Giers," *Südost-Forschungen*, Vol. 34 (1975), pp. 247-274.

BJ36. "The Bulgarian Crisis of 1885-1887 in British Foreign Policy," in: Thomas Butler, ed., *Bulgaria: Past and Present* [Columbus: American Association for the Advancement of Slavic Studies, 1976], pp. 65-70. Paper presented at the First International Bulgarian Studies Conference, University of Wisconsin, 2-5 May 1973.

BJ37. "The Balkan Nations and the Greek War of Independence" in: Nikiforos P. Diamandouros, ed., *Hellenism and the First Greek War of Liberation 1821-1830: Continuity and Change* [Thessaloniki: Institute for Balkan Studies, 1976], pp. 157-169.

BJ38. "The Great Power Protectorate and Romanian National Development, 1856-1877," *Revue des Études Sud-Est Européennes*, Vol. 15 (1977), pp. 681-694.

BJ39. "Russia and the April Uprising," *Southeastern Europe*, Vol. 4 (1977), pp. 217-232.

BJ40. "Diplomatic Problems of an Autonomous State: Romanian Decisions on War and Independence, 1877," *Southeastern Europe*, Vol. 5 (1978), pp. 26-35.

BJ41. "Recent Soviet Publications on the Eastern Question," *Russian Review*, Vol. 37 (1978), pp. 177-187.

BJ42. "Russia and Moldavian Separatism: The Demonstration of April, 1866," in: Alexander Fischer, Günter Moltmann, and Klaus Schwabe, eds., *Russland-Deutschland-Amerika: Festschrift für Fritz T. Epstein* [Wiesbaden: Franz Steiner Verlag, 1978], pp. 73-87.

BJ43. "The Russian Intervention in Wallachia and Transylvania, September 1848 to March 1849," *Rumanian Studies*, Vol. 4 (1976-1979), pp. 16-74.

BJ44. "Negotiating the Treaty of San Stefano," *Southeastern Europe*, Vol. 6 (1979), pp. 171-193.

BJ45. "Commentary," *East Central Europe*, Vol. 7 (1980), pp. 345-348. A commentary on three papers on the theme "The Impact of the Dual Alliance of 1879 on the Austro-Hungarian Monarchy: A Centennial Reappraisal."

BJ46. "Preface" to: Joyce Milton and Caroline Davidson, *One Family, Two Empires: The Spanish Hapsburgs; the Hapsburgs in*

Central Europe [New York, HJB Press, 1980], p. 7. Republished as *The House of Hapsburg* [Boston: Boston Publishing Company, 1987], p. 7.

BJ47. "The Ottoman State and the Study of the Diplomatic History of Southeastern Europe," *International Journal of Turkish Studies*, Vol. 2 (1981), pp. 56-65.

BJ48. "The Abdication Crisis of 1870-1871: The International Aspects," *Revue Roumaine d'Histoire*, Vol. 21 (1982), pp. 89-99.

BJ49. "Romania at the Congress of Berlin: Problems of Peacemaking" in: Ralph Melville and Hans-Jürgen Schröder, eds., *Der Berliner Kongress von 1878* [Wiesbaden: Franz Steiner Verlag, 1982], pp. 189-204.

BJ50. "The Effects of the Franco-Sardinian-Austrian War, the Austro-Prussian War, and the Polish Insurrection on Romanian Political Development," in: Béla K. Király, ed., *The Crucial Decade: East Central European Society and National Defense, 1859-1870* [New York: Brooklyn College Press, 1984], pp. 15-27. A Romanian translation appeared in *File din Istoria Militară a Poporului Român*, Vol. 12 (1984), pp. 76-89.

BJ51. "Russian Balkan Policy in the Era of Revolutions," in: Béla K. Király, ed., *East Central European Society and War in the Era of Revolutions, 1775-1856* [New York: Brooklyn College Press, 1984], pp. 627-642.

BJ52. "Tsarist Russia and Balkan National Liberation Movements: a Study in Great-Power Mythology," in: Roland Sussex and J.C. Eade, eds., *Culture and Nationalism in Nineteenth Century Eastern Europe* [Columbus: Slavica, 1985], pp. 56-66.

BJ53. "British Eastern Policy, 1878-1880: the View from Bucharest; the Letters of William White," *Rumanian Studies*, Vol. 5 (1980-1986), pp. 41-83.

BJ54. "Recent Publications on the Habsburg Empire in the United States," *Études Danubiennes*, Vol. 3 (1987), pp. 45-53.

BJ55. "Tsarist Russia and Greek Independence," in: John T.A. Koumoulides, ed., *Greek Connections: Essays on Culture and Diplomacy* [Notre Dame: University of Notre Dame Press, 1987], pp. 75-101.

BJ56. "Geographic Determinants of Rumanian Foreign Policy," *International Journal of Rumanian Studies*, Vol. 6 (1988), Nr. 1, pp. 7-16. Paper presented at the First International Romanian Studies Congress, Paris, 1986.

BJ57. "Mihail Kogălniceanu: Historian as Foreign Minister, 1876-1878," in: Dennis Deletant and Harry Hanak, eds., *Historians as Nation-Builders: Central and South-East Europe* [London: Macmillan, 1988], pp. 87-105. Paper presented at the 11-14 July 1983 conference in honor of Hugh Seton-Watson, London.

BJ58. "When Diplomats Fail: Austrian and Russian Reporting from Belgrade, 1914," *Wilson Center East European Program Occasional Paper No. 20* [Washington D.C.: The Wilson Center, 1989].

BJ59. "Tsarist Russia and the Balkan Slavic Connection," *Canadian Review of Studies in Nationalism*, Vol. 16 (1989), pp. 209-226.

BJ60. "Tsarist Russia and the Unification of Bulgaria and Eastern Rumelia, 1856-1864," in: Don Karl Rowney, ed., *Imperial Power and Development: Papers on Pre-Revolutionary Russian History* [Columbus: Slavica, 1990], pp. 101-115. Paper presented at the 3rd World Congress on Slavic and East European Studies, 1985.

BJ61. "Ignatiev u Carigradu 1876 godine," *Spomenik. Srpska Akademija Nauka i Umetnosti* CXXXII. Odeljenje istoriski nauka, Vol. 8 (1991), pp. 87-136. "Ignatiev in Constantinople in 1876."

BJ62. "France, the Habsburg Empire, and the South Slav Question, 1914," *Études Danubiennes*, Vol. 7 (1991), pp. 19-31.

BJ63. "The Polish Immigration, 1831-1871: The Challenge to Russia," in École française de Rome, *L'émiration politique en Europe aux IX ième--XX ième siècles* [Rome: École française de Rome, 1991], pp. 235-245. Paper presented at the École française de Rome Conference, March 3-5, 1988.

BJ64. "What the Habsburg Government Knew about the Black Hand," *Austrian History Yearbook*, Vol. 22 (1991), pp. 131-150.

BJ65. "Clouded Image: Critical Perceptions of the Habsburg Empire in 1914," *Austrian History Yearbook*, Vol. 23 (1992), pp. 23-35.

D. Edited by Barbara Jelavich

BJ66. "L'Ambassade russe à Paris, 1881-1898: Les Mémoires de Nicholas Giers," *Canadian Slavic Studies*, Vol. 1 (1967), pp. 1-23, 212-237, 379-403, 587-617; Vol. 2 (1968), 68-85, 219-238, 368-390, 525-541.

II. Works by Charles Jelavich

A. Doctoral Dissertation

CJ1. *Russian Influences in Serbia and Bulgaria, 1881-1897* [Unpublished doctoral dissertation, University of California at Berkeley, 1949], 417 pp.

B. Books

CJ2. *Tsarist Russia and Balkan Nationalism: Russian Influence in the Internal Affairs of Bulgaria and Serbia, 1879-1886* [Berkeley: University of California Press, 1958], x + 304 pp. Reprint edition: [Westport: Greenwood Press, 1978], x + 304 pp.

CJ3. *South Slav Nationalisms: Textbooks, and Yugoslav Union before 1914* [Columbus: Ohio State University Press, 1990], xvii + 359 pp. + 16 pp. of illustrations.

C. Articles

CJ4. "Nikola P. Pašić, Greater Serbia or Jugoslavia?," *Journal of Central European Affairs*, Vol. 11 (1951), pp. 133-152.

CJ5. "Russo-Bulgarian Relations, 1892-1896: With Particular Reference to the Problem of the Bulgarian Succession," *Journal of Modern History*, Vol. 24 (1952), pp. 341-351.

CJ6. "The Revolt in Bosnia-Hercegovina, 1881-1882," *Slavonic and East European Review*, Vol. 31 (1953), pp. 420-436.

CJ7. "The Diary of D.A. Miliutin, 1878-1882," *Journal of Modern History*, Vol. 26 (1954), pp. 255-259.

CJ8. "Some Aspects of Serbian Religious Development in the Eighteenth Century," *Church History*, Vol. 23 (1954), pp. 144-152.

CJ9. "Bulgarian Incunabula," *Quarterly Journal of the Library of Congress*, Vol. 14 (1957), Nr. 3, pp. 77-94.

CJ10. "Slavic Studies and Library Acquisitions," *College and Research Libraries*, Vol. 20 (1959), pp. 118-124.

CJ11. "Die Habsburger Monarchie und die nationale Frage der Südslawen," *Südosteuropa Jahrbuch*, Vol. 5 (1961), p. 61-74.

CJ12. "Yugoslavia," in: George Frederick Howe, *et al*, eds., *The American Historical Association's Guide to Historical Literature* [New York; Macmillan, 1961], pp. 584-590. Annotated bibliography.

CJ13. "The Importance of the Leksikografski Zavod to the Scholar," *Slavic Review*, Vol. 21 (1962), pp. 330-335.

CJ14. "Serbian Nationalism and the Question of Union with Croatia in the Nineteenth Century," *Balkan Studies*, Vol. 3 (1962), pp. 29-42.

CJ15. "The Conference," *Austrian History Yearbook*, Vol. 3 (1967), Pt. 1, pp. 1-7. With R. John Rath. An introduction to the published proceedings of the 1966 Indiana Habsburg Conference.

CJ16. "The Croatian Problem in the Habsburg Empire in the Nineteenth Century," *Austrian History Yearbook*, Vol. 3 (1967), Pt. 2, pp. 83-115.

CJ17. "East Central and Southeast European Studies," *American Council of Learned Societies Newsletter*, Vol. 19 (1968), Nr. 2, pp. 1-11.

CJ18. "Garašanins 'Načertanije' und das Grossserbische Programm," *Südost-Forschungen*, Vol. 27 (1968), pp. 131-147.

CJ19. "Graduate Training and Research Needs" in: Charles Jelavich, ed., *Language and Area Studies* [Chicago: University of Chicago Press, 1969], pp. 1-45.

CJ20. "Zemljopis Srbije i Srpskih Zemalja: An Episode in Austro-Serbian Relations, 1907-1912," *Historijski Zbornik*, Vol. 29-30 (1976-1977), pp. 419-429. In English.

CJ21. "Serbian Textbooks: Toward Greater Serbia or Jugoslavia?," *Slavic Review*, Vol. 42 (1983), pp. 601-619.

CJ22. "American Perceptions of the South Slavs, 1875-1941," *RAD. Journal of the Jugoslav Academy of Arts and Sciences*, Zagreb, Vol. 405 (1984), pp. 195-214. In English, pp. 195-212; Croatian summary, pp. 212-214.

CJ23. "Srbija i Crna Gora u uvodnicima *New York Times*-a 1875-1878," *Mesovite Gradje*, Vol. 14 (1985), pp. 59-111. ("Serbia and Montenegro in the Editorials of the *New York Times*, 1875-1878")

CJ24. "East European Studies Today," *Newsletter of the American Association for the Advancement of Slavic Studies*, Vol. 28 (1988), Nr. 1, pp. 1, 3-4. A summary version of his 1987 AAASS Presidential Address.

CJ25. "Milenko M. Vukičević: From Serbianism to Yugoslavism," in: Dennis Deletant and Harry Hanak, eds., *History and Historians in Central and South-Eastern Europe* [London: Macmillan, 1988], pp. 106-123.

CJ26. "The Issue of Serbian Textbooks in the Origins of World War I," *Slavic Review*, Vol. 48 (1989), pp. 214-233.

CJ27. "Nationalism as Reflected in the Textbooks of the South Slavs in the Nineteenth Century," *Canadian Review of Studies in Nationalism*, Vol. 16 (1989), pp. 11-29.

CJ28. "Serbian Nationalism and the Croats: Vuk Karadžić's Influence on Serbian Textbooks," *Canadian Review of Studies in Nationalism*, Vol. 17 (1990), pp. 31-42.

D. Edited by Charles Jelavich

CJ29. *Selected Problems in the Relations of Federation and Republics and Modern Literary Development in America and Yugoslavia: Reports on the American-Yugoslav Seminar, Zadar, June 18-23rd, 1963* [Ljubljana: Indiana University and the League of Yugoslav Universities, 1968], 498 pp., edited in collaboration with Tihomir Vulović.

CJ30. *Language and Area Studies: East Central Europe and Southeastern Europe. A Survey* [Chicago: University of Chicago Press, 1969], xix + 483 pp. By CJ: Preface, pp. ix-xvi; Postscript, pp. 467-470; Chapter 1, pp. 1-45 [item CJ 19]; Chapter 3, pp. 79-128 [with Barbara Jelavich; item CBJ 11].

III. Works by Barbara and Charles Jelavich

A. Books

CBJ1. *The Habsburg Monarchy: Toward a Multinational Empire or National States?* [New York: Rinehart, 1959], 57 pp. Source Problems in World Civilization Series.

CBJ2. *The Balkans* [Englewood Cliffs: Prentice-Hall, 1965], xi + 148 pp. A volume in the Modern Nations in Historical Perspective Series edited by Robin Winks. A Japanese edition with an additional chapter on 1965-1980 was published by: [Tokyo: Kobunsha, 1982], 248 pp.

CBJ3. *The Establishment of the Balkan National States, 1804-1920* [Seattle: University of Washington Press, 1977], xv + 358 pp. Vol. VIII in the Washington History of East Central Europe Series edited by Peter Sugar and Donald Treadgold. Paperback edition, 1986, xv + 358 pp.

B. Articles

CBJ4. "The Occupation Fund Documents: A Diplomatic Forgery," *American Slavic and East European Review*, Vol. 12 (1953), pp. 343-349.

CBJ5. "The Occupation Fund Documents. Additional Evidence," *American Slavic and East European Review*, Vol. 14 (1955), pp. 390-401. A reply to Paul Blackstock, "The Occupation Fund Documents: A Reassessment of 'A Crude and Ignorant Forgery'," *American Slavic and East European Review*, Vol. 13 (1954), pp. 535 ff.

CBJ6. "Russia and Bulgaria, 1879: The Letters of A.P. Davydov to N.K. Giers," *Südost-Forschungen*, Vol. 15 (1956), pp. 427-458.

CBJ7. "Bismarck's Proposal for the Revival of the Dreikaiserbund in October 1878," *Journal of Modern History*, Vol. 29 (1957), pp. 99-101.

CBJ8. "Jomini and the Revival of the Dreikaiserbund, 1879-1880," *Slavonic and East European Review*, Vol. 35 (1957), pp. 99-107.

CBJ9. "The Danubian Principalities and Bulgaria under Russian Protectorship," *Jahrbücher für Geschichte Osteuropas*, Vol. 9 (1961), pp. 349-366.

CBJ10. "The Call to Action: Religion, Nationalism, Socialism," *Journal of Central European Affairs*, Vol. 23 (1963), pp. 3-11.

CBJ11. "History" in: Charles Jelavich, ed., *Language and Area Studies: East Central and Southeastern Europe* [Chicago: University of Chicago Press, 1969], pp. 79-128.

CBJ12. "Yugoslavia: History," in: Paul L. Horecky, ed., *Southeastern Europe: A Guide to Basic Publications* [Chicago: University of Chicago Press, 1969], pp. 501-515.

C. Edited by Charles and Barbara Jelavich

CBJ13. *Russia in the East, 1876-1880: The Russo-Turkish War and the Kuldja Crisis as seen through the letters of A.G. Jomini to N.K. Giers* [Leiden: E. J. Brill, 1959], xi + 173 pp.

CBJ14. *The Education of a Russian Statesman: The Memoirs of Nicholas Karlovich Giers* [Berkeley: University of California Press, 1962], ix + 241 pp. Reprint edition: [Westport: Greenwood Press, 1982], ix + 241 pp.

CBJ15. *The Balkans in Transition: Essays on the Development of Balkan Life and Politics since the Eighteenth Century* [Berkeley: University of California Press, 1963], xv + 451 pp. Papers published for the Berkeley Center for Slavic and East European

Studies Balkan conference, 13-15 June 1960. Reprint edition: [Hamden: Archon Books, 1974], xv + 451 pp.

IV. Miscellany

M1. Charles Jelavich served as consulting editor for Russia, Eastern Europe, and Europe since 1914 for R.R. Palmer, ed., *Atlas of World History* [Chicago: Rand McNally, 1957]; R.R. Palmer, ed., *Abridged Historical Atlas* [Chicago: Rand McNally, 1958]; for Russia and East Europe on the special map "History of Europe--The Major Turning Points," in *National Geographic*, December 1983; and "Yugoslavia," also in *National Geographic*, August 1990. He edited the following maps for the World History Series of the Rand McNally Educational Publishing Department, Chicago: "Europe in 1914," 88 x 118 cm, 1963, republished in 1987; "Europe, 1922-1940," 88 x 118 cm, 1963, republished 1986, 1987; "Europe After World War II," 124 x 124 cm, 1963, republished 1987; "Expansion of Russia in Asia," 75 x 117 cm, 1980, republished in 1988; "Expansion of Russia in Europe; European Invasions of Russia," 91 x 117 cm, 1980, republished in 1988.

M2. Charles and Barbara Jelavich have contributed individually and together numerous articles on the Balkans and Eastern Europe to *The Encyclopedia Americana* (1985-1991 editions), including "Balkans," Vol. 3 (1991), pp. 91-97; "Brătianu, Ion," Vol. 4 (1991), p. 450; "Brătianu, Ion[el]," Vol. 4 (1991), p. 451; "Iorga, N." Vol. 15 (1991), p. 350; "Pasič, N." Vol. 21 (1991), p. 507; "Yugoslavia," Vol. 29 (1991), pp. 709-729; and to *The New Encyclopedia Britannica: Macropaedia*, 15th edition, including "The Balkans," Vol. 14 (1990), pp. 562-588 (co-authors).

NATIONAL ECONOMY OR ECONOMIC NATIONALISM IN THE BOHEMIAN CROWNLANDS 1848-1914

Catherine Albrecht
University of Baltimore

In the economically well-developed Bohemian crownlands of the Habsburg monarchy, political leaders, economists, and businessmen all were concerned with growing economic competition between Germans and Czechs. Czech national leaders in particular sought to create an economic basis for eventual national self-determination. The goal of Czech national economic policies was to control more of the wealth of the Czech lands, both in absolute terms and in relation to their German neighbors. Czech economic thinkers expected that economic power would bring greater political leverage, most directly in helping them attain property qualifications for suffrage rights. They also sought to reduce the perceived economic dependency of the Czech people, which was seen as paralleling their political dependency. Economic development was seen as a prelude to, but not a substitute for, political power.

The Czech national economic program, which provided a model for other ethnic groups in Eastern Europe, involved two overlapping approaches. The first was self-help. Liberal economic ideas were known in the Habsburg monarchy primarily through popular adaptations of the works of Adam Smith and David Ricardo. Liberalism had a special appeal in the mid-nineteenth century to the Hungarians and the Czechs who opposed the German-dominated administration and sought self-government, an end to feudal restrictions, and the freedom to compete with established German businesses. Among the Czechs, the most unabashed economic liberal was František Ladislav Rieger, who had visited England in 1848 and became convinced of the potential of economic freedom and industrialization to transform his backward society and bring prosperity to the Czech nation. On a more practical level, the slogans of Samuel Smiles--self-help, thrift, duty--appealed to the emerging Czech middle class, as did the optimistic promise of moral and material success embodied in Smiles' writings.[1]

The second approach to achieve economic self-sufficiency was the more exclusive policy of *svůj k svému* or "each to his own."

Svůj k svému reflected the rising protectionist sentiment in Europe in the late nineteenth century. It was a practical extension of Friedrich List's concept of "national economy" to the Czech situation. List's policies had applied to an as-yet-ununified Germany and were intended in part to prepare the ground for eventual political unification of the German territories. List and his followers in Bohemia each emphasized the nation, not the individual or the state, as the basic economic unit. They sought to examine the whole complex of economic operations within the nation: trade, industry, agriculture, transportation. National economic policies reflected the needs, institutions, and goals of a particular nation and were designed to strengthen and unify a nation politically. List advocated a limited form of tariff protection to enable new industries to reach world standards for quality and efficiency of production. Once a nation's industries were sufficiently well developed to compete on the international market, tariff protection could be dropped.[2] "National" economic policies, however, were difficult to apply in ethnically mixed areas. List himself did not believe that the small ethnic groups of eastern Europe could adopt such protectionist policies.[3] The Czechs faced the additional problem of how an ethnic group that lacks the administrative resources, territorial integrity, and authority of a state can implement national economic policies.

Throughout the second half of the nineteenth century, Czech national leaders tried to apply both the liberal principles of self-help and the more protectionist ideas of *svůj k svému* to attempt to create the economic basis for eventual political autonomy. National economic policies encompassed a broad spectrum of responses to economic change; they were intended to encourage Czechs to embrace the opportunities presented by modern industrial society and, at the same time, to protect Czech society from the more wrenching transitions associated with industrialization.[4]

Liberalism: From Self-Help to Entrepreneurship

As early as the 1850s, some Czech political figures called for economic development as a foundation for a strong political movement. Early commentators on economic issues, such as F. L.

Rieger, Karel Havliček-Borovsky, and František Šimáček, all were influenced by the prevailing economic liberalism of the time and saw economic self-help as the best means to achieve prosperity.[5] Self-help implied both individual initiative and, in the spirit of national economic competition, national self-help through economic associations, business and economic education, and cooperation.

Economic associations of all sorts provided networks of support for Czech businessmen and could act as lobbies to influence government policies. The first modern economic association was the *Jednota ku povzbuzení průmyslu v Čechách* (*Průmyslová jednota* or Industrial Union), established in 1833 by "patriotic" nobles. Although founded as a voluntary association, the Industrial Union acted initially as a semi-public institution, mediating between the needs of the business community and the government until this function was taken over by the Prague chamber of commerce in 1850. The Industrial Union sought to promote domestic industry, learn from foreign experience, expand technical education, and spread knowledge of new techniques through publications, exhibitions, and its library. In the 1840s, the Industrial Union lowered its membership dues and began to attract as members Czech artisans and small proprietors who came to dominate the union by the 1860s. The most important activity of the union in the 1860s and 1870s was to sponsor technical education.[6] Another influential self-help association, the business society *Merkur*, was founded in 1862 and came under Czech control after 1868.[7] Many other specialized economic societies focusing on particular industries or trades also were founded in the 1860s and 1870s. They functioned both as interest groups and as organs of national unity.

Business schools, textbooks, journal articles, and public lectures all provided ways of educating the Czech public about the basic principles of economics and sound business practices. The first challenge facing prospective Czech instructors and publicists was to create a vocabulary for business and economics. The introduction of Czech language into spheres like business, in which communication had been dominated by German, was an early goal of Czech reformers.[8] F.L. Chleborad, F.L. Rieger, and Antonín Skřivan wrote the first Czech-language textbooks on economics and business in the 1850s.[9] As Skřivan noted in the introduction to the third edition of his basic bookkeeping text, when he prepared the first edition in the 1840s, he had trouble finding a publisher, since no one believed such a text would sell.[10] In fact, it became the standard work on the subject.

Changes in business law and in the role of the state in the economy, the growing importance of international trade, and the problem of determining which regulations applied to which types of business all created a need for education for businessmen. The Industrial Union organized a weekend course of business instruction in Prague in 1850. Formal education began at the *Prager Handelsakademie* in 1856.[11]

Czech students enrolled in the German-language courses at the Prague Business School and in the weekend courses sponsored by the Industrial Union, but the demand for instruction in the Czech language grew. After several unsuccessful attempts to convince the Prague academy to institute parallel courses in Czech, the Czech students withdrew and the Czech business community, led by the society *Merkur*, organized its own *Československá akademie obchodní* (Czechoslavonic Business Academy) in 1872.[12] Of course, Czech students of business also needed to learn west European languages if they were to trade with those countries; both English and French composition were included in the curricula of the new business academies.[13]

The Czechoslavonic Business Academy became the premier institution for prospective Czech businessmen. It was directed by Eduard Tonner and employed as teachers such economists as Albín Bráf and Josef Kaizl. In the 1880s and 1890s, Czech and German business schools and academies were established in the other major towns of Bohemia.

Another area encompassed by the self-help movement was cooperation. Various cooperative ventures were organized to enable the Czechs to become more independent and to ensure that the profits of Czech labor remained in Czech hands. Credit cooperatives were a particularly successful aspect of the program.[14] Czechs also formed cooperative sugar factories and other types of farmers' cooperatives. Such cooperative ventures were not always well run, however, and their future growth potential was limited by their organizational structure and style of management.

The cooperative movement was integral to the self-help movement in the Bohemian lands for several reasons. First, cooperatives were decentralized, flexible, and under local control. Second, credit associations helped individual Czech proprietors achieve some degree of financial self-sufficiency since they could lend money to support small business ventures. And third, advocates of cooperation like František Šimáček and F.L. Chleborad hoped that if workers were included in cooperative ventures, they would identify their political and economic interests with those of the nation rather than with the aims of the international working class. Thus, cooperatives could contribute to ethnic autonomy, prosperity, and even social cohesion.

One final appeal of economic liberalism and self-help was its connection with various movements for political self-government, including the Old Czech (National party) demands for a restoration of the historic rights and autonomy of the Bohemian crownlands. State right advocates demanded financial autonomy for the provinces and spelled out economic objections to centralism. Antonín Kusý, for example, argued that economic policies formulated in Vienna might not apply to conditions in the Czech lands.[15] Advocates of state right also sought to give provincial diets more control over economic policymaking. Despite their ultimate goal of self-sufficiency, however, Czech national-economic leaders did seek to influence Austrian economic policies. Every new tax law, monetary reform, tariff, social policy, or state loan would have some impact on the economies of Bohemia, Moravia, and Silesia. Without influence in government, the Czechs would not be able to ensure that they would benefit from Austrian policies. As Robert Luft has pointed out, Czech professors of economics, like Albín Bráf and Josef Kaizl, were active in politics, serving both as representatives to the provincial diet or the *Reichsrat* and as ministers in Vienna. The division of Charles University into Czech and German sections in 1882 also gave the Czech professors of economics an opportunity to influence a whole generation of Czech students.[16]

Economic Nationalism and Svůj k svému

The local initiatives associated with self-help succeeded in establishing a network of small businesses, cooperatives, and economic associations. Czech economists attempted to set such activities in the larger context of national economic policies.

As editor of the journal *Obzor národohospodářský* [National Economic Review], Josef Gruber advocated what he called an economics of nationality--or economic nationalism.[17] This broad policy was intended to enable the Czechs to catch up with their German-Bohemian neighbors technologically and commercially, to achieve economic self-sufficiency, and to create a sense of economic solidarity within the nation by overcoming divisions among social classes. Economic and financial self-sufficiency in the Bohemian crownlands was seen as a first step toward (and a prerequisite for) eventual provincial autonomy or even national independence.

To achieve their goal, Gruber and others envisioned a whole raft of specific policies, ranging from renewing the self-help and cooperative movements of the 1860s to asserting Czech rights and demands more aggressively through the *svůj k svému* campaign. In the first issue of *Obzor národohospodářský*, the editors outlined the purpose of their journal.[18] They sought to raise public awareness of economic problems, outline a specific national response to the social and economic issues of the day, help coordinate the disparate activities of various associations and enterprises, and promote an entrepreneurial spirit among the Czechs. Since knowledge of economic processes was essential to determine sound policies, one of the fundamental goals was to encourage greater public discussion of economic issues and to extend economic education, even to the level of primary schools.

This new interest in coordinating economic activities and pushing for greater self-sufficiency arose in response to several changes in the economic and political environment of the late 1880s and early 1890s. The electoral victories of the Young Czechs (National Liberals) created an atmosphere of renewed national competition. Public awareness of the connection between political and economic competition was heightened by the politically motivated boycotts in Moravian towns beginning in the late 1880s.[19] In 1891, the Czechs organized a large industrial exhibition in Prague to celebrate their economic achievements. This jubilee exhibition, held to honor the one hundredth anniversary of the first provincial exhibition in Bohemia, presented the whole picture of Czech economic accomplishments. It demonstrated that Czech economic progress, while lauded by visitors to the fair, remained limited to traditional areas like sugar refining, brewing, the machine-building industry, and various crafts. The jubilee exhibition therefore turned public attention to the future needs of the Czech economy.[20] Finally, a large national economic congress, meeting in Prague, promoted the creation of a *Národohospodářská společnost* [National Economic Society] and the publication of the first issue of *Obzor národohospodářský* in 1896.[21]

The main problem for the leaders of the national economic movement was to determine what sorts of action could substitute for government policies. Ethnic groups that are not independent obviously cannot provide support for new business enterprises in the form of tariff protection, subsidies, preferential taxes, and so on. Likewise, without the authority to enact laws, such ethnic groups cannot influence directly the economic actions and choices of individuals. Instead, a "national" economy required the voluntary cooperation of Czech producers, investors, and consumers.

Education, publicity, propaganda, and pressure could help raise the ethnic consciousness of Czech consumers and manufacturers and thus had the potential to influence the behavior of individuals. The program that best reflected Friedrich List's proposal for limited tariff protection was *svůj k svému*, which had been used by the Hungarians in the 1840s and was adopted by the Czechs in the 1880s. The term had first been coined by František Palacký, whose phrase "svůj k svému a vždy dle pravdy" [each to his own and always by truth] was picked up by František Šimáček as a powerful slogan and program for action.[22]

Some nineteenth-century commentators made a clear distinction between the liberal programs associated with the self-help movement and the protectionist orientation of *svůj k svému*; others saw *svůj k svému* simply as a more active and effective component of self-help. Josef Kaizl rejected *svůj k svému*, arguing that only outright competition could stimulate more efficient Czech production and services.[23] Moderate advocates of *svůj k svému*, like Albín Bráf, promoted giving preference to Czech businesses and products for a limited period of time. In other words, support of national producers was to function as a kind of short-term protective tariff. Bráf argued that Czech manufacturers had the responsibility to take advantage of public support to make their plants more efficient, so that they could compete on an equal basis with their German competitors. Czech merchants were warned not to take advantage of preferential shopping to charge higher prices or sell products of inferior quality. Bráf conceived of the problem as one of the ethics of the marketplace.[24] The more extreme form of *svůj k svému* involved outright boycotts on the basis of nationality, designed not only to benefit Czech businesses but also to harm German and German-Jewish firms.[25] Thus, the programs associated with *svůj k svému* were more negative and did more to undermine Czech-German and Czech-Jewish relations than did self-help.

Boycotts were organized on both sides of the ethnic conflict; Germans in Bohemia and Moravia used boycotts to counter growing Czech political and economic influence.[26] Although the rhetoric was harsh, even the organizers admitted that boycotts failed to prevent people from buying goods from their traditional local vendors.[27] In addition, boycotts were aimed mostly at retail businesses and failed to prevent Czech retailers from selling German-made goods. There was, in fact, a hierarchy of producers and suppliers to consider: merchants, manufacturers, financiers, laborers, and suppliers of raw materials. The boycotts were most effective in setting a combative mood prior to electoral campaigns in which Czechs sought to defeat German candidates for town councils, the provincial diets, or the imperial parliament.

A strong element of antisemitism entered the campaign. It was not unusual for Czech writers to lump German and Jewish businesses together and target Jewish merchants in particular. One anonymous pamphlet on the subject concluded by defining *svůj k svému* as political and economic antisemitism.[28]

Tactics in the boycotts included distributing lists of German and Jewish businesses to peasants on market days, publicizing the names of Czech customers seen patronizing German or Jewish stores, and flying Czech banners and slogans from Czech businesses. Mass rallies were held to motivate consumers, particularly women shoppers. Some observers even blamed the failure of the boycotts on the refusal of women to adhere to the new shopping patterns or to appreciate fully the significance of such economic action.

Entrepreneurship

In the 1890s and 1900s, national-economic leaders also targeted areas like large industry and foreign trade in which Czech participation lagged. Long-range plans for autonomy or independence demanded that the Czechs not only create and support a national business class but that they also extend their influence into areas of industry and business still dominated by German Bohemians. Late nineteenth-century surveys of the occupations of former students of the Czechoslavonic Business Academy show that most graduates were employed in established enterprises or in the government bureaucracy. Few had created new companies or new wealth for the Czech middle class.[29]

These concerns prompted debate over how best to quicken an entrepreneurial spirit among the Czechs. Some commentators complained that the Czechs seemed to lack fundamental entrepreneurial drive, although they tended to place the blame for this failing on the historical exclusion of the Czechs from certain lines of business. In addition, since Czechs generally had less capital available to them, they were more likely to establish joint-stock corporations, which could come under the financial control of other ethnic groups. The social climate and values of the late nineteenth century were also pointed to as undermining Czech trust or interest in business careers. Several widely publicized cases of fraud hurt the image of Czech business.[30]

Other commentators argued that what was lacking was an environment that would encourage risk-taking.[31] Organizational structures to support new enterprises, such as industrial banks (instead of the older credit cooperatives) or preferential taxes, were needed to encourage Czechs to found new businesses. Financiers like Antonín Pimper and Jaroslav Preiss sought to create large investment banks on the eve of the First World War to help the

Czechs compete with German-Austrian cartels on the Viennese capital market.[32]

Czechs also sought to expand their role in the international trade of the Habsburg monarchy. Czech business was directed mostly toward the domestic market, while foreign trade remained dominated by German Austrians. The more liberal of the Czech national economists argued that the protectionist mentality associated with *svůj k svému* needed to be replaced with a more realistic assessment of Bohemia's place in the international division of labor.[33] To this end, scholarship funds were established by the *Národohospodářský ústav* [National Economic Institute] and the Tonner fund to encourage young businessmen to travel abroad to observe modern technical procedures, study advanced approaches to management, and make contacts with foreign firms.[34]

Interest in foreign trade developed concurrently with attempts by Czech political leaders to establish semi-formal contacts with foreign governments that might support Czech demands for political reform of the Habsburg monarchy. It was also stimulated by Neoslavism, and the Czechs were most successful in penetrating the Balkan market.[35] They encountered high trade barriers and official obstinance in their attempts to export Czech manufactured goods to Russia and were only moderately successful in competing with German-made products in central and western Europe.

Conclusion

National economic leaders succeeded in their goal of educating the Czech public about economic issues and demonstrating the important connection between economic development and political power. The self-help movement created a whole range of new cooperatives and associations to support Czech business activities. The growth potential of cooperatives was limited by their structure, and the associations tended to support small businesses, not the large corporate ventures demanded by economic leaders in the 1890s and 1900s.

The example of the Czech national economic movement was followed by other East European ethnic groups--Poles, Slovenes, Ukrainians, and Croats--each of whom also adopted a mix of liberal and protectionist approaches to economic competition.

The national economic movement was less successful in its attempt to create informal structures to substitute for state support of industry and business. *Svůjk svému* was intended to function as a kind of protective tariff, but its effects were more negative than positive. Protectionist trade policies, restrictive currency regulations, and "nostrification" under the First Czechoslovak Republic were all outgrowths of *svůj k svému*. Self-help and *svůj k svému* also failed to achieve their more idealistic goal: to create a national consensus on economic modernization capable of overcoming social divisions within Czech society.

NOTES

[1]A summary of Smilesian optimism illustrates aptly its appeal to East European ethnic minorities: "The essence of Smiles' message is simply this: no matter who you are or what you are, no matter what difficulties and disadvantages you face, if you apply yourself to your affairs with diligence and perseverance, you will be both happy and successful." A.H. Thornton, "Introduction: The Smilesian Philosophy," in: M.D. Stephens and G.W. Roderick, eds., *Samuel Smiles and Nineteenth Century Self-Help in Education* (Nottingham Studies in the History of Adult Education) (Nottingham, 1983), p. 8. See also Asa Briggs, "Samuel Smiles: The Gospel of Self-Help," *History Today* (May 1987), pp. 37-43. Smiles' major works were translated into Czech in the 1870s.

[2]On List, see Keith Tribe, "Friedrich List and the Critique of 'Cosmopolitan Economy'", *The Manchester School* 61/1 (March 1988), pp. 17-36; and W.O. Henderson, *Friedrich List: Economist and Visionary, 1789-1846* (London, 1983).

[3]Henderson, *Friedrich List*, p. 107; Josef Gruber, "Hospodářství a národ," *Obzor Národohospodářský* (hereafter, *ON*) 9 (1904), p. 307.

[4]A comparison of self-help, cooperation, protectionism, and antisemitism in Germany and the Bohemian lands demonstrates clearly the multiple motives of the "national economists." For comparison with Poland, see Rudolf Jaworski, *Handel und Gewerbe im Nationalitätenkampf: Studien zur Wirtschaftsgesinnung der Polen in der Provinz Posen (1871-1914)* (Göttingen, 1986).

[5]On Havliček, see "K hospodářský názorů Karla Havlička," *ON* 9 (1904), p. 135-37, 181-86, 235-37; Em. Chalupný, "Havliček jako hospodář," *ON* 13 (1908), pp. 22-26. On Rieger, see "Význam Františka Ladislava Riegra pro české písemnictví národohospodářská," *ON* 8 (1903), pp. 297-310. For information on Šimáček, see Adolf Srb, *František Šimáček, jeho život a působení* (Prague, 1910).

[6]On the Industrial Union, see [F.L. Rieger], *Geschichte des Vereins zur Ermünterung des Gewerbsgeistes in Böhmen, Herausgegeben bei Gelegenheit der Feier seines 25 jährigen Beständes am 7 März 1858* (Prague, 1858); *Sto let Jednoty k povzbuzení průmyslu v Čechách, 1833-1933* (Prague, 1933); Albín Bráf, "Národohospodářský vývoj český a Jednota ku povzbuzení průmyslu v Čechách," *ON* 8 (1903), pp. 297-310; and "O Prumyslové jednotě před r. 1848," *ON* 9 (1904), pp. 30-32, 80-82.

[7]On the history of Merkur, see "Rozhledy," *ON* 17 (1912), p. 437-440; and *Obchodnický spolek "Merkur" v Praze, na pamět svého 50. letého trvání* (Prague, 1912), pp. 49-71.

[8]For a perceptive discussion of language with particular relevance to economic competition among ethnic groups, see Brian Weinstein, "Language Strategists: Redefining Political Frontiers on the Basis of Linguistic Choices," *World Politics* 31/3 (1979), pp. 345-364.

[9]F.L. Chleborad, *Soustava národního hospodářství politického* (Prague, 1869); F.L. Rieger, *O statcích a pracích nehmotných a jich významu i postavení v národním hospodářství* (Prague, 1850); *ibid.*, *Průmysl a postup výroby jeho v působení svém k blahobytu a svobodě lidu, zvláště pracujícího* (Litomyšl, 1860); Antonín Skřivan, *Český obchodník*, part 1, *O obchodu vůbec* (Prague, 1851).

[10]Antonín Skřivan, *Nauka o kupeckém slohu* (3rd ed., Prague, 1873); Em. Tonner, *Památce Antonína Skřivana* (Prague, 1890).

[11]*Die Prager Handelsakademie von ihrer Gründung bis zur Gegenwart (1856-1906): Festschrift aus Anlass des 50jährigen Jubelfeier* (Prague, 1906).

[12]*Československá Akademie Obchodní v Praze, za dvacetipětletého trvaní svého od r. 1872 do r. 1897* (Prague, 1898); Ivan Nefe, "Vznik středního českého ekonomického školství po

dovršeni průmyslové revoluce," *Hospodářské dějiny* 14 (1986), pp. 117-149.

[13]For information on courses of study, see the annual reports of the various business academies, especially *Zřizovací listina a učební plán Československé obchodní akademie v Praze* (Prague, 1872); and Franz Glasser, *Das commercielle Bildungswesen in Österreich-Ungarn auf Grundläge des elementaren und mittleren Unterrichte und die Kaufmännischen Lehranstalten des Deutschen Reiches* (Vienna and Leipzig, 1893). See also František Fejfar, *Anglická korrespondence obchodní pro vyšší školy obchodní i pro praktické potřeby obchodníka* (Prague, 1896).

[14]For a bibliography on credit cooperatives in Bohemia, see Catherine Albrecht, "Savings Banks in Bohemia, 1852-1914: The Politics of Credit" (Unpublished Ph.D. dissertation, Indiana University, 1986), ch. 3.

[15]Antonín Kusý, "Hospodářský a sociální význam české státoprávní otázky," in: *Státoprávní politika* (Prague, 1903), pp. 52-77; Josef Pilař, "Finanční politika království českého," *ON* 7 (1902), pp. 353-365.

[16]Robert Luft, "Politische Professoren' in Böhmen, 1861-1914," in: Hans Lemberg, *et al*, eds., *Bildungsgeschichte, Bevölkerungsgeschichte, Gesellschaftsgeschichte in den böhmischen ländern und in Europa: Festschrift für Jan Havránek zum 60. Geburtstag* (Vienna, 1988), pp. 282-306; Helmut Slapnicka, "Die Prager Juristenfakultät in der zweiten Hälfte des 19. Jahrhunderts," in: Ferdinand Seibt, ed., *Die Teilung der Prager Universität 1882 und die intellektuelle Desintegration in den böhmischen Ländern* (Munich, 1984); and Josef Gruber, *První česti universitní učitele národního hospodářství* (Prague, 1918).

[17]Gruber, "Hospodářství a národ," p. 251.

[18]"Úvod," *ON* 1 (1896): 1; E.B. Šimek [Frantisek Čuhel], "Několik slov o národním hospodářství," *ON* 1 (1896), pp. 2-3.

[19]Richard Fischer, *Česká svépomoc hospodářská na severní Moravě* (Prague, 1902).

[20]On the exhibition, see the catalog of exhibits, *Sto let práce: Zpráva o Všeobecné zemská výstavě v Praze, 1891: Na oslavě jubilea první průmyslové výtavy roku 1791 v Praze*, 3 vols. (Prague,

1893). Gruber and Bráf frequently refer to the exhibition as a turning point in public awareness of economic issues.

[21]"Česká společnost národohospodářská," *ON* 1 (1896), pp. 161-162; and Státni ústredni archiv, PP-V (1900-07), inv. no. 21/28. In 1907, the *Národohospodářský ústav* [National Economic Institute] was created as part of the new Academy of Sciences, Letters, and Art. See Jana Mandlerová, "Ke vzniku a činnosti Národohospodářského ústavu pri české akademie cisaře Františka Josefa pro vědy, slovesnost a uměni v letech 1907-1914" *Sborník historický* 20 (1973), pp. 107-141.

[22]Jaroslav Purš, "Phase Shift of Protectionism and Economic Nationalism During the Industrial Revolution," *Historica* 28 (1988), p. 43.

[23]Cited in Josef Gruber, "Hospodářství a národnost v poměrech českoněmeckých," *ON* 5 (1900), p. 58.

[24]Albín Bráf, *Národohospodářské potřeby české* (Prague, 1909), pp. 28-30; see also Bráf, *České a německé svůj k svému* (Prague, 1911).

[25]Fischer, *Česká svépomoc hospodářská.*

[26]A strong advocate of German counterboycotts was *Deutsche Rundschau: Wochenschrift zur forderung der nationale Schutzbestrebung der Deutsche in Böhmen.* See, for example, the first issue of the newspaper, 3 July 1895, where the editors ask German Bohemians not to employ Czechs in any position.

[27]Rudolf Jaworski argues that Polish boycotts against German and Jewish firms in Germany were most effective in small towns that had a surfeit of retail shops. Jaworski, *Handel und Gewerbe im Nationalitätenkampf*, p. 84.

[28][Cyrill Horáček], *Naše hospodářské nedostatky* (Chrudím, 1894), pp. 53-54. This entire pamphlet attacks the Jews as the primary economic enemies of the Czechs. Of course, self-help credit cooperatives could also be founded on an antisemitic basis, since they were designed to combat "usury."

[29]O. Sykora, "O obchodním školství," *ON* 3 (1989), pp. 129-130; [Horáček], *Naše hospodářské nedostatky*, pp. 29-31.

[30]Most important was the collapse of the *Svatovaclavská založna* in 1902.

[31]Interest in entrepreneurship was pervasive among Habsburg economists in the early twentieth century. Erich Streissler, "Schumpeter's Vienna and the Role of Credit in Innovation," in: Helmut Freisch, ed., *Schumpeterian Economics* (New York: 1981), pp. 60-83; and Eduard März, *Joseph Alois Schumpeter: Forscher, Lehrer und Politiker* (Munich, 1983).

[32]Jaroslav Preiss, *Průmysl a banky* (Prague, 1912); Antonín Pimper, *České obchodní banky za války a po válce: Nastín vývoje z let 1914-1928* (Prague, 1929). Vlastislav Lacina argues that the Czechs were unable to compete effectively with the large German-dominated cartels in the early twentieth century. Lacina, "Vývoj hospodářské politiky v českých zemích v obodobí imperialismu," *Sborník k dějinám 19. a 20. století* 10 (1986), p. 199.

[33]"Naše průmyslové podnikaní," *ON* 6 (1901), p. 502.

[34]František Fejfar, *Cesty k obohacení obchodní vědomosti v cizině* (Prague, 1902); Mandlerová, "Ke vzniku a činnosti Národohospodářského ústavu."

[35]Paul Vysny, *Neoslavism and the Czechs, 1898-1914* (New York, 1977); Ctibor Nečas, *Na prahu české kapitalové expanze* (Brno, 1987).

KAREL HAVLÍČEK IN CZECH HISTORIOGRAPHY AND THE CZECH INTELLECTUAL TRADITION

Thomas Pesek
Washington State University

One of the more striking features of the intellectual life of Europe's less numerous peoples has been the expenditure of considerable effort on the study of national personalities whose contributions to their nation's past have been deemed great. Perhaps because they are small in numbers, they have felt less endowed with historical artifacts from which to draw a national heritage and, at the same time, hold up to the world something worthy of honor and respect. Following Thomas Carlyle's efforts in the 1840s to show that "great men," and not institutions, revolutions, or ideologies, constitute the prime movers in history, they could hardly have felt compelled to look elsewhere. The French had their 1789, as well as their Danton, Robespierre, and Napoleon; the English their 1689, as well as their Shakespeare, Milton, and Cromwell. And both could claim that the movements, as well as the men, had made important contributions to world history. But for the Magyars, Czechs, Croats, and other peoples of East-Central and Southeastern Europe, their first revolutions had failed and would not bear fruit until the twentieth century, with the achievement of national independence. For the time being, all that remained were those individuals who had first awakened the people and inspired them to action.

As a person whom the Czechs consider one of the great political figures of their past, Karel Havlíček has received a major share of attention in Czech historiography. After Jan Hus, František Palacký, and Tomáš Masaryk, more in fact has probably been written about him than about any other Czech personality. Yet Havlíček's position as a leader is unique in at least one respect: his contributions to his nation's development, coming at particularly difficult times in the Czech national awakening, not only brought him fame, but also made him the object of bitter controversies and altercations. In this, he shares a place with only one other man: Eduard Beneš. Since the last years of his life, he has been debated by historians, politicians, and propagandists of nearly every intellectual and political persuasion, persons who, in the course of over a century, have shown little unanimity of judgment. Instead, each has sought to portray him in a slightly different way, stressing this or that aspect of his thought, minimizing others, and carefully fashioning an image to suit particular interests or convictions.

If one were to look only at Havlíček's own times, the considerations which prompted people to write about him were overwhelmingly political in nature. Both before and during the revolutions of 1848, no one could deny his stature as a national leader and few were oblivious of his stand on controversial issues. Yet none felt motivated, in the intensity of the nation's political struggles, to attempt comprehensive, critical analyses of his policies and thought. It remained for the defeat of the revolution and Havlíček's death a short time later (1856) to provide an impetus strong enough either to attack or to defend him. The constitutional experiments were over, absolutism was restored, and all that remained for disillusioned politicians was to try to explain why events turned out as they did.

Persons who earlier had opposed Havlíček for various reasons were now quick to see in him part of the reason for the Czechs' political defeat: his stand against the creation of a separate Slovak literary language in the early 1840s had driven a wedge between Czechs and Slovaks, weakening both peoples in the ensuing struggle against the dynasty and the dominant nationalities; his refusal to support the abortive uprising of students and radicals in June 1848, and May 1849, had influenced others to do likewise, thus jeopardizing their chances for success; and so on. Simultaneously, many of Havlíček's friends felt that he was being unjustly accused, and they hastened to defend him against his detractors. With this in mind, they eventually wrote their own polemical tracts.

Among later writers, motivation became more diverse. Easier access to Havlíček's writings, as well as the growing remoteness of 1848, enabled some scholars to begin to produce reasonably balanced commentaries on his career. Still, there was never a scarcity of persons whose approach to him betrayed the fact that they wished merely to censure him, or to capture his name in the interest of some political party, theory of history, or socio-economic creed. Common to most was a conviction that their Havlíček, and theirs alone, corresponded to the man as he had actually existed. The result has been an ever increasing number of articles and monographs that offer no substantial popular or scholarly consensus on the meaning of his thought and work.

In general, differences of opinion concerning Havlíček over the years can be attributed to the fact that his "historical legacy" remained, in a sense, incomplete. The brevity of his life and career, together with his lack of opportunity, due to political circumstances, to clarify his stands on controversial issues or to answer his critics, contributed to much misunderstanding about his political philosophy. Unlike his contemporaries Palacký and Rieger, whose lives spanned several important periods of the Czech national awakening and whose careers lend themselves more to analysis from the standpoint of maturation and change, Havlíček remained almost exclusively a figure of the 1848 revolution and its immediate aftermath. His major writings cover a period of but six years. The issues he faced were limited; the possibilities for resolving them even more so. Because he wrote under duress and restrictions of censorship, the principal ideas of his political philosophy often appeared unclear or underdeveloped and were therefore misread or interpreted variously. As a result, Havlíček's legacy has remained open to discussion which has focused at times on his probable response to situations he never faced, or his actual position on issues he addressed only briefly. Herein lies the cause of the controversy.

The first popular image of Havlíček to take root among the Czechs as a whole was that of a national martyr. Common during the late 1850s, it was created in part by his premature death, but even more by the dramatic events that preceded it.[1] Reciting a "dead hero's" political epigrams, especially those with anti-German themes, became a popular practice of the time. In the ensuing years, this contributed to the growth of a veritable Havlíček cult. When a relatively recent writer, Adolf Mokrý, characterized certain Czech politicians of the 1860s and 1870s as persons who "knew little of Havlíček and who, out of a scarcity of information, created fragmentary conceptions...far removed from his true likeness,"[2] he, in effect, could also have been describing these very earliest of Havlíček's devotees; their knowledge of him was just as incomplete, ill-formed, and inaccurate. Still, it is unlikely that they would have acted otherwise. The absolutism of Maximilian Bach was still in force at the time and revolution against Vienna was unthinkable. As a result, the tendency to idolize Havlíček developed largely as an outgrowth of national frustrations and as an endeavor on the part of the Czech people, even though in a small way, to express their dissatisfaction over the lack of political freedom in Austria.

The period of liberalization which dawned in the Austrian Empire in the early 1860s eventually enabled the Czechs to honor Havlíček more openly. Public expressions of respect were no longer suspect or viewed by the government as potential sources of unrest; and instigators of such displays were no longer liable to arrest. It was at this time that there appeared in Bohemia the first scholarly, critical commentaries on Havlíček's career, together with random selections from his literary works. In 1860, some of his lesser-known poems appeared in the literary series *Obrazy života* (Pictures of Life), under the editorship of the nationalist poet Jan Neruda. Two years later, Palacký wrote a brief character analysis of his former colleague, followed by a similar sketch by the German poet Alfred Meissner.[3] Finally, in 1865, a commentary on Havlíček's political program appeared in the second volume of Anton Springer's *Geschichte Österreichs*.

Generally speaking, these writings presented objective pictures of Havlíček and his activities. Few contained recriminations, and most avoided rigid value judgments. Yet all remained, to some degree, fragmentary and incomplete. What seems likely is that lack of access to Havlíček's newspapers and correspondence prevented even well-intentioned people from gaining a total view of him. Their speeches, journal articles, and other expressions of esteem were based almost entirely on personal recollections and, as a result, they fell victim to inaccuracy and a misunderstanding of his true endeavors.

Characteristic of much discussion about Havlíček in the mid-1860s was its political tendentiousness. The feeble, new experiments in constitutionalism, begun in 1860 with the October Diploma and continued the next year by the February Patent, had stimulated among the Czechs a renewed interest in political activities. New political groups began to emerge and old ones were rejuvenated; and party leaders undertook the task of formulating programs, clarifying their "heritages," and searching out new party standards and symbols around which to gather support. Into this maelstrom fell Havlíček. In January 1864, controversy over certain aspects of his political program broke out between the radical Young Czech newspaper, *Národní listy*, and several prominent Old Czechs, including Palacký and Rieger. Each side tried to show that Havlíček belonged more to its own political tradition than to that of the other.[4] The Old Czechs, favoring cooperation with the Austrian government consistent with national interests, stressed Havlíček's support of Austroslavism, the program through which Czech liberals in 1848 had affirmed Austria's need to exist and their own willingness to settle differences with Vienna amicably. The Young Czechs, less ready to compromise, pointed instead to the period after the revolution in which they detected in Havlíček's ideas a much stronger note of opposition to the government. At approximately the same time, old Radical Democratic recriminations were raised again, this time by a minor politician, Jan Sojka, who restated his group's criticism of Havlíček for having refused to support an all-out Czech revolt against the Habsburgs. By the end of the decade, there existed more or less three major interpretations of Havlíček, all centered around one small but important aspect of his activities.

The publication in 1870 of the first volume of Havlíček's writings went a long way toward dispelling erroneous notions about him. Undertaken by a member of the Old Czech political faction, Václav Zelený, and members of the literary-political club "Svatobor," this project received enthusiastic support from much of the Czech public. Two years later, Zelený also completed the first part of a detailed biography, based largely on letters and manuscripts from Havlíček's papers which scholars had never before used.[5] For the first time since his death, there seemed a distinct possibility that controversy over Havlíček would cease. But such was not to be the case. In 1879, the polemics of the preceding decade resumed suddenly, when one of Havlíček's earliest and most severe critics, Jakub Malý, published an extensive study of the Czech national renaissance of the early to mid-nineteenth century.[6]

Unlike earlier commentators who had discussed him primarily in relation to some specific issue or period, Malý attempted to evaluate Havlíček within the broader framework of his entire career. First, he paid his adversary a perfunctory compliment, admitting that he deserved a prominent place among the influential leaders of his time. He also praised his pre-1848 struggle to rid Czech literature of its "excessively patriotic quality." But overriding the positive remarks was his criticism of Havlíček as a person who was incapable of existing "without the arguments and controversies in which his natural character incessantly involved him" and who "frequently went beyond the bounds of discretion and customary propriety in his attacks on others."[7] He further suggested that Havlíček's rigid stand on the issue of Slovak linguistic separatism had divided and weakened the Czechs, declaring flatly that "no responsible person ever agreed with [his] improper denunciation of the Slovaks."[8] Thus Malý's overall assessment was clearly an unfavorable one, his major implication being that, while Havlíček did accomplish some good in his capacity as a national spokesman, his lack of discretion in dealing with important issues ultimately hurt, rather than helped, the cause of his people.

As one might have expected, these comments ignited a new series of disputes, charges, and countercharges which, with few interludes, continued into the twentieth century. The first response of importance came from the Young Czech Party publicist, Karel Tůma, who in 1885 completed the first full-length biography of Havlíček.[9] Admitting his intention to defend Havlíček against those who had "sought to detract from his character," Tůma proceeded to attack both the Austrian government, which had harassed and exiled him, as well as those of his countrymen who had "belittled his admirable struggle" and "betrayed" him.[10] Among the latter, he singled out Malý for special denunciation. But Tůma was not satisfied with writing a mere *apologia* for his hero. Instead, he introduced, as had so many before him, his own characterization of Havlíček's personality and thought, stressing as representative traits almost everything that Malý and the Old Czechs had criticized or rejected.

In Tůma's view, Havlíček personified three things: political liberalism, anti-Germanism, and anti-clericalism. In order to substantiate his opinion, he again concentrated on Havlíček's life between the years 1849 and 1856 and distorted much of the evidence he found, in particular Havlíček's attitudes toward the dynasty and his attacks on church institutions, as expressed in the *Epištoly kutnohorské* (Kutná Hora Epistles). Through a highly subjective selection of facts, yet another Havlíček emerged, considerably removed from the man as he was, but one nonetheless suited to the propagandistic purposes of the author and his political party. To quote from Chalupný an almost classic description of what had taken place:

> Havlíček's name and citations from his statements, chosen one-sidedly from an opposition point of view, became (for the Young Czechs) a sacred arsenal (by which they) terrified representatives of the government and haunted the more conservative elements among the Czech people. Havlíček's true life, its richness and diversity, its metamorphoses and its flaws, receded into the background and Karel Havlíček Borovský became the subject of legend and a little god whose monument was erected on a number of dogmas: the demon Bach, the hell of Brixen, and the premature death of a martyr. And above them all, in place of the saint's halo, flew unyieldingly the red and white flag of the Czechs.[11]

The Young Czech tendency to reduce all of Havlíček's activities to political opposition and radicalism did not go unchallenged for long. In fact, reaction against it set in almost immediately. The Old Czech press, led by *Pokrok* (renamed *Hlas národa* in 1886), rejected Tůma's interpretations, and the polemics between the two camps resumed, although it should be noted that nothing substantial was ever resolved. Even the publication toward the end of the decade of Havlíček's Brixen papers, as well as scholarly new commentaries on his residence and trial in Kutná Hora, failed to settle the many hotly-contested questions concerning his post-1848 activities. The appearance in 1887 of the contentious memoirs of Radical Democrat Josef Václav Frič, one of Havlíček's earliest adversaries, merely added to the controversy.[12] More than thirty years after his death, Havlíček was still the subject of heated debate.

A somewhat different side to the story, though equally interesting, is the development in the late nineteenth century of Havlíček's image among the common people. Throughout earlier decades, scholars had begun gradually to publish the results of research on Havlíček's career which, far from supporting one or another interpretation, pointed convincingly to the fact that his political ideas were quite diverse and that they could not be divided into rigid or mutually exclusive categories. In this respect, scholarly writings pointed up some of the more obvious weaknesses in sensationalistic explanations of Havlíček's thought. But, in spite of the progress, the image of Havlíček which remained most widespread in Czech society as a whole was the distorted one fostered by Tůma and the Young Czechs. The picture of a blameless martyr, deserted in the struggle for national rights by most of his contemporaries, had a strong appeal for a number of mass groups, especially students and members of the Sokol movement. They, in turn, were instrumental in spreading it among the general population during the last years of the nineteenth century. Undoubtedly they too felt themselves part of the national struggle and, lacking more effective means of opposing the government, they sought out symbols of past opposition around which to rally popular enthusiasm. This they did with Havlíček, despite the fact that their uncritical adulation led to a sentimentalizing attitude toward him which was as foreign to his character as anything could possibly have been.[13] Though one could say that change toward a truer picture of Havlíček was transpiring on a scholarly plane, such change at this time had yet to filter down to the level of the general public.

The fortieth anniversary of Havlíček's death in 1896 was the occasion for the publication of a number of new commentaries on his life and career.[14] These served to add additional information to a constantly growing fund of biographical materials, but, in most instances, they resolved no important controversies. The most significant contribution eventually proved to be the work of Tomáš G. Masaryk, at that time professor of philosophy at the Czech university in Prague.

In several respects, Masaryk added important new dimensions to the study of Havlíček. First, he demonstrated more convincingly than any author before his time that Havlíček had been a consistent opponent of armed revolution as a means of effecting political change in the Austrian Empire. This, in Masaryk's opinion, constituted a cornerstone of his entire approach to politics. It was, supposedly, the outgrowth of his conviction that "the progress of individual nations and the whole of mankind [can be] only gradual and slow,...not continuous and without interruptions" and that men must be patient in seeking fulfillment of their just demands.[15] On no account must they resort to open revolt against their society, unjust though that society may be, for each revolution contains within itself the seeds of reaction, and the more violent the revolution, the worse will be the reaction.[16] Revolutionaries therefore err when, in their desire to reform society, they try to do it too quickly and risk everything by failing to see that society must first pass through intermediate stages of development, which temper the impact of change and make it more acceptable to all.

Masaryk's second argument--an exceedingly complex one which defies simple explanation--was that the Czech revolution of 1848, and by extension Havlíček's role in it, constitutes a continuation of the religious struggle of the Czech people begun in the fifteenth century under Jan Hus. The principal causes of the struggle, at least from the standpoint of the Czechs, were a general concern over the role of religion in society during a period of religious decline; unwillingness to tolerate church involvement in secular affairs, which had accentuated that decline; and a desire to reform the church, more in structure and administration than in dogma, in order to make its mission truly catholic. This last consideration, based on the idea that religion exists in order to further the moral and spiritual advancement of mankind, gave the movement a pronounced "humanitarian" character.

In the Czech revolution of 1848, and especially in Havlíček's writings, Masaryk thought he detected similar elements. True, the situation was different; but the national mind toward religion and the Catholic church as a whole seemed sufficiently identical to warrant contention that the religious reform idea had had some continuous existence in Czech history since the Hussite period and had made Czech history unique. Havlíček's anticlericalism and call for church reform were clearly within the spirit of Hussite aims, and he himself had alluded to Hus as one of his chief sources of inspiration.[17] Even Havlíček's liberalism, Masaryk maintained, had a religious slant to it; far from going to the atheist extremes of some of his liberal contemporaries, he (Havlíček) retained an abiding faith and respect for religion and was not so intransigent in his opposition to the official church that he would not accept her preeminent role in Austria were she to end her support of dynastic absolutism and begin to serve the interests of all nationalities.[18]

These interpretations paralleled ones which Masaryk had formulated in another of his major works, *Česká otázka*, concerning the nineteenth century Czech political awakening. There he had viewed Havlíček, and Palacký too, as thinkers in a long line of Czech intellectuals who, by the middle of the nineteenth century, had taken the concepts of "reason" and "humanity" and had applied them to the predicament of the nation. "Humanitarian," an adjective used to describe the whole of the program, was never precisely defined; but in essence, Masaryk considered it in the Enlightenment sense, where it had meant efforts to liberate human beings and society consistent with the dictates of reason. It stressed a belief in progress, the ability of men to find truth through their native rational faculties, and the need for nations and human beings to respect the rights of others. Applied to the Czech situation, it led to the study of the nation's past as a guide to a better future life and to attempts to "create and foster an independent self-sustaining Czech culture" through the cultivation of the national language and a national literature.[19]

In view of Havlíček's supposed relationship to this ideal, Masaryk declared the Slovak Pan-Slav poet Jan Kollár (1793-1852) to be the Czech journalist's most important "humanitarian" predecessor. This was one of Masaryk's main points and it contained an element of irony; for Havlíček had frequently opposed Kollár's "Slavism" as being at least partially detrimental to Czech interests. But Kollár's contribution was unmistakable, and it involved the addition of an idea to the Czech national tradition that became a pre-condition, as it were, to Havlíček's own contributions.

Before the publication of Kollár's poetic masterpiece *Slávy dcera* (The Daughter of Sláva) in 1824, the thrust of the Czech movement had been in the direction of humanizing religion, education, and the like, much in the spirit of Hus and Jan Amos Komenský (Comenius). Little if any attention was paid to the question of nationality. But beginning with J.G. Herder and other German Romantics, intellectuals began to view society not so much as an aggregate of human beings with common citizenship, class structure, or religious beliefs, but more as communities of people sharing the same language, literature, and historical experiences.[20] To Herder, the "State," a political entity, was strictly an artificial concept. It had no life other than the one imparted to it by the nationality or nationalities that comprise it. In order to liberate Man according to reason, one had therefore to foster his development primarily in the area of nationality, which gave meaning to all of his other relationships.

Kollár took this idea and, in the form of *Slávy dcera*, gave it to the Czechs. "Slavism," he believed, represented in the highest degree the notion that nationalities were the basis of society and that only the unhindered flowering of their cultures would ensure their progress and survival. The latter could be accomplished through such things as the formal study of culture and language and by raising the educational level of the people. Reciprocal cultural and literary relations could also be promoted among the various Slavic peoples, especially considering the similarity of their languages and the similar social conditions among them. But the main emphasis remained on nationality; and for this reason Masaryk could say, with justification, that "humanity from an ethical point of view, education according to reason, became [for Kollár] a *national* ideal."[21]

In the writings of both Havlíček and Palacký, this identification of nationality with humanity continued, with two modifications: whereas Kollár's humanitarianism had led him to espouse the mutual self-reliance of *all* Slavs, based on a cultural, *non-political* reciprocity, Havlíček and Palacký extended the program to political reciprocity and restricted it to just certain Slavic peoples. In the minds of Havlíček and Palacký, the most critical area of a people's striving was in its political life; and only in Austria did the Slavs have sufficiently similar, even if not always identical, political interests to justify joint action on their part. There they were all deprived of political power under the same set of circumstances, even while sharing in the linguistic and spiritual heritage Kollár considered characteristic of the Slavic world as a whole.

The result of this change was the program of "Austroslavism," which Masaryk viewed as an integral part of the Czech humanitarian tradition. In his letter to the Frankfurt Assembly in 1848, Palacký had cited the "interests of humanity" as his main justification for wishing to preserve Austria. Were she to be destroyed, he had said, imperial Russia would soon extend her control over the whole of central Europe. Austria's destruction would make it impossible for the nations of the area to develop their respective identities.[22] Federalization alone could achieve the goal, for only federalization would allow development of nationality in the fullest sense, that is, political, in addition to its social, economic, cultural, and intellectual aspects. What Palacký did was to take the idea of Natural Law, the right to total human development as dictated by reason, and derive from it the doctrine of the equality of all peoples.

In evaluating Havlíček, Masaryk saw in him a man who differed from Palacký not so much in the substance of their program as in the way they approached it. As a journalist, Havlíček was considerably more concerned with the practical side of politics. This was in contrast to Palacký, who was by vocation a historian and, by temperament, a philosopher and a statesman. In the latter's writings one could find a great, almost overriding sense of history and the past, which served as a scientific reserve in arguing the validity of present policies. In Havlíček's writings this was less the case. The past was not unimportant to him, but it seldom provided answers to daily problems, which in his opinion had to be treated on a practical, *ad hoc* basis.

Havlíček's journalistic involvements also gave him a considerable appreciation of political tactics. Although it is difficult to generalize, "tactics" to Havlíček meant primarily "intellectual honesty." It meant adhering to convictions and principles--political, philosophical, and otherwise--even at the risk of being wrong or rigid in dealings with others. Masaryk termed this "*opravdovost*," the opposite of expediency. Seldom was Havlíček expedient or compromising in his views simply to gain an advantage over his adversaries.[23]

Finally, and perhaps most strikingly, Havlíček was a man who identified with the common citizen, in which respect he emerged as a more "democratic" leader than Palacký. Throughout his journalistic career, he wrote in an idiom that common people could understand and even used vulgarities when he thought them necessary. He shared little of Palacký's concern for the upper classes and proudly referred to himself as a "simple Czech." In Masaryk's view, this represented a unique expression of the humanitarian ideal. It implied that the flowering of personality and rights, though important to the development of corporate nationality, had also to affect the lives of people as individuals, irrespective of social class.[24]

During the immediate pre-World War I period, disputes over Havlíček diminished. In fact, accord among scholars persisted throughout the twenty-year existence of the First Czechoslovak Republic. There was not, to be sure, complete satisfaction over existing explanations. But the majority of those who at this time contributed studies on Havlíček's career contented themselves with writing journalistic articles, or with editing Havlíček's political writings, correspondence, and epigrammatic poetry. No major revisions of earlier interpretations were attempted.[25] The sole synthetic works of note were those of the sociologist Emanuel Chalupný, who was heavily influenced by Masaryk; but they too were non-contentious in that they merely explained opposing interpretations without attempting to resolve them.[26]

Only after 1948 does one find a resumption in Czechoslovakia of scholarly and other kinds of polemicizing over Havlíček's significance. The seizure of power by the Communist party in February of that year led to efforts by party leaders to rechannel completely the cultural and intellectual life of the people along certain prescribed ideological lines. This, they hoped, would accelerate the nation's transition to socialism. At the same time, attempts were made to discredit certain scholarly disciplines which were thought incompatible with Marxism, or which could somehow be identified with the bourgeois past. Historiography, considered one of the principal means by which the bourgeoisie had tried to explain and justify its dominant influence in the country, became logically one of the first fields to be attacked.

All Marxist accounts of 1848 published in Czechoslovakia up until the mid-1960s depict Havlíček's National Liberal party as having pursued policies detrimental to the interests of the masses of the Czech people. The program of the party, Austroslavism, was of course grounded in the belief that the political and national interests of the Czechs and other Austrian Slavic peoples could best be served by federalizing and preserving the Habsburg Monarchy, rather than through its destruction or breakup into small, self-sustaining units. In the Marxist view, this approach was a result not so much of political considerations as it was of the desire of the program's creators, the bourgeoisie, to protect their economic and social interests against "emancipation-minded" lower classes. Palacký's politics became, according to one Marxist interpretation, an actual instrument of imperial reaction; within a short time, as Austroslavism began to flounder on nationalist dissension between Slavs and Germans, the bourgeoisie were forced to seek additional backing for their chauvinistic goals.[27] This led them to solicit the support of the lower Czech classes, the result being that they diverted the proletariat from the class struggle and thereby made the restoration of absolutism inevitable.[28]

Marxist treatment of Havlíček, however, differed considerably from that meted out to his political party. As a supporter of the political group that had "betrayed the democratic revolution of the Czech people," he could not be exonerated from all of the blame laid on the middle class for the failure of the mid-century uprisings.[29] One writer in fact contended that he almost always acted in accordance with the interests of his class.[30] But, at the same time, Havlíček stood out so strongly as a symbol of opposition to Habsburg absolutism, especially in the years from 1849 to 1856, that he could hardly be said to have compromised popular interests consistently. In that respect, he qualified as a person who might yet be included in a pantheon of progressive figures from the past.

In order to create out of him a sufficiently radical personality, effort was made to show that, in his practical politics, Havlíček never fully belonged to the liberal, bourgeois camp and that, in spirit, he actually stood close to the Radical Democrats, whom he had regarded as his political opponents. The latter identification was accomplished by stressing such things as his somewhat more positive attitude toward revolution during the regime of Bach, and by attributing to him a special awareness of the plight of common people, which he is said to have acquired under the influence of "rising social forces." The fact that certain "proletarian" writers later identified with him was also seen as evidence that Havlíček had links to the beginnings of the Bohemian working class movement.[31] What logically remained for traditional interpretations was either to reject them as too one-sided, or to dismiss them as a bourgeois ploy for blinding the people with notions of rationalism and reform.

During the late 1960s, however, and extending even beyond the Soviet intervention of 1968, relaxation of Communist party controls over intellectual affairs in Czechoslovakia led to some fundamental reevaluations by Czech historians of their nation's past. Writing in the popular historical journal *Dějiny a současnost* (History and Contemporary Affairs), Josef Kočí, for example, argued that many judgments made during the Stalinist era concerning Havlíček's politics and those of the liberal bourgeoisie were no longer acceptable to a majority of scholars. In particular, he objected to the standard Marxist contention that the "betrayal" of the people by the middle class--if, indeed, there was a betrayal--constituted the principal reason for the defeat of the central European revolutions for 1848-49.[32] Given the political conditions of the times--the relative weakness of the nation, emphasis on freedom of nationality as the greatest of all freedoms, and Czech concern over the rampant nationalism of stronger ethnic groups like the Germans and Magyars--Kočí argued that Austroslavism and Havlíček's support of it were entirely logical policies. To maintain that the Czech bourgeoisie, in supporting Austria, were any less "democratic" than the German bourgeoisie, who opposed her continued existence, is specious reasoning; among both groups, the main impetus to action was "nationality," not social emancipation. The latter remained the callword of only a small, boisterous, and largely inarticulate minority. Havlíček and his fellow liberals erred, therefore, not because they sacrificed the needs of the people to absolutism and the interests of their class, but because they saw the needs of the people contained almost exclusively in the narrow concept of "nationality."[33]

In summary, it is clear that a simple reading of the literature on Havlíček affords no uniform picture of him. The ways in which he has been treated suggest, in fact, that those who have written about him, and not Havlíček himself, are the key to understanding his legacy. Attempts to "correct" conceptions of Havlíček, to "vindicate" him, or to impugn or justify his policies have all been common at one time or another. But these tendencies cannot always be evaluated fully, because many are the result of subtle biases and prejudices of which only the authors are cognizant and which they alone can explain.

Virtually all one can say with certainty about the way in which Havlíček has been treated is that the interpretation of each author, politician, or publicist has usually had a strong relationship to his own time, to the social, political, and intellectual milieu in which he wrote or lived. One needs only to consider such a person as Karel Tůma to see that this is true. His publication emphasizing Havlíček's "revolutionary" qualities coincided almost exactly with the first attempts of his Young Czech Party, under Dr. Julius Grégr, to radicalize Czech political strategy in the early 1880s and to wrest the political leadership of the Czech people from the more conservative Old Czech faction, led by F.L. Rieger.[34] Similarly, when Masaryk in the late 1890s advanced the opposite contention--that Havlíček favored the preservation of a democratized Empire and that his Austroslavism precluded open revolt against Vienna--he still believed at the time, in his own political philosophy, that "the Czech nation in its most natural interest needs Austria and that...all of its politics must be directed toward the preservation of Austria."[35] And when Marxist historians tried to attribute to Havlíček the characteristics of a social crusader, they clearly mirrored the broad ideological changes forced on all social sciences in Czechoslovakia during the decade of the 1950s.

One must not, of course, assume that everything which has been written about Havlíček has been unduly colored by writers' personal prejudices or by subtle external influences. In every period of modern Czech history, many authors have managed to rise above their surroundings and preconceptions and write about him in a substantially objective way. But when and where objectivity has been lacking, it has invariably been the result of attempts by a few writers to capitalize on his name for spurious, non-scholarly purposes; and those in turn can be understood only in reference to the Czech people and to the peculiar course of their political development over the past one and one-half centuries.

Every society has symbols which serve to alter or maintain the power practices that exist within it. In the course of their modern history, the Czechs have often been in opposition to the status quo and, hence, they have tended to search out those symbols which denote disaffection and opposition. Karel Havlíček was, and remained long after his death, such a symbol. More than any other figure in recent Czech history, he personified sensible discontent with the old order by espousing a militancy sufficiently strong to bring about change, and yet not so strong that it would lead to the anarchistic extremes of some of his revolutionary contemporaries. This approach has always appealed to the Czech people, because they themselves have been ready to oppose when opposition has seemed warranted, and yet have done so only after carefully and realistically assessing the strength of the forces they felt they had to overcome.

NOTES

[1]Specifically, his trial in Kutná Hora in 1851 and his banishment to the Tyrol.

[2]Adolf Mokrý, *Karel Havlíček Borovský po sto letech* (Stockholm, 1956), p. 12.

[3]See Chalupný, *Havlíček: prostředí, osobnost a dílo* (Prague, 1929), p. 4 for a general discussion of this literature.

[4]*Ibid.*, p. 5.

[5]This detailed study, which treats Havlíček's activities up to the time of his return from Russia in 1844, appeared originally in the historical-political journal *Osvěta* (Enlightenment) in 1872 and 1873. Due, however, to Zelený's death a short time later, the biography, together with a second volume of edited writings, was never completed.

[6]Jakub Malý, *Naše znovuzrození: přehled národního života českého za posledního půlstoletí* (Praha, 1880).

[7]*Ibid.*, pp. 76 and 69. Malý's ambivalence is in some ways reminiscent of comments made earlier by another of Havlíček's political adversaries, W.J. Picek, a spokesman for the new conservatism and reactionary policies of Bach. See W.J. Picek, *Politische Fragmente über Böhmen: ein Beitrag zur Wurdigung der nationalen und politischen Bestrebungen der Čechoslaven* (Prag, 1850), pp. 58-59.

[8]Malý, *Naše znovuzrození*, p. 74.

[9]Karel Tůma, *Karel Havlíček: nejslavnější publicista českého národa* (Kutná Hora, 1885).

[10]*Ibid.*, pp. 6-7.

[11]Chalupný, *Havlíček: prostředí, osobnost a dílo*, p. 6.

[12]A new, three-volume edition of these memoirs, with accompanying commentary, was published in Prague between 1957 and 1963 under the editorship of Karel Cvejn. Most scholars agree that the reminiscences cannot be used as a totally reliable discourse on the events of 1848-49 because of his close identification with the most extreme faction in the Czech political camp. As a purely personal record, however, the memoirs are of considerable value and should not be dismissed lightly.

[13]Chalupný remarks that, while conducting research for his book, he personally encountered persons who thought that Havlíček had been poisoned by Austrian authorities after his release from confinement. Such a belief, needless to say, has no basis in fact and merely served to obscure more the actual occurrences of Havlíček's life.

[14]Notable among these were the personal recollections of Havlíček's friend Antonín Musil, the reminiscences of Havlíček's sister Johanna, Augustin Žalud's *Karla Havlíčka život, působení a význam* (The Life, Work and Significance of Karel Havlíček); and T. G. Masaryk's *Karel Havlíček: snahy a tužby politického*

probuzení (Karel Havlíček: Struggles and Aspirations of the Political Awakening).

[15]Masaryk, *Karel Havlíček*, p. 163.

[16]*Ibid.*

[17]*Ibid.*, pp. 268-290.

[18]*Ibid.*, pp. 287-289. Reaction to Masaryk's book was mixed. Among foreign scholars and politicians, response was largely negative. The Croatian peasant leader Stjepan Radić, a man with some acquaintance with Czech history, together with the French historian Ernest Denis, were in the forefront of those who attacked Masaryk's theses, especially his contention that Havlíček could be explained in reference to earlier Czech religious traditions. In the words of Denis: "Havlíček possessed not even a shadow of mysticism; he was a rationalist and a Voltarian and it is this which constitutes his originality." Denis, *Čechy po bílé hoře*, IV, p. 301.

In Bohemia, Zdeněk Tobolka, a prominent historian and spokesman for a segment of the Prague intellectual community, also criticized parts of the book. In his opinion, Havlíček was more a rationalist and a liberal of the Rotteck-Welcker type, something which Masaryk, especially in the first edition of his book, had been reluctant to concede. But the dean of Czech historians, Jaroslav Goll, as well as other scholars, praised the work as one of the author's greatest. Once again, nothing was resolved and no compromises were reached. If anything, the latest exchange of opinions seemed only to confirm an observation once made by Tůma that Havlíček's writings were indeed so diverse that almost anyone could find in them something that would appeal to him. For further information, see Tobolka's review of Masaryk's study in *Naše doba*, XI (1904), pp. 787-788; and Masaryk's reply, "Havlíček, skutečný a fiktivní," *Naše doba*, XII (1905), pp. 78-80.

[19]See *Česká otázka*, pp. 7-8.

[20]*Ibid.*, p. 21.

[21]*Ibid.*, p. 14. The italics are mine.

[22]*Ibid.*, pp. 81ff.

[23]The preceding and following interpretations of Havlíček are found in several places in *Česká otázka*. See in particular pp. 91-101.

[24]On the basis of the above evaluations, it is the judgment of this writer that Masaryk, more than any other commentator to his time, correctly assessed the significance of Havlíček. Yet even Masaryk's interpretations are far from "normative."

[25]The articles of Karel Kazbunda which appeared in *Český časopis historický* in 1924 and 1926 are perhaps the most significant articles on Havlíček from the inter-war period. They treat respectively Havlíček's confinement in Brixen and his surveillance by Austrian police authorities prior to 1848.

[26]Chalupný's *magnum opus* was first published in 1908 under the title *Havlíček: obraz psychologický a sociologický*. An expanded version, *Havlíček: prostředí, osobnost a dílo*, appeared in 1929. Two condensations of these books were also published in 1911 and 1921 as part of the "Zlatoroh" series on outstanding personalities in Czech history.

[27]*Přehled československých dějin*, II, Part I, p. 41.

[28]*Ibid.*

[29]B. Stanislav [Stanislav Budín], *Karel Havlíček Borovský* (Praha, 1954), p. 5.

[30]*Ibid.*, p. 445.

[31]*Ibid.*, p. 437. See also Václav Procházka and Miloslav Formánek, *Myšlenkový odkaz Karla Havlíčka Borovského* (Praha, 1961), pp. 145-146, for argumentation along much the same lines.

[32]Josef Kočí, "Havlíček a austroslavismus," *Dějiny a současnost*, VIII (March, 1966), p. 10.

[33]*Ibid.*, pp. 11-12. See also the author's two later articles "Havlíček a radikální demokraté" and "Havlíček a čechoslovakismus," *Dějiny a současnost*, VIII (April and May, 1966), pp. 10-12 and 7-10.

[34]Zdeněk Tobolka, *Politické dějiny československého národa od r. 1848 až do dnešní doby*, III, Part 1, pp. 241ff.

[35]From an address by Tomáš G. Masaryk in 1891 in the town of Strakovnice. Cited from Kamil Krofta, *Z dob naší první republiky* (Praha, 1939), p. 10.

HABSBURG EDUCATIONAL REFORM, NATIONAL CONSCIOUSNESS, AND THE ROOTS OF LOYALISM: WEST-GALICIA DURING THE PERIOD OF NEO-ABSOLUTISM

Peter Wozniak
Auburn University at Montgomery

The birth of a modern secondary school system in the Habsburg monarchy may be dated with precision to the promulgation of the *Organizational Outline for the Austrian Gymnasia and Technical Schools* in April 1849. That document was conceived and executed by two pedagogues working for the newly formed Ministry of Education, Franz Exner and Hermann Bonitz. Approved at first only provisionally, the reform received definitive sanction in December 1854, thanks to the untiring efforts of Count Leo Thun, Minister of Education and Religion. The *Outline* redefined secondary education in the Habsburg lands and became the basis of the educational system from 1849 until the end of the monarchy.

This reform focused on the middle schools (gymnasia) because the primary school system was at yet undeveloped, and, in the wake of the revolutions of 1848, the universities were politically suspect. Concentrating on the classical gymnasium as the backbone of the system, the reform's provisions greatly improved the quality of education in the realm, raising it up from the stagnation into which it had sunk during the Vormärz.[1]

The *Organizational Outline* was founded upon the twin conceptions that any educational system must build a coherent whole, and that true educational reform could not be implemented in a piecemeal fashion.[2] Thus, the central government decreed changes in all aspects of middle school education: curriculum, language of instruction, faculty training and supervision, textbooks, and student life. At the core of this educational philosophy was the idea that philological study, especially of the classical languages, was the "inexhaustible source of a truly humanistic education."[3] The framers of the *Outline* firmly believed that this emphasis on the classics trained men effectively for leadership. Philological study served as a kind of "mental calisthenics" enabling students to deal with abstract thoughts, and the analysis of Greek and Roman authors theoretically led to a higher morality.[4] Thus, the purpose and goal of the new system was to mold young minds and help create men loyal to the state and prepared for an active role in society.

Due to the generally poor state of middle school education throughout the Habsburg lands in the first half of the nineteenth century, and to the diversity of local conditions in the provinces, the reform could not be implemented evenly. It took many years to work out various problems in each of the provinces, and often the theory of the reform was not an accurate reflection of the reality of the classroom.[5] Nonetheless, the new system was better organized and more uniform than ever before.

The promulgation of the *Organizational Outline* coincided with the beginning of a new political system for the empire. During the decade of the 1850s the Habsburg state became a highly centralized political entity. Historians have dubbed this either the "Bach Era," after the Interior Minister Alexander Bach, who masterminded the administrative system, or the decade of Neo-Absolutism, referring to the wide-ranging powers that the young emperor Franz Joseph arrogated to himself. The government ruled various provinces under martial law for a number of years, increased the activity of the police force, revamped the administration, and imposed a broad censorship. In 1855, the state signed a concordat with the Vatican which gave the Church wide-ranging prerogatives in secular affairs. Conservative Church, centralized state, and reformed educational system were bound together for the purpose of integrating the various lands and peoples of the Habsburg state into a coherent whole and stamping out any vestiges of the failed revolutions of 1848. During this period, the authorities, hoping to create a conservative, Catholic, state-supporting "Habsburg man," were particularly sensitive to any display of nationalism by the subject peoples.

The Neo-Absolutist state, then, was not known for its espousal of the "ethnic rights" of its many minorities. Those groups among the nationalities clamoring for special consideration or status were suppressed. In the Polish province of Galicia, for example, the regime was resented for its centralization and its Germanizing tendencies, and the historiography on this period has most often portrayed the 1850s as a "dark era" for Polish national development.[6] The political aspirations of the Polish gentry had, in fact, suffered from a series of reverses even prior to the onset of Neo-Absolutism. The failed November Insurrection of 1830, in which many Galician gentry had taken part, an abortive rebellion followed by a bloody *jacquerie* in 1846, and a short-lived revolt during the Springtime of Nations, had taken the wind out of the sails of all but the most fanatic nationalists. The province remained under martial law until 1854. Newspapers and periodicals were suppressed, political clubs were forbidden, and there was an almost total lack of public institutions possessing an exclusively Polish character. After 1848 there was simply no question of active participation in politics.[7] German and Czech bureaucrats inundated the province and once-proud Kraków was turned into a garrison town. In addition, a major portion of the old town in Kraków burned to the ground in July 1850 and natural disasters struck the already poor countryside at periodic intervals. Galicia, in the words of one historian, was in a state "comparable to a hangover."[8]

Thus, it should not be surprising that the Neo-Absolutist period is not often associated with the development of a Polish national consciousness, still less a policy of cooperation with the regime. The government pursued a tendency towards stifling everything Polish and attempted to Germanize the educational system.[9] Habsburg officials had no intention of allowing schools to function as a surrogate forum for political debate or for the nurturing of anti-Habsburg nationalism. For the Jagiellonian University in Kraków, a traditional bastion of Polish nationalism, this signalled drastic changes. The government dismissed all professors hired in 1848 and replaced them with Austrians, many of whom knew no Polish. In 1853, an unprecedented switch to German as the language of instruction led to declining enrollments and encouraged subversive activity. Students meeting in local cafes to discuss politics were arrested for spreading disorder.[10] By the mid-1850s, it had become virtually impossible for students to demonstrate any type of Polish patriotic fervor in public. This picture applied at many, if not most, universities throughout the monarchy.

In spite of the undeniably difficult circumstances in Galicia during the 1850s, however, educated Galician Polish society was anything but stagnant and proved able to contribute to the development of politics and culture in indirect ways. While organized political opposition to the government was impossible, Poles were able to comment on government policy through their reaction to the reforms taking place in the educational system. One vehicle for those responses was institutional, the Kraków newspaper *Czas* (*Time*). Another avenue, far more difficult to trace, may be sought in the multi-faceted activities of the teachers in the West-Galician Schools. Indeed, the foundation of a specifically Polish Galician intelligentsia, which flowered in the subsequent period of autonomy, was actually laid in this earlier period.[11] Finally, attendance statistics serve to reveal something of societies' reaction to the reform. Taken together, these avenues of dialogue indicate that the development of a national egoism and of loyalty to the Habsburg crown were not necessarily mutually exclusive.

In the autumn of 1848, a group of Galician noble landlords known as the "Kraków circle" founded the newspaper *Czas* in Kraków. This daily presented a conservative, clerical view of society and advocated that Poles reject the insurrectionary tradition and accept the status quo.[12] In this, one may discern a predisposition to conciliation and loyalism. Indeed, over the next few years, *Czas* evolved into the prime organ of Galician loyalist politicians. During the Bach era, the paper was able to keep publishing by deliberately not taking an anti-governmental stance on most issues of the day. In its editorials on the educational reform, however, *Czas* proved that it was no mere mouthpiece for official positions. By commenting on the implementation of the reform, the paper seized an opportunity to create a dialogue with both its readers and the government on matters not always strictly limited to pedagogy. It often editorialized on such inherently political issues as the nature and purpose of a unitary state, the necessity of adhering to the principle that all national languages were guaranteed equality, and the desirability of centralization in the Habsburg realm.[13] In addition, the paper often took vehement issue with pedagogical decisions already made by the ministry, especially in regard to the language of instruction, the importance of developing technical schools in provinces as economically backward as Galicia, and on questions of funding.[14] Criticisms of politics and pedagogy were frequently mixed so as to soften, if not mask, their oppositional tone.

The newspaper saw no problem in taking the government to task for what it viewed as flawed or contradictory argumentation. For example, in May and June of 1850, the editors engaged in polemics with the official government organ, the *Reichszeitung*, which had defended the unitary state and written, rather baldly, that the days of national monarchies were over. From a purely practical standpoint, *Czas* replied that in order to be unitary and strong, Austria had to know about each of its nationalities. Thus, the provision in the *Organizational Outline* for lecturing solely on Austrian history in gymnasia was insufficient; national histories must be included as well.[15]

In September, the editors went even further, by tackling the ticklish issue of political centralization and decentralization. While virtually forced to support centralization, the editors included the comment that the multinational structure of the monarchy precluded as thorough a system of centralization as in France. Any centralized Habsburg state was forced to rely on the "strength and vitality" of its component nationalities. Mere recognition of their religion and language was not enough.[16] Furthermore, educating the populace on the history and culture of their own people was essential to progress for both the nation and the state.[17]

It was, however, on pedagogical issues that the editors were able to voice opposition to the government most openly. There, the question of the language of instruction was the prime issue. A stated idea of the reformers had been that all the languages of the monarchy were equal and that each had a natural right to free development, at least in the cultural sphere. The reform document acknowledged the importance of learning one's native language and made provisions for such instruction. Nonetheless, the *Outline* stated that the German language would have to be taught in all schools throughout the empire, due to the fact that is was the most advanced of all languages of the monarchy.[18] Over the first few years of implementation, the Ministry went further than the *Outline* had intended by making German into the primary language of instruction in all schools, arguing that it was best-suited to instruction in advanced subjects. As the decade wore on, more and more subject matter was taught in German. For example, the order of September 12, 1850 decreed that in the West Galician schools German was to be the language of instruction in history, geography, and philosophy from grades three to eight. This evoked a stormy reply from *Czas*. The paper argued that this action was an insult to the principle of equality of languages contained in the *Outline* and to good pedagogy. What did it mean, the editorialist queried, to say "that the language of instruction in Bochnia is Polish" (the official fiction) if these three courses in particular were to be taught in German? For the development of critical thinking--a stated goal of the reform--*Czas* argued that it is important that history, geography, and philosophy be taught in the mother tongue. Furthermore, if students knew German, there should be no need to have passed this law; if they did not, how would they possibly understand the instruction of these difficult subjects? This certainly was not the way, *Czas* thundered, to go about healing "the wounds of the period."[19]

As the decade progressed, however, *Czas* revealed that this opposition to more German in the schools was not based on purely political grounds, nor on any sort of xenophobic nationalism. The paper acknowledged that German was the language of scholarship throughout Europe--there was no denying that. Furthermore, Galician Poles who desired to obtain positions of importance in Austrian society, whether in education or in the bureaucracy, simply had to learn German, and had to learn it well.[20] Through such argumentation, the paper was laying the foundations of a consistent, practical ideology for Poles living under Habsburg rule.

Similarly, *Czas* never missed an opportunity to call for more technical schools in Galicia. In one of the first commentaries on the educational reform as a whole, the paper questioned whether the stress given to the humanistically-inclined gymnasia, which were designed to prepare boys for university study, was misplaced in the Galician context. Was not this training somewhat impractical, *Czas* queried, in a land where the vast majority would not be going on to the university?[21] The paper complained, correctly, that the ministry had not given as much thought to the technical schools as it had to the gymnasia.[22]

Czas would try to fill this gap, arguing that a technical institute should be practically oriented, offering basic instruction in agricultural techniques and in industry, and should attempt to impart some "practical knowledge."[23] Above all, instruction needed to be in Polish in order to improve attendance. Throughout the decade, the paper would periodically compare the poor attendance ratio of Galician schools to other provinces. Inevitably, the column would end with a comment that these statistics might improve if there were more technical schools.[24]

This support of technical education showed that the editors of *Czas* were not quite as hidebound to tradition as is sometimes surmised. In fact, their support of technical education revealed the influence of the reform program of the Polish National Education Commission in the eighteenth century, as well as an implied belief in the role education plays in enhancing economic growth. In its fulminations against the backward state of Galicia's economy the paper was encouraging attitudes perhaps best described as "positivistic".

All in all, *Czas* felt free to criticize the ministry when it saw fit. The editors were consistent throughout the decade in their support of the principle of the equality of language development and in their support of technical education. While the paper had no power--it cannot be said that any of *Czas*' arguments were heeded in Vienna--the paper's editorials certainly show that intellectual life in Galicia was not stagnant. In fact, these editorials open a small window on the process of a developing Galician Polish attitude that would come to fruition in the period of autonomy.

While the exact relationship of schooling to society in general, let alone to the concept of nationalism, is still a matter of some debate among historians of education, the activity of teachers in West Galicia shows that there was certainly an active intellectual response to the reform where it mattered most--in the schools. The faculties of the five gymnasia of West Galicia, located in Bochnia, Tarnów, Rzeszów, Nowy Sącz, and Kraków, each underwent radical change as a result of the reform. By the end of the decade, a solidly professional body of teachers had been created.[25] These teachers were mostly native-born Galician Poles intimately familiar with the province, and not Germans or Czechs, as was the case with the provincial bureaucracy. In at least three areas: curriculum, textbooks, and relationship with students, teachers revealed themselves to be pedagogues dedicated to nurturing a Polish, as well as a loyal Habsburg, mentality among their students. In fact, their actions sometimes reveal a distinctly anti-governmental bias.

Pride of place among all Galician towns was accorded by tradition to Kraków. Independent of the monarchy until 1846, the city had significantly remained Polish in character. In addition, Kraków schools, above all the gymnasium of St. Anne's, had been deeply influenced by the reforms of the National Education Commission more than half a century earlier. That reform had been based less on the classical and more on modern foreign languages and included much more emphasis on practical subjects such as geometry and modern foreign languages than did the Habsburg reform. The Ministry's disregard of the earlier Polish reforms only compounded resentment among teachers, students, and the population in general. For these and other reasons, Kraków emerged as a center of discontent with Habsburg rule and proved to be difficult for the reformers to integrate into the new system.

It was on changes in the curriculum that Galician teachers were first afforded a chance to comment on the government's policy. In general, the Galician faculty implemented the reformed curriculum as best they could. Only in Kraków was there consistent opposition. There, the faculty often complained about the over-attention paid to the classics to the detriment of such "more-useful" languages as French and Russian. Even the teachers of classics tended to disagree with the ministry about the importance of Greek for the Roman Catholic Poles. The crucial issue of curriculum reform for most teachers, however, turned out to be the language of instruction.

It should be noted that there was never any question that the level of fluency in German for the school-going population of Galicia had to be improved. Even in Kraków the faculty recognized this. During several faculty meetings at St. Anne's in the summer of 1850, the German teacher Rev. August Otremba lobbied for an increase of hours.[26] In July, he stated quite bluntly that at least half of the seventh grade students could not read

German at all. Professor Walenty Kulawski, a full lecturer at the Jagiellonian University and part-time instructor in history at the gymnasium, agreed that student's knowledge of history would also be better if their command of German was improved. Neither, however, advocated that instruction itself should be in German.

Although a glance at the official curricula charts over the decade will show that German was increasingly used as the language of instruction in all the schools, these official reports do not necessarily provide an accurate reflection of the reality of classroom life. Instruction in Polish often continued, largely because individual faculty members could not, or would not, instruct in German. In Kraków, for example, starting in 1854, the records show that mathematics was supposed to be taught in German. Most likely, however, it was not. The teacher for this entire period was one Ignacy Gralewski. A product of Kraków's school system himself, Gralewski was widely respected by his colleagues and loved by his students. His spoken German was poor. It seems that he would use German only when the director or the supervisor were in the classroom, switching to Polish when they left the premises.[27] Gralewski was also approved for teaching physics, so it may be assumed that a good deal of instruction in that subject too was in Polish.

The situation in St. Anne's was not anomalous. As late as 1858, in the Nowy Sącz school, courses that were supposed to be taught in German were actually taught in Polish. Similar instances may be found in each of the schools, except for Tarnów, long considered the most "German" school in the province. Thus, although the curriculum was officially Germanized, that cannot be said of either the faculty or the students.

Teachers' work on textbooks was also an important avenue for stimulating both pedagogical progress and the development of a Polish consciousness. Several teachers, often in conjunction with *Czas*, led community-wide drives to collect books for the school libraries in order to supplement the very meager allotment of funds provided by the ministry for this purpose.[28] Others tackled a serious problem head-on by translating various German and Latin texts into Polish. The net effect of this activity was to increase the holdings of gymnasium libraries rather substantially.

A controversy over history texts provided an instance where Polish national feelings actually induced the ministry to make some changes. At first, the major complaint about the standard history text, Wilhelm Puetz's *Grundriss der Geographie und Geschichte*, was that most students' knowledge of German was insufficient to comprehend the text. Thus the book was dropped for pedagogical reasons. In the opinion of the provincial school board, the secondary text approved by the ministry, Theodore Welter's *Lehrbuch der Weltgeschichte*, was even worse due to the "emotional manner in which [the author] describes the partitions."[29] It too was dropped and the difficulties compounded. In February 1853, a third textbook, *Die Weltgeschichte* by Johannes Bumüller, described as "a model for the handling of historical instruction," was accepted as a reference work for students and faculty. By November of that year, however, objections arose on the question of Bumüller's portrayal of the partitions as a "necessary punishment for the behavior of the state."[30] The ministry agreed with the school board that this passage was objectionable, but still maintained that the rest of the work was balanced and useful. Since abandoning Bumüller altogether would have left the schools in the position of not having any suitable textbook at all, a compromise was reached. Volume one of Bumüller would be used without alteration; volume two, covering the partitions, would be edited and then distributed in pamphlet form.

A third field of teacher activity concerned faculty-student relations. By their interaction with the gymnasium youth outside the classroom, teachers played an important role in the intellectual and social development of their students. Father Felix Dymnicki, one of the most beloved teachers in all of Galicia, used to ride his wagon all over the province during the summer vacation in an attempt to raise money for poor boys who otherwise could not afford to go to school. His efforts paid off in 1875 when he had collected sufficient funds to build a dormitory in Rzeszów. Many faculty members housed students in their homes for little or no recompense. Others took the boys on outings during which otherwise forbidden patriotic songs would be sung. Still others made a point of teaching the boys the work of Adam Mickiewicz and other Polish romantic authors. Memoirs show that these teachers made lasting impressions on the minds of their students. While the extent of this influence may only be surmised, it undoubtedly provided a welcome counterbalance to the oppressive political atmosphere.

An idea of the response of Polish Galician society as a whole to the reformed system may be gauged by an examination of attendance statistics. The general patterns of enrollment show that, after an initial period of uncertainty, and then a decline in 1851-53, enrollment began to rise. From 1851 to 1853, noble and peasant alike had suffered substantial material losses from natural disasters and bad harvests.[31] Many were unable to afford the time, others the tuition necessary, to send a son to school. By 1853, however, the bottom had been reached; after that year enrollment steadily increased.[32]

An interesting situation evolved in Kraków. There, St. Anne's exhibited the most dramatic increase in attendance of all West-Galician schools, so much so that by 1855 parallel classes had to be created and, in 1858 a whole new school. Named after St. John, the school was constituted with German as the language of instruction and was meant to accommodate a growing number of students who wished for more and better instruction in German than was available at St. Anne's. This phenomenon, which seems to contradict the notion of Kraków as a hotbed of anti-Habsburg feeling, was due mainly to the emerging cosmopolitan nature of the city. In the 1850s, the population of Kraków was steadily expanding. As the seat of the West Galician governmental apparatus, the city was home to many German-speaking bureaucrats. Officials from all over Galicia, whether Polish, Czech, or German, tended to send their sons to Kraków rather than to the smaller schools. In addition, the Jews of Kraków preferred St. John's to St. Anne's. There is evidence too that many Polish parents enrolled their sons in an attempt to ease the boys' chances for job prospects in the future. Both the head of the Kraków city government and the school inspector reported cases of Polish parents explicitly requesting that instruction be given in German.[33] In the first year, roughly 30% of the students in St. John's were Poles.

As a discussion in the Ministerial Conference showed, however, it was also governmental policy that influenced the establishment of St. John's. Habsburg ministers considered it *politically* desirous to separate German students from Poles, not just in parallel classes, but in an entirely separate institution, fearing contamination from nationalistic Cracovians.[34] Significantly, virtually all of the Polish students attending St. John's were from outside of Kraków. The native Cracovians preferred the "Polishness" of St. Anne's. Thus, Kraków's schools were being pulled in two directions.

Some idea of the social origin of students is also important in assessing the impact of schooling. Although this information is difficult to uncover, it is true that at least the upper classes of the gymnasia were dominated by sons of the nobility. It was they, and not peasants' sons, who would go on to university and to careers in government and public life. Clearly, even within this reformed system, it is too early to speak of any democratization of education.[35] Memoirs show that the Tarnów gymnasium had traditionally been a bastion of the nobility, while the school in Nowy Sącz was a mixture of nobles and poor mountain people. *Czas*, which kept close track of all attendance figures and focused on matters sometimes ignored by the ministry, claimed that St. Anne's had the highest percentage of sons of gentry in all of Galicia.[36] This statistic reflects the fact that Kraków was beginning to serve as a magnet for the *szlachta* from all over the province. Most significant is the fact that it became increasingly common for the son of a relatively well-to-do country squire to spend his middle school years at three and sometimes four different schools, and then finish at St. Anne's. Kraków, a city noted for its traditional advocacy of Polish causes, but increasingly also the home of a developing loyalist mentality, was clearly becoming an important center for students.

In summation, the idea that the Bach Era had little or nothing to contribute to a growing sense of national consciousness or to the development of the idea of Polish loyalty to the Habsburgs merits reevaluation. While there was no possibility of political opposition, Polish society was able to evince a maturing sense of national identity by means of varied responses to the educational reform. In the editorials of *Czas*, for example, one may trace clearly enunciated Polish concerns in a manner totally acceptable to the censors. In the activities of teachers, who were neither Germanized nor "purged" of their national consciousness, one may see important formative influences on the minds of the young men that would later go on to make a mark on the politics and culture of Galician society. It seems clear that some Poles, at least, maintained and even nurtured that rather amorphous phenomenon called national consciousness.

At the same time, it is not true that the harshness of the political regime engendered nothing but the equally harsh, sullen attitude discernible among the university students and faculty of the period. The attendance figures of the gymnasia indicate a society coming to terms with its political and socio-economic condition. While attendance increased in an even more marked fashion after the later polonization of schools during the autonomous period, that should not detract from the fact that attendance also increased in the 1850s. This is especially noteworthy when one considers that the pattern for university study ran in the opposite direction. The evidence would seem to indicate that the reformed smoothly-functioning middle school system was attractive and won steady, if grudging, acceptance in Polish society.

The West Galician model indicates that the educational system offered Poles the opportunity to assert their national identity while simultaneously developing a loyalist mentality unmatched in either of the other Polish partitions. Although it was not until after the political settlement of the 1870s that Galicia witnessed the "flowering" of Polish society, at least one of the institutional preconditions for that development, that is, a reformed educational system, was laid in the 1850s. By the last quarter of the nineteenth century, Galicia would be both the most "Polish" of the partitions and the most comfortable with the political status quo.

NOTES

[1]The state had summoned various commissions for years throughout the reign of the emperor Francis, but had, characteristically, actually done very little good. Administrative changes that reversed direction too often, poor textbooks, and a resurgence of the more traditional elements of the curriculum all combined to frustrate educators. See Richard Meister, *Entwicklung und*

Reformen des österreischsichen Studienwesens (Vienna, 1963); and Helmut Engelbrecht, *Geschichte des österreichischen Bildungswesens* (Vienna, 1984).

The *Organizational Outline* fits what Detlef Müller has called the stage of "system emergence." During this stage uneven and sometimes unrelated developments occur in differing areas of the educational structure. In effect, the situation of Habsburg education in the 1850s was one of a system in the making. See Detlef Müller, "The process of systematisation: the case of German secondary education," in: *The Rise of the Modern Educational System. Structural change and social reproduction 1870-1920*, eds. Detlef Müller, Fritz Ringer and Brian Simon (Cambridge, 1989), pp. 16-17.

[2]It is perhaps significant to note that the reform, although implemented in the 1850s, was not really a child of that period. Its origins are to be sought in the eighteenth century and in the Vormärz, deeply rooted in the pedagogical philosophy of Herbart and in the traditions of Bohemian Reform Catholicism.

[3]*Entwurf der Organisation der Gymnasien und Realschulen in Österreich* (Vienna, 1849), p. 5. Hereafter cited as *Organizational Outline*.

[4]Lenore O'Boyle, "A Possible Model for the Study of Nineteenth Century Secondary Education in Europe," in *Journal of Social History*, vol. 12, #2, Winter 1978, pp. 236-244.

[5]This was especially true in regard to the language of instruction.

[6]See Konstanty Grzybowski, *Galicia 1848-1914: historia ustroju politycznego na tle historii ustroju Austrii*, (Kraków, 1959) pt. IV, pp. 194-200. Also, Piotr Wandycz, *The Lands of Partitioned Poland*, (Seattle, 1974), pp. 150-151.

[7]One Polish scholar wrote, "During the Bach era, there could be talk of working along with Austria only if one did not put forth any demands." Stefan Kieniewicz, *Galicja w dobie autonomicznej (1850-1914)*, (Wrocław, 1952), XII. Also, Marcin Król, "Konserwatyści Krakowscy 1831-1865," in: *Archiwum Historii Filozofii i Myśli Społecznej*, (Warsaw, 1973), t. 19, pp. 175-196.

[8]Stefan Kieniewicz, *The Emancipation of the Polish Peasantry*, (Chicago, 1969), p. 133. On the condition of Kraków, see Lawrence D. Orton, "The Formation of Modern Cracow (1866-1914)," *Austrian History Yearbook*, vol. XIX-XX, Part 1, (1983-84), pp. 105-117.

[9]Waltraud Heindl, "Universitätsreform und Politisches Program. Die Sprachenfrage an der Universität Krakau im Neoabsolutismus," in: *Österreichische Osthefte*, #20, 1978, p. 86. Heindl shows how the majority of the Ministerial Conference, the Reichsrat, the chief of police, and the emperor himself supported a strict policy of Germanization.

[10]Marian Zgórniak, "Młodzież akademicka Uniwersytetu Jagiellońskiego wobec wydarzeń politycznych lat 1846-1866," in *Studia z dziejów młodzieży Uniwersytetu Krakowskiego od Oświęcenia do połowy XX wieku*, ed. Celina Bobinska (Krakow, 1964), tom I, pp. 107-164.

[11]Peter Wozniak, "Middle School Teachers in West Galicia during the Period of Neo-Absolutism (1849-1859)," *The Polish Review*, vol. XXXVI #3, 1991, pp. 283-308.

[12]Marcin Król, "Konserwatyści Krakowscy", 195; Jakub Forst-Battaglia, "Paweł Popiel," in: *Twórcy Polskiej Myśli Politycznej Zbiór Studiów* (Warsaw, 1978), p. 10; and Lawrence Wolff, "Czas and the Polish Perspective on the Austro-Hungarian Compromise of 1867," *The Polish Review*, vol XXVII, #1-2, 1982, p. 65. The founders of *Czas* included Adam Potocki, Lucjan Siemienski, Wincenty Kirchmajer, Paweł Popiel, and Kazimierz Wodzicki.

[13]*Czas* #45 February 23, 1850, #105 May 7, 1850, #127 June 6, 1850, and # 218 September 12, 1850.

[14]*Czas* #205 September 6, 1850, #226 October 1, 1850, # 241 October 18, 1850, #252 October 31, 1850, #45 February 25, 1852, #173 July 31, 1852, and #223 September 30, 1853.

[15]*Czas* #105 May 7 and #127 June 6, 1850.

[16]*Czas* #218 September 21, 1850.

[17]*Czas* #45 February 23, 1850.

[18]*Organizational Outline*, p. 7.

[19]*Czas* #252 October 31, 1950.

[20]*Czas* #201 September 2. 1959.

[21]*Czas* #205 September 6, 1850.

[22]*Czas* #226 October 1, 1850. Changes in technical education proceeded at a slower pace, though these too followed the lines laid down in the *Organizational Outline*.

[23]*Czas* #241 October 18, 1850.

[24]*Czas* #45 February 25, 1852 and #223 September 30, 1853.

[25]Peter Wozniak, "The Habsburg Middle School Reform 1849-1860: With Special Reference to West Galicia," (Unpublished Ph.D. dissertation, Indiana University, 1987), pp. 218-235.

[26]Archiwum Państwowe Miasta Krakowa. (Krakow) GLN 2., *Protokołły z Sesyi Zgromadzenia Nauczycielskiego Liceum Krakowskiego Świętej Anny* #7 June 11, 1850, #10 July 2-3, 1850, and #18 August 13-14, 1850.

[27]See memoirs of Tarnowski and Chłędowski in: Antoni Knot, ed., *Galicyjskie wspomnienia szkolne* (Kraków, 1955). The school inspector's report of November 1855 backs this up. He wrote that, while professors may have had a command of German sufficient for scholarly purposes, their spoken language was poor. Verwaltungsarchiv (Vienna) *Bestand-Unterricht* fasc. 2114 sig. 10 Galizien #25886-855 ad 18150.

[28]*Czas* #70 March 25, 1850. The editors took this opportunity to cite examples of the same sort of collection going on in England, a country unrivaled for its tradition of local initiative.

[29]APKr. GLN 25. *Normalien* p.o. See also Tarnowski's comments in Antoni Knot, *op. cit.*

[30]APKr. GLN 25. *Normalien*, p. 664. Letter from the Provincial School Board to St. Anne's November 28, 1853.

[31]*Czas* #107 May 12, 1853.

[32]For attendance statistics see various issues of the *Zeitschrift für die österreichischen Gymnasien*; G.A. Schimmer, *Statistik der Lehranstalten des oesterreichischen Kaiserstaates 1851-57, Cenzura Ogólna Uczniów Liceum Krakowa Święta Anna*; various yearly reports from each of the schools; and the school inspectors biannual visitation reports.

The school in Bochnia recorded a substantial decrease in attendance after it was demoted to a four-year school in 1852. There was no net decrease in overall attendance, however, because Bochnia's students simply transferred to nearby St. Anne's in Kraków. That school thus exhibited a dramatic increase. The

Rzeszów attendance rate remained relatively stable throughout the period, while that at Tarnów grew notably. Nowy Sącz increased its attendance even more than Tarnów.

[33]Archiwum Główne Akt Dawnych (Warsaw) 202u and 206u. Letter from Heinrich Clam-Martinic to the ministry September 29, 1856, report of Hofrat to ministry (prepared by school inspector Andreas Wilhelm) dated May 16, 1857.

[34]Haus-Hof-und Staatsarchiv. (Vienna) *Kabinettskanzlei* MCZ 2995/1857 July 26, 1857.

[35]For a fascinating discussion of the concept of democratization in schooling see the debate over segmentation and systematization contained in Muller, *The Rise of the Modern Educational System*.

[36]*Czas* #107 May 12, 1853.

MIKLÓS HORTHY AND THE JEWS OF HUNGARY

Thomas Sakmyster
University of Cincinnati

Perhaps the most intriguing aspect of the career of Miklós Horthy, Hungary's head of state from 1920 to 1944, was his relationship with the Jews of Hungary. His political career, in fact, began and ended in national crises that deeply involved the Jews of Hungary. Horthy rose to national prominence in 1919 in an outburst of violence against Communists and Jews known as the White Terror. Through his participation in this campaign of violence, Horthy gained the unsavory reputation abroad as perhaps Europe's most vicious anti-Semite. Horthy was not necessarily embarrassed by such notoriety; on a number of occasions in the interwar period he was to boast that he had been the first statesman to take vigorous action against the Jews.

Yet in World War II, near the end of his tenure as regent of Hungary, Horthy was influential in resisting Nazi Germany's demands for drastic measures against the Jews. Hungary for a time became a haven for the Jews of East Central Europe. When in 1944 German troops occupied Hungary, and the Jews were dispatched by Adolf Eichmann to the gas chambers of Auschwitz, Horthy at first acquiesced in the action but finally stepped forward to halt the deportations and save the lives of most of the Jews of Budapest. In a final ironic twist, after the war Horthy and his family were sustained in exile in Portugal by subsidies from affluent Hungarian Jews who wished to show their gratitude to the former regent.

What was the nature of Miklós Horthy's anti-Semitism, and how can we explain his seeming transformation from an enemy of Jews in 1919 to an apparent protector and even liberator in 1944? For the first fifty-one years of his life before he mounted the Hungarian political stage in 1919, almost nothing is known of Miklós Horthy's attitude toward Jews, or, for that matter, of any of his political and social views. He grew up in a Calvinist, gentry family on a small estate in southeastern Hungary where few Jews lived.[1] During his years of training and service as an officer in Emperor Franz Joseph's imperial and royal navy, Horthy seems to have had little direct contact with Jews. His stint in Vienna as *aide-de-camp* to Franz Joseph from 1909 to 1914 did, however, expose him to the virulent anti-Semitic forces that were stirring in the imperial capital and that had a major impact on Adolf Hitler, whose residence in Vienna coincided almost exactly with Horthy's. Like Hitler, Miklós Horthy learned and accepted the rhetoric, stereotypes, and mythmaking of the vulgar anti-Semitism that had taken strong roots in *fin de siècle* Vienna. For the rest of his life, Horthy would never be able fully to eliminate the dislike for, and suspicion of, the Jews that he acquired in this period.

Yet the greatest influence on Horthy seems to have been the emperor himself, who presided over a political and social regime that was relatively tolerant of Jews, granting civil liberties and providing many opportunities for Jews to excel in the world of finance and the professions. István Tisza and the governing elite in Hungary shared this view and were able to establish a symbiotic relationship with the assimilated Jews. As a result, despite the fact that Jews represented only 6% of the population of Hungary, by the early twentieth century they had achieved a dominant position in Hungarian banking and industry and a leading role in such fields as medicine (59.9% of doctors), law (50.6%), journalism (34.3%), engineering (39.2%), and music (28.6%).[2] Like his revered king and the conservative political establishment in Hungary, Horthy apparently came to appreciate the valuable contributions to society made by the assimilated Jews of Vienna and Budapest.

This relative tolerance toward the Jews in Austria-Hungary, however, was soon to end. Defeat in the Great War, a brief but traumatic experience of Bolshevism in the form of Béla Kun's Soviet Republic, and the dismemberment of Hungary carried out under the terms of the Treaty of Trianon had a shattering impact on Horthy, indeed on virtually all Hungarians.[3] The temptation was overwhelming to place the blame for these traumatic events on a convenient scapegoat. For politically unsophisticated thinkers like Admiral Horthy, the explanation was simple and obvious: the Jews were responsible for all the calamities that had befallen Hungary. From this period comes the earliest record of Horthy's views of the Jews. Echoing a view that had become commonplace in Hungary by 1919, Horthy asserted that the most important national task was liberating the country from all alien racial elements, especially the Jews, who, he believed, had instigated the revolutions that had ravaged Vienna and Budapest.[4] Noting the preponderance of Jewish intellectuals and activists in the ruling elite of the Hungarian Soviet Republic, Horthy now became convinced that the Communist Revolution in Hungary was a gigantic Jewish conspiracy.

Horthy's antagonism toward the Jews in 1919-20 was sharpened by close association with the proponents of the "Szeged idea," an indigenous radical right-wing movement that emphasized a violent anti-Communism, anti-Semitism, and fervent nationalism. Such rabid anti-Semites as Gyula Gömbös, Pál Prónay, and other military officers convinced Horthy that the Jews and Communists represented so invidious a force that only a relentless campaign of terror could bring about the "purification" of the nation. Horthy, who throughout his political career was to prove quite malleable, seemed readily to embrace the language and methods of these Hungarian harbingers of Fascism and Nazism. Agreeing that those who had participated in, or shown sympathy for, Béla Kun's regime needed to be punished, Horthy authorized a violent campaign that came to be known as the White Terror. Among the hundreds of victims of the White Terror in 1919 and 1920 were many Jews who were executed in pogrom-like actions by special officer detachments.[5]

Horthy's collaboration with his extremist officers in 1919 and early 1920 brought to the surface his darkest and most sinister impulses. Convinced of the need to destroy the "Bolshevik poison," Horthy began to speak the violent language of Gömbös and Prónay. "I am capable of anything," he told a colleague. "If necessary, I'll use strychnine poison and employ the basest methods. After all, our enemies have treated us like corpses to be desecrated."[6] When liberal and socialist newspapers in Budapest began to publish articles about atrocities committed in the White Terror and to denounce the officer detachments, Horthy was irate. In public, he indignantly denied that his officers were involved in terrorist actions. Privately, however, he acknowledged that he had under his command men who "with a cold smile will do away with anyone who stood in his way." On several occasions, Horthy vented his antipathy on left-wing journalists in the capital city. When the time came, Horthy told his officers on one occasion, he would have those "Jewish scribblers" hanged "till they rotted in the noose."[7]

It was this kind of intemperate, violent language that implicated Miklós Horthy in the most sensational atrocity of the White Terror. At a gathering of commanders of several officer detachments in late December 1919, someone brought in a copy of a recent article by Béla Somogyi, the Jewish editor of the Social Democratic newspaper, *Népszava*. Banned by the military censor, the article was sharply critical of the officer corps as an instrument of terror. Amid the consternation and outrage evoked by the article, it was suggested that the time had truly come for this "Jewish imposter scribbler" to be tossed into the Danube River. At this point Horthy pounded angrily on the table and declared: "This requires action, not just words!" One of the officers present, Captain Gyula Ostenburg, took this to be a directive from the Commander-in-Chief and proceeded to plan and carry out the murder. In mid-February 1920 the mutilated corpses of Béla Somogyi and Béla Bacsó, one of his fellow journalists, washed up on the banks of the Danube.[8] The news of this caused an uproar in the Hungarian Parliament, and the funeral several days later was turned by the Social Democrats into one of the largest mass demonstrations in Hungarian history.

This unexpected turn of events created a predicament for Admiral Horthy, coming as it did on the eve of the election by Parliament of a regent to serve as temporary head of state. Having benefitted from the wave of revulsion against the Soviet Republic and the yearning for a restoration of orderly government under a man of authority, Horthy was the leading candidate for the regency. He was thus upset to hear of Somogyi's murder; he had apparently forgotten that he had instigated such a thing, if indeed he had ever intended his earlier outburst to be taken literally.[9] In any case, he now upbraided Ostenburg for his clumsy methods and poor timing, but at the same time made it clear that he intended to conceal his complicity and protect the guilty officers from prosecution. In this he was successful, for Horthy's expressions of regret over the incident and his private thwarting of the judicial investigation left the mystery of the crime unsolved. Horthy was thus elected regent in March 1920 by a substantial majority. The murder of the Jewish editor of *Népszava* was to remain, however, Horthy's "darkest secret" for the rest of his life, forcing him for many years to appease the radical officers lest they incriminate him publicly.

Shortly after his election as regent in 1920, Horthy gave his full approval to Europe's first post-war legislation prejudicial to the Jews, the so-called *numerus clausus*. This law stipulated that enrollment of students of various "races and nationalities" in Hungarian universities was to be limited to their percentage in the general population. Thus, the Jews, who were not specifically mentioned in the legislation, but figured prominently in the parliamentary debate, could henceforth not constitute more than 6% of university student bodies.[10] Passage of the *numerus clausus* seemed to confirm Horthy's reputation as one of Europe's most notorious anti-Semites. Jewish organizations and left-wing newspapers throughout Europe deplored developments in Hungary. Demonstrators in Paris, London, and even far away Cleveland, Ohio denounced Horthy as a "butcher of Jews." Yet there are indications that privately Admiral Horthy felt ambivalent about the White Terror and that he by no means shared the racial or biological anti-Semitism that animated such radical officers as Gyula Gömbös and Pál Prónay. Except for his indirect complicity in the assassination of Béla Somogyi, Horthy did not participate personally in the White Terror; on several occasions he did attempt, albeit in oblique or convoluted ways, to lessen its severity. It is worth noting, for example, that in this period, and indeed throughout his political career, Horthy refrained from making any public condemnation of the Jews. Horthy's increasing cautiousness and restraint perplexed Pál Prónay, who complained of his commander-in-chief's "timid conduct" and "pacifistic tendencies." Privately Prónay wondered who could be giving Horthy such bad advice. His wife? The "Jew-loving aristocrats?"[11]

Most disappointing to his Szeged colleagues was Horthy's decision to prevent an unleashing of the full fury of the White Terror in Budapest, or "Judapest" as the enemies of the Jews mockingly called the capital city. As in so many cases, Horthy was deeply ambivalent in his attitude toward the Jews of Budapest. On the one hand he despised the left-wing Jewish intelligentsia who, in his opinion, had inspired and led the revolutions that had nearly ruined Hungary. For these Jews--whom Horthy often referred to privately using the vulgar German expression "Scheissjuden"--the sternest punishment was justified. Yet even as the White Terror was raging in the Hungarian countryside in 1919, Horthy was reverting to the pre-war idea that there were good, patriotic Hungarians who made valuable contributions to the nation, particularly in economic life. Late in 1919 he met with a delegation of prominent Budapest Jews and for two hours listened patiently and respectfully to their arguments and explanations. Horthy assured his visitors that as Hungary recovered its health, he would work to eliminate injustices against the Jews. For their part, the leaders of the Jewish community should exercise a calming influence in Budapest and report to him if any outrages were committed.[12] It did not escape Horthy's notice that most of these establishment Jews and their organizations subsequently supported his candidacy for the regency.

After 1920, as the shock and bitter memories of Béla Kun's regime began slowly to fade, Admiral Horthy gradually reverted to his pre-1918 views. He was skillfully guided along this path by Count István Bethlen, who became the regent's most trusted advisor and served as Prime Minister until 1931. Bethlen regarded the shrill anti-Semitism of the Szeged movement as degrading, vulgar, and detrimental to the interests of the country. Bethlen's careful and persistent arguments and his skill in isolating Horthy from his radical right-wing friends explain the fact that by the late 1920s the pre-war tacit alliance between the conservative political establishment and the community of assimilated Hungarian Jews had been to a large extent re-established. The *numerus clausus* was no longer rigorously enforced, and Hungarian Jews, mostly highly assimilated and in many cases even converts to Christianity, continued to play a leading role in the Hungarian economy, finance, and many of the professions. Certainly anti-Semitism remained in many baleful guises, particularly in the press and propaganda in general, but Horthy and Bethlen succeeded in restoring to Hungary the rule of law and limited civil liberties that had provided a large degree of safety and security to Hungarian Jews before the Great War.

One reason for Horthy's support of Bethlen's quasi-liberal policies was his growing conviction that the Jews who resided in Budapest were by and large "good indigenous types,"[13] that is, patriotic Hungarians who were making useful contributions to society. It is worth noting that in the 1920s, for the first time in his life, Miklós Horthy came to know certain Jews as individuals. Several of the leading Hungarian industrialists and bankers became Horthy's regular bridge partners and informal advisors on economic matters. Perhaps Horthy was awed by their great wealth; perhaps, as Budapest pundits suggested at the time, he sought their company because they allowed him to win consistently at the bridge table. Whatever the case, Horthy developed feelings of friendship and even affection for such men as Ferenc Chorin and Leo Goldberger.

Yet, despite his association with prominent Jews and his approval of Bethlen's tolerant policies, Regent Horthy continued to regard himself as, and to speak the language of, a convinced anti-Semite. He was never able to shake loose from the vulgar prejudices he had picked up earlier in life. He spoke with particular contempt of the so-called "Galician Jews," the largely unassimilated, Orthodox Jews who lived primarily in the northern part of the country and were to be found in significant numbers in those parts of Slovakia and Transylvania regained by Hungary in 1938, 1939, and 1940. Like Pál Teleki, who served as Horthy's Prime Minister in 1920-21 and again in 1939-41, Regent Horthy regarded these Jews as foreigners who had infiltrated the country but remained alien to the Magyar nation.[14] That the "Galician Jews" were a menace to Christian society was accepted as a social and political axiom by Horthy, even though he apparently never questioned how these largely impoverished and isolated Jewish communities could possibly be a threat.

It was thus not surprising that anti-Semitism in general, and callousness toward the unassimilated Jews in particular, also permeated the Horthy household. His son Miklós Jr. would later speak of the distaste for Jews that he had acquired from his parents.[15] Yet the anti-Semitism that Miklós Horthy imparted to his children must have been relatively moderate or shallow, since both his sons as adults maintained good relations with the Jewish community and were branded as philosemites by the German and

Hungarian radical right-wingers. Indeed, Miklós Horthy, Jr. was to play a key role in 1944 as a liaison between his father and the Jewish Council. Also interesting is the fact that Horthy's wife, Magda Purgly, also gained a reputation as a friend of the Jews.

Throughout his political career, Admiral Horthy remained a prisoner of the rhetoric on which his regime was based, particularly the emphasis on, and commitment to, "Christian nationalism." The use of the word "Christian" in this context had definite anti-Jewish connotations in Horthy's Hungary. It reflected a widely shared desire in the counterrevolutionary camp to curtail what was considered undue Jewish influence in society and enhance the prestige of the churches after the official atheism of the Béla Kun regime. An organization described as "Christian" would thus likely be one in which Jewish membership was prohibited and so-called Jewish influences had been eliminated. Miklós Horthy certainly thought in these terms. When, for example, he met in 1922 with the visiting Secretary-General of the American YMCA, Horthy is said to have greeted him with the words: "I am delighted to meet the head of such an important anti-Semitic organization."[16]

The story might be apocryphal, but it does capture the earnest but ill-informed and often naïve nature of Admiral Horthy's extemporaneous remarks on social and political matters. Incorrigibly garrulous and indiscreet, Horthy lectured many a visitor on the alleged danger the Jews posed for European civilization. In Horthy's imagination, the Jews were "a people whose hand was against every man and a people whose only God was Gain." Under the malicious direction of the "Elders of Zion," Jews exploited other people's misfortunes, fomented trouble, committed sabotage, and, in general, paved the way to Bolshevism. Horthy admitted that in peacetime, in a well-governed state such as England, the Jews could hold responsible posts and have a real stake in the welfare of the country. But things were different in Central and Eastern Europe, where the Jews monopolized economic life. How unpleasant it was, Horthy asserted, to visit Hungarian factories and be welcomed at each one by what seemed to be the same five Jews.[17]

Admiral Horthy seemed not to notice the contradiction between his privately expressed anti-Semitic prejudices and the tolerant official policies of his regime. Many of his anti-Jewish utterances, in fact, seemed to be mechanical recitations to which Horthy had never given serious thought. Perhaps, as a fervent Anglophile, Horthy was unconsciously making the point that Hungary, which supposedly resembled England in its parliamentary and constitutional traditions, was as well governed as England and thus, unlike other countries in Eastern Europe, could allow its talented Jews to make important contributions to society. Whatever the case, Regent Horthy would no doubt have continued to foster the tacit alliance between Hungary's conservative political establishment and the community of assimilated Jews to the end of his political career had extraordinary events not occurred.

The Great Depression gave a boost to extremist movements throughout Europe, notably Germany. In Hungary, Count Bethlen yielded his place to Gyula Gömbös, three months before Hitler came to power in Germany. At this key juncture, Regent Horthy made one of the most important decisions of his career. Given his previous collaboration with Gömbös in the Szeged movement, Horthy might well have allowed Gömbös to enact new anti-Jewish legislation, if only as a way of diverting public attention from economic problems. But Horthy rejected this option. Indeed, in appointing Gömbös the Regent insisted on a pledge that no anti-Jewish laws would be enacted. For the next several years, Horthy resisted the clamor from the Hungarian radical right-wing parties for a close alliance with Nazi Germany and for drastic action against the Jews of the kind being undertaken by Hitler. Admiral Horthy found much to admire in Hitler's policies, particularly his strident anti-Communism and his commitment to revision of the Paris peace treaties. But he was averse to the introduction of Nazi-like practices and institutions into Hungary. This would undermine the foundations of the conservative political establishment of which he was now very much a part. By this time he had also come to regard Hungary's most important radical right-wing party, the Arrow Cross, with contempt. Its leadership consisted, in his opinion, of vulgar, uncultured individuals who were less faithful and valuable to the Hungarian nation than the Jews.[18]

The attempt of Admiral Horthy and his conservative advisors to ride Hitler's coattails and gain territorial revision without becoming infected with the Nazi virus proved a dismal failure. One tactic approved by Horthy in this period had a most deleterious impact on Hungary's Jews. In an attempt to appease Germany and to "take the wind out of the sails of the Arrow Cross," the Hungarian Parliament passed a series of anti-Jewish acts beginning in 1938. These measures were increasingly rigid, finally adopting a definition of a Jew similar to that of Germany's Nuremberg Laws.[19] It is conceivable that the Regent, whose prestige and authority by the late 1930s were immense, could have prevented, or at least forestalled, these anti-Jewish laws. But Horthy remained a prisoner of his ingrained prejudices, and he was unwilling to struggle against the now powerful anti-Semitic current in Hungarian society that he had helped to foster. Moreover, he could rationalize his actions by noting that such a respected statesman as Pál Teleki, as well as many prominent intellectuals and even the spokesmen of the Christian churches, approved the actions against the Jews as a "civilized anti-Semitism" that merely restored a more vigorous version of the *numerus clausus*.[20] Apparently Horthy also reasoned that the "Galician Jews" would bear the brunt of these discriminatory actions. In his view, these foreign elements could be "eliminated from national life," but he would see to it that good, patriotic Jews were not molested.[21]

Miklós Horthy thus played a major role in fostering an intolerance and hostility toward the Jews that would later facilitate Eichmann's work in Hungary. But he did so reluctantly, without enthusiasm. He insisted that exemptions be granted to converted Jews and those who had served the Hungarian nation with distinction. As he explained to the American minister in Budapest, he had consideration for the "patriotic Jew(s) long resident in the country who had helped to make it prosperous and who were as much Hungarian as was he." He would not permit such Jews to be deprived of their livelihood.[22] The most explicit statement of Admiral Horthy's view appears in a letter he wrote to Pál Teleki in October 1940. The most striking passage:

> I have perhaps been the first to loudly profess anti-Semitism, yet I cannot look with indifference at inhumanity, senseless humiliations, when we still need

> them. In addition, I consider, for example, the Arrow-Cross men to be by far more dangerous and worthless for the country than I do the Jew. The latter is tied to this country from interest, and is more faithful to his adopted country than the Arrow-Cross men, who...with their muddled brains want to play the country into the hands of the Germans.[23]

The historian might well observe that Horthy's views about the Jews also had a "muddled" quality, but it is clear that from 1938 on he became more and more uneasy about the brutal treatment of Jews in Germany. In the wake of the "night of the broken glass," an outpouring of violence against German Jews on November 10, 1938, Horthy privately deplored Germany's treatment of the Jews as "brutal" and "inhuman."[24] Thus, as Hitler's "final solution" was being implemented after June 1942, Admiral Horthy rejected persistent German demands for expropriation of Jewish property, wearing of a yellow star, ghettoization, and deportation of the Jews from Hungary. Certainly Hungarian Jews suffered great hardships, especially in the Jewish labor battalions, but, when informed of the situation, Horthy took steps to mitigate these conditions.

During a visit to Germany in April 1943, Horthy was subjected to a litany of complaints about Hungary's lenient treatment of the Jews.[25] Ribbentrop, the German Foreign Minister, expressed astonishment that Jews were still allowed to be members of the Hungarian Parliament. Horthy's response was a discourse on the sanctity of the Hungarian constitution and a profession of complete confidence in his Prime Minister, Miklós Kállay, whom his German hosts were excoriating for his protection of the Jews and his alleged secret peace feelers to the Western Democracies. No doubt to the amazement of Hitler and Ribbentrop, Horthy even confessed how ashamed he was of the enormous death toll of Jews in the labor battalions on the Eastern Front. Summarizing his policies towards the Jews, Horthy added that "he had done everything that could be done against the Jews, but, after all, he couldn't murder them or do away with them in some other way." Ribbentrop responded bluntly that there was no other solution to the Jewish problem than killing them or sending them to concentration camps. Hitler added that the Jews had to be treated like tuberculosis bacilli, and nations that failed to take proper precautions would perish.

Horthy's assertion that he couldn't murder the Jews or "do away with them in some other way," which was not meant to be sardonic, indicates that at this late date, April 1943, Miklós Horthy was still unaware of the true meaning of the "final solution." Certainly many Hungarian officials knew in general terms of the horrible fate awaiting the Jews deported to "the East."[26] And Horthy's trusted advisors must have used persuasive evidence to convince him to take a firm stand in resisting German demands for deportation of Hungary's Jews. Nonetheless it seems clear that before 1944 Horthy did not grasp the true nature of the unfolding Holocaust, that is, the systematic massacre of the Jews in death camps. Horthy's understanding of events, whether historical or contemporary, was quite simplistic and unsophisticated. For him an event became "real" and entered his consciousness only when it could be described in terms of compelling stories or anecdotes. Thus, he knew in 1943 that horrible things were happening to Jews in German-controlled areas of Europe and that it would be inhuman to subject Hungarian Jews to that fate, but he knew nothing of the actual procedures of deportation or the barbaric conditions in the death camps. Perhaps, like many statesmen both in Europe and North America, he found the subject so painful to contemplate that he consciously or unconsciously refrained from a careful investigation of the matter.

Some historians have interpreted Horthy's relatively tolerant policy toward the Jews as blatant opportunism aimed at creating an insurance policy should the Axis Powers lose the war, a way of demonstrating to the victorious Western Powers that Hungary had not been Hitler's lackey.[27] But this ascribes to Admiral Horthy a degree of calculation and cleverness that he did not possess. His refusal to comply with the most radical of Hitler's demands was not a pragmatic response to Germany's declining fortunes in the war, but rather a matter of principle to which he stubbornly clung from 1939 on. As he privately explained to both pro- and anti-Nazi Hungarians with whom he consulted, there were limits to the anti-

Jewish actions he could approve, since "inhumanity is alien to the Magyar character."[28]

Whatever the basis for Horthy's actions, it was largely through the influence of Horthy and the pro-Western conservatives on whom he relied (notably Bethlen, Miklós Kállay, and Ferenc Keresztes-Fischer) that Hungary by late 1943 had become a haven for Jews in the heart of Hitler's Europe. Of course, the Germans would not long tolerate such a situation, and in March 1944 Wehrmacht and Gestapo units occupied Hungary. Horthy's advisors urged him to resign and dissociate himself from the German puppet government, but his sense of duty compelled him to stay on and salvage what he could: a captain must not abandon his ship. Significantly, leaders of the Jewish community urged the Regent to stay on, for it was believed that Horthy alone stood between them and the Nazi menace.

In the spring of 1944, Horthy's main objectives were to find a way to persuade Hitler to withdraw his troops, to prevent a Soviet occupation of Hungary, and to salvage what he could of Hungary's regained territories. At first, the fate of the Jews was a secondary consideration for him. Indeed, he made the fatal error of allowing two notorious and fanatical anti-Semites, László Endre and László Baky, to be placed in charge of Jewish affairs and informed his Cabinet that he washed his hands of all responsibility for actions against the Jews.[29] In the false hope that it would speed the German withdrawal, Horthy also agreed to Hitler's demand for a large number of Hungarian Jews to serve as workers in German war industries. He assumed it would be the unassimilated Jews of the countryside, the "Galician Jews," who would be sent to their uncertain fate. At his postwar trial, László Baky claimed that in April 1944 Horthy told him: "I abhor the Communists and Galician Jews--out of the country with them! Out! But at the same time you must admit, Baky there are some Jews who are just as good Hungarians as you or I. For instance, take Chorin and Vida. I cannot allow them to be deported, but I don't mind about the others."[30] Like his counterparts in Romania and Bulgaria, Horthy thus seemed to be saying: "You can take the foreign Jews, we are glad to get rid of them, but we do not agree to the deportation of our Jews."[31] Horthy seemed to cling to the naïve belief that, with the war at a critical point, these Jews would indeed be used as forced laborers in Germany. He did not suspect that they would be taken directly to the gas chambers of Auschwitz. Yet Horthy was not alone in what now seems to be cynical indifference and inhumanity: even the leaders of the Jewish organizations in Budapest cooperated with the Germans and cautioned against resistance in the hope that somehow things would work out.[32]

Horthy refused to believe the first reports that reached him of the pitiless cruelty of the Hungarian gendarmes and the horrible fate of the deported Jews in Auschwitz, even when László Ravasz, the head of the Hungarian Reformed Church, voiced his personal concern to the Regent. Horthy's response to Ravasz was that the Jews were only going to Germany as workers. They would not be mistreated and not "a single hair on their heads would be harmed."[33] But when in June an eyewitness report of these horrors was sent to the Regent by the Jewish Council, Horthy was truly shocked and resolved to end the deportations.[34] Unfortunately, never a very adroit or imaginative statesman, Horthy could think of no expeditious way to carry out his intentions. He now faced the greatest crisis of his regency virtually alone, for all of the advisors on whom he had relied in the past were either in prison or in hiding. Moreover, his Cabinet and Chief of Staff warned against defying the Germans, and the Regent's order that Baky and Endre be relieved of their duties and that atrocities against the Jews cease was treated in a dilatory fashion. Döme Sztójay and most other civilian and military leaders procrastinated because they feared offending the Germans and the fate of the Jews was of no concern to them.

Matters reached a climax in late June, when within the space of a few days messages of concern and admonition from all over the world acted as a kind of "bombardment of Horthy's conscience."[35] The King of Sweden urged Horthy to take humanitarian action on behalf of the Jews. In an open telegram, Pope Pius called on the Regent, as the leader of a "noble and chivalrous nation," to spare the Jews further suffering. Likewise, President Roosevelt warned of severe reprisals if the deportations did not stop. Finally, and perhaps most important of all, Horthy received a memorandum drawn up by Count Bethlen, who was still in hiding. Bethlen deplored what he called the "inhuman, foolish, and cruel persecution of the Jews" which had already permanently disgraced the Hungarian nation. Not only did Bethlen call for an end to the deportations, but he offered Horthy a step-by-step plan for carrying this out, removing Sztójay from power and establishing a new government.[36] All the pieces were now in place. The pope's message gave Horthy a moral imperative; the eyewitness report on the horrors of Auschwitz had galvanized his conscience; Roosevelt's telegram was a grim warning; and his most trusted advisor offered a viable plan of action. Reports of an imminent *coup d'ètat* by radical right-wingers intent on deporting the Jews of Budapest provided the final impetus; in early July, Admiral Horthy managed to arrange for the transfer of loyal troops to the capital city. His order that all deportations of Jews be ended could now be backed up with military power.[37]

Scholars have perhaps underestimated the significance of Horthy's defiance of Hitler, which occurred after the Allied landings at Normandy but before the assassination attempt on Hitler in July. Through the summer of 1944 Admiral Horthy remained firm in his decision to protect the Jews of Budapest, collaborating with Raoul Wallenberg, the Red Cross, and those neutral countries working to rescue the Jews. Ironically, an offer by Horthy in this period to facilitate the emigration of some Hungarian Jews proved discomfiting to the Western Powers, who were reluctant to allow any more Jews to settle in their territories.[38] After Horthy was deposed by the Germans in mid-October, Hungary's Jews were subjected to renewed terror, but the war was almost over and most of the Jews of Budapest, numbering more than 200,000, were to survive.

Yet the question remains: how was it that a man who was a self-proclaimed anti-Semite, who after World War I became notorious as a persecutor of the Jews, could emerge in World War II as an apparent protector of Jews? It seems quite clear that Horthy felt uncomfortable with, and ultimately rejected, the violent racial anti-Semitism of the Hungarian and German radical right wing. His attitude toward the Jews was a more traditional one, shaped, in large part, by his experiences in prewar Austria-Hungary. One historian has noted that in late nineteenth and early twentieth century Austria it was not uncommon for educated, well-respected members of society to express in private strong, even vulgar prejudices against the Jews, yet act tolerantly toward, and even socialize with, Jews in public.[39] This description would seem to fit Miklós Horthy, who might well have adopted the phrase attributed to Karl Lueger, the popular major of *fin de siècle* Vienna: "I decide who is a Jew." For those he considered "good Jews," Horthy came in time to develop a grudging respect and, for certain individuals, even affection.

Horthy's policies towards the Jews were also influenced by the example of Emperor Franz Joseph, whom the Hungarian Regent regarded as an exemplary head of state to be emulated whenever possible. Certainly Horthy never went so far as to declare, as had Franz Joseph, that "there will be no Jew-baiting in my land."[40] But Horthy's increasing tolerance toward the Jews during the 1920s, and his insistence during World War II that he would not inflict "senseless humiliations" on the Jews because that would be uncivilized and unbecoming the Hungarian nation, did seem to echo the sentiments of his former king and emperor.

That Admiral Horthy nonetheless contributed greatly to the intensification of anti-Semitism in Hungary after World War I and was implicated in several repressive actions against Hungarian Jews can be attributed to the exaggerated nationalism and fervent anti-Communism that pervaded his thinking in the post-war period. Profound indignation over Hungary's loss of the war and humiliation by the Paris Peace Conference and by her victorious neighbors led Horthy to resent and suspect any remaining foreign or alien elements in Hungary, including the Hungarian-Germans. This explains Horthy's callous attitude toward the "Galician Jews," whom he regarded as latecomers who had never fused into the Magyar nation. At the same time, it helps explain Horthy's more protective view of the Budapest Jews, whom he came to regard as real patriots who had made important contributions to national life in finance, athletics, science, and other areas.

Above all, it was Horthy's fervent anti-Communism, which remained to the end the guiding principle of his political life, that shaped and perverted his policies toward the Jews. Admiral Horthy regarded Bolshevism as an insidious poison that must at all cost be eradicated from Hungarian and European society. Because Jews had played so prominent a role in Béla Kun's government, Horthy came firmly to believe that they had some sort of peculiar affinity for what he considered to be an abominable political doctrine; hence his willingness to sanction drastic action against Jews on those occasions when Communism seemed to pose a direct threat to Hungary. But in both the White Terror of 1919 and the deportations of 1944, Horthy's main motive was to strike a blow against Communism, not to punish the Jews. Thus his attitude in both cases was ambivalent and he ultimately rejected the most radical plans of the fanatical German and Hungarian anti-Semites.

Frustrated by the Hungarian government's refusal in 1943 to take harsher measures against the Jews, Joseph Goebbels grumbled that Horthy was too tangled up with the Jews and mistakenly tried to employ humanitarian and liberal arguments.[41] Admiral Horthy was certainly not a liberal, although, as William McCagg has argued, during World War II he did choose as advisors individuals who might be termed "closet liberals."[42] But the historian can detect a spark of humanitarianism in Horthy's policies. This was not based on religious principles, for Horthy was not a religious man and, as has been seen, the word "Christian" had in any case been put to perverse uses in Hungarian political life. Rather, like a "latter-day knight"[43] Horthy seemed ultimately guided by an archaic sense of chivalry, a code of honor to which a Habsburg officer and gentleman had been expected to adhere. This code of honor prescribed gratuitous violence against one's enemy, not to mention against women and children. In Admiral Horthy it produced a limited kind of humanitarianism, to be sure, but in Hitler's Europe humanitarianism of any sort was a virtue in very short supply.

NOTES

[1]For useful, though brief, biographical sketches of Miklós Horthy, see Peter Gosztony, *Miklós von Horthy. Admiral und Reichsverweser* (Göttingen, 1973); and Loránd Dombrády, *A legfelsőbb hadúr és hadserege* (Budapest, 1990).

[2]Andrew C. Janos, "The Decline of Oligarchy: Bureaucratic and Mass Politics in the Age of Dualism (1867-1918)," in: *Revolution in Perspective, Essays on the Hungarian Soviet Republic*, Andrew C. Janos and William B. Slottman, eds. (Berkeley, 1971), pp. 33-38. For the role of Jews in the professions, see Ezra Mendelsohn, *The Jews of East Central Europe between the World Wars* (Bloomington, 1983), pp. 100-102.

[3]For the impact of the Great War and the Hungarian revolutions on Horthy, see Thomas Sakmyster, "From Habsburg Admiral to Hungarian Regent: The Political Metamorphosis of Miklós Horthy, 1918-1921," *East European Quarterly*, 17, no. 2 (1983), pp. 129-148.

[4]Aladár von Boroviczény, *Der König und sein Reichsverweser* (Munich, 1924), p. 16.

[5]Gruesome details of the White Terror can be found in the diary of Pál Prónay, *A határban a halál kaszál. Fejezetek Prónay Pál feljegyzéseiből*, Ágnes Szabó and Ervin Pamlényi, eds. (Budapest, 1963), *passim*. See also Ervin Hollós and Vera Lajtai, *Horthy Miklós a fehérek vezére* (Budapest, 1985).

[6]Anton Lehár, *Erinnerungen: Gegenrevolution und Restaurationsversuche in Ungarn, 1918-1921* (Munich, 1973), p. 159.

[7]Lehár, p. 146.

[8]Ernö Gergely and Pál Schonwald, *A Somogyi-Bacsó gyilkosság* (Budapest, 1978), pp. 106, 181-182.

[9]Historians hostile to Horthy have branded him guilty of murder. For example, Ernö Gergely (p. 106) concluded that "Horthy thus pronounced Béla Somogyi's death sentence." On the other hand, C.A. Macartney suggested that Horthy was no more guilty than was Henry II for Thomas Becket's death. C.A. Macartney, *October Fifteenth. A History of Modern Hungary, 1929-1945*, 2 vols. (Edinburgh, 1961), vol. 1, p. 494.

[10]On the *numerus clausus* see Mendelsohn, *Jews of East Central Europe*, p. 105; and Nathaniel Katzburg, *Hungary and the Jews. Policy and Legislation, 1920-1943* (Jerusalem, 1981), pp. 60-64.

[11]Prónay, *A határban a halál kaszál.*, pp. 130-31, 160.

[12]Ferenc Pölöskei, *Horthy és hatalmi rendszere, 1919-1922* (Budapest, 1977), p. 98; Gostony, *Horthy*, pp. 25-26; and József

Patai, "A fövezérnél és a kormányzónál," *Múlt és Jövö* (April, 1930), pp. 140-142.

[13]William McCagg, "The Role of the Magyar Nobility in Modern Jewish History," *East European Quarterly*, 20, no. 1 (March, 1986), pp. 43-44. This phrase was used by the influential Hungarian historian, Gyula Szekfü, in his *Három Nemzedék*. Horthy is unlikely to have read Szekfü's work, but this concept of the "good Jew" was prevalent in many quarters of Hungarian society.

[14]Randolph L. Braham, *The Politics of Genocide. The Holocaust in Hungary*, 2 vols. (New York, 1981), vol. 1, pp. 141-143.

[15]Miklós Horthy, Jr. told a Jewish colleague in 1944: "I have been an anti-Semite since my birth and even by virtue of my education. It could hardly have been otherwise in our home, since this was the prevailing attitude when discussing Jews in my parents' home. For example, it would be inconceivable for me to marry a Jewish woman, or to consider that my children have Jewish blood." Quoted in Béla Vágó, "Budapest Jewry in the Summer of 1944. Otto Komoly's Diaries," *Yad Vashem Studies on the Jewish Catastrophes and Resistance*, 8 (1970), p. 99.

[16]George Clare, *Last Waltz in Vienna. The Rise and Destruction of a Family, 1842-1942* (New York, 1982), p. 83.

[17]See Horthy's comments to various British dignitaries and diplomats, as found in Public Record Office, FO371, 12180/C5330-/58/21 (June 15, 1927); mission in Budapest, Austrian State Archives, NPA, K885/2-4/594; K885/18-20/22799.

[18]Horthy's letter to Pál Teleki of October 14, 1940. Miklós Szinai and László Szücs, eds., *The Confidential Papers of Admiral Horthy* (Budapest, 1965), pp. 150-152. Cited hereafter as "Horthy Papers."

[19]For the anti-Jewish laws, see Braham, *Politics of Genocide*, vol. I, pp. 118-198.

[20]*Ibid.*, pp. 140-141.

[21]In July, 1942 Horthy made comments along these lines to a pro-German member of the Hungarian Cabinet. German Foreign Ministry records, National Archives Microcopy T-120, Roll 1096, 452385-87.

[22]Report of John F. Montgomery, Jan. 12, 1939, U.S. State Department records, National Archives (Washington), 762.64/133.

[23]Horthy Papers, pp. 150-152.

[24]Horthy's comments as recorded in a memo by the wife of Béla Imrédy on December 10, 1938, on deposit in the Macartney Archive, Bodleian Library (Oxford, England).

[25]Andreas Hillgruber, ed., *Staatsmänner und Diplomaten bei Hitler*, 2 vols. (Frankfurt, 1970), II, p. 245.

[26]Döme Sztójay, Hungary's Minister in Berlin, knew by late 1942 that deportation to "the East" was a euphemism for mass annihilation of the Jews. Sztójay's information was passed on to the Foreign Ministry. Braham, *Politics of Genocide*, vol. 2, p. 71.

[27]Thus Zvi Erez asserts that Horthy's relatively tolerant policy toward the Jews was designed "for the benefit of London and Washington," and did not represent "an honest attempt to remedy the abuses which had long since been officially sanctioned and carried out rather pitilessly." Zvi Erez, "The Jews of Budapest and the Plans of Admiral Horthy, August-October, 1944," *Yad Vashem Studies*, 16 (1984), p. 618. See also Andre Biss, *A Million Jews to Save* (London, 1975), pp. 85-91.

[28]Gyula Kádár, *A Ludavikától Sopronkőhidáig* (Budapest, 1978), p. 636.

[29]György Ránki, *Unternehmen Margarethe. Die deutsche Besetzung Ungarns* (Vienna, 1984), pp. 301-302. Horthy's decision to "wash his hands" of government policy toward the Jews has been sharply condemned by some historians. Asher Cohen writes: "By this stand, Horthy, who possessed enormous moral authority over and above his formal powers, was in effect forsaking his Jewish citizens." Asher Cohen, *The Halutz Resistance in Hungary, 1942-1944* (Boulder, 1986), p. 53.

[30]Eugene Levai, *Black Book on the Martyrdom of Hungarian Jewry* (Zurich, 1948), p. 113.

[31]Béla Vágó, "The Reaction to the Nazi Anti-Jewish Policy in East Central Europe and in the Balkans," in: Francois Furet, ed., *Unanswered Questions. Nazi Germany and the Genocide of the Jews* (New York, 1989), p. 225. For a full discussion of Horthy's role in acceding to the German request for "Jewish workers," see Braham, *Politics of Genocide*, I, pp. 369-72, 377-82; and Mario D. Fenyö,

Hitler, Horthy, and Hungary. German-Hungarian Relations, 1941-1944 (New Haven, 1972), pp. 163-206.

[32]Concerning this seeming "conspiracy of silence" on the part of Hungary's Jewish leaders, see Braham, *Politics of Genocide*, vol. 2, pp. 691-731.

[33]Ernö Munkácsi, *Hogyan történt? Adatok és okmányok a magyar zsidóság tragediájához* (Budapest, 1947), p. 142.

[34]Gosztony, *Horthy*, p. 109; Braham, *Politics of Genocide*, vol. 2, p. 745.

[35]Gerald Reitlinger, *The Final Solution. The Attempt to Exterminate the Jews of Europe, 1939-1945* (South Brunswick, 1968), p. 432.

[36]For a detailed discussion of Horthy's decision to end the deportations, in which the author emphasizes Horthy's fear of a coup d'ètat by radical right-wing forces, see Tsvi Erez, "Hungary. Six Days in July, 1944," *Holocaust and Genocide Studies*, 3, no. 1 (1988), pp. 37-53.

[37]Horthy Papers, pp. 307-315.

[38]Béla Vágó, "The Horthy Offer. A Missed Opportunity for Rescuing Jews in 1944," in: Randolph Braham, ed., *Contemporary Views on the Holocaust* (Boston, 1983), pp. 23-45. Horthy was unaware of the controversy and diplomatic activity that his "offer" caused. He makes no direct mention of the "Horthy offer" in his otherwise exculpatory memoirs.

[39]On this phenomenon, see Sigurd Paul Scheichl, "The Contexts and Nuances of Anti-Jewish Language. Were all the 'Antisemites' Antisemites?" in: Ivar Oxaal, *et al*, *Jews, Antisemitism and Culture* (New York, 1987), pp. 89-110.

[40]Robert S. Wistrich, *The Jews of Vienna in the Age of Franz Joseph* (New York, 1989), p. 176.

[41]Louis P. Lochner, ed., *The Goebbels Diaries* (Garden City, 1948), p. 357.

[42]On this and other related questions, see the comments of István Deák and William McCagg in "Genocide in Hungary: An Exchange," *The New York Review of Books*, May 27, 1982, pp. 55-56.

[43]The term is used by István Deák in his *Beyond Nationalism. A Social and Political History of the Habsburg Officer Corps, 1848-1918* (New York, 1990), pp. 126-138.

THE CAMP OF NATIONAL UNITY: A POLISH EXPERIMENT IN "STATE NATIONALISM," 1936-1939

Edward D. Wynot, Jr.
Florida State University

The decades between the world wars witnessed a surge of extreme nationalist movements throughout Europe. This trend assumed especially virulent forms in Eastern Europe, where the venerable liberal parliamentary ideals of the West had little intrinsic permanent basis. Consequently, various proto-fascist groups appeared in virtually every land east of Germany and Italy, often in response to developments in those two countries. In nearly every instance, the movement focused its attention and efforts upon strengthening either the state or the nation.[1]

Although Poland, too, possessed a native fascist movement, it was an insignificant force in domestic politics. Far more important was the organization sponsored by a leading faction within the government that, after 1936, promoted a program of "state nationalism" that offered a unique blend of fascist doctrine with Polish political traditions and contemporary nationalist theory. The result was the formation of an ideology unique to Eastern Europe and having major value as a precedent for political developments following World War II. This essay will focus on the theoretical framework of this ideology of "state nationalism." It will attempt to illuminate the intellectual dynamics of a movement striving to unite the two major entities of nation and state into a coherent program for socio-economic modernization as well as political survival in an increasingly hostile international environment. Space restrictions limit this discussion to the doctrine of the movement at the expense of recounting its activities, which have been treated elsewhere.[2]

The "Camp of National Unity" (*Obóz Zjednoczenia Narodowego*, or OZN) originated in the midst of an acute domestic political crisis. In May 1926, Marshal Józef Piłsudski had forcibly overthrown the existing government, establishing in its place a regime that, while not a classical personal or totalitarian dictatorship, became a centralized authoritarian oligarchy.[3] The group of men who followed the Marshal became known as the "Sanitation"

(*Sanacja*) camp for their vows to cleanse Poland of the evils that had proliferated during the five years since the enactment of the constitution in 1921. This document, inspired by the French governmental system, had thrust the legislative branch forward as the supreme organ in the state, thereby fostering, in Piłsudski's view, the widespread growth of political parties and the rapid turnover of cabinets that rendered the normal governing process virtually impossible. This "partisan" (*partyjny*) spirit, he concluded, was only dividing the Polish people and nation when they should be firmly united around the state, and so the Sanacja resolved to attack it on a broad scale.

The resulting offensive against the existing government structure after 1926 operated on several fronts. One involved the formation of a parliamentary coalition known as the "Nonpartisan Bloc for Cooperation with the Government" (*Bezpartyjny Bloc Współpracy z Rządem*, or BBWR) to rally support for Sanacja programs within the existing legislature. Spanning the entire ideological spectrum of Piłsudski's supporters, including deputies representing the national minorities, the Bloc's primary objective was to draft a new constitution along lines more acceptable to the Marshal. Simultaneously, the regime launched a campaign of intimidation and harassment against those political parties hostile to the Sanacja, culminating in the infamous "Brześć Purge" of opposition leaders in 1930-1931. Manipulation of the electoral process finally produced a workable parliamentary majority, and, after considerable disputes involving terminology and provisions, the legislature completed its assigned task with the enactment of a new constitution on April 23, 1935.

As the final state document signed by Piłsudski, who died three weeks later, the so-called April Constitution legitimized the situation that had existed in Polish politics from the coup nine years earlier.[4] Its dominant feature was the reduction of Parliament to secondary importance, while concentrating power in the executive branch. The constitution defined the role of the state in terms that rendered impossible any misunderstanding. Article 4 declared that "the life of the community rests upon and forms itself within the framework of the State," which was to assure "the free development" of that life by "directing and coordinating its conditions when the public welfare requires this." While personal liberties were available to all citizens, they were clearly limited by "the common good" (Article 5). The state was charged with "uniting all of its citizens in harmonious cooperation for the common good," and hence "no activity shall be counter to the aims of the State, as expressed in its laws" (Articles 9-10). Indeed, with its emphasis upon a strong, centralized executive and the total subordination of all spheres of life to the best interests of the state, this document was the exact antithesis of the 1921 constitution, and its revision formed one of the leading goals of the opposition, left weakened but not completely impotent.

Piłsudski's death on May 12, 1935 precipitated a crisis of both leadership and ideology within the regime. The Sanacja contained many diverse elements, each with its own distinctive political, social, and economic philosophies; the sole adhesive that bound these unlikely allies together was Piłsudski's dominating personality. Unfortunately for his successors, the Marshal formulated and conducted his policies without any formal body of doctrine to serve as an ideology. For Piłsudski, the ruthless realist, the acquisition and maintenance of Poland's independence was the only goal to which he aspired. The means to this end were simple: a powerful army, a strong centralized state apparatus, and a country free from internal strife. Through the sheer force of his personal authority and prestige, Piłsudski gained the acquiescence of most Poles irrespective of political disposition for his programs. An ideology *per se* never existed; under Piłsudski, one was never required.

His removal from Polish political life, while not unexpected, created a gaping void within the regime. The architects of the new state structure, with its powerful executive, clearly envisioned Piłsudski as the first president to occupy that branch. But along with a body of coherent political doctrine, the Marshal had also failed to bequeath his followers a clearly designated political heir. The resulting succession struggle lasted over a year before finally producing an uneasy compromise that shared power and governing responsibility between the current president, Ignacy Mościcki, and the Inspector General of the Armed Forces, General (later Marshal) Edward Śmigły-Rydz. Since neither could approach the magnitude of personal authority that Piłsudski had exuded, the leadership would have to base its actions and authority on some kind of ideology. In the circumstances, this had to be constructed on the spot, and the need for swift, decisive action was pressing; as a contemporary rival politician observed, for the Piłsudski-ites "to govern the country without ideas is to dig graves under themselves and under Poland."[5]

As he gradually emerged as the dominant partner in the new order, Śmigły-Rydz sought to bolster his authority by creating a solid organizational base for his power, while simultaneously filling the regime's ideological void. Hence, in May 1936 he announced the formation of the Camp of National Unity, which made its formal debut on February 21, 1937 with the publication of its "Ideological-Political Declaration."[6] This document, complemented by subsequent statements of the organization's leadership and the resolutions of its advisory Chief Council (*Rada Naczelna*), provided the ideology so vital to the post-Piłsudski Sanacja.

The most crucial problem in this sphere was defining the political legitimacy of the Camp and, through it, Śmigły-Rydz himself. The leadership solved this dilemma by attempting to form a chain of associations linking the army, through the person of Śmigły-Rydz, to the community on one end and to Piłsudski on the other. They portrayed Piłsudski as the font of the Camp's ideology, and took great pains to emphasize that Śmigły-Rydz was indeed the designated continuator of his will and work. This process commenced well before the Camp's actual appearance in the form of speeches and press editorials by Śmigły-Rydz backers.[7] Not surprisingly, the one element indisputably connected to both Piłsudski and Śmigły-Rydz--the army--received new emphasis. The regime published the latter's earlier speeches to his troops as proof that as early as 1936 he had perceived the need for military participation in politics, since the army, not the politicians nor the masses, was the true originator and bearer of the ideal of Polish independence. "If we view contemporary relations in Poland we must state," felt the newly-promoted Marshal, "that the Army is the center around which grows all that is powerful and healthy in the community, which understands the citizens' duties in relation to the State--in short, it is that Poland, which wishes to be powerful and understands her historic mission."[8] The Camp's program declaration singled out the army as one of the basic foundations of the Polish state, second in importance only to the constitution, and asserted that "the Army will be surrounded with the love and respect of the entire community, who understands its role and its needs...."[9] Press editorials and articles hammered home this point ceaselessly, and the Sanacja provided extensive publicity coverage of everything connected with the military, such as maneuvers, decorations, and parades.

In these circumstances it followed logically that the regime attempted to create a cult of the army's "Chief" around the person of Śmigły-Rydz. Himself a somewhat retiring individual without any real charismatic appeal, Śmigły-Rydz thus gained the exposure and fame necessary in his new role of political and moral leader, while simultaneously benefiting his fledgling political organization. This was a radical departure from the policies of Piłsudski, who, distrusting any outburst of spontaneity among the masses, shunned the appeal to a collective national catharsis and emotional rededication to Poland in the form of himself. Instead of firing the political consciousness of the populace, Piłsudski sought to depoliticize the nation by subordinating it to himself and his circle with no advance fanfare. Consequently, the drive to portray Śmigły-Rydz as the personified political, spiritual, and moral ideal of the Polish Nation was a new venture for the Piłsudski-ites.

The regime launched a massive propaganda campaign aimed at building up the image of the once-forgotten Division Commander. Books began to appear that related biographical anecdotes about Śmigły-Rydz, each generously laced with assertions that he alone after Piłsudski had been endowed with those spiritual, mental, and moral qualities essential to the Leader of the Nation.[10] Speeches praised the idea of the omnipotent Leader in general, and Śmigły-Rydz in particular, as vital to national survival in dangerous times. Typical were the sentiments expressed by General Stanisław Skwarczyński, last head of the Camp, who asserted that the person of the Leader "must be surrounded with devotion, love and enthusiasm, not only by the Army but also by the entire Nation."[11] To charges that this cult of personality was totalitarian, he defiantly replied that "Poland does not need to be ashamed of such totalitarianism."[12]

These cults of personality and the army were in themselves insufficient to form an ideological base and to justify the Camp's intended activity, however; the regime still needed a solid, incontestable idea. It found this in the principle of "defense of the State" ("*obrona Państwa*"), conceived of in a broad, sweeping context and first stated when Śmigły-Rydz announced his intention to form the Camp of National Unity. Speaking to the XIII General Congress of Polish Legionnaires on May 24, 1936, he asserted that the slogan of defense of the state will provide "the road that will lead us to the liberation of the moral and creative forces in the nation, to their assembly, to the creation of those new values so vital to us." He predicted that organizing a movement in pursuit of this goal would not be easy, for its leaders would have to employ either "a friendly word or a harsh order, knowing neither exceptions nor pardons," and warned that "whoever feels that he has his own, better way of thinking...whoever thinks that only he is wise...can leave us."[13]

The concept of "defense of the State" became the cornerstone of the regime's ideology. It was the decisive factor in permitting the Camp to define its own legitimacy as a political movement. By invoking this principle, it could not only associate itself with Śmigły-Rydz and, through him, with Piłsudski himself--expressly venerated as the "Creator of the Polish State"--but could also justify the totality of its programs. Its declaration insisted that "the defensive power of the State, emanating directly from its well-organized and directed internal life, is the most natural and simultaneously the most cardinal idea under which the community should gather itself, forgetting about barren and demoralizing controversies, personal rancors, debts from the past, and niggardly nit-picking."[14] A leading spokesman went further, defining the principal elements of a strong Poland as "a powerful Army, invincible, surrounded by the love and highest solicitude of the entire nation, a powerful State organization and a community cooperating with it, disciplined and cohesive, united under the slogans of national defense and entrusted to the Commander-in-Chief as the first Sentry and Director of Polish defense readiness."[15] Indeed, the first leader of the Camp, Colonel Adam Koc, expressly defined its chief task as "political consolidation [of the nation] under the banner of Defense of the State and the cult of the Army and its Commander."[16]

Having solved the problem of its legitimacy, the Camp turned its attention to the type of preparation necessary to ready the country for proper defense of the state. Since the new constitution had already reorganized the latter along strengthened lines, the Camp focused its efforts on mobilizing the Polish nation. In the preamble to its organizational statute, the Camp declared the Polish nation to be "an immortal value, to which must be subordinated the aspirations of individuals, social strata, and even the immediate objectives of a living generation."[17] This nation, according to leading regime spokesman Bogusław Miedziński, was not a linguistic, territorial or political concept, but rather "the Will of this and no other formation of history, a Will running, not through one generation, but through centuries, a Will striving to realize its own ideal of life, its own ideal of Man." This spirit was often silent, deep, an internal rather than external phenomenon; "to make this Will, from misty instinct, from undefined impulse, from a will-o'-the-wisp feeling, from unconscious reaction--through effort, work, conscious action--to make it a Truth, a truth dominant above all other--that and only that is to create the power of the Nation."[18]

But the nation could not realize its historic destinies alone; hence, the necessity of a close connection between State and Nation. Miedziński defined the nature of this relationship:

> The State creates the possibilities of a forced concentration of all its citizens' efforts into one, the assembly of dispersed forces into the whole, the State gives the Nation the mechanism of power--a political and material, legal and physical mechanism. But, as even the most powerful army, having at its disposal the greatest mechanism, is helpless when the mind of the Commander does not direct it--so does the best political system of a State not guarantee strength, when it lacks an "organized, uniformly-directed human will." Not only through law and discipline,

> but also through a person's own decision can this will become a tangible action from a hazy idea, a coordinated effort from a patriotic sigh.[19]

The principle of "Defense of the State," as formulated in the Camp's organizational statutes, provided the answer to the Polish dilemma: "At the moment when the slogan of 'a nation in arms' resounds ever more powerfully in the world, when particular states are drawing entire societies into the orbit of their actions, the Polish Nation, as the master who, through the struggle and sacrifice of her best sons, resurrected the Polish State, cannot remain unconsolidated and disorganized."[20] The movement's program declaration left no doubts on its stand, asserting emphatically that "the State is the only form of the real and healthy existence of the Nation. It gives the Nation the mechanisms of power and organizes its eternal development. There are no contradictions between the interest of the Nation and that of the State." In view of this, Miedziński drew the obvious conclusion: "The organization of the Polish Nation, the rallying and directing of its vital forces as an expression of its collective power...behold the important task that the Camp of National Unity took up. It is the further continuation and indispensable complement of the work on the Republic's political structure already achieved."[21]

Regime spokesmen insisted that theirs was a "new nationalism," creative and working *for* the state, and not, as universally practiced in the nineteenth century and still exploited in Poland by the rival Nationalist movement, directed against it. The Sanacja press promised that "this nationalism for tomorrow will socialize the State and make society state-conscious," in the process "erasing the tragic division of today between Nation and State."[22] An official of the Camp defined the issue more expansively in 1938:

> Therefore nationalism, conceived as the aspiration to strengthen the developing power of the Polish Nation, is the principal factor in the strength of the State. Our nationalism is a creative nationalism, a

> state nationalism, which is to serve as the architect and power of the Polish State....This fact places upon us the obligation of a more powerful organization of the community, because only a strong organization of the nation can, in conjunction with the principles of the Constitution, produce the greatest energy of its forces.[23]

In advancing itself as the guardian and nurturing force of the Polish nation, the Sanacja set out on a collision course with that institution that for centuries had claimed these roles as its own exclusive domain: the Roman Catholic Church.[24] Prior to 1935, most Church leaders had aligned themselves, *de facto* and in actual political activity, squarely behind the rival Nationalist movement, in opposition to the Piłsudski regime with its traditionally anti-clerical orientation. Despite intense lobbying pressure, the hierarchy did not attain an improved legal position in the revised constitution, and thus looked upon the emergence of a new support base in governing circles with ill-disguised hostility. Accordingly, in an attempt to improve the already-strained ties between Church and state, and lay the foundation for a more cooperative future relationship, the Camp reserved a separate section of its program declaration for the role of the Church in Polish life. After observing that "the Polish Nation has been spiritually joined from the birth of its civilization with the Catholic Church, and has unequivocally acknowledged its devotion by the heroic act of shedding blood" on its behalf, the declaration concluded that the Church "should be treated with solicitous care." However, the Camp also noted that "in relation to other denominations, we stand on the position outlined in the Constitution that results from the Polish tradition of religious tolerance"[25]--a qualifier that largely nullified whatever gains may have accrued from the preceding sentiments.

In the challenging circumstances surrounding their efforts, regime officials required a novel organizational principle with which to institutionalize their "new nationalism." Some proposed the formalization of the position of the "Commander" as the permanent link between the nation and state as the most simple solution. Proponents of this viewpoint argued that "the will of the Commander becomes the realization of the traditional will of the Nation in historic moments. Does this mean that the will of the Commander is not the will of the Nation? On the contrary: the will of the Nation is incarnated in the will of the Commander in such moments."[26] Others preferred a more impersonal approach. Departing from the premise that the guiding imperative had to be "the supremacy of the national interest over the egotistical aspirations and interests of social groups or individuals," they hailed the end of the era of classical Western Liberalism, with its concern for protecting the individual against the State.[27] Instead, they triumphantly ushered in a new epoch of collective organization around and by the state. Minister of Finance and Vice Premier Eugeniusz Kwiatkowski, generally considered to head the "liberal" wing of the Sanacja, proclaimed that "we do not aspire...to create a totalitarian state, monoideology or monoparty, but neither do we wish to be a liberal democracy, a democracy of slogans and phrases."[28] Other spokesmen were more extreme in their view of the new order best suited for Poland. Those associated with the weekly publication *Zaczyń* coined the term "Statist" (*"Państwowiec"*) to describe those within the Camp who were committed "not to forming a political party, but a world outlook...a radical way of thinking." This radicalism was "not of deed, but of thought," for it did not "tie itself to any burdensome traditions but tolerates only those that do not stifle new creativity...it is maximalist, i.e., it selects the widest from among all possible horizons of new creativity and establishes the farthest-reaching changes."[29] *Zaczyń*'s writers left no doubts that such changes could only be accomplished by introducing a rigid totalitarian political system into Poland, and promoted its immediate adoption.[30] However much they differed on what should replace it, though, all regime officials agreed that they could never permit Poland to return to a system of parliamentary democracy, where chaos, deceit, and uncertainty reigned, and no constructive activity was possible.

In place of that discredited "demoliberalism," the Camp advanced the novel concept of "directed democracy." Koc first unveiled it in June 1937, when he told a gathering of Camp activists that "we have as our goal the creation of a new democracy, directed by the good of the Nation and State, in which the interests of the individual and the State are immutably connected."[31] Another official explained that the Camp would use this new theory as the doctrinal basis for joining together into one coherent whole the diverse issues of defending the state, the cult of the Commander, and the political, social, and economic organization of Poland. In February 1938, the leading Sanacja press organ further clarified the revised definition of "democracy" in an editorial entitled "The Fatherland--That is the Great Collective Duty:"

> Our democracy, a new democracy educating a new man and citizen in Poland, is not the method of binding a man to the doctrinaire formula of supposed personal freedom in a condition of separation from the collective, nor the continued perpetration of the opposition lie of the clash between the "interests" of the State, materially understood, but rather a democracy that binds, with a moral tie of trust, the State-collective to the citizen-individual....Only thusly comprehended and joined in a common effort can democracy advance us to our goal, without which the greatness and future of Poland will always be frighteningly unknown to all. This goal is the reconciliation of the principle of force with the principle of freedom, of the State with the citizen, making into reality the social canon of the Constitution that the State is the common good of all its citizens....[32]

Later pronouncements streamlined this ideal even more into "a certain internal-political synthesis, built on the principle of a governed and organized democracy--a democracy mobilized in the name of a systematic and disciplined construction and strengthening of the development of the four basic elements of the power of Nation and State...[our] political, economic, moral and cultural values."[33]

The scope of the Camp's organizational activity was to be all-embracing. In Koc's words, "we want to organize this life, not on narrow, class principles, excluding those broader reaches beyond the interested spheres, but in the name of a national consolidation, for a sense of national solidarity lives in all strata...embracing the nation and not a class, group or profession."[34] Both the atmosphere in which this consolidation occurred and the means to expedite it were of vital concern. Regarding the former, Zdzisław Stahl, who after 1937 emerged as the Camp's chief ideologue, felt that the best solution would involve the proper combination of force and law, for "compulsion and force are not only the inseparable comrades and necessary guardians of the law, but are the eternal, principal agents for conditioning the community, and must be applied to insure conditions favorable to the State's development."[35] Stahl envisaged a total commitment and absolute subordination of everything and everyone to the Nation-State, and unhesitatingly rejected any chance of compromise with other political parties or movements as a "ludicrous delusion."[36] He promised that the Camp, "believing in the justness of its principles, will struggle in their name with opponents, as well as win over followers for their development," and warned that "in this struggle it will not count on any easy and fleeting successes, but on essential and absolute victory."[37] Stahl reserved special venom for rival political parties, insisting that "the developing State must eliminate, liquidate and destroy all formations of this type, as residual and anachronistic remnants of the past--or also as foreign agents."[38] That the idea of a "new, directed democracy" did not evolve quite along the lines originally envisioned by its creators is evident from the final form it had assumed.

In formulating their ideological guidelines, regime theorists found that it was one thing to speak of "consolidating the nation," and quite another to define exactly what those terms actually meant. In a country where one-third of the population was ethnically non-Polish, the issue of "national minority rights" provided fuel for continual controversy and conflict. The Nationalist movement and its allies, who had controlled the state prior to Piłsudski's coup, had pursued a program of compulsory Polonization and discrimination against the Ukrainians, Belorussians, Germans, and Jews who, along with other minority groups, enjoyed Polish citizenship and the constitutional guarantee of their rights.

Determined to avoid domestic unrest, Piłsudski had tried, with mixed results, to prevent the more blatant anti-minority activities of his predecessors. His death encouraged the Nationalists to resume their pressure against the non-Polish population, thereby arousing understandable concern among the latter. In the face of Nationalist-sponsored proposals for restrictive legislation against the minorities, Premier General Felicjan Sławój-Składkowski sought to reassure them that Piłsudski's departure did not necessarily mean the end of his moderate nationality policies. Speaking to Parliament in December 1936, he warned that such acts as the extremists advocated would create "an inflammatory atmosphere harmful for the State." Noting that in a country with an ethnically heterogeneous population "there is a natural tendency to a certain amount of both coexistence and antagonism," Składkowski expressed his belief that "among the citizens of our State there should take place a natural struggle for survival, a powerful struggle within the legal bounds of the State, which would elevate those citizens most useful and willing to perform positive deeds for the State, without paying any attention to somebody's name and origin." He concluded by reflecting that "a policy which stated that, despite the existence of minorities, there is only one nation in the State and all must work exclusively for it, would be the most popular, but would also be a short-sighted policy and a search for some cheap popularity."[39]

Initially the Camp of National Unity officially endorsed this line of thought. After stating that "the promulgation of racial hatred is alien to the Polish spirit," the program declaration went on to define the regime's stand on this delicate issue:

> Our guideline in relation to the national minorities is the wish for fraternal, citizenly coexistence on that land, for which in the course of centuries we have shed blood, setting up centers of civilization and defending them before the onslaught of barbarism. In the historical processes, our fates have become intertwined. Wedges of interests foreign to us and to them have been driven into our coexistence. After

> years of slavery we found ourselves once again within the framework of one Republic. We realize the distinctions establishing differences between them and us. We acknowledge these differences, as long as they do not clash with the interests of the State and to the extent that they are not deliberately exploited to throw up a chinese wall and to stir up hatred between us.[40]

A scant year later, apparently the Camp had succumbed to the dangerous temptations against which the Premier had cautioned. Lest talk of reconciliation create a misunderstanding about its nationality policies, the organization's activists were told that "the Polish Nation is the only Master in its State, and no obstacles can stand in the way of its development and the serving of its vital interests across the vast expanses of dispersed population." Moreover, they were assured that the minorities would receive "social justice" only if they recognized the complete integrity of Poland's borders.[41] The revised organizational statute left no doubts regarding the group's true nature, declaring at the outset that "the Camp of National Unity is the political organization of the Polish Nation, and as such has as its goal the inclusion in its ranks of all creative and active individuals of Polish nationality for the realization, through common strength, of the slogans contained in the Ideological-Political Declaration of 21 February 1937."[42] Subsequent pronouncements underscored the Camp's intent to use control of the state apparatus as a weapon against the non-Polish inhabitants, especially the Ukrainians and the Jews.[43] Clearly, the "Nation," of which Sanacja and Camp officials spoke so glowingly, was an exclusive club, restricted to those who met the proper ethnic and religious criteria.

Such was the political-ideological basis of the group that governed Poland after 1935. Employing the Camp of National Unity, it used the principle of "Defense of the State" to claim its legitimacy through the army and its commander, Marshal Śmigły-Rydz, to Piłsudski himself, and demanded the development of an organized, revitalized Polish nation to join with the state in producing a uniquely Polish answer to Polish geopolitical problems. As the atmosphere became more strained with the passage of time, so did the Camp's ideology tighten up; it is a long road from Koc's "new directed democracy" to the overtly totalitarian concepts of Stahl. Yet, despite their concerted efforts, the Sanacja could not replace the authority of their departed founder with a body of doctrine--and the organizational framework to implement it--that ensured support from an increasingly restive and dubious population. The "consolidation," of which officials spoke so optimistically in 1936, was no closer to reality when the Polish state collapsed in September, 1939 than it had been at the conception of the attempt three years earlier.

NOTES

[1]For a general discussion of fascist and extremist movements in interwar Eastern Europe, see especially Peter Sugar, ed., *Native Fascism in the Successor States, 1918-1945* (Santa Barbara, 1971); Peter Sugar and Ivo Lederer, eds., *Nationalism in Eastern Europe* (Seattle, 1969); Joseph Rothschild, *East Central Europe between the Two World Wars* (Seattle, 1974); and appropriate chapters in S. J. Woolf, ed. *European Fascism* (New York, 1969), and Eugene Weber, *Varieties of Fascism* (New York, 1964).

[2]Edward Wynot, *Polish Politics in Transition: The Camp of National Unity and the Struggle for Power, 1935-1939* (Athens, 1974).

[3]For the coup and subsequent developments, see Joseph Rothschild, *Pilsudski's Coup d'Etat* (New York, 1966).

[4]The full text of the constitution was printed in *Monitor Polski* of April 24, 1935, and in 1967 the Polish Government-in-Exile published a dual English-Polish text (London, 1967).

[5]Władysław Grabski, *Idea Polski* (Warsaw, 1935), p. 4. Grabski, a former Premier, belonged to the moderate wing of the opposition National Party.

[6]The declaration was printed in its entirety in the regime's semi-official organ, *Gazeta Polska*, on February 22, 1937. All citations from the Declaration are from this source.

[7]For examples, see the speeches by Minister of Military Affairs Gen. Tadeusz Kasprzycki in February, 1936 (*Gazeta Polska*, February 21, 1936), and Premier Gen. Felicjan Sławój-Składkowski the following June (*Gazeta Polska*, June 5, 1936). Col. Bogusław Miedziński, chief spokesman for this group, in a major editorial, referred to the emergence of Śmigły-Rydz "as a recognized moral authority" who "assumed command not only of the army but of the moral forces of the Nation."--*Gazeta Polska*, May 31, 1936.

[8]Edward Śmigły-Rydz, *Byście o siłę nie zapomnieli. Rozkazy, artykuły, mowy, 1904-1936* (Warsaw, 1936), pp. 160-73.

[9]*Gazeta Polska*, February 22, 1937.

[10]In addition to his above-cited collection of speeches, which included a lengthy adulatory preface, the public received such works as *Opowieści żołnierskie o Generale Śmigłym* (Warsaw, 1936), written in elementary terms and aimed primarily at the soldiers, and his "official" biography, *Edward Śmigły-Rydz, Inspektor Generalny Sił Zbrojnych* (Warsaw, 1936), by Kazimierz Cepnik.

[11]*Gazeta Polska*, February 22, 1938.

[12]*Ibid.*, October 31, 1938.

[13]Śmigły-Rydz, *Byście o siłę nie zapomnieli.*, pp. 255-261.

[14]*Gazeta Polska*, February 22, 1937.

[15]Editorial by Zdzisław Stahl, *Gazeta Polska*, May 7, 1939.

[16]Archiwum Akt Nowych (Warsaw), file *Obóz Zjednoczenia Narodowego*, folder 1--"Notatki do Deklaracji programowej O.Z.N." Hereafter, documents from this collection will be cited as AAN/OZN.

[17]AAN/OZN, folder 32--Statut organizacyjny O.Z.N. [May-June, 1938].

[18]*Gazeta Polska*, May 31, 1936.

[19]*Ibid.*

[20]AAN/OZN, loc.cit.

[21]Bogusław Miedziński, *Wczoraj, Dziś, Jutro* (Warsaw, 1938), p. 179. Hereafter cited as *WDJ*. See also two other essays in the same work: "Organizacja Państwa a Organizacja Narodu" (pp. 27-30) and "Naród i Państwo" (pp. 31-33).

[22]*Gazeta Polska*, April 12, 1938.

[23]Speech of Colonel Stefan Dąbrowski in *Gazeta Polska*, July 11, 1938. See also his speech of March 7 in *ibid.*, March 8, 1938.

[24]For a broad discussion of Church-state relations during this period, see Edward Wynot, "The Catholic Church and the Polish State, 1935-1939," *Journal of Church and State*, 15 (1973), 2, pp. 223-240.

[25]*Gazeta Polska*, February 22, 1937.

[26]*Gazeta Polska*, May 26, 1939.

[27]*Ibid.*

[28]*Gazeta Polska*, October 17, 1938. See also editorials in the issues of December 30, 1938, February 6, 1939, April 25, 1939, and May 7 and 31, 1939.

[29]November 4, 1937.

[30]For example, see the editorial "Rola Naczelnego Wodza w życiu państwa" in the issue of January 3, 1938.

[31]*Gazeta Polska*, June 1, 1937.

[32]February 12, 1938.

[33]*Gazeta Polska*, October 31, 1938.

[34]*Gazeta Polska*, March 2, 1937.

[35]*Gazeta Polska*, June 1, 1939.

[36]Zdzisław Stahl, "Co to jest konsolidacja?", *Idea i walka* (Warsaw, 1938), p. 32.

[37]"O co komu chodzi?," *Idea i walka*, p. 128.

[38]*Gazeta Polska*, March 9, 1938.

[39]*Gazeta Polska*, December 22, 1936.

[40]*Gazeta Polska*, February 22, 1938.

[41]AAN/OZN, folder 17--*Instrukcja dla dzialaczów O.Z.M. (luty 1938 r.).*

[42]AAN/OZN, file 23, loc.cit.

[43]For a detailed examination of the relationship between these two population groups and the regime, see the articles by Edward Wynot: "The Ukrainians and the Polish Regime, 1937-1939," *The Ukrainian Historian*, 7 (1970), pp. 44-60; and "'A Necessary Cruelty': The Emergence of Official Anti-Semitism in Poland, 1936-1939," *American Historical Review*, 76 (1971), pp. 1035-1058. On the Germans, see Edward Wynot, "The Polish Germans, 1919-1939: National Minority in a Multinational State," *The Polish Review*, 17 (1973), pp. 23-64. Roman Szporluk underscored the

traditional nature of this approach in an unpublished paper presented at the conference on interwar Poland held February 21-23, 1985 at Indiana University-Bloomington, and elaborated upon the practice in his article on interwar Czechoslovakia, "War by Other Means," *Slavic Review*, 44 (1985), 1, pp. 20-26. See also the response in the same issue by F. Gregory Campbell, "Politicized Ethnicity--A Reply" (pp. 27-29).

TRADITION AND RITE IN TRANSYLVANIA: HISTORIC TENSIONS BETWEEN EAST AND WEST

William Oldson
Florida State University

Delegates of the Romanian Orthodox Church of Transylvania, meeting in the Grand Synod of 1697, committed themselves to reuniting with the Roman Catholic Church. Led by their Bishop Teofil, they received confirmation of this alteration in their religious, and hopefully their legal, status from Vienna in an Imperial Diploma dated March 19, 1701. This same document also specified that the former Orthodox and now Greek Rite (a.k.a. Uniate) bishop would have at his side as a counsellor a Western adviser bearing the title of "Theologian." This office of "Theologian" would become the focus of the discontent among the Romanians over the extent of Latin influence on their culture and liturgy as well as a symbol from that point on of Western condescension towards the Eastern Rite.[1]

Background for this putative change in the religious orientation of all of the Romanian Orthodox of Transylvania came first in the creation of the Congregation for the Propagation of the Faith by Gregory XV in 1622. To facilitate healing the breach of 1054, Rome cautioned against the traditional animosity of the Latin West towards the rite and cultural usages of Eastern Europe. These were no longer to be attacked or even treated as merely tolerated. The Eastern Church's liturgy now entered under at least the theoretical protection of the Holy See. Unfortunately, this fond wish became tainted with the concept of "Uniatism" and the interaction of mutual suspicions between the practitioners of Latin and Eastern rites.[2]

From Rome's point of view, the essentials of this reintroduction of the Transylvanian Orthodox of Romanian ethnic heritage into Roman Catholicism resided in their acceptance of the "Four Points" in the course of 1699. Having accepted the primacy and teaching authority of the Pope, the existence of Purgatory, the "Filioque" clause of the Nicene Creed, and the use of unleavened bread in the Eucharistic service, the Romanians of Transylvania were considered Eastern Rite Roman Catholics or Uniates. The Habsburg authorities, newly returned to a Transylvania reconquered from the Ottomans, thus obtained a Catholic majority in that province through the supposed conversion of the entire Romanian population. The Uniates, for their part, received from Emperor Leopold I the never quite fulfilled promises of legal and constitutional equality with the other inhabitants of Transylvania.[3] Most importantly from the point of view of those recently abjuring their ties with the Orthodox Church, they received assurances that their rite could remain unadulterated by Latin influences or innovations. One of the many unfortunate complications of this bargain grew out of the suspicion on the part of the Western Catholics that these former Orthodox (now Uniates) were not sincere. This charge haunted the Uniate bishopric from the very beginnings of the Union with Rome and necessitated, in the Vatican's eyes, the appointment of the Jesuit "Theologian" to guarantee the orthodoxy and good faith of the Uniate hierarchy.[4]

Tradition and rite, dogma and liturgy, politics and economics came together, then, in the Uniate movement from 1697 onwards to confuse and antagonize both Eastern and Western sides of the discussion. For the mass of the Romanian peasantry and most of the clergy, doctrinal matters, even that of the much contested "Filioque" clause, fell not only beyond their ken but, more importantly, outside the pale of their fundamental religious preoccupation; namely, the preservation of their rite, especially the liturgy. Dogma simply equalled words, while the broad outlines of the Eastern Church's rite had long been equated with traditional ethnic values and security. Rite had long since, then, become the distinctive characteristic of the Romanian self-image. Their peculiar ritual, not *ipso facto* the special beliefs of their communion, marked them off in their own eyes from all the other peoples of Transylvania. It assumed a secular dimension as well, summing up their consciousness as a discrete ethnic group. Largely uneducated, the bulk of Transylvania's Romanians, clergy and laity alike, saw the core of their faith in the method of worship, not in theological concerns. Despite, and complicated by, the union with Rome, religion and rite functioned as a single entity in the eyes of the formerly Orthodox Romanians.[5] With this general approach in mind, the Romanians who accepted the Union with Rome viewed it as only a general set of principles. Their prime adherence remained to the Greek Rite. Throughout the eighteenth century, the Romanian Uniates saw themselves engaged in a desperate struggle to prevent the "latinization" of their rite. Although they had accepted the "Four Points" and the new ties with Rome, they believed this necessitated no substantial change. A modicum of doctrinal rewordings would be camouflaged behind the traditional usage of the Greek Rite. To their great dismay, however, they perceived a determined effort, despite the proclamations of the Propaganda Fide and the initial documents of the Union, to latinize their Church. The Romanian Uniates of Transylvania, to some considerable extent, came to believe that the intent of the Church authorities of that province focused not on reuniting them with the Vatican, but rather on assimilating them into the Latin Rite.[6]

Graf Leopold Cardinal von Kollonitsch, Primate of Hungary and Archbishop of Gran, both reported accurately this Romanian fear of latinization and stood out as its prefigurement in their eyes. Besides his clerical posts, the Cardinal had also served as the president of the court exchequer in both Pressburg and Vienna. In Transylvania, he had preponderant moment for the social-economic concerns of the new Uniates as well as the ultimate authority over their religious anxieties. In brief, he possessed more influence than any other courtier at Leopold I's court.[7] Writing to the Propaganda Fide in 1701 he reported the mistrust generated by dread that those following the Greek Rite had for all things Latin. He likewise constructed a brief regarding the outright hatred of the Latin Rite by the overwhelming majority of those still Orthodox, among whom the Uniates still lived. In turn, Kollonitsch had his judgment confirmed by members of the Society of Jesus whom he considered the only Roman Catholic clerics sufficiently versed in the language and culture of the area to serve as guides for the Uniates. Gabriel Hevenesi, the foremost Jesuit superior of that time and region, testified to this widespread aversion towards Catholic influence especially when it impinged on the fashion in which worship was offered. Indeed, the assessment of modern Romanian historiography continues to reflect this extreme reaction, maintaining that all but the few who embraced the Union preferred emigration to conversion or substantive Latin incursions into their rite.[8] Feeding this fear and rancor of those practicing the Greek Rite for those of the Latin was the condescension, indeed contempt, of the latter for anything that differed from the post-Reformation liturgy and mores of Rome. Even the highly educated Jesuits, specially trained and selected to work among the Eastern Christians, looked down upon the other rite. This approach to the culture and traditions of both the Uniates and Greek Orthodox dated from the beginning of the Union with Rome and persisted throughout the eighteenth century. Though the worst of it and the most visible manifestation (that is, the establishment of the Jesuit "Theologian" at the side of the Uniate bishop to ensure his compliance with Rome's ways) disappeared with the suppression of the Society of Jesus in 1773, the Vatican's attitude, not merely towards the Orthodox world but also towards its most recent group of Uniates in Transylvania, stood forth unmistakable in the words of Leopold Cardinal Kollonitsch. Despite the fact that he and his church had accepted Bishop Teofil's pledge of faith and assent to the "Four Points," Cardinal Kollonitsch labelled all such hierarchs not simply as schismatics but as persons "without faith." Presumably including the Uniate leader under his blanket indictment, the Cardinal left no doubt in his readers' minds as to the atheism [sic], inclinations towards simony, and lack of valid ordination/consecration of all Orthodox prelates. The pervasive attitude of distrust and suspicion which Kollonitsch manifested towards Uniate and Orthodox alike can best be summed up in the list of "errors" which he forwarded to the Jesuits working among the Romanians of Transylvania. This odd mixture of religious antipathy and patronizing of ethnic inferiors encompassed more than the long-standing dispute over the primacy of the Pope and its corollaries going back through all the confessional dispute to 1054. The Hungarian Primate also charged the Romanians with refusing Latin priests the use of Eastern Rite churches and with granting divorce simply upon request. With uncommon suspension of disbelief, Cardinal Kollonitsch even relayed the bizarre canard that Greek Rite priests obliged their parishioners to kill Roman Catholics, enticing them to do so with the promise of forgiveness of their sins.[9] Following the prescripts of the Council of Florence, Kollonitsch, like the Latin Church in general, accepted the theoretical legitimacy and dignity of the Oriental rites. Unhappily in his view, given the past errors and abuses of the Romanian Uniates, he had to be on his theological guard constantly. The lack of trained clergy to be found among those recently reunited with Rome compounded this difficulty. Ultimately, of course, for him and the Habsburg cause in Transylvania, the Protestant faction had to be combatted both in secular and religious terms. To "exterminate" the Protestants, the Romanian Orthodox had to be "converted" *en masse*, whatever their level of canonical preparedness or *bona fides*. Unfortunately, neither the political necessities of the Habsburgs nor the aspirations of the Romanians to be other than "pariahs" in their homeland (namely, to enjoy the same constitutional and societal rights as the Magyars, Saxons, and Secklers) could erase the tensions between the two rites.

From the Romanian viewpoint, the entire structure of the Union, most especially the fact that the Jesuit "Theologian" peered over their bishop's shoulder, made it a suspected agent for transforming them into cultural Roman Catholics. This deeply felt skepticism about Latin intentions erupted in 1701, when due to the suspicions of the Latin Rite authorities Cardinal Kollonitsch decreed that Bishop Atanasie would have to be reconsecrated. This gave credence and tangible support for the misgivings of those following the Greek Rite. It certainly flowed naturally from Kollonitsch's personal apprehensions concerning the validity of Orthodox ordinations and consecration of bishops. Moreover, it stemmed directly from Catholic wariness over the extent of Magyar Calvinist influence on the Uniate bishop, indeed queasiness over the role the Calvinists played in providing the political and financial support that enabled Atanasie to be made a bishop in the first place.[10] At the price of an uncertain conversion of an undetermined number of formerly Orthodox Romanians, Kollonitsch and the Habsburgs had obtained an instant "majority" in Transylvania. Rather than an insignificant 30,000 members of their confession, they could now make the claim to one-third of a million inhabitants of the province and hence to a majority. Unanswered, of course, were the questions of actually granting the promised equality to the Uniates and the hierarchical relationship between Latin and Eastern Rite Roman Catholics. Not unexpectedly, the religious intolerance of the seventeenth century spilled over into the eighteenth. While not violent as in the West, this animosity between sectaries also eroded the affairs between varieties of Catholics. Matters of rite assumed a significance proportional to those between sects. Increasingly in the course of the eighteenth century, the centrality of the Greek Rite for the Romanians of Transylvania would become more pronounced. Indeed, it assumed a singular importance surpassing what would later be termed nationalistic considerations embracing the entire religious-cultural identification of the Romanians.[11]

The possibilities for misunderstandings, and the magnitude of the difference in emphasis, became obvious from the issuance of the initial manifesto dealing with the Tranyslvanian Romanians' Union with Rome. In 1698, both a Latin and a Romanian language version of this document was forthcoming. In the context of tensions over preserving the pristine quality of the Greek Rite for the Uniates, the Romanian copy spent almost half its time dealing with this issue. In contrast, the Latin rendering limited itself to an implicit reference to the background commitment dating from the original negotiations "to observe the Greek Rite."[12] With a centuries-old history of antagonism and jurisdictional jousting, the stage obviously was set for skirmishes between Uniate and Latin Rite Roman Catholics. As if to alert the Romanian Uniates to this danger, and to arouse their worst fears, Cardinal Kollonitsch seemed from the start to place a vastly different interpretation on the admonition "to observe the Greek Rite." In 1704, even in the process of establishing a foundation for the education of Uniate seminarians, he urged that these Romanian priests-to-be should be ordained according to the Greek Rite "in so far as is possible." Otherwise, they might receive orders in the Latin Rite.[13] This loophole allowing ordination into the Latin rather than the Greek Rite would become, in the eyes of the later nationalists, an invitation to become a Magyar, to denationalization. But even in the mid-eighteenth century, such alienation from the Romanian ethos was clearly sensed and rejected. Though differing from twentieth century nationalists in evoking a variant ethnic villain as an adversary, those who continued Orthodox warned that to become Uniate meant becoming a "German."[14]

Certainly for any Romanian versed in his religious traditions, even if now a Uniate, the Orthodox emphasis upon culture and liturgy remained an integral part of his intellectual makeup. Dogmas, precisely defined or not, fitted more naturally into the *modus operandi* of the Latin Rite Roman Catholic or the various kinds of Protestants to be found in Transylvania. Indeed, the level of theological ignorance and casualness about dogmatic issues lingered not merely at the point of not recognizing basic Christian tenets, but more basically at a stage of not being able to declare whether one was Uniate or Orthodox. The Transylvanian Romanian, whether newly reunited with Rome or embracing the faith of his immediate forebearers, continued fundamentally to take his bearings from a religious culture expressed through popular traditions. The Latin orientation, with its theoretical and dogmatic characteristics, seemed, in his eyes, the reflection of the birthmark of a different people's heritage.[15] Also reflected in these differences, was the realization that because of the influence of folkways on the Greek Rite the Latins looked down upon the Uniate. We have already seen how Cardinal Kollonitsch allowed for Romanian seminarians to shift from their native rite to that of the West. If any further indication of the disparaging attitude towards Uniate culture were necessary, one which both contemporaries and later observers have bitterly commented on, it could be found in the Roman hierarchy's concern for the formerly Latin Rite priests who now worked among the Uniates. Due to the lack of native priests and the "extraordinarily uncultivated" nature of Romanian converts, a certain number of Latin missionaries had changed over to the Greek Rite. This, the former Western priests felt to be a horrendous burden. Forced to conduct the Greek liturgy as their normal ministry, they begged to be permitted the "solace" of saying the Tridentine Mass in the privacy of their own chapels.[16] This complex of attitudinal discrepancies between Eastern and Western rite Roman Catholics in Transylvania existed from the very foundation of the Union. It explains the persistent *cri de coeur* from the open stages of the Union, primarily from those remaining Orthodox but also from the Uniates themselves, that "as we have lived, so we wish to continue." This emotionally charged reaction to all things Latin, and to the temptations of denationalization, also explicates the emigration that began in the eighteenth century and spilled over into the nineteenth. A considerable portion of the Uniate peasantry simply voted with its feet, taking itself off across the Carpathians into the Danubian Principalities.[17]

So deeply did this resistance to the Latin Rite West's influence run that, for many, it transcended simply preserving the Orthodox cult, as important as that may have been. Resisting "foreign" impact on the Eastern religious tradition presented itself as the only way "to lead a decent life." The specter of "latinization" hovered in the background, then, for both Uniate and Greek Orthodox, threatening the religious practices of their forebearers and, possibly leading to apostasy.[18] The cutting edge of this threat the Uniates saw first of all in the continuing, if sporadic, practice of allowing Romanians to make the transfer from the Greek to the Latin Rite. Nothing could have been a clearer signal as to the unacceptability of Eastern folkways to the Western observer. That this feeling of condescension, perhaps even contempt, stood out glaring for all to see can be found in the pointed references to how the Uniate clergy dressed. After more than half a century of Union with Rome, the Uniate Romanian Bishop in Transylvania was still perceived as wearing the garb of a "schismatic." The robe and headdress of the Orthodox rite, which the Uniates supposedly possessed the right to continue to use, seemed to undermine their allegiance to Rome. They could not be other than suspect since their traditional appearance aligned them with a contumeliously regarded history and region.[19] Along with these cultural factors, very real practical considerations came into play. Both eighteenth century contemporaries and later Romanian critics perceived a situation in which a talented young man of ambition had to abandon his accustomed ethnic religious patterns for career purposes. The Latin Rite became the key for advancement. Not infrequently, members of the Romanian nobility in Transylvania found that to progress very far in the state bureaucracy they had the Hobson's choice of either embracing the Latin liturgy or becoming Calvinist. In either instance, from the customary point of view, they were lost to their people through apostasy. They had, as a later commentator explained, "thrown away their nationality."[20] Such defections by the upper classes had, of course, occurred before and across numerous generations. These became especially galling, however, after the Union with Rome at the end of the seventeenth century. Whatever the political and economic motivations at work then, from the Romanian viewpoint the Union was based on an explicit promise that their church would retain its ethnic character. More specifically, they were to have not only an independent church, but one marked off from the Latin by its distinctive rite and discipline, namely that of the Eastern Church. The original Romanian subscription to the cause of Rome, therefore, had as its most prominent feature the pledge that in "no way" would their rite suffer admixture. Indeed, they went so far as even to stipulate the nature of the church calendar they were to employ.[21]

Having been promised not simply the integrity of their rite in general, or even just their calendar, but "all their ceremonies and holidays," the Uniate Romanians might have expected the dignity that comes with having their children continue in this regimen. Unfortunately, one of the very promises made at the time of the Union came to work against them. Among other concessions they received from the Habsburgs, they were to have the right to send their sons to the schools run by the Latin Rite Catholics. Obviously, if they wanted to have any hope of effectuating the similar guarantee of access to all offices open to other ethnic groups, then they had to prepare their children properly.[22] By the mid-eighteenth century, though, concerned onlookers were commenting on how this "right" was miscarrying. To at least some, the Roman Catholic educational experience was being employed to latinize Romanian scholars. Since the privileges promised at the time of Union would have upset the existing socio-economic order in Transylvania, few Uniates ever came into full possession of them. Passage to the Latin Rite, accorded to a restricted few, circumvented this obstacle. And attendance in the various schools run by Latin clergy facilitated both the attainment of otherwise almost impossible to acquire perquisites, as well as the acquisition of the Western religious mentality.[23] Within a generation after the Union with Rome, the politically astute clearly understood that upward mobility depended not on acceptance of the "Four Points" and becoming a Greek Catholic, but rather on transferring between rites. "Not Catholicism, but Catholicism of the Roman rite," made the difference in one's status. Rite emerged early and definitively, then, as the clearest indicator of social status. To be Greek Rite, meant the condition of a serf most likely. To become Latin Rite signalled loss of ethnic identity and alienation from one's cultural roots. From the perspective of the more aggrieved modern Romanian historian, such efforts accelerated at the end of the eighteenth century. This historiography maintains that economic as well as administrative and educational lures were used to drag as many Uniates as possible into the embrace of Latin Christianity. Ironically, lack of access to schooling during the seventeenth century had protected the Transylvanian Romanians against Calvinist inroads. After the Union with Rome, denial of schooling constituted a major revetment to a similar danger: latinization. For most Transylvanian Romanians, Uniate or Orthodox, *legea* (i.e. the "law", "religion", "tradition") remained not simply the extent of their religious knowledge, but the core of it.[24] The identification of the Romanians with the physical/visual expression of their faith constituted a given, one stubbornly adhered to throughout centuries of resolute assault. As modern researchers have noted, Romanian religious sensibilities centered, then and now, on the familiar lines of the observable traditions about them. These, in turn, took on the broader lineaments of their existence as a distinct group, of their "national and social character."[25] In the post-Vatican II world of ecumenism, Romanian historians have gone beyond seeing this conflict of rites as being merely "detrimental" to the culture and religious unity of their eighteenth century Transylvanian ancestors. "Latinization" is proclaimed to be the prime and necessary outcome of the whole Uniate movement. The Union with Rome amounts, in this interpretation, to "an opportunistic papal propaganda effort...to tear believers from the Orthodox Church and incorporate them into the Roman Catholic Church...." The Uniate rite, then, "formed a part of a papal expansionist drive, a Catholic ecumenism aimed at eradicating the Orthodox Church, since it was only a phase in the total absorption of Orthodoxy into Roman Catholicism."[26] More eloquently, though not more violently, put than would have been the case by partisans in the eighteenth century, these quotes capture the vehemence of the conflict between Eastern and Western appreciations of rite. They certainly help introduce us to the quandary in which the Habsburgs found themselves while trying to both balance the opposing parties and capitalize on the political significance of the Union.

Despite the political necessity of obtaining a larger measure of Catholic presence among the Transylvanian population, the Habsburgs, from the very beginning, had regarded the Romanian acceptance of the Four Points with considerable reservation. From Vienna's vantage point, the Uniates had not so much espoused Catholic belief as capitulated to *force majeure* in the realms of rights and economics. Ambivalence, at the very least, marked the treatment of the subscribers of the Union. Carol VI, for instance, issued a decree requiring that, in areas where the two rites were intermixed, the Greek Catholics must celebrate the feast days of the Latin Rite. To obtain the full flavor of the decree, the reader should appreciate the fact that the Latin participle employed to highlight the participation of these Romanians in the Greek Rite can be rendered as both "assigned to" and "alienated by." Certainly this helps explain the way the affront was interpreted by contemporary Greek Rite observers.[27] These (and similar efforts) the Uniates saw as none too subtle attempts to compel conversion to the Latin form of worship. They quite easily espied their being lumped with religious deviants by their Latin brethren. The conviction then and now persisted that, due to traditional and ritual divergencies, the Latins did not regard the Uniates as "true Catholics;" and all of this in the face of official pronouncements to the contrary. Indeed, during Maria Theresa's reign Latin Rite adherents received an imperial order to recognize the Eastern Rite as worthy of respect, not to be altered in any way, and "holy." Western priests had to be formally cautioned not to attempt to entice crossovers between rites by implying an invidious comparison between the two forms of ritual.[28]

In the mid-eighteenth century, Maria Theresa's government did make substantial legal efforts to uphold the rights and dignity of the Greek Rite Roman Catholics. Unhappily, the situation remained such that imperial decrees and the actions of the diet had repeatedly to single out the Uniates. To combat the prejudice engendered by rite and folkways, these documents had to stress that "both rites," that "also those of the Greek Rite," were to enjoy tolerance and liberty.[29] In the spring of 1745, when widespread agitation against the Union as destructive of the Greek Rite occurred, the Empress felt the need again to enjoin her representatives in Transylvania to do everything possible to maintain the Uniate Church. The staying power of such edicts, and the likelihood of their impinging in any significant manner on the established order of this province, can be judged by the list of Uniate complaints submitted to Maria Theresa in 1748. Prominent among these was the charge of on-going latinization, both through solicitation to change rites and alteration of the Eastern ritual itself.[30] The Habsburgs responded, then, when Romanian reaction to Western forays into their traditional religious culture reached crisis proportions. The Governor of Transylvania, Ioan Haller, attempted to soothe frayed heterodox sensibilities in 1745 by declaring that there existed no desire or intent to modify the Greek Rite. In contrast to the consistent Romanian evaluation of Western attitudes since the eighteenth century, Maria Theresa promulgated a rescript insisting that "Uniates of the Greek Rite are as much Catholic as those of the Latin Rite...."[31] Though none of this occasioned a shift in the mentalities involved, the Empress' rescript did elicit a profession of *bona fides* from the Transylvanian authorities. These ecclesiastical and secular functionaries touted their absolute opposition to latinization of the Uniates. In fact, their response to Vienna contended that no intention to transmute Greek Catholics into Latin adherents had ever existed. Whatever the Transylvanian chancellery and the Court in Vienna published for public consumption, their closest held sentiments strayed markedly from that benchmark. Within the decade, the Governor's chancellery had accused the Uniates of not simply being insincere, but of clinging to "schismatic" ways and of "detesting" Latins. The reiterated public underpinning of things Uniate savored more of exigency than fundamental commitment.[32] Vienna's outward guise of support for the Union position did not seem to assuage either Romanian discontent or Latin suspicions. Maria Theresa's postulate that her throne never contemplated forcing the abandonment of the Greek Rite simply added fresh rhetoric which the Uniate hierarchy might quote in the contest with Transylvanian religious and lay powers. The official stance arrested at the bald assertion of no latinization in practice or strategy.[33]

As mentioned at the beginning of this discussion over ritual and disciplinary differences between Eastern and Western rites, the post of the Jesuit "Theologian" achieved symbolic importance from the start of the Union with Rome. Whether as the Western hierarchy's insurance regarding the doctrinal legitimacy of these new Catholics, or as the Eastern clergy's *bete noire* of their traditional mode of worship, this Jesuit custodian summed up the clash of religious cultures. The suppression of the Society of Jesus in 1773, therefore, marked the end of an epoch for the Uniates as well as Western Christianity as a whole. And this Jesuit era covering the first three generations of the Romanian Union with Rome saw congealed once and for all certain animosities that endure until today. Simply put, the "Theologian's" office, in the Romanian view, centered on the latinization of their rite. Even the most charitable of Greek Rite views catalogs the role of the Jesuit "Theologian" not primarily under the heading of assisting an admittedly ill-educated Uniate clergy, but rather under the classification of "Western prejudice."[34] Despite Jesuit support of the Greek Rite and, indeed, on occasion even criticism of the office of the "Theologian" itself, the tone detected by those not Latin in orientation was one of mastery and disrespect. Throughout this introductory and critical phase of tutelage by Rome, the Jesuit "Theologian" represented the sullying of ethnic pride and treasured pietistic customs. A contemporary screed stated categorically that "the Uniate Bishop had the Latin Theologian placed at his side in order that all [Uniates] might more easily be led over to the Latin Rite."[35]

In 1773, the year the Jesuits disappeared from the Uniate stage, the Greek Rite hierarchy still chanted the same sad dirge. Though the galling symbol of Latin airs of superiority had vanished, the Uniate experience still remained that all Romanians were lumped together. Whether united with Rome or Orthodox, the legacy of almost a hundred years stigmatized any and all votaries of the Greek Rite. That a minor motif in this patrimony included sporadic Habsburg summons to preserve the Greek Rite (and hence, perhaps, preclude any further peasant disturbances in the province) did not change Romanian impressions then or later.[36] In that pivotal year at the end of the eighteenth century, the Uniate Church maintained that the Jesuit "Theologian" had had a continuing prejudicial effect upon the Greek Rite. That institution had limned in graphic fashion the inference that the Romanians were an inconstant people, one whose commitments could not be trusted. In its twentieth century polemical form, this indictment eventually became one taxing Rome with a type of covetous aggrandizement which could not tolerate cultural dissimilarities. Even during the Communist period, Romanian historians played vigorously on this theme. Under the Ceauşescu dictatorship, whatever its ideological props, being Uniate became equated with not only undue Western influence, but also with being a second class Christian (one differing from both the Orthodox and the true Catholics). This position also allowed the Romanian government to maintain the façade that the Uniate Church had not been suppressed, but had chosen to reintegrate with the cultural community from which it had sprung.[37]

We must observe, then, that at the end of the Jesuit schooling of the Uniates they garnered the aversion of the Orthodox and the Latin Rite Catholics alike, that for themselves and others they constituted a "third law." Illuminating the tensions and sensitivities between East and West as early as 1773, we have confirmation of the dislike of the term "Uniate" with its implication of inferior status. The Habsburg authorities in Transylvania at that time gave great moment to the fact that emphasis (and, perhaps, dignity?) had to be given to this group by referring to them as "Greek Rite Catholics." The true measure of the disregard between the rites can, perhaps, best be epitomized in the prohibition the Transylvanian chancellery had to enact on the activities of Latin missionaries trying to evangelize Greek Rite Catholics.[38] As would be in the case in the following century, eighteenth century Romanians whether, Orthodox or Greek Catholic, relished "a fundamentalist faith in which the outward symbols and popular traditions rather than theological subtleties dominated...."[39] When the Transylvanian Romanians accepted the Four Points and became Greek Rite Catholics, they obviously did not abandon their folklore and customs. Such traditions and practices possessed abiding consequence for them after the Union just as before. Unfortunately, with the exception of a few rare and largely anachronistic cautions, this cultural obligation received scant attention and less esteem. Tradition and rite continued destined to be of paramount prestige, embodying enduring stresses between East and West.[40]

NOTES

[1]B. Bărbat, S.I., "L'institution de l'office du 'theologien' dans l'Eglise Roumaine Unie," *Orientalia Christiana Periodica*, XXIX (1963), 1, pp. 155, 157.

[2]Wilhelm de Vries, *Rom und die Patriarchate des Ostens* (Freiburg/München, 1963), pp. 202-203; Cirillo Korolevskij, "L'Uniatisme," *Irénikon*, II(5/6) (Amay sur Meuse, 1927), pp. 22, 26.

[3]G. Bariţiu, "Din cronic'a lui Michailu Cserei. 1661-1711," Transilvani'a, II(1869), nr. 16, p. 182; Nicolao Nilles, S.J., *Symbolae ad illustrandam historiam ecclesiae orientalis in terris coronae S. Stephani*, I (Oeniponte, 1885), pp. 165-170; Nicolae Albu, *Istoria învăţământului românesc din Transilvania până la 1800* (Blaj, 1944), p. 113.

[4]Nilles, *Symbolae ad illustrandum*, pp. 167-168; Bărbat, "L'institution de l'office du 'théologien'," p. 160.

[5]Lucian Blaga, *Gîndirea românească în Transilvania în secolul al XVIII-lea*. George Ivaşcu, ed., (Bucureşti, 1966), pp. 39-40, 90-91; Petrus Bod, "Brevis Valachorum Transylvaniam incolentium Historia," mss., 1764, Romanian Academy, Cluj, Manuscrise Latine # 29, p. 49.

[6]I. Bianu, "Vito Piluzio, Documente inedite din Archivulŭ Propagandei", *Columna lui Trainanu*, IV(1883), pp. 272-273; Blaga, *Gîndirea românească în Transilvania*, pp. 42-44, 92-93.

[7]Mathias Bernath, *Habsburg und der Anfänge der Rumänischen Nationsbildung* (Leiden, 1972), p. 57; Ferdinand V. Zieglauer, *Harteneck, Graf der sächsischen Nation und die siebenbürgischen Parteikämpfe seiner Zeit, 1691-1703* (Hermannstadt, 1869), pp. 64-65.

[8]Collectio Hevenesiana, mss. Tom. 24 (Eötvös Loránd Tudományegyetem Központi Könyvtára), pp. 273-276, 281-283, 317-320, 355-366; Silviu Dragomir, *Istoria Desrobirei Religioase a Românilor din Ardeal în secolul XVIII*, I (Sibiu, 1920), p. 42.

[9]*Corespondenţa episcopului Moise Dragoş, 1747-1784.* Mss. original, Academia Română Filiala Cluj Biblioteca. Manuscrise româneşti 550, f. 74-75; Bărbat, "L'institution de l'office du 'théologien'", pp. 162-164, 178.

[10]Georgie Bariţiu, *Părţi alese din istoria Transilvaniei pre două sute de ani din urmă*, I (Sibiu, 1889), pp. 20, 227-228; Octavian Bârlea, *Ostkirchliche Tradition und westlicher Katholizismus, Die Rumänische Unierte Kirche zwischen 1713-1727* (Monachii, 1966), p. 77; Bărbat, "L'institution de l'office du 'théologien'", p. 162.

[11]Bârlea, *Ostkirchliche Tradition*, pp. 13-14, 20; Bariţiu, *Părţi alese din istoria Transilvaniei*, pp. 14-15.

[12]Alexandru Gama, *Cestiunĭ din dreptului şi istoria bisericei românească unite*, I (Blaşiŭ, 1893), pp. 7-8.

[13]Augustin Bunea, "Istoria autonomieĭ bisericescĭ," *Discursurĭ Autonomia bisericéscă, Diverse* (Blaş, 1903), pp. 284-286; Antal, Hodinka, *A munkácsi gör. szert. püspökség okmánytára*, I (Ungvár, 1911), pp. 418-419.

[14]Constantin C. Giurescu, *Istoria Românilor*, III (Part 2) (Bucureşti, 1946), p. 917; Eudoxiu de Hurmuzaki, *Documente privitore de Istoria Românilor*, VII (Bucurescĭ, 1876), p. 4.

[15]Keith Hitchins, *The Rumanian National Movement in Transylvania, 1780-1849* (Cambridge, 1969), p. 1; Helmut Klima, "Die Union der Siebenburger Rumänen und der Wiener Staatsrat im theresianischen Zeitalter," *Südost-Forschungen*, VI(1941), Heft 1/2, pp. 250-251.

[16]*Collectio Hevenesiana*, Tom. 24, pp. 293-295, 297.

[17]Alex. Lăpĕdatu, "Pater Ianoş," *Prinos luĭ D. A. Sturdza* (Bucureşti, 1903), pp. 305-309; I. Nistor, "Emigrările de peste munţi," *Analele Academiei Române.* Memorile Secţiunii Istorice, Seria II. XXXVII(1914-15), p. 844.

[18]Sterie Stinghe, *Documente privitoare la trecutul Romînilor din Şchei.* I (Braşov, 1901), pp. iv, 61-62; Gheorghie Şincai, *Chronica Românilor.* III., 2nd ed. (Bucuresci, 1886), p. 424.

[19]Augustin Bunea, *Episcopii Petru Paul Aron şi Dionisiu Novacovici, saŭ istoria Românilor transilvănei de la 1751 până la 1764* (Blaş, 1902), pp. 5, 25, 401-402.

[20]Dragomir, *Istoria Desrobirei Religioase*, p. 183; Bunea, *Epsicopii Petru Paul Aron şi Dionisiu Novacovici*, pp. 401-402.

[21]Bunea, "Istoria autonomiei bisericesci," pp. 290-294, 358; Samuelis Klein, "Historia Daco-Romanoroum sive Valachorum," *Instructiunea Publica*. A. Treb. Laurianu (ed.), 1861 (March/April), pp. 92-93.

[22]Nilles, *Symbolae ad illustrandam*, pp. 202-207; Klein, "Historia Daco-Romanorum," p. 93.

[23]Samuil Micu, *Scurtă cunoştinţă a istorii romînilor*, Cornel Cîmpeanu, ed. (Bucureşti, 1963), pp. viii-ix; Bod, *Brevis Valachorum Transylvaniam*, p. 432.

[24]Endre Ivánka, "The Rumanian Greek-Catholic Church," *The Eastern Churches Quarterly*, VIII (1949), #3, p. 156; Korolevskij, "L'Uniatisme," p. 15; Bariţiu, *Părţi alese*, p. 411; Mathias Bernath, *Habsburg und die Anfänge der Rumänischen Nationsbildung* (Leiden, 1972), p. 73.

[25]Stefan Meteş, *Mănăstirile româneşti din Transilvania şi Ungaria* (Sibiu, 1936), pp. xxi-xxii; Gabriel Patacsi, S.J., "Die unionsfeindlichen Bewegungen der orthodoxen Rumänen Siebenburgens in den Jahren 1726-1729," *Orientalia Christiana Periodica*, XXVI(2), pp. 356-358.

[26]Cezar Vasilu, "Relaţiile dintre Biserica Romano-Catholică şi Biserica Ortodoxă de la anunţarea Conciliului Vatican II (ianuarie 1959) pîna în decembrie 1970," Teză de doctorat în teologie, *Ortodoxia Revista Patriarhiei Romane*, XXVIII (1976), #1, pp. 118, 150.

[27]Bârlea, *Ostkirchliche Tradition*, p. 12; Bariţiu, *Părţi alese*, pp. 407, 736-737.

[28] Bunea, *Episcopii*, pp. 384-385; Augustin Bunea, *Episcopul Ioan Inocenţiŭ Klein (1728-1751)* (Blaş, 1900), p. 119.

[29]Bunea, *Episcopul Ioan Inocenţiŭ Klein*, pp. 101, 276.

[30]*Ibid.*, pp. 186, 189-190, 277-286.

[31]Dragomir, *Istoria Desrobirei Religioase*, Anexe, pp. 38-40, 46-48.

[32]Edoxiu de Hurmuzaki, *Documente privitoare de Istoria Românilor*, XV (Part II), N. Iorga, ed., (Bucureşti, 1913), pp. 1649-1652, 1656-1658, 1675-1676.

[33]Stephano Katona, *Historia Critica Regum Hungariae Stirpis Austriacae*, 20 (Budae, 1809), pp. 320-321; Nicolao Nilles, S.J., *Symbolae ad illustrandam historiam ecclesiae orientalis in terris coronae S. Stephani*, II (Oeniponte, 1885), p. 571.

[34]Eudoxius Freiherrn von Hurmuzaki, *Fragmente zur Geschichte der Rumänen*, II (Bucuresci, 1881), pp. 105-106; Korolevskij, "L'Uniatisme," pp. 12-14.

[35]Nilles, *Symbolae*, pp. 186-187; *Objectiones contra Canonizationem Episcopatus Graeci Ritus Magno Varadiensis*, Mss contemporan (sec. XVIII), Academia Romana Filiala Cluj Biblioteca. Manuscrise latine 481, f. 15.

[36]Ioan Moga, "Contributiuni privitoare la tipărirea cărţilor bisericeşti în veacul XVIII pentru Românii din Transilvania şi Ungaria," *Omagiu Înalt Prea Sfinţiei Sale Dr. Nicolae Balan Mitropolitul Ardealului* (Sibiu, 1940), p. 593.

[37]Zenovie Pâclisanu, "Din istoria bisericească a Românilor ardeleni. 'Teologul' vlădicilor uniţi," *Memoriile Secţiunii Istorice*, Seria III, Tom. I (1923), p. 187; Onisifor Ghibu, *Catolicismul unguresc în Transilvania şi politica religioasă a statului român* (Cluj, 1924), p. 201; Vasiliu, "Relaţiile dintre Biserica Romano-Catholică şi Biserica Ortodoxă de la anuntarea Conciliului Vatican II (ianuarie 1959) pînă în decembrie 1970", [Teză de doctorat în teologie], *Ortodoxia Revista Patriarhiei Române*, XXVIII, Nr. 1(1976), pp. 117, 149, 184.

[38]*De ortu, progressu conversione Valachorum, Episcopis item archi-Episcopis et Metropolitis eorum.* Mss contemporan (1774), Academia Româna Filiala Cluj Biblioteca. Manuscrise latine 396, f. 11; Korolevskij, "L'Uniatisme," p. 27; "Protocollum Sessionum Anno 1773 Viennae Celebratum." Mss (1773), Copie. Academia Romana Filiala Cluj Biblioteca. Manuscrise latine 420, f. 22-24.

[39]Keith Hitchins, *Orthodoxy and Nationality, Andreiu Saguna and the Rumanians of Transylvania, 1846-1873* (Cambridge, 1977), pp. 195-196.

[40]Emanuel Turczynski, "The National Movement in the Greek Orthodox Church in the Habsburg Monarchy," *Austrian History Yearbook*, III (Pt. 3), 1967, pp. 83, 87.

CEAUŞESCU'S NATIONALISM: ANCIENT DACIAN TRANSLATED INTO MODERN ROMANIAN

James Ermatinger
University of Nebraska at Kearney

Romanian politicians after the Second World War increasingly sought to negotiate a policy between the Soviets and the West. Throughout Nicolae Ceauşescu's reign, this was marked by voicing public opposition to Moscow. Such "independence" enabled Romania to acquire western foreign loans. As part of this "independence," Romania emphasized its peculiar identity as "a Latin island in a sea of Slavs." This nationalism, in turn, enabled Romania to be viewed by the West as standing in opposition to Moscow.

The recent rise of democracy in Eastern Europe allows us the opportunity to review critically the post-war communist regimes and their political philosophies. Romania provides an excellent example of nationalistic propaganda whereby President Nicolae Ceauşescu attempted to link his regime with Romania's ancient past, particularly that of the Dacians. Moreover, by using ancient history, he hoped to bolster his country's claim to certain disputed geographical regions, especially Transylvania.

The Romanian use of their Dacian heritage is somewhat akin to other nations using popular stories about their heritage. Unlike most national popular stories which attempt to teach morals, Ceauşescu sought to create a political heritage. This was not done without controversy, however; Transylvania is a continual source of conflict in Romanian and Hungarian historiography. Romanians argue that when Rome abandoned Dacia in 270 A.D. the native population remained behind. The counter claim, put forward by the Hungarians, is that the inhabitants left and were replaced by successive invaders.[1] To combat the latter, Ceauşescu's regime exalted the history of Dacia, especially the reign of Burebista (50 B.C.).[2]

Archaeologists have discovered massive fortifications in Northwestern Romania attesting to Burebista's power and wealth. These strongholds became natural areas for the accumulation of wealth. The Dacians had been able to gain their independence from the Celts. The height of the Dacian kingdom occurred from 50 B.C. to 100 A.D.[3] Rome's expansion, however, soon brought the two powers into conflict. In 88 A.D. the Legio V Alaudae and the emperor Domitian's praetorian prefect, Cornelius Fuscus, were slaughtered by Decebalus.[4] This disaster was further complicated when Domitian not only bribed the Dacians, but gave them military technicians and engineers as hostages in exchange for the barbarians' evacuation of the Roman provinces south of the Danube. The emperor Trajan (97-117 A.D.) defeated and killed Decebalus after two quick wars in 105-106. Trajan then annexed Dacia, mainly the area of Transylvania. With its capture, Dacian gold flooded the Roman market.[5]

Rome transplanted numerous colonists into the region, mostly ex-soldiers who cultivated the rich valleys. The native population, however, was not displaced or exterminated, but rather were absorbed by the Romans. Nearby lay "Free" Dacia, that is, Muntenia and Moldavia, which although Rome never conquered nevertheless influenced. The process of Romanization in Dacia, however, began before its conquest and lasted after the Roman government withdrew in 270 A.D. Why was this region so easily Romanized in so short a period? As Vasile Pârvan argued, Dacia was a great kingdom based upon a solid and homogeneous ethnic population. Because of this single ethnic base, Rome could more easily influence the entire region.[6]

Although Dacia was ultimately overrun by Germanic tribes, the Huns, and finally the Slavs, according to Romanian scholars the native population remained and fused with the invaders. Other scholars counter that the present population is descended from shepherds who had migrated from Yugoslavia and Albania after the Slavic invasions, and are therefore not Romanized Dacians. This view, however, has problems, First, there is no solid evidence of a massive depopulation of the region after Rome's departure. Second, the number of shepherds needed would have been more than 200,000. Finally, the evidence used does not take into account the archaeological evidence supporting continuity during the fourth and fifth centuries.[7]

The Communist regime has used the persisent Dacian language as an example of continuity. The Dacian language is exceedingly difficult to reconstruct. Of the words which we possess, only about 130 are still used in modern-day Romania. From epigraphy, we can recognize 2050 words of which 1150 are personal names and 900 geographical, of little or no use. The Thracian language is similar and there seems to have been some intermixing, since the modern Romanian language has two phonetic groups, consonant and palatable like *centem*, and a spiraits (s,z) like *satem*. The combinations are not usually found in one language. Unfortunately, it is impossible to determine which words came from which language.[8]

Of the 70-80 common words, 30 have no sure etymological source, 27 are from botony, and 15 from medicine. Most of the words were derived from the local natives taking their own Dacian words and transcribing them into Latin. Of the 130 words still in use, only 16 are common, and another 48 are average, used in rural areas, or confined to poetry. In addition, the grammar of the Dacian language is even more complex since we have no primary Dacian documents. Thus, the knowledge which we possess concerning the Dacian language is minimal. Certain conclusions can, however, be drawn.

First, Dacian is an Indo-European language. Second, it is closely related to Thracian, and, in all probability, the two had a common recent or peripheral proto-type, Traco-Dacian. Third, both languages arrived late into the Balkans, and were preceded by Greek and Hittite. Fourth, elements of both the *centum* and *satem* constructions are present. Finally, the majority of words preserved are rarely used. From this meager evidence of the Dacian language, Ceauşescu's regime embarked on a propaganda campaign to encourage national pride and international prestige.[9]

Ceauşescu's early propaganda efforts claimed a descendency from the Dacians. A problem with this policy, however, soon appeared: the Dacians had been conquered by Rome. The similarity between Rome and the Soviet Union became apparent. Instead of proclaiming the continuity of the Dacians, the shift to the previous inhabitants, the Thracians, occurred.

What goals did Ceauşescu hope to achieve by emphasizing the ancient Dacian language in modern Romania? There appear to be two. Internally, the communist regime hoped to create a strong national unity using a continuously inhabited nation from the fifteenth century B.C. onwards. In 1975, the *Anale de Istorie* published an article about the Moldavian Museum of History in Iaşi, stressing the evolution of the unified Romanian society in Moldavia. This region could date its history to the time when it was under the control of King Burebista. The communist regime claimed this society to be a slave state and not free, since Burebista controlled the region. The archaeological evidence purportedly pointed to an ethnically pure population. The Ceauşescu regime further stressed that this population was not only pure but culturally superior to any invader.[10]

The theme of keeping Romanian national and ethnic identity pure over the conquering migrations henceforth became a common theme in Romanian historiography. The superiority of Romanian civilization over the subsequent invaders, in particular the Slavs and Magyars, highlights modern historiography. Unfortunately, the evidence and the process has not been so pure.

After 1971, culture (history included) in Romania was determined not by trained specialists, but by the *culturnics*, party-trained activists who had no special training. Appointed and supported by the Communist Party, their job was to develop new myths about the past, in particular the Traco-Dacian period, according to party directives. According to historian Vlad Georgescu, the intellectuals were silenced, and those directing the trends in research were not professionals. The goal of the Communist Party through the *culturnics* was nationalism.[11]

The ethnogenisis of Romanian historiography occurred in 1966 with the identification of the present age with the Roman period. This form of identification came with the push to show the modern Romanian language as Latin-based. Later, a movement began which emphasized the pre-Roman Dacian state. Although this move was resisted by I. Pătrăşcanu, a party leader, by 1975 the Central Committee officially established that Burebista had come to power in 70 B.C. They purposely selected this year so that Romania could celebrate its 2050th year of Dacian or Romanian nationalism in 1980. That year witnessed a series of international congresses and was celebrated with much fanfare. Unfortunately, there is no evidence that Burebista became king in 70 B.C.; in fact, the evidence is that he became king in about 50 B.C. The *culturnics* had chosen the date purely for political reasons.[12]

The Dacian question was the *culturnics*' first obsession. The Party and the *culturnics* went further. They began to stress the Thracians in place of the Dacians, a reasoning based on the fact that the Thracians were older. Since the Thracians had remained free, unlike the Dacians, the Communist Party may have desired to stress their "independence" instead of domination, similar to post-war Romania and the Soviet Union.

Their obsession did not end there. The *culturnics* promoted the theory that the oldest people in the world were from Romania. The origins of man and civilization did not start in Africa and Mesopotamia, but in the mountains at Bugiulieşti. A subsequent discovery at Scorniceşti, Ceauşescu's birthplace, was said to be even earlier.[13]

Romanian historiography has attempted to stress certain periods. The first, beginning in 1948, exaggerated the Slavic influence, undoubtedly forced upon them by the Russians. The second phase, beginning in the mid-1960s, stressed the Traco-Dacian ancestry, preferring the indiginous culture to Rome. The continual internal program became national unity using these new theories. The originator of these theories was Ceauşescu, rather than the academicians. Like the *culturnics*, Ceauşescu had no qualms about inventing history. For example, he claimed that the medieval feudal states of Romania were more advanced than their Western counterparts. Morever, the constitution and organization of these feudal states created economic and social conditions greater than the West. Ceauşescu's evidence for these statements came from the Communist Party. This continual emphasis on the Dacians and the "discovery" of archeaological evidence pointing to the oldest people became a joke in Romania.[14]

But this national link with the past and the use of the Dacian language had foreign ramifications as well. Since the shift had moved away from the Slavic influence, Ceauşescu was seemingly expressing an anti-Soviet view. The Romanians stressed the Traco-Dacian era, instead of the Roman occupation, in order to link themselves with their free past. This anti-Soviet view, however, was not exceedingly dangerous. Ceauşescu capitalized on the sentiment both at home and abroad by having ties with China and Israel but without upsetting the Soviets too much.

The use of Dacian specifically, and language in general, nevertheless attacked Soviet influence. Since Romanian is a Latin-based language, it has obvious ties with the West. Since 1953, when the alphabet was reorganized by the Soviets, this western significance had declined while the Slavic influence increased. Resistance to this reorganization came not from the pre-war scholars, as one would expect, but from the Communist trained philologists. The change primarily involved the letters "â" and "î". Since both are phonetically the same, and occur side by side, the change may seem minor. But this change de-emphasized the Latin, for example *pâine* (Latin *panem*) became *pîine*.

Some changes have occurred since 1953. In 1965, Romania began to replace "î" with "â" in the word România and its derivatives. The movement to revert back to "â" was led by Adrian Paunescu, a writer born in 1944, who wrote:

> Renouncing the letter (â) was an error, much more than a mere fault. It was an error, because it manifested itself, not only in the field of linguistics, but also in the much broader field of molding the national spirit and of retaining our specific national character. When the (â) was dropped, it was not only a letter which was dropped, but a part of our history.[15]

But this attack was not successful. The Party adamantly oppossed any change. Although Ceauşescu allowed discussion, the people were reminded of their past and they could vent their anti-Soviet views; the change did not take place.

Ceauşescu's use of ancient Dacian had political ramifications. It allowed his regime continually to claim Transylvania and to make claims on Soviet Bessarabia. In both instances, the use of the ancient language aroused national sentiment for support of his ideas. The use of Ancient Dacian for political propaganda had its roots in the changes in Romanian historiography.[16] Beginning in 1945, the education system was controlled by the Party. The use of

Ancient Dacian went through three main Communist historiographical stages during Ceauşescu's reign. The first stressed Romanian genetic character. Here, the Romanian Communist Party overemphasized the biological foundations of the Traco-Dacians stating that the fundamental traits of the present Romanian population remained unchanged. The second stage was the Euphoric character. In this instance, everything in Romania was bigger, better, or more significant than anywhere else. Belonging to this phase is the concept of the ruler cult. The final stage was the Anniversary character, where everything is commemorated to stimulate patriotic feelings. In so doing, the genetic character produced an anti-Marxist response, the euphoric an anti-scientific, and the anniversary an anti-patriotic. In all three instances, the opposite effect occurred.

The use of Ancient Dacia has incorporated all three aspects of historiography. The genetic character, anti-Marxist, is the obsession with the Traco-Dacian question, even when information is lacking. The Euphoric, or anti-scientific phase, concentrated on the cult figures: Burebista, Decebalus, and, of course, Ceauşescu. The final phase, the Anniversary or anti-patriotic, is quite evident with the 2050th year of Romanian unity occurring in 1980, even though the anniversary is incorrect.

Ceauşescu's Romania attempted to use the Ancient Dacian language for political reasons. First, Romania has had a long tradition of being invaded, but they continually profess an ethnic stability and purity. Second, the major influence comes from the Roman period, as witnessed by the modern Romanian language. Third, the evidence for the Dacian language itself is rather scant; most words are either names or topographical. Only 130 words, of which a mere 16 are used in everyday common speech, 48 in rural or poetic, and nearly half never used, exist. Fourth, the Dacian language which we do possess is in actuality derived from two languages, Thracian and Dacian, and it is impossible to determine which words come from which language. Fifth, Ceauşescu's government employed the *culturnics*, controlled by the Party, and not trained specialists to formulate policy. Sixth, the *culturnics* and the party hierarchy were not above professing and attempting to prove their theory with blatant lies. Finally, Romanian historiography concentrated on three main phases often producing the opposite effect: genetic or anti-Marxist, euphoric or anti-scientific, and anniversary or anti-patriotic.

As such, although the study of the Ancient Dacian language is important, during the Ceauşescu regime it became a farce. Only time will tell whether new research will be performed by trained philologists (and not *culturnics*) so that a truer picture of the relationship of Ancient Dacia to modern Romania may emerge.

NOTES

[1]For the different theories see below. The argument that the Romans completely evacuated the province of Dacia rests solely on Eutropius who wrote 100 years later. In addition, scholars have rarely examined Eutropius' reasons, prejudices, and historicity. Like all Roman historians, his motive for writing was to instruct the Romans; to accept his arguments without critically assessing them is therefore dangerous.

[2]The Thracians arrived in Romania during the Halstatt era around the twelfth century B.C. In the eighth century B.C., the Scythians settled in Transylvania and Wallachia, remaining there until the Celts in the fifth century B.C. pushed them out. The Scythians in Romania were culturally inferior to the other tribes. The Scythians and Thracians seemingly intermixed and became almost identical. The Getae, a member of the Thracian race, adopted the Scythian culture to hold them at bay. Ultimately the Celts overran the region. Around 200 B.C., we see Dacia becoming stronger, with massive fortifications constructed of large square blocks of limestone quarried and brought from considerable distances. For the history of pre-Roman period see Vasile Pârvan, *Dacia* (Cambridge, 1925).

[3]The height of the Dacian kingdom was during Burebista's reign, when the western Dacians were the main participants. For this period see Constantin Preda, *Traco-Dacia* (Bucureşti, 1976), 263ff.

[4]Lino Rossi, *Trajan's Column and the Dacian Wars* (Ithaca, 1971), p. 22.

[5]For Rome's expansion into this region, see R.M. Errington, *The Dawn of Empire* (Ithaca, 1972); W.V. Harris, *War and Imperialism* (Oxford, 1979); and P.A. Brunt, *Italian Manpower* (Oxford, 1973). For the conquest by Trajan, see Lino Rossi, *Trajan's Column and the Dacian Wars* (Ithaca, 1971); and H. Daicoviciu *Dacii* (Bucureşti, 1965).

[6]Pârvan (above note 2) argued that since Rome did not have to conquer many tribes with different languages and political institutions as in Gaul or Spain, Rome could concentrate on the political and cultural institutions. Du Nay's argument (see below) regarding the limited influence on the rural population is unconvincing.

[7]For the various theories of continuity, see Gheorghe Bichir, "The Natives Did Not Leave Their Country," in: *Romania, Pages of History*, vol. 1 (1976), p. 52; Stefan Olteanu, "Demographic Realities in Transylvania in the 8th-10th Centuries," in: *Romania, Pages of History* vol 3 (1978), p. 145; Vasile Netea, "In Answer to Historian Endre Haraszti," in: *Romania, Pages of History*, vol. 3 (1978), p. 220; Ilie Ceauşescu, "Transylvania From the Dacians until 1918," in: *Romania, Pages of History*, vol. 4 (1979), p. 99; and Andre Du Nay, *The Early History of the Rumanian Language* (Denver, 1977). Du Nay, a pseudonym for a Romanian writer, has attacked the Romanian theory of continuity. For a history of Romania's communist party, see Robert King, *History of the Romanian Communist Party* (Stanford, 1980).

[8]Dacian is an Indo-European language related to Hittite, Celtic, Venetic, and Iranian. These languages comprised the major tongues of the ancient northern Asia Minor-European world. It also appears that Dacian is a descendent of the Indo-Germanic prototype, with elements similar to Albanian and Armenian. For a discussion of the Dacian language see Gunter Reichenkron, *Das Dakische*, (Heidelberg, 1966), pp. 76-119.

[9]The relationship between Dacian and Thracian is complicated. There are two views: Russu believes that there was one language with two dialects; Gheorghiev believes in two distinct languages. For Russu and Gheorghiev's views, see Hadrian Daicoviciu, *Dacii*, (Bucureşti 1965), pp. 20-21. See also Crosslands, *Actes Du II Congres International de Tracologie*, (Bucureşti 1980), p. 38. For

the view of native Dacian craftsmen ignorant of Latin, commissioned by provincials also ignorant of Latin but who desired to copy the Roman models, see I.I. Russu, *Limba Traco-Dacilor*, (Bucureşti, 1963), 48-49. The common words still used are: *a băga*, (to put or place), *băiat* (boy), *căciula* (fur cap), *codru* (forest or hunk of bread), *copil* (child), *a fărîma* (to crumble), *a feri* (to protect), *a găsi* (to find), *hot* (a thief), *mare* (great), *mic* (small), *pat* (bed), *sat* (village), *a ţipe* (to cry), *a zgîria* (to scratch), *zgură* (cinders). Words such as *a băga, băiat, copil, a găsi, mare, mic, pat* and *sat* are used in everyday speech. Words like *căciula, codru, a farîma, a feri, a ţipe, a zgîria* and *zgură* are peculiar to an area or time.

[10]See *Radio Free Europe Reports, Eastern Europe: Romania*, July 24, 1975, pp. 10-11.

[11]For the history of the *culturnics,* see Vlad Georgescu, *Politica şi Istorie* (München, 1981), pp. 81ff. Georgescu was a political refugee from Romania whose views are echoed by many other refugees who left during Ceauşescu's regime.

[12]The multiple number of congresses occurring in 1980 in Romania highlighted this anniversary. For example there was an international congress on the Roman Frontier, economic and social history, and language. See, for example, the *Actes du II Congres International de Tracologie* (Bucureşti, 1980).

[13]For this and other examples, see Georgescu (above note 11). That Ceauşescu is continually used as a source, see, for example, Mircea Muşat, *Izvoare şi Martunrii Străine Despre Strămoşii Poporului Român* (Bucureşti 1980).

[14]See *Anale de Istorie* vol. 20, no. 5, pp. 5-6; and Machael Cismarescu, "Das neue Programm der Rumaenischen Kommunistischen Partei," in *Oesterreichishce Osthefte* 18:2 (1976).

[15]See Georgescu, *Politica*, p. 113, note 46.

[16]The concentration on the Dacians even led to the formulation of courses at the universities, and often the notes proving the history are from Ceauşescu himself.

ON THE CONDITION OF WOMEN IN WARTIME SLOVAKIA AND CROATIA

Yeshayahu A. Jelinek
Ben-Gurion University of the Negev

Three Slavic states belonged to the camp of the Third Reich's satellites: Bulgaria, Slovakia, and Croatia. Bulgaria was an independent (yet revisionist) state before the Second World War, and joined the Nazis voluntarily. However, unlike Bulgaria (which will not be discussed here), the Slovak state was Berlin's direct creation (14 March 1939), while Rome shared with Berlin the "honor" of the establishment of the "Independent State of Croatia" (10 April 1941). Before gaining "independence," both nations lived within multinational states. However, various grievances had alienated large portions of the Slovak and Croat populations from the dominant nations, the Czechs and Serbs respectively. These grievances eventually paved the way for cooperation between oppositionist local groups and the Axis powers.

But the resemblance did not end there. Both nations, overwhelmingly Catholic, assigned to their faith a leading role in independent statehood. Each rejected parliamentary democracy, choosing instead an authoritarian structure.[1] The dominant power in Slovakia was Hlinka's Slovak People's Party (whose members were nicknamed "L'udaks"), which, until the Fall of 1938, was essentially a conservative, staunchly nationalistic force. This party was a strong and established power in Czechoslovakia, although it never succeeded in capturing a majority vote in Slovakia and even among the Slovaks its plurality was contested.[2] Only in cooperation with Berlin, and under the influence of the radical segments within the party, did the L'udaks take the authoritarian direction. In Croatia, it was the Ustasha Croatian Liberation Movement which ruled. Prior to its taking the helm, Ustasha was a minor underground movement, hardly endangering the domination of the principal Croatian political unit, the Croatian Peasant Party. Living partly in exile and partly in hiding at home, Ustasha became involved with authoritarian ideologies almost from the outset. It could be counted with the radical rightist elements of Europe's body politic.[3] Clergy and committed Catholics ("clericals") commanded the Slovak state, while secular politicians, often only outwardly Catholic, ruled Croatia. Nevertheless, it was the intransigent nationalism, the Catholic faith, and the anti-democratic, oppressive system, which gave the decisive coloring to both satellites and their treatment of women.

Regarding the role of women, one should recall that both countries studied and frequently copied the practices of Nazi Germany and Fascist Italy. Moreover, views in Slovakia and Croatia on the role of women in society were firmly embedded in the famous German phrase "*Kinder, Kirche, und Küche*."

It is with this background that we shall examine the position and status of women in Slovakia and Croatia. We shall probe their role in the dominant political forces, the ideology of the governments in regard to their standing, and the situation of women in the communal life. A comparison with women belonging to ostracized groups such as Jews and Serbs will shed further light on the issue.

The Ideology

Religious Catholic principles, more than anything else, guided the determination of the status of women: the woman's place was in the home. Her calling was sacred. She was the life-giver, the preserver of the family nest. A healthy family was regarded as the best insurance for the nation's well-being. The bond connecting family and national life, the importance of motherhood, and the preservation of morality in personal as well as communal conduct were the frequently repeated axioms in public addresses, in the press, and in the scholarly world.

In Slovakia, Dr. Jozef Tiso, President of the Slovak state, acted as its principal spokesman. In his pronouncements on family and women, he followed closely the habitual Catholic thought, which was similar to the conservative European approach to womanhood.[4] Jozef Sivák, Minister of Education and Public Enlightenment, was responsible for shaping state education and, in this capacity, served as an important spokesman on the subject. When designing education for girls, he expressed his fundamental belief that "the life-calling of the woman is the family life."[5]

The Croatian media also explained to their consumers the advantages the new state extended to women. They pointed to the alleged discrimination suffered in Yugoslavia and to the advantage of having an independent state.[6] As Dr. Ante Pavelić, the *Poglavnik* (leader) of the Independent State of Croatia, exhorted a visiting delegation of women:

> The Lord granted the women with the task to be the cornerstone of their families, and therefore the eternal cornerstone of the fatherland and the nation. The woman is the carrier of survival, through herself is the nation alive, she regenerates it; she transmits to the future generations all assets, all values, and the life itself.[7]

Sivák's Croatian counterpart, Dr. Mile Budak, also celebrated the noble task of motherhood.[8]

Scholars enlightened the people's perceptions. A philosopher told young men to prepare themselves for numerous vocations, but the young women were to be ready for but one: the guardianship of the family flame.[9] A female educator reminded her sisters that, while demanding equality, they should not try to displace men, but rather divide responsibilities and teach women the crafts necessary in their spouses' calling.[10] Theologians prepared treatises designed to instruct in the art of being good wives and mothers.[11]

As such, it seemed then that the population could expect only blessings from the hands of the new rulers. However, the reality was not always that cheerful.

Education, Vocations, and Professions

The new authorities wanted to discourage and, if possible, prevent women from gaining higher education and entering professional life. They expressed the fear that the departure of a woman from the traditional home, and her engaging in an independent career, would threaten the preservation of time-honored values, the well-being of the family, and the survival of the nation. While demonstrating the social importance of mothers by placing them just below the clergy, one journalist-priest charged that the:

> Emancipation of women, expounded by the Judeo-Bolsheviks, is a heresy, a sin of the nations, as it is today clearly seen in the fertility of various states....What shall we gain from having lady-scientists, lady-professors, lady-officials, lady-pilots, and God knows what else, if there are no mothers?[12]

To prevent girls from getting higher education and entering the professions, the Slovak Ministry of Education prepared plans to limit their enrollment in universities. These included hampering them in taking the matriculation examinations (*abituriat-matura*), a requirement for admission to an institution of higher learning. The Ministry further prescribed a *numerous clausus* on admission. No more than 105 female students were to enroll annually.[13] The Croatian Minister of Education thought along similar lines. He wanted to ban women from studying law and medicine.[14] In both countries, co-education, common under the old regimes, was officially terminated.

Apparently the public in general, and women in particular, did not accept this obscurantist activity lightly. A Croatian study showed that mixed schools continued to flourish in that country.[15] In Slovakia, women journalists defended their sex's right to an education and a career. Against the arguments of "pseudo-progressive ideas of corrupted women," they raised the "ancient desire of equality with men," and pointed to the importance of education for self-esteem.[16] Time and again, the state-fathers were compelled to pacify the public, and averred that there was no intention of discriminating against educated women. The reforms were meant to contribute to their well-being and thus strengthen family ties.[17] It seems that the plans to curtail women's education in Slovakia never got off the ground.

Concerning the teaching profession, the Ministry ordered teachers not married by the clergy out of the classroom.[18] Authorities sought ways to exclude all married women from education, leaving it to unmarried ones only. Initiators of this plan argued that a pregnant woman in a classroom did not present a nice, aesthetic example.[19] Many married female teachers were indeed removed from schools for economic reasons, as we shall see. In Croatia, however, the ruling Ustasha welcomed educated women, and bestowed upon them professional and public functions.[20] Female students were abundant in Zagreb's university.[21] It was evidently hard to set the clock back, but some of the movement's members at least gave it a try.

As the war progressed, the growing need for labor opened the gates to vocations initially considered improper for women. One example was public transportation in Croatia. While in 1942 the Zagreb municipal administration excluded women-drivers from working in this area, a year later they were recruited and put to work on the Sarajevo tramways.[22]

Nevertheless, female labor did not fare well. Women were the first to lose their jobs in times of unemployment. Their salaries were always lower than those of men. After becoming independent, Slovakia faced a serious economic recession, and, although thousands went to the Reich to work in German war industries, unemployment remained considerable.[23] The order in the Fall 1939 to expel all married women from education, thereby vacating positions for men, touched off a sharp reaction. Also affected by a similar order were public officials, government employees, and some other professionals.[24] Government spokesmen argued that it would be an inequity to have two incomes in a single household when others had no income whatsoever. The place of the woman was in the family, they stated, and thus wives should return to their husbands who would earn enough to support them. Moreover, girls remaining at home would have a favorable impact on the marriage rate. Since the law of minimum wages did not include women, they did not bring home much money anyway and, therefore, their working did not make a difference in the couple's income.[25]

Croatia evidently suffered from the same maladies congenital to Slovakia, and hit upon similar remedies. It too hoped to solve the problems of the labor market, overstaffing of government offices, and family coherence, by the dismissal or statutory retirement of married women.[26] Although women constituted more than one-third of Croatia's labor force, social and labor legislation dealt primarily with males and family units.[27]

An ironic note concerning women's unemployment was the problem of housemaids. Racial legislation in both countries forbad Jews from keeping housemaids,[28] another example of aping Nazi racial legislation. Yet, what was to be done with those maids who lost their income? In Croatia, Jewish families, having been forced to dismiss their maids, were then ordered to pay heavy indemnities to them.[29] Slovakia found another solution to assist unemployed maids. The government commanded households with a defined, higher monthly (or yearly) income to employ one or two maids. This "ordinance with the force of law" also extended to Jewish households but with the stipulation that the maids be over forty.[30]

Nevertheless, as the war continued, the status of women on the labor market changed and improved. The growing need for workers, especially due to increased military recruitment (particularly in Croatia) made female labor sought-after and better rewarded.[31] At the same time, the flourishing black market and shortage of supplies compelled women and mothers of low-income families to seek employment in order to make ends meet.

Morality and Public Conduct

The worship of women as life-givers had a corollary of suspicion and mistrust. Slovakia's Prime Minister, Professor Vojtech Tuka, warned that "the destruction of many states in the past occurred because of women."[32] Separation of schools by gender, attempts to close higher education to women, and several labor laws all were expressions of this misgiving. In his explanation of the termination of coeducation, the Slovak Minister of Education remarked: "I want to make it certain that only our best wishes, and the supreme good of women's dignity, value and honor led to our decision to abolish coeducation."[33]

There were also other means to guard "women's dignity, value and honor" and to reduce temptation for the male. The Slovak Minister of Interior outlawed parties and public dancing.[34] High schools were forbidden to organize balls for their students and graduates.[35] Common entertainment was curtailed considerably. Sivák's Ministry put books discussing the relations between the sexes and sexual guides on the index.[36] Clergy pressed for the strict prohibition of open bathing, since it revealed human flesh and led to sin.[37] The journal of Catholic Action (a lay organization), *Katolické Noviny*, demanded surveillance of bathing sites and punishment of those revealing too much of the body, committing the intransigent to the Slovak incarceration center, the notorious Ilava Prison.[38] Authors asked the public to keep a watchful eye on theaters performing comedies "ironical of virginity," joking about "marital fidelity," and propagandizing "free love." Movies should be controlled, since they might be "harming the holiness of the family."[39] It was little wonder that priests objected to girls acting in amateur theaters, for fear of their moral corruption.[40] Thus, the behavior of the public, in particular of the youth, was closely supervised.

Croatian authorities exceeded even the fathers of the Slovak state as they set out to enforce morality. The gendarmerie of the city of Osijek published an order prohibiting two-piece women's bathing suits at local swimming grounds, and prescribing the minimum size of male trunks. Transgressors could be prosecuted, fined, or imprisoned.[41] Budak, in a public address, called on women to stop using make-up, and beautifying themselves: "The highest degree of beauty is a good family with many children."[42] The Mayor of Zagreb forbade female employees of the city from using make-up, and smoking while at work.[43] The *Poglavnik* and the Ustasha Supreme Staff ordered female youth, and female members of the movement, to go without make-up, and threatened offenders with punishment.[44] Even as late as the Summer of 1944, when a large part of the country was already controlled by enemies of the state, the Secretary of the Ustasha's political section and office of the Prime Minister reminded female officials of the strict prohibition against nail polish, and the wearing of silk stockings (as well as talking during working hours).[45]

Cities like Zagreb, Sarajevo, and Osijek banned dancing and even dance music in public places. Dancing was restricted to private parties, and if youth were to participate, then it could only be under the supervision of adults.[46] The *Poglavnik* warned Ustasha and state functionaries against visiting prostitutes ("because they may harbor enemies"), not to curse God, mothers and fathers (he probably was aiming at a rather popular sexual swearing), not to play cards or gamble, to abstain from violent conduct, not to drink alcoholic beverages, and to lead virtuous and exemplary lives. The Ustasha were also bothered by swearing, and repeatedly called on the man in the street to desist from this vice.[47]

Yet, if rules of conduct concerning males and females mostly affected the public aspect of behavior, many prescriptions aimed at females attempted to impose a code for private behavior. Or, looking at it another way, if all orders pertaining to the male way of life involved female conduct as well, numerous permissions and prohibitions affected the latter only. In other words, women deserved and needed outside guidance.

Motherhood and Family

Slovak and Croat politicians and public figures repeatedly honored the holy calling of women: child-bearing and motherhood. Festivities celebrating mothers of many children, as well as motherhood in general, were staged in both countries. The Hlinka Party proclaimed a day in the month of May as the national Holiday of the Slovak Family. It charged branches to keep lists of mothers with eight or more children, and the President conferred diplomas on those having a dozen offspring.[48] The Slovak Minister of Interior, Alexander Mach, proposed taxing childless (or even those with a single child) families heavily. He also started a campaign against bachelorhood. The statesmen proposed barring bachelors and members of childless families from advancement in their jobs.[49] Ustasha celebrated a Mother and Child Day of its own, glorifying motherhood and women with big families.[50]

The close attention to the natality rate grew out of religious and national sources. Since the numerical strength of the nation was believed to ensure not only national survival, but also an international role and prestige, attention was given to the propagation of natality.[51]

Slovakia vowed to prosecute artificially infertile families and to fight against abortion. An anti-abortion law was placed on the books.[52] Yet, in its battle against abortion, Croatia dwarfed Slovakia. There a law stipulated when, and under what conditions, a fetus could be removed. It carried heavy penalties for anyone encouraging an expectant woman to stop pregnancy, and for those performing illegal abortions. Under certain provisions, if a physician, a druggist, a midwife, or anyone previously prosecuted for performing illegal abortions repeated such an operation, the punishment was death. Also, anyone causing an abortion without the knowledge of the expectant woman, or forcing her to lose the fetus, was liable to capital punishment.[53] This law did not go unheeded; midwives and other so-called convicts were indeed punished harshly, including execution by firing squads.[54] On the other hand, rapists were also put to death.[55]

It should be remembered that human life was very cheap in the "Independent State of Croatia." People were systematically courtmartialed and executed without much ado; this, apart from the massacres committed in the countryside and in concentration camps. Tiso justly took pride in the fact that the Slovak state, from its foundation until the Slovak National Uprising of August 1944, had not seen a single execution on the country's territory.[56] Apart from the objective conditions of continued warfare, and varied local traditions, the supremacy of the secular in Croatia, and of the clerical in Slovakia, accounted much for the differing values placed on human life.

Charity, social services, wage increases, and similar steps were there to support the child-breeding of the needy, and of unwed mothers. During the summer, Croatian female students replaced working mothers to enable the latter to spend time with their families.[57] Charitable organizations extended grants in kind and in monetary assistance. Both countries structured a special charitable network, fashioned after the Nazi *Winterhilfe*, called *Zimná pomoc* (winter relief) in Slovakia, and *Pomoč* (relief) in Croatia.[58] These organizations were purely propagandistic, with the secondary aim of extracting from the public means for the charitable activities which the government did not want to (or could not) perform directly. Therefore, any assistance given through the Winter Relief was accompanied by major publicity.[59] Pavelić's own family habitually granted sums for various social purposes, including families in need, mothers of numerous children, young mothers, poor children, etc.[60] The money did not come out of private pockets and was aimed at boosting the *Poglavnik*'s shaky popularity.

The various provisions and pensions given to families of soldiers, to widows and orphans of the fallen, and to diverse kinds of needy persons of past fame and prominence also belong to the category of social assistance to mother and child. There was a special arrangement in Slovakia which allowed a girl to marry a sweetheart absent at the front and thus to secure for herself his name and his privileges.[61]

Croatia's problems also included the victims of the war, especially the masses of refugees. These naturally included countless mothers and children, and their misery was great. Neither the Croatian government and local charitable organizations, nor the German military assistance, could alleviate the untold suffering. The living conditions of the poor went from bad to worse as the war progressed, but the governments could not provide any remedy.

Related to social conditions was matrimonial legislation. In both countries, this sphere of activity was very much under the control of the Church, which demanded changes in matrimonial legislation, forcing Catholic norms onto the population.[62]

Although motherhood ranked high on the list of values in Slovakia and Croatia, the reality in which women lived left much to be desired. In some fields they advanced, in others they stagnated, but in many they actually regressed from pre-war achievements.

The Party and the Regime

The Hlinka Party was predominantly a male organization, but it did contain a women's section--one of the several female societies in Slovakia faithful to the cause of nationalism--with Božena Tuková, the Prime Minister's wife, as its nominal head. But, until 1940, the section exhibited hardly any activity. However, after German intervention in Slovakia's internal affairs in August 1940, the clerical majority reorganized the party with the aim of better resisting its Nazi-guided radical minority.[63] It revamped the women's section as well. In the Party's secretariat, a women's bureau took on the task of coordinating activity among the ladies. A new head, younger and more dynamic (Anna Sokolová, wife of the Parliament's Speaker), and a new secretary, aimed at setting up branches all over the country, which were to get involved in social and cultural work, but which were to perform independently from (the male) branches of the party. A leader of each local "women's section" was to be included in extended city and district secretariats,[64] but there was to be no mixing between the male and female local branches, and neither one had the right to intervene in the activities of the other. Naturally, the male branch was predominant.

The Party called on women to cooperate with other women's organizations in the state, with the final aim of securing a decisive influence over the great majority of the nation's females. Women's sections were expected to cooperate with the (male) secretaries for social affairs, and were in charge of such activities as the preparation of the Day of the Slovak Family.[65]

There were no female units in the Party's storm troopers, the Hlinka Guard, but there were separate female battalions in the Hlinka Youth. This party youth movement divided boys and girls into subdivisions according to age, but without mixing the genders; adult women commanded the girls. Compulsory youth labor was for males only.

Moreover, the State's elite included no women. Not a single woman deputy sat in the parliament, the State Council, or any other important state institution. Although there existed in Slovakia several celebrated female writers, journalists, singers, and actresses, their official standing had no significance. One hardly ever read about women professionals, doctors, or scientists. Altogether, women did not cut an important figure in the Slovak state. And in the Communist and non-Communist undergrounds which existed in Slovakia, only one of them could boast of an outstanding woman participant (Květa Viestová, Czech by descent). The few women in the underground or in resistance movements were mostly Jewish or Czech.

Conditions in Croatia were different. Although there too women did not stand out in the Ustasha elite or the state's institutions and political administration, a woman did serve on the Ustasha Supreme Staff from the outset. She was in charge of the female members of the movement. In spite of the inferior position of women in the state, it seems that the Ustasha recognized and appreciated female assistance. Therefore, important Ustasha women were readily seen at public functions, appearances, and in the media. We may, however, question their actual influence on public affairs.

The Ustasha Women's Lodge was officially constituted in October 1941,[66] although a women's section started to act earlier. The Lodge's operation was to be similar to other sub-units, and it was charged with the task of absorbing all existing women's organizations in the country.[67] Like males, members had to swear allegiance to *Poglavnik* and to the movement. Social and charitable work, with occasional other tasks, were the chief obligations of the Lodges.

Female students congregated in a separate faction of the compulsory Ustasha Student Organization.[68] The Ustasha Youth included girl battalions. Female high school graduates were recruited to National Service equally with, but separately from, their male colleagues.[69] Education in the female units concentrated on indoctrination, propaganda, and revolved around the calling of wives and mothers.[70] The loyalty of the members was carefully checked.[71]

A Croatian specialty was women serving in auxiliary military (including combat) units. *Poglavnik*'s Bodyguard, the Ustasha elite troop, had a special unit (the Women's Auxiliary Service) which was also stationed at Zagreb.[72] There were also female Ustasha guards at the women's concentration camp of Stara Gradiska who were noted for their cruelty. Others participated in armed confrontation with partisans, thus granting to the Ustasha many heroines and martyrs.[73] In the Muslim village of Fazlagica Kula, fifty-six women allegedly assisted the men in repelling a partisan attack in June 1941, and the regime expressed its appreciation by bestowing honors upon them.[74]

Croatia also boasted many renowned sopranos, outstanding actresses, artists, authors, scientists, and scholars, who often appeared in the media or before the public eye. Some of these, including the entire staff of one theater, joined Tito's partisans. Resistance activity engulfed the Croatian women and they fought with the partisans in the underground; as such, they were repeatedly victims of the Ustasha courts which sent several of them to their deaths.[75]

It seems that Croatian women were more efficiently deployed; they enjoyed a higher standing than their Slovak sisters. Their freedom of action was wider, and organizational limitations less. But this was true only primarily for the urban population. In the countryside, women were probably less affected by the profound changes in the cities, and this was even more so within the Muslim community which was limited by peasant traditionalism and its conservative religion.[76]

Women of the Persecuted Minorities

Both Slovakia and Croatia were made up of multi-national communities, but they both treated the various nationalities unequally. Ethnic Germans and Magyars in both enjoyed privileges, while the Slovak Jews and Gypsies, and the Croatian Serbs, Jews, and Gypsies were persecuted. In theory, the legislation held for the entire population but, in practice, the privileges were reserved for the dominant nations and nationalities, and the rest suffered discrimination. Moreover, there were also distinctions between Catholics and Protestants in Slovakia, and Catholics and Muslims in Croatia.

The privileged nationalities were occasionally bestowed with particular legislation prepared for them only; the fortunes of their women were better than the rest. Laws curtailed the freedoms of the persecuted minorities, and their females would suffer even more because of their gender. Here we shall mention only a few selected topics in order to show the double standards of the local ruling elite.

In the spring of 1942, Slovak authorities decided to send Jewish youth to "work in the East." Berlin, supported by local radicals, ethnic Germans, and often by the clerics, was clamoring for the solution of the "Jewish Question." As the German war industry continued to ask for additional labor, Slovak authorities were looking for a solution.

However, fewer and fewer Slovak workers were willing to travel abroad as employment in the country improved; working conditions in Germany had deteriorated, and they wished to stay with their families. Therefore, it was felt that the dispatch of Jewish labor would satisfy the German needs for workers, reduce the pressure for the "solution," and also reduce the number of Jews in Slovakia. In his trial after the war, Tiso asked why Jews could not go abroad to work if the Slovaks could![77] But this was only a cover as Tiso and the others had been aware already of Nazi misconduct towards the Jews in the East.[78] Senior officials in the Slovak Foreign Office termed the destination of the transports "Never-to-see-again in the East" (*Niemehrwiedersehn in den Osten*)[79] although the facts of the exterminations were not then known. Slovak workers left voluntarily in regular trains, and had secured communication with their homes, but the Jews were loaded under guard into boxcars and abandoned.

The first Jews from Slovakia to be deported were women aged eighteen to thirty-five, but when it was found that there were not even one thousand girls in this age group available for the first transport, authorities lowered the age to sixteen. Spouses of childless families were separated and deported, and aging parents were left without support. The authorities concentrated the girls in several locations where Slovak guards beat, robbed, and even raped them, and then shipped them off to the extermination camps in Poland.[80]

The next transport included males, many of them young husbands; they went to Auschwitz. And now for "humanitarian reasons," families were no longer separated, but went to the Polish ghettos and the gas ovens together.[81] The horrible truth about the "Osten" trickled into the country in the summer of 1942, but even then the prominent notable, Bishop Msg. Ján Vojtaššák, still contended that the Jews only wished to evoke pity and that life in Jewish camps might be quite good.[82]

Ustasha regarded the Serbs as the prime enemy of Croatia, and their suffering was akin to that of the Jews and the Gypsies. There are few episodes reflecting Ustasha honor for womanhood and motherhood. Most of our information comes from Yugoslavian sources, but we possess also German and Jewish documentation.

In 1942, the Axis waged a campaign against the partisans in the Kozara mountains and destroyed many villages; Serbian orphan toddlers from these villages were sent to the concentration camp

Stara Gradiska and allegedly gassed there.[83] Grisly details of sexual (and other) outrages permitted by the Ustasha ranking officer Victor Tomić in Serm (Sirmium) in 1943 alarmed even the Germans, who made efforts to have him removed from command and from the public eye.[84] The Wehrmacht opened graves of Serbian women killed by the Ustasha unit from the Jasenovac concentration camp and reported that the victims' breasts had been cut off, eyes torn out, and that death had been from torture.[85]

Jewish women fared no better. In the women's concentration camp of Djakovo, the guards raped and killed the inmates, thereafter throwing them into quicklime.[86] In another camp, Kruščica, hungry inmates--women and their children--saw the carloads of parcels sent to them by the Jewish community of Zagreb being burned before their eyes, without these starving creatures being able to take any nourishment.[87] Wanton cruelty and sadistic passion marked the path of the Ustasha moralists.

These are grave testimonies of the double standards followed by the authorities of the two states. The obscurantist fundamentalism accorded to their own womanhood was matched by a harsh and frivolous treatment of alien females. "Women" meant "Aryan" women, and none of the "protection" or "reverence" supposedly accorded them ever did any good at all to any other women.

Summary and Conclusions

Two different approaches were possible in this study: we could probe how women related to their societies, or how the societies related to them. We devoted our attention to the latter or, more precisely, to the inter-relationship between women and the official agencies of Croatia and Slovakia. In both cases, the rulers did not represent the free will of their citizens, but rather the will imposed on them by foreign powers. Therefore, rather than answer to the public, they were expected to please their foreign masters. However, the rulers were relatively free to impose arbitrary policies on anybody, including women. There were no checks or balances. Instead, the ultimate decisions rested in Croatia in the hands of the *Poglavnik* and in Slovakia, after February 1941, in the hands of the *Vodca* (leader) Tiso.

Public opinion had no formal channels through which to make itself heard. Nevertheless, there were informal ways of influencing and molding governmental decisions, as proved by the shelving of plans to curtail higher education for women. In several cases, authorities debated with, or catered to, public opinion. The pressure of conservative-religious groups could be matched (or even opposed) by these not easily perceived feelings emanating from the masses. If the banning of coeducation or the restrictions imposed on bathers angered many, approval by even larger numbers kept the governmental orders in place. Routine, habit, and custom, rather than direct opposition, wore down the Ustasha female legislation. Coercion had only a limited effect, and so the rulers of Slovakia--less embattled and with more time on hand to gain public support--could achieve more than the struggling and short-of-breath Ustasha regime. When they relied on accepted values or accustomed means, and when they evoked instincts or pleased emotions, the ruling elites could expect an accommodating atmosphere or at least not outright rejection. Such was the case with the deportation of Jewish girls from Slovakia, with the exclusion of women from government, and with countless other issues.

Both governments were closest in conduct to one another when playing up motherhood and expanding social activities on behalf of the family. Ustasha was more radical on the abortion issue, in handling "morality," and in dealing with personal conduct. In both countries, the male elite wished to keep girls and women behind bars in their family homes, and did not trust the females' readiness to maintain themselves within traditionally and conservatively defined freedoms. Bratislava handled these problems with certain subtlety; Zagreb immediately moved in with a big stick.

The main differences were in labor and the acceptance of a female role in the political/social life. Here, too, one may consider the Ustasha more liberal than the L'udaks. Doubtless both would have liked to have excluded women from the professions and the labor market, but the needs of war brought the Croats to their senses and they allotted to women a not insignificant share in the nation's production. When Slovakia too recognized these objective needs, it still appeared uncomfortable with sending females to perform the masculine task of bread-earning. On the other hand, women in the upper classes, familiar with Western modern traditions, chaffed at the obscurantist innovations of the regimes. They too constituted an obstacle to the regimentation of society.

The distance between the two nations was the greatest when assigning women a share of power and public activity. Faithful to the authoritarian spirit, the L'udaks could not omit women from the sphere of party control and political deployment; yet, even then, the L'udaks required the females to fulfill the traditional role of dispensing charity. If barred completely from legal political manipulation, there existed a danger that women would turn to opposing political centers. (In fact, such was the case with the Slovak intelligentsia which, displeased by the clerical limitations on intellectual life, tended to accept the radical lead.)

But the Hlinka party had been a conservative force since its foundation. Father Andrej Hlinka and his heir Tiso were surrounded by ecclesiastic brethren; the clergy were unaccustomed to female political activity and did not desire it, perhaps feeling threatened and tempted by it. And so, only charity remained for the women.

Ustasha was somewhat different. As a skeleton underground organization immersed in conspiracy, it had been in great need of help from whatever source, including that of women. Females had been close to the Ustasha heart, and performed various important tasks in the movement, including assisting in the assassination of King Alexander. And so, the good-will gathered in the past could not be relinquished in the present and consequently, conscious of female contribution in the earlier days, the women could not be excluded from later action. Therefore, Ustasha women ranked higher on the public ladder than their L'udak counterparts.

Taking into account female participation in underground and resistance activities, one is invited to broaden one's considerations and speculate over both the societies under discussion. Croatian society was probably the more progressive, liberal, and permissive, and this can explain similar and dissimilar patterns of behavior of both establishments. In Croatia, women either actively supported or opposed the regime; in Slovakia they did neither. It would be impossible to charge the Slovak clergy and clericalism with the sole responsibility for the particular treatment of women. After all, in some respects the Slovak clergy moderated and channeled the more extremist passions within their own society, as the abstention from capital punishment proved. In Croatia, some elements of the clergy also tried to tone down excesses, although others surpassed in radicalism (the most notorious example being Tomislav Filipović-Majstorović, a defrocked Franciscan, nicknamed the "Devil"). One would perhaps have expected the Slovak clerics to induce extremism, and the Croatian to call for restraint, but this was not the case. Both ecclesiastic bodies grew in their respective societies and both influenced (and were influenced by) the populace. The Croatian people would not accept or understand a too radical departure from the traditional standing of women; the Slovaks found the changes not too far-reaching, and therefore easily accommodated. The authoritarian regime contributed the peculiar twist of toughness, but failed to set binding, guiding values. In a pluralistic society, however, such toughness would encounter opposition. If a formal sanction were required, the regimes would have a harder time turning their prejudices into official anti-female policy.

The hypocrisy and double-dealing are particularly apparent when considering the females of minorities. The combination of secular nationalism with some patterns of religious-philosophical doctrines provided for (and justified) the double standards. In any event, what was right and good for the nation's own women did not apply to alien females. Naturally, foreign Nazi influence bears a great deal of responsibility for the horrors, but local sources and resources cannot be exempted or exonerated. As such, a conclusion can be drawn that conservative Catholicism, reckless nationalism, and an authoritarian government shaped the condition of women in wartime Slovakia and Croatia.

NOTES

[1]See: Yeshayahu A. Jelinek, *The Parish Republic: Hlinka's Slovak People's Party, 1939-1945* (Boulder, 1976); and Fikreta Jelić-Butić, *Ustaše i NDH* (Zagreb, 1977). In my previous works, I described the Slovak political-ideological system as "Clerical Fascism." It seems to me now that this term has never been adequately defined and analyzed, despite its frequent use in both

the West and East. Moreover, while scholars append it usually to states ruled by Catholic authoritarian parties and movements, they neglect to inquire into the nature of the deeply religious (Romanian Orthodox) League of the Archangel Michael, or the (Norwegian Protestant) National Samling. While the term "Clerical Fascism" may indeed well elucidate the structure and spirit of Salazar's Portugal, Dolfus' and Schuschnigg's Austria, and Tiso's Slovakia, it cannot be accepted on face value alone.

[2]See: Yeshayahu A. Jelinek, "The Slovak Right: Conservative or Radical? A Reappraisal," *East Central Europe* IV, 1 (1977), pp. 20-34.

[3]Jelić-Butić, *Ustaše*, pp. 11-57.; Mladen Colić, *Takozvana Nezavisna Država Hrvatska 1941* (Belgrade, 1973), pp. 9-82.

[4]Štefan Polakovič, *Tisová nauka* (Bratislava, 1941), pp. 333-335.

[5]*Slovák* (Bratislava), 22 June 1939.

[6]See examples in *Nova Hrvatska* (Zagreb), 13, 27 January 1942.

[7]*Donau Zeitung* (Belgrade), 25 November 1942; Cf. *Hrvatski Narod* (Zagreb), 27 July and 1, 2, 4 August 1942.

[8]*Hrvatski List* (Osijek), 23 June 1941.

[9]V. Horbačevský, "Poslanie ženy," *Národný Pracovník*, III (1942), p. 235.

[10]Margita Kovačová. "Národná pracovníčka na dedine," *Národný Pracovník*, I (1941), p. 61.

[11]Book reviews in *Národny Pracovník*, IV (1943), pp. 94, 126, 127.

[12]O. Formanek, "O význame matky," *Našé Novinky*, reprinted in *Slovák*, 3 January 1940.

[13]Jelinek, *The Parish Republic*, p. 111.

[14]United States National Archives, Washington, D.C., Military Division, OSS, Report No. 18842, 29 April 1942.

[15]*Ibid.*; Jelinek, *The Parish Republic*, pp. 111-112; *Naša domovina*, (Zagreb), 1943, pp. 852, 857, 862.

[16]Rozalia Benická. "Má vzdelaná žena zaistenú budúcnosť'?," *Slovák*, 16 June 1939; Jozef Lapin, "Slovensko v prerode a ženská otázka na Slovensku," *Slovák*, 11 February 1940.

[17]Polakovič, *Tisová nauka*, p. 334; Sivák in *Slovák*, 22 May 1939.

[18]Jelinek, *The Parish Republic*, p. 110.

[19]Cf. Andrej Siracký, *Klerofašistická ideologia l'udáctva* (Bratislava, 1955), p. 112. One may suspect that the desire to see more girls entering convents also contributed to this initiative.

[20]Like Olga Osterman, a Principal to the Third High School of Zagreb (*Nova Hrvatska*, 28 July 1943), or Engineer Marija Marišić, a Commander of Labor Services (Archives of the Institute for Military History [AIMH], Belgrade, 39/6-2, K171-17, Command of the Ustasha Youth to the Supreme Ustasha Staff, Zagreb, 4 February 1944).

[21]Federal Archives, Koblenz, Südost Europa Gesellschaft (SOEG), Wochenbericht Nr. 28, 27 June 1942; *Donau Zeitung*, 7 February 1943; *Neue Ordnung* (Zagreb), 27 August 1943.

[22]*Neue Ordnung*, 19 April 1942; *Hrvatski Narod*, 23 April 1943.

[23]*Organizačné Zvesti* (Bratislava), III 3 (March 1942), p. 10. The government specified that unmarried girls going to work in Germany should not be under the age of twenty, and should have been gainfully employed in Slovakia at least two years before leaving.

[24]National Archives, Microcopy T-81 (The Institute for Germans Living Abroad), R 528, 5295615; 407 married female teachers were dismissed between Fall 1939 and Fall 1940.

[25]Polakovič, *Tisová nauka*, pp. 334-35; Minister of Interior Ferdinand Ďurčanský in *Slovák*, 22 October 1939; also *Slovák*, 2 and 8 March 1941.

[26]*Hrvatski List*, 2 August 1941; *Südost Echo* (Budapest), 24 October 1941.

[27]Such was the case in Slovakia as well, where the emphasis on family wages was believed to solve the economic problems of individual households and decrease the need for a wife's salary. SOEG, Bericht Nr. 165, 26 June 1942; OSS, Report No. 38183, 16 June 1943; *Za Dom* (Zagreb), 1 July 1943, 1 July 1944; Polakovič, pp. 335-336.

[28]In Croatia, the age limit was 45. Colić, *Takozvana Nezavisna Država Hrvatska*, Appendix XI, p. 419. In Slovakia it was 40. Anton Vašek, *Protižidovské zákonodarstvo na Slovensku* (Bratislava, 1942), p. 109.

[29]*Hrvatski List*, 8 August 1941.

[30]*The Slovak Collection of Laws*, No. 209, 3 September 1940. The ordinance was abrogated on 16 June 1942 (*Slovak Collection*, No. 114).

[31]The few statistical details available underscore this. By the end of 1942, 215,888 workers (including 129,487 males) were insured by the Croatian Social Security. A year later, there were 196,034 workers registered, yet the number of men declined 9.2% and women increased 2.2%. That year the authorities permitted women to work at night, something prohibited the year before. *Sudöst Echo*, No. 19, 7 May 1943. Eighteen months earlier, the number of males insured was increasing and women declining. *Sudöst Echo*, No. 43, 24 October 1941.

[32]*Slovák*, 20 August 1939.

[33]Jelinek, *The Parish Republic*, p. 111.

[34]T-175 (Reichsführer SS and Chief of the German Police), R519, 937671, of 17 February 1944.

[35]*Slovák*, 12 January 1940.

[36]Moresheth Archives, Israel. The Slovak Collection, The Presidium of Ministry of the Interior, Circular letter, 28 May 1943; *Slovák*, 30 March 1940. The permitted ones were "Christian" in their spirit. *Národný Pracovník*, IV (1943), p. 188.

[37]Msg. Ferienčík in *Slovák*, 14 March 1941.

[38]T-75, R 530, 9401413, of 8 June 1941.

[39]*Slovák*, 30 December 1939, 3 March 1940.

[40]Siracký, *Klerofašistická ideologia l'udáctva*, p. 96.

[41]*Hrvatski List*, 7 July 1941.

[42]*Hrvatski List*, 23 June 1941.

[43]*Hrvatski List*, 7 July 1941.

[44]AIMH, 39/6-2, K170-A, Command of the Ustasha Youth to the branches, 4 February 1944.

[45]AIMH, 40/8-1, K170, Circular letter, 17 July 1944.

[46]SOEG, Wochenbericht Nr. 149, 9 March 1942, Nr. 150, 10 March 1942, Nr. 205, 29 March 1943; AIMH, Command Ustasha Youth, Sarajevo, 10 February 1944.

[47]AIMH, 20/1-1, K161, Gendarmerie order, 17 June 1942; 7/15-1, 2, K85, Poglavnik's Supreme Staff, Circular Letter, 22 March 1942; *Hrvatski Narod*, 28 April 1943, 30 March 1944; *Zbornik*

zakona i naredaba Nezavisne Države Hrvatske, I, 4, No. 369, p. 279, 4 July 1941.

[48]*Organizačné Zvesti*, IV, 5 May 1943.

[49]*Slovák*, 12 December 1939, 14 January 1941; T-81, R550, 5324162.

[50]*Donau Zeitung*, 31 May 1942.

[51]Polakovič, *Tisová nauka*, pp. 353-354; *Slovák*, 2 December 1939, 30 April 1940, 21 May 1940, 14 January 1941, 19 February 1941, etc.

[52]Polakovič, *Tisová nauka*, p. 335; *Slovák*, 2 December 1939, 21 May 1940.

[53]*Zbornik*, I, 3, No. 229, p. 17, 10 June 1941.

[54]SOEG, Wochenbericht Nr. 150, 18 March 1942; *Neue Ordnung*, 23 August 1942.

[55]*Hrvatski Narod*, 10 August 1941.

[56]T-175, R 524, 9393956, SD Vienna to RSHA, 21 March 1944.

[57]*Donau Zeitung*, 27 June 1942.

[58]*Zbornik*, I, 8, No. 816, p. 703, 29 September 1941; *Organizačné Zvesti*, II, 8-9 (August-September 1941).

[59]Polakovič, *Tisová nauka*, pp. 361-370; *Donau Zeitung*, 23 December 1941, 11 January, 1942, 26 February 1942, etc.; *Za Dom*, 22 February 1944.

[60]*Donau Zeitung*, 1, 10, and 17 January 1943, 5 May 1943; *Hrvatski Narod*, 6 and 9 January 1942.

[61]T-81, R 550, 8324384, of 19 July 1941.

[62]*Slovák*, 29 and 30 May 1940; Cf. The Political Archives of the German Foreign Office, Bonn, Inland II g 256, Kasche to the German Foreign Office, 21 September 1942.

[63]See my "Slovakia's Internal Policy and the Third Reich, August 1940--February 1941," *Central European History*, IV, 3 (September 1971), pp. 250-251.

[64]*Organizačné Zvesti*, II, 10 (October 1941), III, 5 (May 1942).

[65]*Organizačné Zvesti*, III, 7 (July 1942), IV, 3 (March 1943).

[66]SOEG, Wochenbericht Nr. 134, 19 November 1941; *Hrvatski Narod*, 17 November 1941.

[67]SOEG, Wochenbericht Nr. 134, 19 November 1941.

[68]*Neue Ordnung*, 31 January 1942, 3 January 1943, Ustashi, both military and civilian, were performing a rather mystical swearing ceremony.

[69]*Donau Zeitung*, 7 February 1943; *Hrvatski Narod*, 19 March 1943.

[70]OSS, Report No. 18842, 29 April 1942; *Zbornik*, I, 10, No. 982, p. 857, 4 April 1941.

[71]AIMH, 44/3-1, 114B, Command Ustasha Youth Sarajevo to the branches, 17 September 1943; 16/5-1, K171-A, Leader of the Labor Service to the Travnik branch of Ustasha youth, 14 October 1943.

[72]AIMH, 22/6-1, A-171, Command Ustasha Youth to the branch of Laska-Pliva, 14 January 1944.

[73]AIMH, 16/6-1, A-171, Command of Ustasha Youth, Propaganda Section, to branch Travnik: commemoration of Jelena Santić, 16 November 1943.

[74]*Hrvatski Narod*, 30 March 1944.

[75]*Donau Zeitung*, 26 October 1941; *Hrvatski Narod*, 27 September 1942, 15 April 1943.

[76]However, women were virtually excluded from political functions in Bratislava and Zagreb, although Zagreb appeared more relaxed than the stringent and morose Bratislava.

[77]*Pred súdom národa*, Bratislava 1947, Vol. II, p. 15.

[78]Jelinek, *The Parish Republic*, pp. 155-156.

[79]T-120 (German Foreign Ministry and Chancellery Records), R 4744, K403488, Note to files, Ludin, 2 December 1941.

[80]Yirmiyahu Oskar Neumann, *Im Schatten des Todes* (Tel Aviv, 1956), pp. 95-96; Aron Gruenhutt, *Katastrophenzeit des slowakischen Judentum* (Tel Aviv, 1972), pp. 94-95. The rumor that they were being sent to German military brothels was probably untrue.

[81]Livia Rothkirchen, *The Destruction of Slovakian Jewry* (Jerusalem, 1961), p. 20.

[82]*Ibid.*, pp. 22-23; Vilém Prečan, *Slovenský kato-licizmus pred februarom 1948* (Bratislava, 1955), p. 50.

[83]Mirko Peršen, *Ustaški logori* (Zagreb, 1966), pp. 104, 109.

[84]Federal Military Archives, Freiburg, RH 31 III/9, Note for discussion, Glaise with Pavelić, 8 Novermber 1943.

[85]AIMH, 22/4-15, 16, K76, Commander of the local gendarmerie to the command Banja Luka, 28 October 1942.

[86]Jewish Historical Museum, Belgrade, Reg. No. 1835, Dr. Pavle Vinski, "O progonima Židova okruga Osijek."

[87]Central Zionist Archives, Jerusalem L17/188, Dr. Dragutin Rosenberg, "Kurze Darstellung der juedischen Verhaeltnisse in Jugoslavien," Switzerland, April 1944.

THE EASTERN QUESTION AND THE EUROPEAN STATES SYSTEM: LINKAGE FROM A SMALL POWER PERSPECTIVE

Lawrence J. Flockerzie
University of Dayton

In a recent essay on the European states system during the nineteenth century, Paul W. Schroeder described the Eastern Question as "the most complicated, persistent, and dangerous question in European politics."[1] From the end of the Napoleonic wars to the outbreak of the First World War, the issues surrounding the decline of the Ottoman Empire, especially in regard to its Balkan provinces, exerted a steady pressure upon the policies and actions of the European great powers. The leading role played by the great powers simultaneously on the European continent and in the "Near East" served to link the Eastern Question to the European states system. Throughout the nineteenth and early twentieth centuries, the various crises emerging from the Eastern Question constantly threatened, directly or indirectly, to spill over into European affairs. Some examples point this up. The revolt of Egypt's Mehemet Ali against the Sultan in 1839 not only drew the great powers once again into the quagmire of Ottoman politics, but also precipitated the Rhine Crisis of 1840, which threatened central Europe with a French invasion and threw the German Confederation into turmoil. The Crimean War of 1854-56 is well known as an accelerator of German and Italian unification. Finally, the various Balkan crises from 1875 to 1914 played a key role in eroding Bismarck's European alliance system and in ultimately leading the great powers--and all Europe--into the long-feared general war.[2] The ability of the great powers for the most part to effectively manage and contain the numerous crises surrounding the Eastern Question is one of the noteworthy achievements of the international system between 1815 and 1914. Nonetheless, the avoidance of general upheaval over this issue until 1914 was never a foregone conclusion, and the modern European states system was from the start highly susceptible to events in the Near East.[3]

A most precarious time in this relationship was during the post-Napoleonic consolidation of 1815 to 1818. During these years, statesmen and diplomats struggled to complete the reconstruction of the postwar European states system that had merely begun at the Congress of Vienna and with the general settlement of 1815. Despite the vast network of mutual obligations and multilateral agreements erected at Vienna and Paris, much in fact remained incomplete or deferred by the end of 1815. This unfinished business included complex and bitter border disputes, the future status of defeated France in the international community, the final shape of the German Confederation, and the structure and scope of the European alliance system. This last issue was indeed central, for the Allied great powers of Austria, Great Britain, Russia, and Prussia--united in the Quadruple Alliance--had emerged from the difficult negotiations of 1814-15 with their solidarity sorely tested. By the end of 1815 it remained an open question if the great powers would carry their wartime solidarity into peacetime or revert to the more competitive spirit of eighteenth century diplomacy. Far from ushering in the long desired age of peace and repose, the period after 1815 was one of frustration, uncertainty, and tension in European affairs. Only with the successful conclusion of the Congress of Aachen in late 1818 did many of the vexing problems left over from 1815 begin to reach resolution, so that by 1820 the settlement of 1815 had finally achieved a relative stability. Until that time, however, the European states system existed in a highly provisional and uncertain condition.[4]

Unfortunately, this rather delicate period in European affairs was paralleled by a revival of the Eastern Question, which had lain dormant since the latter stages of the Napoleonic wars. The issue that signalled renewed tensions in the Near East was the Russian claim that the Ottoman government had not adequately complied with the Treaty of Bucharest, which had ended the Russo-Turkish War of 1806-12. In 1816, Baron Stroganov was sent to Constantinople to demand that the Turks comply with the treaty. The Turks proved recalcitrant, and very quickly rumors of an impending Russo-Turkish conflict began to spread across Europe. Many diplomats feared that Tsar Alexander I harbored ambitious plans for the conquest of the Romanian Principalities of Moldavia and Wallachia, nominally held by the Turks. Particularly unsettling to many was Russia's refusal to demobilize its massive wartime armies and the rumored concentration of Russian troops between Kiev and

Mohilev, a convenient staging area for thrusts into both the Principalities and central Europe.[5]

Baron Stroganov continued his futile and sometimes acrimonious negotiations with the Ottoman government throughout and beyond the postwar years. Only the Greek rebellion of 1821, which brought the active intervention of the great powers, managed to break the impasse. Nevertheless, the early years of the Stroganov mission constituted a simmering, persistent threat to the general peace. Although secondary works tend to ignore the period before 1821, contemporaries clearly understood the broader implications of an explosion in the east. That the great power leaders were conscious of the potential linkage between the Eastern Question and Europe is indicated by the fact that during the negotiations of 1814-15, British, Austrian, and Russian statesmen made a number of attempts (all unsuccessful) to include the Ottoman Empire in the legal and territorial settlement of 1815.[6] Similarly, in a memo on the state of Europe written in mid-1817, a Prussian foreign office official wrote:

> At this moment the Ottoman Porte attracts the attentions of all Europe. The differences that have arisen between it and Russia regarding the execution of the [Treaty] of Bucharest are of the highest importance, not in their causes or by their object, but in the consequences that they can produce.[7]

I would like to consider the Eastern Question's impact on European international relations from the unusual vantage point of the small, central European kingdom of Saxony.[8] As a small power, Saxony had much to fear from the "consequences" that an explosion in the east could produce. By examining the Eastern Question through the eyes of Saxon diplomats and statesmen, we gain an important, but often ignored, small power perspective. For while the Eastern Question was predominately an arena for *great power* politics, Saxony and the other small powers of Europe were bound to be affected by virtue of the dual role played by the great powers: if the great powers came to blows in the east, there would almost certainly be repercussions in Europe and particularly upon the smaller and more vulnerable states. This was especially the case after 1815, when the leadership of the great powers and the interconnectedness of the European states system had been developed to an unprecedented degree.

The Saxons had special cause to worry about the impact of an eastern crisis upon Europe. After 1815 they were convinced that the fate of their small kingdom was tied to the fate of the general settlement. At the Congress of Vienna, Saxony had barely escaped extinction and absorption into Prussia. After a bitter struggle among the great powers, the Saxon state survived but was forced to cede to Prussia about half its territory and population. While the Prussians returned home extremely bitter over not having gained all of Saxony, the Saxon leadership left the congress convinced that at the first opportunity--such as a new war, prolonged diplomatic crisis, or a general revision of the 1815 treaties--Prussia would move to incorporate the remaining parts of the now defenseless kingdom, which contained 1.2 million subjects as well as the cities of Dresden and Leipzig. It should be noted that after 1815, the Saxon foreign office, under the direction of *Kabinettsminister* Graf Detlev von Einsiedel, did not consider the possibility of exploiting a new upheaval in order to regain its lost lands. In the wake of the devastating partition of 1815, Saxony was a wounded state desperately hoping to hold on to what had been left it by the great powers at Vienna. Nor did the Saxon leaders feel they could depend exclusively upon the friendship of a single great power. Although Dresden tended to lean on Austria in German affairs, one of the bitter lessons they had learned at the congress was that they could not trust completely any great power. Einsiedel believed therefore that Saxony's salvation, at least during the period of postwar consolidation, was not to be found in the protection of a Big Brother or in the kingdom's own meager resources, but in the survival of the overall legal and territorial status quo of 1815. Thus it was imperative that the great powers maintain their solidarity, avoid conflict, and dedicate themselves to completing the unfinished parts of the 1815 settlement. Einsiedel constantly admonished his diplomats to watch carefully the activities of the great powers, since the "political relations among the great powers [were] of the utmost importance for all the others...."[9] Throughout the postwar years Einsiedel assiduously followed up all reports and rumors of "discord," "cooling," and "approaching rupture" among the great powers.[10] At the same time, the *Kabinettsminister* constantly sought assurances that these powers, despite their persistent differences, would remain united and "occupy themselves with the consolidation of their work."[11]

Although postwar Europe offered the Saxon foreign office numerous trouble spots toward which to direct its anxieties, the Eastern Question stands out in Saxon diplomatic reports and memoranda as an underlying threat to great power unity and the settlement of 1815, as well as the dreaded "opportunity" for a Prussian move against Saxony. As early as February 1816, Einsiedel began to receive reports that Russia's new initiative in the east was straining great power relations. In a despatch dated January 31, the Saxon *chargé d'affaires* in Vienna, von Griesinger, noted that:

> the negotiations [Baron] Stroganov will open in Constantinople on the numerous unfulfilled points of the last treaty of peace, concluded at Bucharest, are drawing the concern of the court of Vienna, and it is feared that Russia might be planning new incursions into Moldavia and Wallachia.[12]

Soon the issue of bilateral negotiations between Russia and the Ottoman Empire became enmeshed with the all important question of war and peace. On February 10, Griesinger reported that according to reports from Constantinople "nearly all the Pashas have placed their contingents in readiness."[13] About one month later, Einsiedel learned indirectly that on a recent visit to Vienna, the British envoy to Constantinople expressed fear of an imminent outbreak of a Russo-Turkish war.[14] Russian-Turkish differences over the Treaty of Bucharest were rendered more ominous for the Saxons by the above mentioned build-up of Russian forces in western Russia. Beginning in April, Einsiedel and his diplomats began to express concern about the possible use of these forces. Einsiedel's April 13 despatch to his envoy in London, in which he asked for information regarding British attitudes on this matter, is a typical example:

> People are beginning to believe in the possibility of an impending break between Russia and the Porte. What is at least certain is that [Russia] has assumed a very threatening attitude toward the south, which is suggested by the...large quantity of troops reported to be assembled between Mohilev and Kiev.[15]

One week later, the Saxon embassy in Vienna reported early signs of a possible anti-Russian coalition:

> One is constantly convinced [in Vienna] that the Russians [will move] on Moldavia and Wallachia and that this is the motivation for their armaments. According to M. Hudalist, Austria is most determined that Russia does not come into contact with Transylvania and Hungary [and will seek] to avoid such a blow through the intervention and support of its allies.[16]

Throughout the remainder of 1816 and the entire postwar period, Einsiedel and his diplomats attempted to follow the ebb and flow of the Russian-Turkish negotiations as well as reactions of the other powers. As the above sample of despatches suggests, however, the Saxons found themselves considerably removed from the sources of information. In general, incoming reports on developments surrounding the Eastern Question were sketchy, and clearly based on second-hand information. Although reliable intelligence on this matter was of considerable importance to the Saxons, their means for attaining such information were extremely limited. Saxony's bitter experiences at the Congress of Vienna, and its reduced financial and military circumstances following the partition, had moved the foreign office to scale back considerably its international presence. After the Congress of Vienna, Saxony withdrew from active participation in European affairs and maintained embassies in the great power capitals primarily as observation posts. Only within the regional confines of the German Confederation did the Saxons hope to play a moderately active role. In keeping with this policy of retrenchment, Dresden did not reactivate its diplomatic mission in Constantinople, which had been abandoned at the end of the Napoleonic wars.[17]

A handicap more serious than lacking an envoy in the Ottoman capital was Saxony's status as a small power, which greatly limited access to reliable and current information on great power involvement in the Eastern Question. Indeed, even in Europe, plotting the movements and activities of the great powers proved a difficult and frustrating exercise for Saxon diplomats. Typical is the lament from the Saxon ambassador in London, who answered Einsiedel's query for precise information on great power policy with the complaint that "in regard to *grande politique*, it is always very difficult here, except for those initiated to the source, to learn the true state of affairs."[18] Saxony's exclusion from the inner councils of the great powers was by no means unique among the smaller powers. Since the final stages of the Napoleonic wars, the great powers had arrogated for themselves the right to set policy and undertake actions in the name of all Europe. At the Congress of Vienna, for example, the great powers organized themselves into a "council of five," through which they held exclusive control over the agenda and disposal of affairs. This directorial trend continued after 1815, and the representatives of the small powers were generally excluded from the diplomatic meetings of the great powers. While the great power leaders argued that in doing so they greatly streamlined diplomatic work and facilitated Europe's reconstruction, these exclusionary practices nonetheless engendered anger and fear among the smaller powers.[19] The Saxons had special cause to be wary of great power secretiveness. At the Congress of Vienna they had been excluded from all negotiations regarding Saxony's fate and tended to learn of great power decisions concerning their homeland "at the moment at which they [were] carried out."[20] Considering this experience, as well as their precarious position after 1815, the Saxons were particularly concerned at being unable, despite their efforts, to "learn the true state of affairs" about great power politics and the Eastern Question.

Of all the great powers observed by the Saxon foreign office after 1815, Russia appeared to hold the key to events in both Europe and the Near East. For better or worse (and the Saxons contemplated both alternatives), Russia represented the principal link between the post-Napoleonic European states system and the simmering Eastern Question. In regard to the still fragile settlement of 1815, Russia alone seemed to possess both the will *and* the ability to uphold the treaties of 1815. As one of the greatest winners to emerge from the Napoleonic wars, Russia naturally had a stake in defending the status quo. Moreover, far more than any other power, the Russian empire had the means (purportedly over 800,000 troops) to swiftly and independently assert its will in Europe. By late 1815 Russia had, according to the Saxon envoy at Paris, "reached a point where it no longer feared anyone."[21] That Russia would use its vast power to preserve rather than overthrow the order of things was suggested to the Saxons by the opinions and reputation of Tsar Alexander I following the Congress of Vienna. Through his efforts at reconciling the defeated French, his authorship of the Holy Alliance, and his oft-repeated commitment to the settlement of 1815, the Russian autocrat assumed for a number of Saxon diplomats the spiritual and political leadership of post-Napoleonic Europe.[22]

If Russia appeared to the Saxons as the greatest hope for the consolidation of the settlement of 1815, this power also seemed, ironically, the settlement's most serious threat. Clearly, Russia's enormous power and prestige was a double-edged sword. The ultimate goals of the Russian Empire and its charismatic tsar remained unclear to the other great powers. After 1815, the tsar's diplomats and "agents" seemed to be everywhere engaged in asserting Russia's newfound power, and Saxon diplomats reported signs of deepening concern in London, Vienna, and Berlin over the possible hegemonial designs of Russia.[23]

For the Saxons, the equivocal nature of Russian power and ambition appeared most dangerous when linked to the Balkans and Constantinople. Unlike other areas of diplomatic activity after 1815, the Eastern Question existed on the periphery of the European states system and thus subject to few of its international controls. The Saxons were well aware that the Eastern Question lay outside the all important "legal" network of the 1815 treaties. Russia, moreover, had a long tradition of unilateral and aggressive policy against the Ottoman Empire, a policy that predated its commitment to monarchical solidarity and international cooperation. To make matters worse, Russia's principal antagonist in this region, the Ottoman government, existed entirely beyond the restraints of Restoration statecraft. Saxon reports generally depicted the Ottomans as stubborn and unpredictable in their dealings with the Russians. More than any other European great power, the Russian Empire straddled two separate but connected arenas of international politics; Europe was regulated by a complex series of multilateral agreements while the Eastern Question appeared to exist primarily in the realm of power politics.

This dualism in Russian interests caused Einsiedel much anxiety, and the Saxon foreign minister constantly had to weigh whether Russia's massive armaments were being maintained to ensure "the exact fulfillment of all that was stipulated and promised at Vienna and Paris"[24] or to carry out the "conquest of Moldavia and Wallachia."[25] From Saxony's vantage point, the Russian Empire's unmatched power and prestige endowed it with an uncomfortably broad range of options. Despite Alexander's continual protestations of peace, it was feared that ambitious advisors might "sooner or later seize some pretext in order to make use of the superiority of forces that Russia has at its disposal."[26] The volatile, unregulated Eastern Question appeared in Dresden to threaten to furnish such a pretext. Commenting on the tsar's general policies, the Saxon envoy to St. Petersburg confirmed that "the Emperor indeed desires peace, but he is no less resolved to see realized all the promises that have been made to him by the Turks."[27]

Saxon uncertainty over the ultimate direction of Russian foreign policy was indicated in Dresden's reaction to the Holy Alliance of September 26, 1815. Conceived and drafted by Alexander, this treaty called upon all Christian monarchs to forsake war and to dedicate themselves to the Christian principles of justice, charity, and peace.[28] On the one hand, the Saxons greeted this unorthodox pact, if nothing else, as a manifestation of the tsar's dedication to peace. On the other hand, Einsiedel and his diplomats had to consider the possibility that the Holy Alliance was merely a screen for Russian adventurism in the Near East. Soon after his first reports of this "*alliance extraordinaire*," the Saxon ambassador in Paris, Uechtritz, began to consider the Holy Alliance in the context of traditional Russian foreign policy and the Eastern Question, seeing it as a possible Russian attempt to "paralyze" Austria and Prussia (two of the original signatories) in case of a clash in the east. Uechtritz went on to suggest strongly to Einsiedel that the tsar's enthusiasm for Christian ethics might be "masking some ulterior motive against the Ottoman Empire."[29] Somewhat later, when the Saxon foreign office learned that the tsar planned to publish the Holy Alliance in St. Petersburg, Einsiedel wondered if this constituted a ploy to intimidate Constantinople and to "make the Ottoman Porte more pliant" in the upcoming negotiations with Stroganov.[30]

Given the Eastern Question's detachment from the treaties of 1815, as well as the ambiguity of Russia's direction, Einsiedel was greatly concerned that the tsar might sooner or later become entangled in an open conflict with the Ottoman Empire. At the very least, this would divert from Europe the attention and energies of the settlement's greatest protector. More likely, a Russo-Turkish conflict would unleash geopolitical rivalry among the great powers and place considerable strain on the critical principle of great power unity. Since Great Britain and Austria were Russia's principal rivals at Constantinople and in the Balkans, the Saxons generally feared that a Russo-Turkish war would quickly undermine the Quadruple Alliance and initiate a dangerous period of diplomatic realignment, bilateral alliances, and possibly a general war. Dresden assumed that Saxony would become a prime bargaining chip in any such transformation. A combination threatening in the eyes of the Saxons was a close alliance between Austria and Prussia. Sandwiched between these two powers, the Saxons saw their survival at the Congress of Vienna as due in part to Austria's desire to maintain a buffer state between itself and its traditional rival, Prussia. Ever since Prussia had become a great power, one Saxon memo of 1816 reads, "Saxony has existed only as a buffer between Prussia and Austria. Should Saxony not, therefore, fear all the more their union?"[31] Russia's military threat along Austria's eastern frontier since 1816 appeared to be a leading motive for such a union. As Russian armies were reported to be massing between Mohilev and Kiev, Austria was believed to be gravitating toward Berlin for support. It was feared in Dresden that if Austria and Russia clashed in the east, Prussia might bargain for the remnants of Saxony "in exchange for its alliance against Russia or its neutrality."[32] An explosion in the east also brought up for the Saxons the possibility of an equally fatal Russo-Prussian understanding. In an April 1817 despatch from Vienna, ambassador Schulenburg noted that some sources in the Austrian capital maintained that if Russia wished to launch a strike against the Ottomans, it would endeavor first to gain the support of another great power. In a thinly veiled reference to Berlin's persistent designs upon Saxony, this opinion held that Prussia of all states would be most open to a deal with the Russians since Berlin "has certainly not renounced...its plans to increase its territory at the expense of its closest neighbors."[33]

From Dresden's vantage point, these fears converged in regard to the postwar reconstruction of central Europe, where Russian involvement in the Eastern Question threatened to undermine the still unformed German Confederation. This union of thirty-nine German states and free cities, of which Saxony was a founding member, had been created by the Final Act of June 8, during the last days of the Congress of Vienna. Austria was to preside over this confederation, and held the permanent presidency of the confederation's federal diet, located at Frankfurt am Main. As with so much else concerning the settlement of 1815, the German Confederation had been created in 1815 but by no means placed upon a firm foundation. The necessity to conclude the Congress of Vienna in order to meet the challenge thrown up by Napoleon's escape from Elba had obliged the German negotiators to draw up the confederation's constitution, or Federal Act, in haste. The Federal Act did little more than establish the general outline of the confederation. Much was left unresolved. Vital questions such as the competence of the federal diet, political and economic relations between member states, and the organization of a common defense were left unanswered. These and other issues were to be worked out by the federal diet, which was to begin its work on September

1, 1815. The provisional nature of things after 1815 is seen in the fact that the federal diet did not actually convene until November 1816 (fourteen months later) and did not complete the elaboration of the Federal Act until 1820/21.[34]

The consolidation of the confederation was crucial to the Saxons, who saw the Federal Act as a legal bulwark against its Prussian neighbor, since articles 2, 3, and 11 guaranteed the sovereignty and inviolability of all member states. Saxon trepidation about the immediate future of the confederation focused on doubts over the commitment of the two German great powers to uphold the Federal Act. After 1815, Einsiedel and his diplomats fully trusted neither Austria nor Prussia to fulfill their roles as pillars of the new confederation. The Saxons were utterly convinced of Prussia's determination to bring not only Saxony, but all north Germany, under its scepter. Dresden generally credited the Austrians with desiring to carry out its assigned leadership role in Germany, but, at the same time, believed the Austrians to be increasingly pessimistic about their ability to exert effective leadership over all Germany, as called for in the Federal Act. It was feared in Dresden (as in other small power capitals in Germany) that Austria and Prussia might take advantage of the uncertain conditions prevailing after 1815 and move to overthrow the Federal Act before it or the general settlement of 1815 became consolidated. In its place, Vienna and Berlin were suspected of wanting to erect a more convenient partition of Germany into Austrian and Prussian spheres of influence. As a north German state, the Saxons had no illusions as to their fate in a sphere controlled exclusively by Prussia.[35]

The Saxons saw the non-German great powers as playing an important role in making sure that the Federal Act was respected in Vienna and Berlin. As signatories of the Final Act of the Congress of Vienna, Russia, Great Britain, and France were also, indirectly, guarantors of the Federal Act, since this document had been incorporated into the more general Final Act. The Saxon foreign office seemed fairly convinced that neither Austria nor Prussia would attempt a *putsch* against the confederation without the consent of the other great powers. It was Dresden's hope that a situation would never arise in which this consent would be given, either directly as a result of a general revision of the treaties of 1815 or by default through the outbreak of a general war, which in any case would render the "legal" efficacy of the Federal Act irrelevant. Thus one begins to appreciate why, especially during the postwar years, Dresden often contemplated the relationship between Saxony's fate, Germany's future, and great power stewardship over the unfinished settlement of 1815. As with the entire postwar settlement, the Saxons saw Russia as a primary protector of the Federal Act. The interests and desire of both France and Great Britain to uphold the status quo in Germany were duly acknowledged in Dresden, but the ability of defeated and occupied France or insular England to render immediate aid in central Europe was questioned. Only Russia could intervene quickly and decisively, its armies, noted one foreign office official, "equally disposable against the infidel and the saints of September 26, 1815."[36] The Saxons moreover believed that the Russians would move to defend the Federal Act not only because of the tsar's commitment to the treaties of 1815, but also for strategic interests. Any partition of Germany into two halves would inevitably, predicted one Saxon diplomat, "be reunited under one head, be it Austria or Prussia." And such a unified Germany would constitute an intolerable threat to Russia's western frontiers.[37] Yet what if Russia's power and interests were, even temporarily, directed elsewhere? The connection between events in the Near East and central Europe thus becomes evident. The Eastern Question, and Russian involvement in it after 1815, appears to have exerted a steady pressure on the confederation as an opportunity for--or catalyst to--an Austro-Prussian coup against the confederation and the Federal Act. In late November 1815, as Russia began to move against the Turks for non-compliance with the Treaty of Bucharest, the British diplomat George Rose reported to London that the Saxon government was most fearful that:

> at the first opportunity, for instance, when Russia shall have aggrandized herself at the expense of Turkey, [Austria and Prussia will] strengthen themselves according to a previous understanding at the expense of the smaller German powers, particularly

> Austria encroaching upon, or swallowing up Bavaria, and Prussia treating Saxony in a like manner."[38]

If such was the mood in Dresden in late November 1815, it could hardly have improved when, in early December, the Saxon envoy to the federal diet suggested that Austria and Prussia were conspiring to delay the opening of that body [already three months late] in hopes for an impending change in the balance of power. Once again, the Eastern Question was a central factor:

> The oft-postponed opening of the federal diet and the conspicuous indifference of the Austrian and Prussian courts toward the progress of deliberations feed the anxiety that both powers are aiming to gain time and, if their hands are freed through repose in France and Russia's involvement with the Turkish Empire, to execute their joint expansion plans against Germany.[39]

The constant uncertainty surrounding Russia's involvement in the Eastern Question between 1815 and 1818 served to add considerable anxiety to Saxon observers as they attempted to gauge the state of relations between Berlin and Vienna.

Saxon fears over the survival of the settlement of 1815 abated considerably after the Congress of Aachen in late 1818. This congress, which was the first great power meeting since 1815, proved to be a turning point in Saxon perceptions of post-Napoleonic Europe. The feared breakdown of great power unity did not occur and the four Allied great powers renewed their Quadruple Alliance. Moreover these powers, along with a "rehabilitated" France, publicly re-affirmed their commitment to upholding the treaties of 1815 in the so-called Declaration of Aachen. Although they were neither invited to the congress nor kept abreast of its discussions, the Saxons nonetheless greeted both the renewal of the Quadruple Alliance and the declaration with noticeable relief.[40] While these developments were in themselves quite encouraging to Einsiedel, they were backed up by more direct assurances. Enroute to the congress in September, Tsar Alexander had visited Leipzig, where he personally affirmed to Einsiedel and the Saxon king his unswerving determination to protect the settlement of 1815.[41] For the Saxons, the Congress of Aachen and the tsar's personal assurances gave the settlement of 1815 a solidity that it had not previously enjoyed. After 1818, Saxon diplomatic records show a marked decrease in rumors of war, upheaval, and realignment. From Dresden's vantage point, it appears that the events surrounding the Congress of Aachen made Europe's continued reconstruction less susceptible, if not entirely immune, from being derailed by a crisis in the Near East.

One might question whether the observations of the Saxon foreign office and its diplomats constitute a useful vantage point from which to follow European and Near Eastern developments. After all, Einsiedel was hardly initiated into the plans of the great powers and Saxon diplomats were forced to always view the Eastern Question and the *Grosse Politik* of the great powers through the skewed and dim perspective of a small, central European state. Yet it can also be argued that these very limitations gave to Saxon observers a heightened awareness of the dangers confronting their own and Europe's future. Along with most small powers in the age of great power ascendancy, the Saxons were constrained to practice politics as the art of the possible which consists, as Enno E. Kraehe suggests, "not only in sensing what can be attained but also in appreciating the full range of what can happen."[42] This was especially so in regard to the impact of the Eastern Question upon European affairs. Although the dark projections that haunted the Saxon foreign office between 1815 and 1818 did not come to pass, their fears concerning linkage between Europe and the Eastern Question were nonetheless perceptive--and in some cases far-sighted.

As seen above, the Saxons gave much thought to the attitudes and plans of Tsar Alexander. Einsiedel and his diplomats were gratified at the tsar's open commitment to the settlement of 1815, but, at the same time, were fairly dubious about his ultimate goals in the Near East. Dresden feared that these two areas of Russian foreign policy activity would not long remain isolated from one another. This tension surrounding Russia's foreign policy, so clear in the Saxon records, remained acute until the Congress of Aachen and the tsar's visit to Leipzig. The natural tendency perhaps is to impute Dresden's reactions in this matter to the anxieties of a threatened and ill-informed small state. Yet recent research on Russian foreign policy after 1815 suggests that the Saxons were on target in their concerns, for there apparently existed a genuine tension between Russia's desire to conduct a conservative foreign policy in Europe and its traditional tendency to play rough with the Turks. That the Russians refrained from moving against the Ottomans between 1815 and 1818 has been attributed by scholars to Alexander's determination not to endanger the European settlement.[43]

Saxony's central fear that the settlement of 1815 and its own existence would be endangered by an explosion in the east was by no means unfounded. Such was evidenced in the so-called Polignac Plan of 1829. This French diplomatic initiative sought to redraw the map of Europe in the wake of the Russo-Turkish War of 1828 and in anticipation of an imminent collapse of the Ottoman Empire. According to this plan, Prussia was to be allotted the Kingdom of Saxony in the massive reorganization.[44]

Although the Eastern Question did not precipitate the much-feared Austro-Prussian alliance, it did nonetheless exert an important, long term influence upon the balance of power in Germany and particularly upon the balance of power between the two German great powers. In all the partition scenarios contemplated in Dresden, Prussia was the instigator and chief culprit. One finds in the Saxon records not an ounce of faith in Berlin's commitment to either the letter or spirit of the Federal Act. Austria, however, was viewed in a more generous light. The Saxons generally gave Vienna full credit for its conservative ideology and its desire to maintain its leadership in the German Confederation. If Russia and the great powers managed to keep the general settlement of 1815 intact, then Austria would gain the security and repose necessary to defend the Federal Act. At the same time, however, Dresden saw the Austrian Empire as an overextended state, distracted from its central European interests not only by its overwhelming domestic problems, but also by its growing alarm at Russian power along its eastern frontiers and in the Balkans. After

1815, the Saxons believed that this fear of Russia was causing Vienna to slowly gravitate toward Berlin, thus giving the Prussians increased leverage in German affairs. The Saxons feared that despite its good intentions, Austria might be unable or unwilling to uphold the Federal Act against the partition schemes of the more aggressive Prussia. In this they were prophetic.[45]

NOTES

[1]Paul W. Schroeder, "The 19th-Century International System: Changes in the Structure," *World Politics* 34 (October 1986), p. 6.

[2]On the 1840 Rhine crisis, see Robert D. Billinger Jr., "They Sing the Best Songs Badly: Metternich, Frederick William IV, and the German Confederation During the War Scare of 1840-41," in Helmut Rumpler, ed., *Deutscher Bund und deutsche Frage, 1815-1866* (Vienna and Munich, 1990), pp. 94-113. The author gives an extensive bibliographical overview of this issue on page 95, note 5. The impact of the Eastern Question upon European diplomacy from mid-century on is covered in Winfried Baumgart, *Vom Europäischen Konzert zum Völkerbund* (Darmstadt, 1974), pp. 1-55.

[3]Three stimulating articles dealing with the European states system during the nineteenth century are: Richard B. Elrod, "The Concert of Europe: A Fresh Look at an International System," *World Politics* 28 (January, 1976), pp. 159-174; Paul W. Schroeder, "The 19th-Century International System," pp. 1-26; and Wolf D. Gruner, "Deutschland und das Europäische Gleichgewicht seit dem 18. Jahrhundert," in: Wolf D. Gruner, ed., *Gleichgewicht in Geschichte und Gegenwart* (Hamburg, 1989), pp. 60-133.

[4]The standard works on great power relations from 1815 to 1820 are: Alfred Stern, *Geschichte Europas seit den Verträgen von 1815 bis zum Frankfurter Frieden von 1871* (Berlin, 1894); Charles Kingsley Webster, *The Foreign Policy of Castlereagh, 1815-1822* (London, 1925); Herta Frielinghaus, *Preussen und England vom Wiener Kongress bis zum Tode Castlereaghs 1822* (Cologne, 1932); Gertrud Steckhan, *Preussen und die Neuorientierung der europäischen Staatengesellschaft auf dem Aachener Kongress, 1818* (Berlin, 1934); Bertier de Sauvigny, *Metternich et la France après le Congrès de Vienne* (Paris, 1968); and Karl Hammer, *Die französische*

Diplomatie der Restaurations und Deutschland 1814-1830 (Stuttgart, 1963).

[5]Eberhard Schütz, *Die Europäische Allianzpolitik Alexanders I und der Griechische Unabhängigkeitskampf, 1820-1830* (Wiesbaden, 1975), pp. 1-30; M.S. Anderson, *The Eastern Question, (1774-1923)* (New York, 1966), pp. 28ff.

[6]Charles Kingsley Webster, *The Foreign Policy of Castlereagh, 1812-1815* (London, 1931), pp. 427-434; Schütz, *Allianzpolitik*, pp. 23-24.

[7]"Tableau général de la situation et de la politique des États de l'Europe au commencement de Juin 1817," *Zentrales Staatsarchiv* Merseburg, R 92, Nachlass Hardenberg, G 17, p. 113.

[8]Saxon diplomatic papers and reports dealing with Europe and the Eastern Question after 1815 are located at the Staatsarchiv in Dresden. Much of the material used in this essay was gathered in Dresden while on a Fulbright/IREX dissertation research grant. See "Between Legitimacy and Expedience: The Saxon Question After the Congress of Vienna, 1815-1818" (Unpublished Ph.D. dissertation, Indiana University, 1987).

[9]Einsiedel to Just, 6 September 1817, *Staatsarchiv Dresden, Geheimes Kabinett*, (Hereafter cited *StaD GK*), Loc. 30021, p. 381.

[10]Einsiedel to Just, 12 May 1816, *StaD GK*, Loc. 30021, pp. 316-317; Einsiedel to Breuer, 20 May 1816, *StaD GK*, Loc. 606, unpag.

[11]Einsiedel to Uechtritz, 5 May 1816, *StaD GK*, Loc. 624. unpag.

[12]Griesinger to Einsiedel, 31 January 1816, *StaD GK*, Loc. 30017, pp. 17-18. The Russians had occupied the Principalities during the Russo-Turkish War of 1806-12, but were required to withdraw from them by the Treaty of Bucharest.

[13]Griesinger to Einsiedel, 10 February 1816, *ibid*, p. 23.

[14]Griesinger to Einsiedel, 23 March 1816, *ibid.*, p. 50.

[15]Einsiedel to Just, 13 April 1816, *StaD GK*, Loc. 30021, p. 312.

[16]Griesinger to Einsiedel, 24 April 1816, *StaD GK*, Loc. 30017, p. 72.

[17]Saxony's postwar foreign policy was most clearly delineated in the instructions for Baron Wilhelm August von Just, who headed the Saxon embassy in London. "Instructions et lettre de créance du Baron de Just," (Hereafter cited "Instructions for Just") (24 January 1816), *StaD GK*, Loc. 30021.

[18]Just to Einsiedel, 14 June 1816, *ibid.*, p. 127.

[19]On the development of the great power directory over Europe see, Charles Kingsley Webster, *The European Alliance* (Calcutta, 1929), passim; Wolf D. Gruner, *Die Rolle und Funktion von "Kleinstaaten" im Internationalen System 1815-1914: Die Bedeutung des Endes der Deutschen Klein-und Mittelstaaten für die Europäische Ordnung* (Stuttgart, 1985), pp. 6-14; and F.R. Bridge and Roger Bullen, *The Great Powers and the European States System: 1815-1914* (London, 1980), pp. 1-19.

[20]Walter Kohlschmidt, *Die sächsische Frage auf dem Wiener Kongress und die sächsische Diplomatie dieser Zeit* (Dresden, 1930), p. 117.

[21]Uechtritz to Einsiedel, 18 December 1815, *StaD GK*, Loc. 624, p. 359.

[22]Uechtritz to Einsiedel, 16 September 1815, *ibid.*, p. 95; Georg von Einsiedel, "Réflexions sur les principes qui doivent régler la conduite du ministre du Roi en Russie..." (Hereafter cited as G. Einsiedel, "Réflexions"), *StaD GK*, Loc. 617, p. 71.

[23]The general fear of Russia among the great powers after 1815 is discussed in Charles Kingsley Webster, *The Foreign Policy of Castlereagh 1815-1822* (London, 1958), pp. 88 ff.

[24]Einsiedel to Schulenburg, 20 March 1818, *StaD GK*, Loc. 30017, unpag.

[25]Einsiedel to Just, 30 April 1816, *StaD GK*, Loc. 30021, pp. 314-315.

[26]Griesinger to Einsiedel, 21 August 1816, *StaD GK*, Loc. 30017, p. 158.

[27]Georg Einsiedel to Einsiedel, 15 April 1817, *StaD GK*, Loc. 617, p. 79.

[28]Instructions for Just, *StaD GK*, Loc. 30021, p. 9.

[29]Uechtritz to Einsiedel, 3 October 1815, *StaD GK*, Loc. 624, pp. 128-129.

[30]Einsiedel to Uechtritz, 20 February 1816, *ibid.*, unpag.

[31]Friedrich Biedermann, "Réflexions au sujet du nouveau projet de Confederation Germanique" (Hereafter cited as Biedermann, "Réflexions") (25 May 1816), *StaD, Aussenministerium* (Hereafter cited *Aussen.*), nr. 823, pp. 7-8.

[32]*Ibid.*, p. 8.

[33]Schulenburg to Einsiedel, 7 April 1817, *StaD GK*, Loc. 30017, pp. 66-69.

[34]On the development of the confederation during the Congress of Vienna see Enno E. Kraehe, *Metternich's German Policy: Vol. II: The Congress of Vienna, 1814-1815* (Princeton, 1983). An overview of the principal issues confronting the confederation between 1815 and 1821 is found in Ludwig Bentfeldt, *Der Deutsche Bund als nationales Band 1815-1866* (Göttingen, 1985), pp. 52ff.

[35]On Saxon perceptions of Austria and its German mission after 1815 see my article, "Saxony, Austria, and the German Question after the Congress of Vienna, 1815-1816," *The International History Review* 12 (November 1990), pp. 661-687.

[36]Biedermann, "Réflexions," *StaD Aussen*, nr. 823, p. 7.

[37]Georg Einsiedel, "Réflexions," *StaD GK*, Loc. 617, p. 75.

[38]Rose to Castlereagh, 23 November 1815, Public Records Office, Foreign Office, 64, 100, p. 253.

[39]Görtz to Einsiedel, 2 December 1815, *StaD Aussen*, nr. 2835. unpag.

[40]Schulenburg to Einsiedel, 4 November 1818, *StaD GK*, Loc. 30017, pp. 227-234; Uechtritz to Einsiedel, 19 November 1818, *StaD GK*, Loc. 624, pp. 630-635.

[41]Einsiedel to Schulenburg, 9 October 1818, *StaD GK*, Loc 30017, pp. 374-375.

[42]Enno E. Kraehe, *Metternich's German Policy: Vol. I: The Contest With Napoleon, 1799-1814*, (Princeton, 1963), p. 191.

[43]Schütz, *Allianzpolitik*, pp. 1-36; Ulrike Eich, *Russland und Europa: Studien zur russischen Deutschlandpolitik in der Zeit des Wiener Kongresses* (Cologne and Vienna, 1986), pp. 292-331, 416-420.

[44]On the Polignac Plan see Alfred Stern, "Der Grosse Plan des Herzogs von Polignac vom Jahre 1829," *Historische Vierteljahrschrift*, 1 (1900), pp. 49-77.

[45]Flockerzie, "Saxony, Austria, and the German Question," pp. 685-687.

EUROPEANS, OTTOMAN REFORMERS, AND THE *REAYA*: A QUESTION OF HISTORICAL FOCUS

Gerasimos Augustinos
University of South Carolina

Since the nineteenth century, when reform was implemented in the Ottoman Empire, the involvement of Europeans and the impact on the non-Muslim peoples, the *reaya*, has proved an intriguing issue for historians. Both the intent, the implementation, and the significance of the Tanzimat, the reform movement in the Ottoman Empire, has been the subject of continued historical debate. Recently, one scholar of the Near East described the issue in this way:

> The dilemma of the Tanzimat reformers was that, whatever their hopes that in the very long run their reforms might produce consent for their rule, in the short term they were sure that many of their non-Muslim subjects could only be held within the empire by force. To use force against Christians required the assent of at least some of the major European powers. The great crises of the Eastern Question arose mainly from the European efforts to prevent the Ottomans from enforcing their authority. One face of the Tanzimat was therefore concerned with creating the instruments through which the state could enforce its will and the other with restricting the use of those instruments.[1]

During the nineteenth century, many representatives of the European powers depicted the empire in unflattering terms, commenting negatively on the governance of the empire and the condition of the non-Muslim peoples. Since then, historians have questioned whether the representatives of the European powers in the Ottoman Empire helped or hindered reform and for whose benefit they sought it. Was the reform of the "sick man of Europe" a hopeless cause because Europeans thought so and thus made the reformers' goals unattainable? Were the interests of the

Europeans and the Ottoman reformers incompatible or misaligned? In the past, the statements and activities of the most prominent and strong-willed European figures at the imperial center, like Stratford Canning, have been the basis for judgment. But how did the lesser luminaries among the European representatives, including those on the periphery, see the issue of reform and their role as they carried out their assignments? The purpose of this essay is to shift the focus of the subject slightly, and thus contribute to the search for historical perspective.

Mindful of its strategic interests in the Mediterranean and points eastward to imperial India, Britain supported the territorial integrity of the Ottoman Empire from the 1830s on. In England, Lord Palmerston, who served as foreign secretary and prime minister at various times between 1830 and 1858, most fully elaborated this policy. A firm diplomatic presence was provided on the spot by Britain's ambassador to the Porte, Stratford Canning (later Lord Redcliffe) who represented, and some say made, British policy there as the second stage of reform, the Tanzimat, commenced.[2]

But, diplomatic interests aside, the Ottoman Empire literally represented a sizeable investment for Britain by the mid-nineteenth century. England exported as many goods to the Ottoman Empire as to her neighbor across the channel, France, and more than to her rival, Russia.[3] From the late 1830s, when a major commercial convention was signed between the two states, Britain worked steadily to open up market opportunities in the sultan's domains for the rising volume of manufactured goods its industries were producing.

Because of its international commitments, its search for economic advantages in the Near East, and an articulated vision of what a progressive society ought to be like, Britain was a seriously interested party to any Ottoman schemes for reform. For its part, the Porte could hardly afford to ignore British interests or advice in the aftermath of the Crimean War. Did the British, however, view the attempts at reform in the Ottoman Empire as the means to revive the state's former political as well as military power, or was it the opening of a new era to be marked by far-reaching change and progress as some of the reformers hoped?[4] Here, perceptions are perhaps as important as the social and political dynamics of the reform.

Britain supported the "Crimean system," the diplomatic front to meet a perceived Russian threat to stability in the Near East and the culmination of almost two decades of vigorous political activity in the area. Motivated by the desire to curtail Russian influence in the Ottoman Empire, Canning was also heavily involved in negotiations with Ottoman statesmen that led to the Imperial Rescript of 1856.

The discussions that led to the proclamation of the *Hatt-i Hümayun* are ample evidence of the fact that the Ottoman Empire had become practically a client state of the European powers, which collectively agreed to guarantee its territorial integrity.[5] Moreover, the great powers, no doubt to the annoyance and resentment of many Muslims, had made a special clientele of the empire's Christian population. Acting on their perceptions of the empire's condition and its needs, Europeans left their mark on the content, pace, and even the manner of the actual workings of the Ottoman reform. At the time, the British, who held a commanding lead in economic and political capabilities, exercised the prime influence in the empire among European states.

At the end of his tenure as minister to the Porte, Stratford Canning, apparently not a little weary about the progress of reform, gave his assessment of the situation. Two-and-a-half years after the *Hatt-i Hümayun* had been proclaimed, the British minister still could see little being done to implement it. He was concerned not only with the slow pace of the reform, but with the adverse consequences to the sultan's position because of the lack of progress. There was the danger that "...His Majesty would be exposed to the whole weight of discontent engendered by innovation on the one hand, and irresolution on the other."[6] As it turned out, Canning had gauged the situation correctly. A few months later, early in 1859, the Kuleli revolt broke out in the capital. Abd ül-Mecid had to contend with both camps, the reformers and the traditionalists. All the while, he looked out for his own interests, for his position was not impregnable.[7]

British perceptions of the state of affairs at the time were that the empire was not lacking in resources, both material and human, to bring about improvements. Efforts to do so were hindered, Canning believed, by the weight of the past:

> The difficulties are principally moral, the results of religious prejudice, of defective education, and of inveterate abuses in every administrative Department....The Koran, the harem, and a Babel of languages, are no doubt so many obstacles to advancement in a Western sense.[8]

If this burden were to be lifted, Stratford Canning argued that it could not be done by the Ottomans themselves. Europe, "with its science, its labour, and its capital" must take a hand.[9] But in the process, the contrast between old and new, native and foreign, would be sharpened. Dealing with this problem seemed the real challenge to Europeans. As for the reform, those Ottomans who supported it saw in it both a challenge and an opportunity.[10]

Stratford Canning's successor as minister to the Porte, Henry Bulwer, chose to look at the Tanzimat from a prudent and lofty perspective:

> Whether the Turks have done a great deal, or very little, depends on the point of view from which we look at the subject. If we compare Turkey as she is with what she was twenty-five or thirty years ago, the change is marvelous. On the other hand, when you compare Turkey as she is to what she ought to be, in order to stand side by side on equal terms with the first and most civilized States in Europe, the progress she has already made appears almost insignificant.[11]

Once he became familiar with the Ottoman political and social scene, Bulwer advocated a policy from which he believed the Ottoman government might best profit, and with which his own government could live. His tactic was to offer "friendly encouragement on the one side, and friendly remonstrance on the other, demonstrative of the absolute and rigorous necessity of further changes."[12] After the *Hatt-i Hümayun* was proclaimed, the sense of urgent need for reform that marked Stratford Canning's, and by extension Britain's, dealings with the Ottoman government, became a more measured stance with the Foreign Office leaving its ambassador to encourage change.

When it came to implementing the clauses in the *Hatt-i Hüma-yun* that were to place Christians and Muslims on an equal footing, Bulwer's advice was revealing:

> The changes to be made here must be made gradually; because in the first place, the Rayahs themselves could not be made fit at once for vast or sudden ones; and secondly, because the Mussulman population, on whom, for some time at least, the Sultan can alone count as an army, would not, without disgust, bear violent and abrupt ones.[13]

The specter of social upheaval pitting non-Muslim against Muslim weighed heavily on the ambassador's mind. In his search for ways to ameliorate the inequalities among the Ottoman populace, this conservative representative of the progressive West instinctively favored methods that might enhance, rather than diminish, social stability.[14]

Taking a page from Ottoman history and displaying an imperial perspective, the British ambassador suggested that the sultan's government build up a supra-national elite, something like the once-influential Fanariots, drawn from the talented laymen of the various ethnic communities. "Animated by a feeling of nationality on the one side, and linked by position and interest with the ruling Government on the other, they would finally become a constituted and moderating power." Bulwer found little merit in the reformers' vision of a common Ottoman citizenship. In his view, "We are apt in Europe to imagine that Turkey is a nation composed of various races, which should each see the benefit of being united. But to an inhabitant of Turkey, the Turkish Empire is as nothing. His nation is the particular portion of the Empire to which he belongs."[15] There was no point, therefore, "to attempt to amalgamate entirely into one common system the different sects and races. Each now in great measure governs itself and is accustomed to its own habits and mode of administration."[16] The question is whether he was being realistic or perceiving an advantage for Britain in the multi-ethnic character of the empire.

Both the British minister and the men of the Tanzimat recognized the liabilities of the traditional, non-national state at a time when western Europe was a thriving region of powerful states, whose societies were now aligned along capitalist and national lines. They differed, however, in their estimation of the manner and the extent of the change that was needed in Ottoman society and for whose benefit. Was it to establish stronger links between the state and the people, increase the power of the government, promote economic development, or establish equality among the subject peoples? Neither Europeans nor Ottoman reformers had illusions about the nature of the empire and whose interests were to be served.

The imperial rescript of 1856 broached the idea of opening up positions in state service to all subjects, Muslim and non-Muslim, if they were qualified. Bulwer, as we have seen, was in favor of the idea if it was applied with care. Other European ministers were also intrigued by the possible benefits of this proposal. Baron Prokesh, Austria's minister in Istanbul when the *Hatt-i Hümayun* was drawn up, had several discussions with officials at the Porte. On this matter he was cautiously optimistic, commenting that admitting non-Muslims into state service would be "the bridge by which the Christians will enter the fortress, not in order to destroy it but to defend it. The danger that they might gradually invade the whole administration will be for the Muslims the most appropriate challenge stimulating them to compete."[17] Some years later, when his observations were made public by the Austrian government, they were picked up and reprinted in Greek-language newspapers in the empire, but without comment.[18]

There was, of course, another dimension to the European factor in the Ottoman Empire; the presence of consulates in the cities across the sultan's domains. By the mid-nineteenth century, in Anatolia alone, the British had established the most extensive diplomatic network, covering both the coastal areas and the less accessible regions of the interior.[19] The European states manned these posts with men drawn from their diplomatic corps as well as local residents. In the British case, the latter were often merchants, native Englishmen or subjects of England, who were given positions as vice-consuls. For the most part, they faithfully and judiciously executed the instructions sent from their embassy. But in their dealings with the local populace, the foreign consuls sometimes exhibited a marked sympathy for one or another side, Muslim or non-Muslim (see appendix). In doing so, they often clashed with the local Ottoman authorities, resorting to threats such as having their ambassador intervene with the Porte, if they did not get their way.[20] Some abused their power and privileges, selling the protection of their flag to locals and outsiders for a fee.[21]

As the Tanzimat was implemented in the provinces, foreign representatives often assumed they should play a significant role. When the Foreign Office contemplated moving the British consulate from Kayseri, the official there protested the idea on the grounds that:

> before my arrival, no one here whether European, Mohammedan or rayah, could consider his business and property, or even his person secure. All this has now given place to a better state of things. The certainty that any irregularities are made known to the Porte, serves as a powerful check in deterring the authorities and others from acts of injustice. The provisions of the Tanzimati-Khairie, before as a dead letter, are now in a great measure carried out, the free course of commerce is unimpeded, and all enjoy a freedom and tranquility before unknown. The wanton vexations to which the Christians were formerly subjected are no longer attempted, and...the European dress is at present almost universally adopted by them.[22]

The presence of a forceful foreign agent often offended the sensibilities of local Ottoman officials.[23] But beyond this reaction, which one would expect to occur, the activities of the consuls illustrate a reality of life in the countryside and how much certain aspects of the reform movement were affected by European involvement. They point up the fact that non-Muslims were more apt to avail themselves of the opportunity to press for change, if only to be rid of past discriminatory regulations such as dress codes. The paradox is that adopting new ways contributed to an even greater sense of division between Muslim and non-Muslim.

From the examples given above, the following observations may be made. British officials in the Ottoman capital, like Bulwer, who involved themselves in the reform plans and who observed the efforts to implement them, felt that setting the correct pace for change was the key factor if they were to prove successful. Moving too rapidly might trigger an explosive counter-reaction; not enough movement left the impression that there was no determination, on the government's part, to prevail. Second, while the representatives of a great power like Britain felt that the empire needed to import Western technology, ideas, and capital to improve its material and military posture, they did not believe this would obliterate the long-standing religious and economic divisions between the various peoples. What they hoped might result from reform was the amelioration of inequality among the subject peoples and, equally important, an increase in material development.

There are also the European consuls and their interventionist activities in the affairs of the empire to be considered. Historians have argued that they only muddled things because they did not correctly assess the subject peoples' legitimate grievances and the complicating factor of separatist nationalist movements.[24] But it is important to note that a number of European diplomatic agents were constructively familiar with conditions in the empire. Men like consul Blunt (see appendix) were quite aware of how much ethnic shearing was occurring between Muslims and non-Muslims and in the *reaya* social fabric as well, and that the empire was not a many-colored mosaic of subject peoples that could be legitimately managed through coercion. By the middle of the century there were enough examples of nationalist movements in the Balkans to enlighten even the most superficial observer.

In the thinking of European diplomats like Bulwer, who advised the Ottoman statesmen, the only practical way for Ottoman reformers to cement the subject peoples' loyalty to the imperial center in Istanbul, was to encourage both effective administration and material prosperity. Yet, at the same time, they doubted the ability of the imperial administrative service to pull itself, much less its people, together through reform. From the perspective of the British representatives, both in the capital and the provincial towns, reform would be most beneficial if it provided the political stability for material and social progress to develop. This, they believed, the Ottoman Empire needed if it were to be considered a player on the European diplomatic game board.

While sometimes there was tension between Europeans and those Ottomans who sought to imitate Western ways, there was also the contradiction between form and essence in the reform movement itself. Both Europeans and Ottoman reformers supported the implementation of Western practices in administration, education, and technology. Yet each, for their own purposes, also believed that there were limits to what could and should be accomplished in the name of reform. As for the *reaya*, who were caught between the two interested elites, they sought to gain whatever advantages they could from both groups.

APPENDIX

In a letter dated November 6, 1857 (FO 195/527), from which excerpts are reproduced here, Charles Blunt, the British Consul in Smyrna (Izmir), instructed the new vice-consul in Adalia (Antalya) about his duties. It provides an informative view of how the knowledgeable representatives of the European powers in the Ottoman Empire perceived their role during the Tanzimat era and illustrates their attitude when they dealt with the Ottoman authorities and the non-Muslim subject peoples.

"I must further request that, you will keep me correctly informed upon the state of the Country within your vice Consulate district, and any important public movement you will advise me by express--the manner in which the Council is composed, and how the Greek Bishops and Christian members of the Council are treated therein--the feelings of the Mahometans towards the Christians--the general character and deportment of the Governor, the changes of the Local Governor, the causes, if the result of complaint made by the inhabitants, whether by the Christians or Mahometans, and the nature of the complaint--the appearance of Pirates--the arrival and sale of Slaves, state from whence, the flag, and name of the vessel by which they were imported....

In reporting upon the system of administration generally as you are a stranger both to the Country and to the languages, I must warn you not to be too ready in giving credence to the reports of the Greek Christians, of the Oriental Church, whom I know from long experience, seldom confine themselves to facts in their representations against the Ottoman Authorities and Turks, but more generally cloak them with the more fabulous exaggerations.

It is more than probable that you will be called upon by the Greek Bishops of the Diocese or the Clergy of the district to give your advice and assistance towards saving Christians from embracing Islamism, and it may often occur that the individual to be saved is a mere child. I would therefore beg you to bear in mind that Children under twelve years of age cannot by Turkish Law be accepted as Converts; with respect to adults in your arguments while admitting the right of freedom of religious persuasion you must at the same time give the authorities clearly to understand that anything bearing on coercion cannot be admitted, further, that in such an event it will be your duty to report all the circumstances as being in opposition to the benevolent wishes of the Sultan. You may in some instances meet with Turkish Governors who will not object to your presence, or that of your interpreter, when the investigation and declaration is made either for, or against apostasy, but you must remember that you cannot demand as a right the admission of your interference.

You will have to bear in mind that Her Majesty's Consular Servants in the Ottoman dominions are specially authorized and called upon by Her Majesty's Secretary of State for Foreign Affairs to give assistance to Jews, subjects of the Porte, in all cases when the laws are not justly administered on their behalf,...you will call the attention of the Authorities to your instructions....

In all your communications with the Turkish Authorities I would recommend a dignified but at the same time friendly spirit, which you will soon find to your advantage rather than adopting a captious deportment. This is the more necessary when giving them your friendly council in reference to oppression or other matters relating to the administration of the district.

You will probably frequently receive written applications for assistance by intercession against oppressions and cruelties towards Christians of all denominations, Jews and Mahometans, these you can communicate to the Authorities 'officieusement' and with reserve as to the truth of the statement; and when you find your intercession against glaring Cases of Tyranny and oppression unheeded, and that no attention whatever is paid to your friendly council, you will then report the case to me with all the particulars, well attested.

In your more friendly, or rather non official intercourses with the Authorities and better class of Turks (for I should cultivate a friendly footing with both) I would advice [sic] you never to lose sight of the opportunity of moral council and remarks, no people appreciate such observations more than the Turks but most unfortunately few profit by them.

From the tenor of my observations you will understand that I advocate a spirit of Philanthropy in your general deportment which will not only be in conformity with the wishes and views of Her Majesty's Government, but will shortly establish your influence with the Authorities and people, making at the same time, the British name justly appreciated throughout the jurisdiction of the vice-Consulate. It is unhappily too much the custom with Consular Authorities in Turkey (I include in the remark Consuls of all nations) to exercise what too many of them term philanthropy, according to the religious creed of the applicant, hence the result, that much of the good which might, and ought, to be done is lost, rather than disturb their spirit of unchristian fanaticism."

NOTES

[1]M.E. Yapp. *The Making of the Modern Near East 1792-1923* (London, 1987), p. 114.

[2]Canning served as ambassador to the Porte in 1825-1829, 1831, 1841-1846, 1848-1851, 1853-1858. For British policy up to the Crimean War and evaluations of Stratford Canning's role in Ottoman reform, see Frank Edgar Bailey, *British Policy and the*

Turkish Reform Movement (New York, 1970, a reprint of the 1942 edition), Ch. VI. Bailey argued that during Palmerston's tenure as foreign secretary and when Canning was minister in Istanbul, Britain recognized the need for reform in the empire. But it promoted reform slowly, because it was secondary to its primary concern, which was to maintain its strategic diplomatic and economic interests in the area. Also see Harold Temperley, *England and the Near East* (Hamden, 1964), Chs. VI, IX.

[3]Bailey, *British Policy*, p. 219.

[4]Niyazi Berkes, *The Development of Secularism in Turkey* (Montreal, 1964), p. 148, argues that the British viewed the Tanzimat as an effort by the Ottoman government to restore the political system to its earlier vigor by revitalizing the traditional order. The French press, on the other hand, true to its historic legacy, saw it as a revolutionary change marked by Westernization. It is difficult, however, to categorize by country the opinions of Westerners regarding the reform. For the social and political dynamics of the reform see Norman Itzkowitz, "'Kimsiniz Bey Effendi,' or A Look at *Tanzimat* Through Namier-Colored Glasses," in: *Near Eastern Round Table 1967-68*, ed. R. Bayly Winder (New York, 1969), and Halil Inalcik, "Applications of the Tanzimat and its Social Effects," *Archivum Ottomanicum* V (1973), pp. 97-127.

[5]See Roderic Davison, *Reform in the Ottoman Empire 1856-1876* (Princeton, 1962), pp. 52-53, 81-82, and appendix A for Canning's role as well as that of the French minister, Thouvenel, in the making of the *Hatt-i Hümayun*.

[6]Great Britain, *Papers Relating to Administrative and Financial Reforms in Turkey 1858-61* (London, 1861), p. 8. de Redcliffe to Malmesbury, October 6, 1858.

[7]*Ibid.*

[8]*Ibid.*, p. 11. Memorandum of de Redcliffe, October 22, 1858.

[9]*Ibid.* Lord Kinross in his *The Ottoman Centuries: The Rise and Fall of the Turkish Empire* (New York, 1977), p. 480, states: "From the middle of the century onward the spirit of reform within the Empire was losing its vigor. The influence of Stratford Canning, for all his successes, had failed in its efforts to reform the prisons, to improve road communications, to suppress corruption, to

ameliorate the Empire's finances. Nor, for all his preoccupation with the religious problems, had he succeeded in achieving any real degree of equality between Christians and Moslems. His noble efforts had produced more concessions in words than in deeds."

[10]Itzkowitz, "A Look at *Tanzimat*," pp. 47-51. Carter V. Findley, *Bureaucratic Reform in the Ottoman Empire* (Princeton, 1980), pp. 152-220.

[11]Great Britain, *Papers Relating*, p. 14. Bulwer to Lord Russell, July 26, 1859.

[12]*Ibid.*, p. 19. Bulwer to Russell, August 16, 1859. On June ll, 1860, Bulwer sent out a questionnaire to all the British consuls in the empire concerning the condition of the Christian population. The responses, which Bulwer forwarded to London, were printed as a report of Parliament. See *Reports Received From Her Majesty's Consuls Relating to the Conditions of Christians in Turkey 1860* (London, 1861).

[13]Great Britain, *Papers Relating*, p. 19.

[14]Bulwer was even ambivalent about the value of the *hat*. In a dispatch to the Foreign Office, dated November 16, 1860, he opined: "The Hatt-i Hümayun itself was merely valuable as a declaration of principles which might serve as a landmark for future legislation. It did nothing itself in the way of legislation, and I doubt much whether, by pointing too suddenly and extensively at an entire alteration in manners and feelings, it did not give rise to many of the evils which usually follow such experiments, and actually followed those of the same kind made in France in the eighteenth century." *Ibid.*, p. 66. Bulwer, who came down on the side of caution, nevertheless believed that the Ottoman Empire had "to be Europeanized to cope with its enemies or rivals in Europe; and I own I do not see any way in which it can be so with sufficient rapidity to be in time to meet coming events, unless by the agency of Europeans." Great Britain, *Papers Relating*, p. 16.

[15]*Ibid.*, pp. 102-103.

[16]*Ibid.*, p. l5.

[17]A. Schopoff, *Les reformes et la protection des chretiens en Turquie 1673-1904* (Paris, 1904), pp. 89-90.

[18]*Amalthia*, February 16, 1868, p. 3.

[19]By contrast the Greek Kingdom established consulates in Asia Minor mainly along the Black Sea and Aegean littoral where the greatest concentration of Greek Orthodox lived, as well the nearby islands.

[20]FO 195/527, June 26, 1856, Smyrna.

[21]Davison, *Reform*, pp. 72-73, describes the negative aspects of the presence of Europeans and their proteges in the Ottoman lands. His account points up the disdain that some diplomats exhibited at the time towards the "Levantines." In the interior of Anatolia, possessing a foreign passport was not necessarily in itself a guarantee of privilege or safety. The British consul in Kayseri remarked that there were "many persons here, either natives or long established in the country, who have Russian or Greek passports. They were treated as rayahs, but they tell me a great change was manifest towards them, as soon as the intelligence of my being on the way hither was received." FO 78/492, February 26, 1842.

[22]FO 78/796 March 20, 1849, Kayseri. FO 78/492, February 26, 1842, Kayseri. FO 195/527, November 6, 1857, Smyrna. FO 78/796, November 10, 1849, Erzerum. Anastasios Levidis, *Istorikon Dokimion* (Zincidere, 1909), p. 192. Henry J. Van Lennep, *Travels in Little-Known Parts of Asia Minor* (London, 1870), I, pp. 11-12, remarks that "the Rayas are treated with far greater gentleness from fear of European interference....Yet there is but little change in such parts of the interior as are the most isolated from foreign contact."

[23]The British, who had a large stake in the success of the reform measures, were aware of the problem. Lord Russell wrote to Bulwer offering this advice: "Each Consul is eager to press his own view on the Pasha of his jurisdiction; if he succeeds, he raises his country's reputation, and perhaps, his own. But he weakens the authority of the Porte, and excites jealously among the other Consuls of Christian Powers. It is very desirable to introduce regularity and concert in making these laudable efforts. If each Consul were, unless in very urgent cases, to report to his own Ambassador or Minister at Constantinople, and if the Ambassadors were to communicate in a friendly manner to each other respecting an ill-governed district and frequent outrages on justice, they would

have a better claim to be attended to than the separate Consuls can hope to establish by their desultory efforts." Great Britain, *Papers Relating*, p. 17. See also Anonymous, "Mysteries of Administration in Turkey," *Contemporary Review*, 37 (March, 1880), p. 362.

[24]Serif Mardin, *The Genesis of Young Ottoman Thought*, (Princeton, 1962), p. 15.

THE HOTEL LAMBERT AND FRENCH FOREIGN POLICY IN THE BALKANS 1840-1848

Robert A. Berry
Salisbury State University

In the study of nineteenth century diplomatic history, writers almost invariably confine themselves to looking at the actions of the Great Powers seeking solutions among themselves for the problems with which they were concerned. Seldom, if ever, are the objects of this diplomacy considered as viable actors with their own legitimate concerns. Rarely do historians seek to analyze the interests and actions of smaller states or groups which have a vital interest in diplomatic resolutions to problems, and which may even play significant roles affecting and guiding the activities of the powers themselves. The reasons for this narrow approach are often based upon the belief that only major powers can play a significant role in the resolution of major events. However, such studies may provide only a partial understanding of events and thus offer erroneous conclusions. One such case involves French diplomatic activities in the Ottoman Empire following the resolution of the Second Near Eastern Crisis, where a close reading of the evidence suggests that the French played a relatively passive role, accepting for the most part and implementing policies developed by the exiled Polish leader Prince Adam Czartoryski and his Hotel Lambert organization.

In his evaluation of French actions at the Sublime Porte in this period, James Edgar Swain stated:

> The French did not remain inactive...after their failures connected with Mehemet Ali. The loss of prestige seemed to be an impetus for renewed activity. M. de Bourquenay, who had for some time been connected with the French Embassy in London, was appointed *chargé d'affaires* at Constantinople. He was instructed to use his influence to gain the confidence of the Sultan and build up French prestige. The success that crowned his work even under adverse conditions is suggestive of what can be done in the field of diplomacy by a skillful diplomat.[1]

In fact, a study of the Hotel Lambert's diplomatic correspondence between Constantinople and Paris indicates that Bourquenay relied heavily on the advice and counsel of Czartoryski and his chief agent, Michał Czajkowski. For many reasons Czajkowski and Prince Adam sought to give credit for their actions to the French ambassador[2], yet over a broad range of activities the initiative clearly came from the Poles.

The Establishment of Franco-Polish Diplomatic Ties

In November 1830, the Poles rose against the Russians in a futile attempt to gain their freedom. That failure caused a veritable flood of refugees. Estimates indicate that in the period 1831-1839 some 7,000 emigrés settled in the West, 5,500 of them in France and some 700 in Great Britain. The remainder scattered throughout Western Europe and the United States.[3] The emigrés shared a common goal: to effect as prompt a restoration of a Polish state as possible. The leaders of the Great Emigration understood that their numbers were too few to reach this goal alone. They needed the support of both France and Great Britain. Education and the experience of the Napoleonic period led the majority of emigrés to view France as their benefactor. French thought and culture had already heavily influenced Polish political thought in the nineteenth century.[4] Based on the historical record, most Poles were convinced that France would actively support their cause.

This generation of emigrés, despite all its activity, never attained any real success in the quest for Polish independence, though their presence served to keep the Polish question alive in the West for a generation. The realities of power politics ensured that only through a European-wide conflict could the country be restored. Neither France nor Great Britain was willing to take this step for a nation which had disappeared from the map of Europe at the end of the eighteenth century. Nor would they go far in any diplomatic representations against either Russia or the Habsburg Empire--against the state viewed as the most powerful land force in Europe, or against the legitimate empire which controlled Central Europe. The risks involved were too great.

Although united by a common goal and influenced by the same outside forces, the Polish Emigration quickly divided into two major camps, differing ideologically in the manner by which they hoped to achieve the restoration of Poland. One faction, strongly imbued with the Napoleonic concept, advocated the policy of fomenting and supporting revolutions throughout Europe. In this manner, they hoped to provoke a major conflagration, one result of which would be the rebirth of a Polish state. In a Europe tired of war and, for the time, dedicated to keeping the peace at all costs, the republican faction had little chance for success.[5]

In contrast, the group which coalesced around Prince Adam Czartoryski and which took its name from his residence in Paris, the Hotel Lambert, adopted a more traditional, even monarchist, view. Its basic approach was diplomatic and evolutionary. Czartoryski's aim was to establish the Hotel Lambert as an independent force in international relations. He hoped that by achieving successes in political problems which concerned Europe to create *faits accompli* for France and Great Britain which they would use for their political advantage and which would obligate them to the Poles and, by extension, to Poland.[6]

The organization into which Prince Adam molded this wing of the Emigration, and over which he maintained control until his death, quite naturally mirrored the experiences and thought of its founder. It largely reflected his background, family and education, as well as his experience in the government of Tsar Alexander I, tempered by his own later reflective thought, and by the experiences of the Emigration itself.[7]

Of immediate importance to the attitudes of the Poles, whatever their political persuasion, was the psychological effect of being emigrés after their previous experiences. The growth of Romantic nationalism as a motivating force during this period, characterized by Mazzini in Italy, also affected Polish thought. The emphasis on personal sacrifice to the point of martyrdom for the Holy Cause of "nation" is clearly expressed in the writing of the Polish national poet, Adam Mickiewicz:

> For the one who remains in his fatherland and endures servitude in order to save his life, in that case he loses both his fatherland and his life. But the one who leaves his fatherland to defend liberty at the peril of his life, then he will save his fatherland and he will live eternally.[8]

French philosophers and their ideas strengthened these feelings. Of them, the most influential was Saint-Simon, whose effect on the emigrés was quite different than that on the French themselves, for whom the social consequences of Saint-Simon's thought were of prime importance. It was rather his religiously Utopian vision which influenced the Poles; a future where men would treat each other as brothers, where all would contribute to the general well-being of mankind, the idea of ameliorating the lot of man, association instead of war. In addition, Poles drew many of their views from the thought of Philippe Buchez, Pierre Leroux, and Lamennais. A believer in the general law of progress, Buchez most influenced the Poles through his theory that each man must devote and sacrifice himself to a work outside himself, to the mission of his age, of his species. From Leroux, the emigrés drew a concept of the love of man, of identity with God, of humanity's existing to perfect man, and man's existing to perfect humanity. Lamennais was read and known by all the Poles since he, like Mickiewicz, portrayed the view of a martyred people, which the emigrés equated with Poland itself. His writing, dedicated to serving God and liberty, was exactly what the emigrés desired to hear and his romantic concept of the nation as the common fatherland struck a responsive chord in the hearts of all Poles, causing the emigrés to identify with the concept of a Holy Mission unique to themselves. Religiosity became a fundamental element of their psychology, political faith, and action.[9]

Despite this apparent sympathy between the Poles and the French based on tradition and culture, and the consequent predisposition for the Emigration to attempt to align itself with French policies, Czartoryski did not move his Hotel Lambert strongly in this direction until 1840. The reasons for this were due partly to Czartoryski's own political conceptions and partly to the existing international situation during the 1830s.

Czartoryski's early education led him to derive a general set of political principles which his program of the 1830s and 1840s attempted to implement. Drawn substantially from the ideas of the Enlightenment prevalent in Prince Adam's youth, these concepts may be termed a policy of aristocratic liberalism. Its major elements were: national independence based on nationality; the right of a nation to develop free from outside interference; the necessity for the advancement of civilization; and the establishment of liberal representative governments.[10] These views easily combined with the growing concept of Romantic nationalism. Czartoryski articulated them in his *Essai sur la diplomatie*, his attempt to define a philosophical base for the practice of diplomacy, written during the 1820s and published in France in 1830.[11]

In the early days of the Emigration, the resources at Czartoryski's command were too few to attempt to translate his basic principles into a European-wide program. In order to achieve any success, the Hotel Lambert required a focal point for its activities. After early efforts to pursue military actions failed to evoke any significant Great Power support, Czartoryski turned toward diplomatic activities. He found his focal point in the Eastern Question, in the problem of the continued existence of the Ottoman Empire, and of the future of the Balkan peoples.

While serving as Tsar Alexander's Foreign Minister (1803-1806), Prince Adam came to view the Balkans as significant and assigned the area a prominence in his plans for Russia. At that time, to combat the Napoleonic threat to Europe, Czartoryski had advocated the establishment of federative states in the Balkans, placing the Slavic peoples under the protection of Russia.[12] One result of this project was to awaken in him a concept of Slavism, a belief in the uniqueness and merits of Slavic civilization. His native patriotism convinced him of the ability of the Poles to lead their brother Slavs to a fuller realization of their potential greatness.[13] In 1840 this concept reached fruition.

Czartoryski's political thought harbored both the concepts of aristocratic liberalism and Slavism for decades. Prior to 1832, however, they had not fused into any viable program. For this, a catalyst was necessary. The psychological effects of the Emigration provided such an agent. Exile created within the Poles a need to justify their existence, a sense of mission. The goal of restoring Poland originally satisfied this, but as it became more apparent that there would be no early restoration, this need had to be expressed in some form of action. The result was an active policy for the political development of the Balkans directed against Russia and which Czartoryski endeavored to join to the diplomatic programs of both France and Great Britain. Czartoryski believed that his Balkan activities would eventually serve the cause of Poland, that the Hotel Lambert's aid would earn the Poles a debt of gratitude both in the West and among the Balkan peoples.

Entering exile, Czartoryski first proceeded to London in order to work for the Polish cause. Here he met no immediate success and soon left for Paris. At the urgings of his wife, and because of his desire to remain close to the heart of the Polish Emigration, he established his permanent residence in the Hotel Lambert, which quickly became the center of Polish social and cultural life in France and the headquarters of his diplomatic activities.

Throughout the 1830s, despite his proximity to the French government, Prince Adam oriented his activities toward British diplomacy. Through his nephew, Władysław Zamoyski, who acted as his chief deputy, Czartoryski maintained close contact with many leading diplomatic figures in Great Britain.[14] However, neither Czartoryski nor Zamoyski fully understood that personal sympathy for their cause and British reasons of state were not compatible. While Czartoryski believed that Palmerston, as Foreign Minister, would lead Great Britain to a break with Russia, Palmerston's assessment of the situation left no room for British foreign policy to antagonize the Tsarist government and would not allow for the possibility of a Polish restoration. Zamoyski thought that a relationship with the Tory opposition would be fruitful. However, when Aberdeen became Foreign Minister (1841-1846) he did nothing for the Poles.[15]

In general, conditions in France during the 1830s proved inhospitable to the Polish exiles. The presence of such large numbers of emigrés proved to be both an embarrassment to the monarchy and a drain on governmental resources. The French policy was to place the majority of emigrants, who had arrived in 1831-1832, into several resettlement camps throughout the provinces. Only gradually were they allowed to settle elsewhere.[16]

The conditions facing the Hotel Lambert were much more favorable. Czartoryski's rank, his prestige as a statesman, his close ties to Europe's ruling classes, and his role as a political leader, all made it easier to exercise influence. Although on a personal level, Prince Adam never maintained cordial relations with Louis Philippe, the Hotel Lambert nevertheless enjoyed generally close and friendly contact with the Foreign Ministry.[17]

As early as 1833, Czartoryski had attempted to interest the French in his program. He proposed to send a Polish mission under French auspices to the Ottoman Empire for the purpose of gaining information about the Russian army and the Black Sea defenses. The government did not respond to this initiative but Czartoryski later used this idea as the basis for a British-supported effort under General Wojciech Chrzanowski.[18]

As Czartoryski's diplomatic program evolved, he found the resources to send agents into the Balkans to explore the feasibility of cooperative efforts with the various nationalities. By the late 1830s, several, including Dr. Adam Łyszczyński, Michał Czajkowski, and Janusz Woronicz-Werner, had undertaken missions to Serbia and the Danubian Principalities. Preliminary reports indicated not only that Polish efforts would be welcome, but also that these could be tied to the policies of the Western powers.

In 1838, Woronicz investigated the possibility of action among the Romanians. In Bucharest, he established contact with Felix Colson, the Secretary of the French consul, who introduced Woronicz to Colonel Ion Cîmpineanu, a Wallachian leader opposed to the activities of the ruling prince, Alexander Ghica. Ghica's subservience to Russia had aroused the opposition of many independence-minded Romanians. Colson, who was actively anti-Russian, probably exerted more influence in Bucharest than the actual consul, Chateaugiron. On the basis of the information Woronicz received and transmitted to Czartoryski, the Hotel Lambert actively began to seek support for the Wallachians in their struggle against Ghica in both Paris and London.[19] To this end, Czartoryski sponsored Cîmpineanu's journey to the Western capitals in 1839 in an attempt to gain their support. These early Polish efforts to direct the course of events failed, due more to Cîmpineanu's poor personal showing, to his inability to persuade the respective governments of the need for support, than to any weakness in the Hotel Lambert's own program.[20]

The Mohammed Ali crisis of 1839-1841 decisively caused the Hotel Lambert to reorient its program toward alliance with French policies. Sultan Mahmud's attempt to overthrow his vassal in 1839, and the subsequent Ottoman military defeats, caused near panic in Constantinople. The Egyptians made demands which would have spelled the *de facto* disintegration of the Ottoman Empire. The European powers, fearful of such an outcome, took immediate action. The rapid intervention of the British fleet prevented an Ottoman capitulation and served notice that Europe would not condone any change in the status quo in the Levant. In August, the Porte in effect requested that the powers make a settlement with Mohammed Ali on its behalf.

France, while not in favor of complete independence for Mohammed Ali, nevertheless regarded Egypt as a potential client state and desired to secure some of the fruits of his victory. The Egyptian leader relied heavily on French officers and experts in his military. France also had strong commercial interests in Egypt. In addition, a powerful Egypt under French influence appeared to be a useful tool to prevent British predominance in the Eastern Mediterranean. Consequently, France remained intransigent in its support of Mohammed Ali's claims.

This Anglo-French antagonism provided Russia an opportunity to break the Anglo-French *entente* which had been such an important factor in European politics in the 1830s. In London, the Russian envoy, Brunnow, and Palmerston conducted negotiations toward this end. For several months, efforts were made to find a solution to the crisis acceptable to France, but her attitude became more uncompromising and unrealistic. Finally, on 15 July 1840, representatives of Great Britain, Russia, Austria, and Prussia signed a series of agreements in London with the representative of the Porte, Shekib Effendi. These effectively gave the Ottomans the protection of the four powers and restricted Mohammed Ali to control of Egypt. Russia, in signing these agreements, repudiated the exclusive rights she had gained with respect to the Ottoman Empire in 1833 with the treaty of Unkiar-Skelessi, removing one of the basic problems which had affected Russian-British relations. The French remained violently opposed to the agreements but took no steps toward conflict with Great Britain to settle their differences.[21]

The events of 1840 created a dilemma for Czartoryski. On the one hand, Great Britain had reaffirmed its support for the continued existence of the Ottoman Empire, a key point in Prince Adam's own program. However, the London agreements effectively aligned Britain with Russia, the chief enemy of the Poles. France, on the other hand, although it supported Mohammed Ali, demonstrated to the Poles a strongly anti-Russian attitude. Faced with this situation, and with the growing disappointment at his inability to achieve any practical results with the British, Czartoryski reoriented his organization toward French policies. Reasons of state dictated that the Poles align themselves with a power opposed to Russia. France now appeared to be the only state so oriented.[22] The fact that the London agreements actually strengthened the British position with respect to Russia was totally overlooked by the Hotel Lambert.[23]

Growing religious motivations in Prince Adam's plans for the Balkan peoples also impelled him toward alignment with France. While Czartoryski was a devout Catholic, the Pope's tacit support for Russian policies with respect to Poland after 1831 disturbed him greatly. As a consequence, the Hotel Lambert's activities in the Balkans often were designed to enhance the Polish image at the Vatican and to erode the demoralizing effects of Papal attitudes toward Russia.[24]

Polish-French Cooperation in the Balkans 1840-1848

Continual contact with French culture over the years strongly affected Czartoryski's ideas. Although he recognized and valued the uniqueness of Slavic civilization, he viewed French civilization as the ideal toward which the Slavs should aspire. His desire to gain the support of the Church, the psychological need to fulfill a mission, and his attitudes toward France produced in Prince Adam a concept of a *mission civilisatrice*. The Catholic orientation of the

Hotel Lambert convinced Czartoryski that only France would support his Balkan program.

An early, informative example of Czartoryski's attempt to tie all aspects of his program together occurred in 1840. By this time, the Hotel Lambert had established close ties with the French Lazarist order which maintained several missions in the Ottoman Empire. In this same year, Prince Adam devised a project calling for the establishment of a Slavic society to undertake an educational and religious mission in the Slavic areas of the Ottoman Empire. One aspect of his plan envisioned the society spreading French culture and civilization in cooperation with the Lazarists. Working primarily in the field of education, the society would establish a printing press in Paris to publish textbooks in the various Slavic languages of the Balkans. It would also develop a system of primary schools throughout the region which were to be attached to small religious establishments under the leadership of both the Lazarists and the Sisters of Charity. Each center would have a significant Polish element. Support in the form of teacher training and free passage on French ships was to be sought from the French government.[25]

The elements of the program were clear: enhance the Hotel Lambert's standing with the Church; help spread French culture into a backward area of Europe; ensure a strong Polish presence whose actions would incur a moral debt both from the French and from the Balkan nations. Although this particular project never came to fruition, significant elements of it were later incorporated into other Hotel Lambert projects. The initiative's most serious weakness was the hope that the Orthodox population would be amenable, even indirectly, toward Catholicism. This naïve view almost foredoomed the religious aspect of Czartoryski's program to failure. One Polish writer has commented that the linking of service for Poland with that for the Church was a fatal blunder.[26]

In organizational terms, the Hotel Lambert's French orientation proved advantageous. Czartoryski's chief agent in Constantinople after 1841, Michał Czajkowski, established a close relationship with the French ambassador, Bourquenay. František Zach, a Czech in the service of the Hotel Lambert, served for a time in the French consulate in Belgrade and later maintained close ties with the consul there, Durand de St. Andrée. Several agents, among them Ludwik Zwierkowski-Lenoir, who worked in Belgrade in 1841-1842, possessed French passports.

The Hotel Lambert also made regular use of the French diplomatic post to carry its correspondence from Paris to the agencies in the Balkans and elsewhere. At approximate ten-day intervals, dispatches would be forwarded along the diplomatic routes. As chief agent, Czajkowski in Constantinople would add his commentary to Zach's reports and then forward these, along with his own, to the Hotel Lambert's headquarters. In Paris, Czartoryski would prepare his instructions for his agents and then send them along the same path. Czartoryski most often confined himself to general directives. Czajkowski enjoyed considerable autonomy in developing specific instructions for other agents in the field. Using this system, the Hotel Lambert maintained a reliable, secure, and efficient method of communications. Certainly, if the French government had not found the Polish services valuable they would not have permitted such an extensive use of diplomatic privileges.

In 1842, an uprising in Serbia led by the Constitutionalists overthrew Prince Michael Obrenović and placed on the throne Alexander Karageorgević. The revolt was led by Toma Vučić-Perišić and Avram Petronijević, who were openly anti-Obrenović. The Porte had, nevertheless, earlier named them as regents for Michael following the abdication of his father Miloš. Dislike for Michael's policies led the regents to engineer his overthrow. Prior to these actions, in 1841 Czajkowski had met the Serbs in Constantinople and had been impressed by their seeming anti-Russianness. Consequently, he took on the role as their political mentor, viewing this as an opportunity to further Polish aims within Serbia. As events later proved, the two Serbs were interested only in maintaining their own positions of power and sought support wherever they could find it. Czajkowski, in his advisory role, continually stressed to them the necessity of remaining loyal to the Porte.[27] However, after their return to Belgrade before the overthrow, the two Serbs ignored Czajkowski's advice and initiated the plot against their own ruler. Despite this failure to heed his counsel, Czajkowski and Ludwik Zwierkowski played more than a passing role in the uprising and the subsequent election of Alexander Karageorgević as ruling prince.[28]

This coup led to international repercussions when, early in 1843, Russia, with Austrian support, objected to an election which had confirmed Alexander as prince of Serbia. Nicholas I sent his personal envoy, Baron Lieven, to Constantinople where he demanded new elections and the expulsion of Vučić and Petronijević from Serbia as a punishment for their participation in the affair.[29] At this point, the Serbs turned to the Hotel Lambert for aid.

The re-election of Alexander was accomplished with little difficulty.[30] The return of Vučić and Petronijević to Serbia, however, required diligent effort and the cooperation of Western diplomats to overcome both Russian objections and pressures on the Porte. Here the Hotel Lambert, with its ties to the French embassy and the Serbs, and its well-developed connections with the Porte itself, could work effectively.

In the course of the next two years, the Hotel Lambert conducted an intense diplomatic campaign to secure the safe return of the two Serbian ministers. The purpose of the Hotel Lambert's activities went beyond this simple fact; it also desired to ensure the continuation of the Karageorgević government and to weaken Russian influence in Serbia.[31] In Paris, Czartoryski sought Guizot's backing against Russia. His nephew and deputy in London, Władysław Zamoyski, had the task of persuading the British government to support the Serbs. Czajkowski, temporarily in Paris, was dispatched to Belgrade to offer recommendations to the government there. He soon continued on to Constantinople where he engaged in the sending of diplomatic notes to the Porte and cooperated closely with the French ambassador. Throughout the diplomatic maneuverings, Bourquenay sought Czajkowski's advice and counsel. In return, Czajkowski supplied the French with information concerning the Serbs and acted as their intermediary.[32]

The Polish-French efforts in support of Vučić and Petronijević met with difficulties from the outset. The Serbs were their own worst enemies. They were reluctant to heed the advice from Constantinople or to comply with the terms of their exile. This exacerbated French initiatives on their behalf and left the French to seek Czajkowski's aid. In August 1843, Cor, the French dragoman, requested that Czajkowski inform Vučić and Petronijević of the need to leave Serbia since their continued refusal to do so hampered French actions. Czajkowski complied with the French request, but in his letter to the Serbs advocated that they first secure assurances from the government that they would not be replaced, a measure which Czajkowski felt would insure them against a permanent exile.[33] Their departure at the end of August cleared the way for further steps.

Throughout the fall of 1843, even after the Serbs had fully complied with the terms of their exile, Baron Lieven, in Belgrade, continued a campaign of harassment against the two leaders within the Serbian government. Despite an Ottoman promise to protest Lieven's protracted stay in Serbia, for which he had no justification, by September the Porte had yet to take any action. At this point, Petronijević wrote to Czajkowski who, in his turn, sent notes on the matter to Sarim Effendi and to Bourquenay.[34] His actions soon brought results. On 12 October, Cor, under orders from Bourquenay, presented a formal protest against Lieven's presence in Belgrade. He argued that the deportation of Vučić and Petronijević had ended any Ottoman obligation to Russia and that the Porte should now cease its harassment of the Serbs. In a subsequent note to Czajkowski, Cor stated that Rifaat Pasha had been deeply embarrassed by the issue, that he would cease bothering the Serbs, and would, instead, actively support their return.[35]

By early 1844 the initiatives appeared to be working well.[36] Bourquenay informed Czajkowski that both he and the British ambassador, Canning, strongly supported the Serbian cause and advocated that the Poles intensify their efforts in Paris and London.[37] In Serbia, František Zach, who had become the Hotel Lambert's agent in Belgrade in 1843, undertook to guide the Serbian government in the best means to present its case to the Porte.

In late April, news from Belgrade appeared to indicate a successful end to the problem. The Russian consul, Danilevski, informed the Serbian government that Nicholas had agreed to allow Vučić and Petronijević to return. Zach received this news skeptically, preferring to wait for confirmation through action rather than words.[38] Indeed, no action followed the Russian announcement; though a victory in principle had been achieved, the two Serbs had not yet been permitted to return home. In Constantinople, Czajkowski suspected that the Russian ambassador, Titov, was purposely delaying their return for political reasons. He suggested to Bourquenay that the ambassador put pressure on Titov through the Austrian ambassador to the Porte, Stürmer. Czajkowski advised Bourquenay to state, through Stürmer, that "if the next ship does not bring the answer [from St. Petersburg giving the Tsar's consent to the return], the French embassy, even though it is not supported by the British, will have to act for the benefit of Serbia and the Porte." Bourquenay took this to heart and followed Czajkowski's directions exactly. On the day after Bourquenay's discussion with Stürmer, St. Petersburg issued permission for the return of Vučić and Petronijević.[39] Though it may have been coincidental, it is more probable that Czajkowski's spirited actions helped resolve the problem.

Finally, in September 1844, Vučić and Petronijević returned to Belgrade. Outwardly a triumph for the Hotel Lambert, the affair appeared to vindicate the organization's worth as a diplomatic force. However, after their return, Vučić and Petronijević demonstrated a marked coolness toward their benefactors. This loss was only partially offset by a growth of influence over Serbia's foreign minister, Ilija Garašanin, and Prince Alexander.

Although the 1843 election had confirmed Alexander as prince with a life title, his position within Serbia remained weak. He lacked a strong personality and his internal support resulted from his being an alternative to Michael. There was no guarantee that he would not be overthrown. Czartoryski feared this situation. Serbia effectively lacked internal stability as he saw it and the country could plunge into turmoil at any time. These conditions also left a way open for Russia and Austria to interfere in Serbian affairs. To remedy this, Czartoryski felt it necessary to obtain the right of hereditary succession for Alexander, an inherently difficult problem to resolve. Only the Ottoman government could grant this right. The Serbs would not only have to present a formal request, but Alexander would also have to demonstrate that he had both the support of the Serbs and the personal qualities to make him worthy of such a concession.[40]

As before, the Hotel Lambert undertook the coordination of efforts to ensure a successful outcome. It was, however, a hopeless cause. Although the Hotel Lambert, with some French support, had a modicum of success in persuading the Porte to consider hereditary rights, their position was weak. Timid, parsimonious, easily controlled by those around him, Alexander generated no enthusiasm among the French or the British. In 1845, Bourquenay indicated clearly the lack of French enthusiasm when he informed Czajkowski that he would personally second Polish efforts at the Porte, but that the Poles should not expect any encouragement from the French government.[41]

Polish involvement in Bosnian affairs began late in 1843, when Franciscan representatives from that region approached Zach in Belgrade, seeking the Hotel Lambert's support in an ecclesiastical quarrel known as the Barišić affair. Bosnia was legally under the jurisdiction of the Ottoman Empire, but the church in Austria exerted control over its Catholic clergy. Both the Pope and the Sultan bestowed privileges on the chapters and orders located there.[42] What the Bosnian Franciscans sought was a confirmation of their local religious autonomy and freedom from Austrian control manifested through the Papacy.

Problems in Bosnia had begun in 1832 with the Holy See's selection of a new bishop, Rafo Barišić, to head the order locally. Barišić was devoted to Austria and to a program for the modernization of the church in Bosnia. The majority of the Franciscans, who were less cosmopolitan and closer to their native roots, protested Barišić' actions vigorously. They even accused him of exceeding his authority over them. Though Papal investigations of these charges led to banning Barišić from Bosnia temporarily, by the early 1840s, Austrian pressure ensured the bishop's return. At this point, one faction of Franciscans strongly opposed to Barišić and feeling that Rome supported Austrian policies detrimental to their interests turned toward the Porte, their temporal suzerain, seeking a redress of their grievances. At this juncture, they encountered the Hotel Lambert which viewed the situation as an opportunity to increase Polish influence in the region.[43]

From late 1843 through 1846, Zach guided the Bosnians' actions toward Rome. Czajkowski worked diplomatically, seeking the support of Bourquenay and the Lazarist leader, Leleu, in Constantinople, for the Bosnians. By June 1844, the Hotel Lambert's actions among the French and the Ottomans secured a qualified victory when Rome forbade Barišić from returning to Bosnia.

The Franciscans, however, suffered from a basic naïveté and soon found their position deteriorating. By the fall of 1844, the leader of the Bosnian delegation in Belgrade, Pašalić, went to Constantinople in an attempt to gain direct governmental support. Czajkowski now took command of the affair. He sent notes outlining the problem to Shekib Effendi, then minister of Foreign Affairs and to Emin Effendi, director of police. He also approached the French embassy and wrote Czartoryski for advice.[44] Prince Adam's reply stressed the need for care and suggested that the Bosnians somehow demonstrate their loyalty to the Holy See.[45]

Czajkowski's subsequent actions aimed at persuading the Porte to request Barišić' withdrawal from office.[46] Barišić soon arrived in Constantinople to plead his case. Stürmer's intervention on his behalf led Czajkowski to approach Bourquenay seeking French support.[47] Throughout 1845, Czajkowski continued to send a series of notes to the Porte and to guide the Franciscans through the intricacies of Ottoman politics. In August, he arranged a meeting between the brothers and Shekib Effendi. Shekib received them cordially and suggested that they should place their case in the hands of the Armenian Catholic Patriarch, arguing that the Porte itself was unfamiliar with the rights and privileges of the Franciscans. Shekib stated that the Ottoman government would forward the Patriarch's recommendations concerning the matter to Rome, along with the Franciscans' specific requests.[48]

Czajkowski now turned to Leleu, the French Lazarist leader in Constantinople, seeking his aid to convince the Armenian Patriarch of the justness of the Franciscan cause. He believed that, in this instance, Leleu's intervention would be more beneficial than Bourquenay's.[49] Despite Rome's intransigence toward the Bosnians, and the continued pressure by Austria on the Porte, the Polish efforts, supported and encouraged by the French embassy and the Lazarists, succeeded in effecting a favorable solution. The Porte, in January 1846, through Reshid Pasha, decided to give its full support to the Bosnian dissidents against Barišić.[50]

Meanwhile, Czartoryski's organization was promoting other programs in the Balkans designed to increase Catholic influence and to strengthen the Polish position with the Holy See. These initiatives primarily concerned the development of education in Bulgaria and support for an independent Bulgarian Orthodox Church.

As early as 1842, Czajkowski had formulated a broad-based plan for Bulgaria. He sought Lazarist cooperation in this venture and presented his views to Leleu. Czajkowski argued that providing local instruction in both the native language and native spirit would ensure that Bulgaria could "easily be restored" to Catholicism and a Uniate church could be established. Catholic involvement in education would increase the church's influence and lead to a religious union. Czajkowski advocated the use of Polish teachers as being most useful in the area. Although Leleu agreed with Czajkowski's presentation, he stressed a need for caution, fearing that this action could arouse Ottoman suspicions.[51] Though relatively tolerant of religion, the Ottomans could easily interpret this venture as overt proselytizing and unwarranted intervention in their own internal affairs.

In the spring of 1844, Czajkowski requested that a joint exploratory mission be undertaken to Bulgaria. Both Czartoryski and Leleu acquiesced and in May, funded by the Lazarists, the mission departed. It included a member of the Lazarist order, Scaffi, and one of the Hotel Lambert's agents, Chmielewski.[52] Satisfactory reports led Czajkowski to propose, in June, the establishment of a normal school in the Bulgarian region.[53]

Initial enthusiasm was high, but both the Hotel Lambert and the Lazarists realized that, to accomplish such a project, outside aid was necessary. Czajkowski turned to Bourquenay who expressed his favor and told Leleu that he would request backing from the French government for this project.[54] By September, plans had progressed to the stage where Leleu approached Czajkowski with a request for funds and for a Polish teacher to staff a school already under construction. Czajkowski forwarded the Lazarist appeal to Czartoryski, urging that he seek French aid to implement the request.[55] However, Czajkowski's note effectively culminated a three-year effort to implement a Polish concept of educational development which had first seen light in 1840. Neither the Hotel Lambert nor the Lazarists could provide the necessary funds or personnel. The French government evinced no willingness to back such a project. Barely able to provide agents for itself, the Hotel Lambert did not even attempt to find suitable instructors and thus had to abandon the project.

Events though soon led Czajkowski and the Hotel Lambert to champion a new cause which they felt could lead to the establishment of a Bulgarian Uniate church.

In 1824, a native religious movement designed to create an autonomous Orthodox church free from Greek ecclesiastical influences arose in Bulgaria. Previously, the Greek clergy had dominated the Bulgarian church at the highest levels and this movement soon escalated into a drive to replace them with Bulgarian clergy throughout the country. When, in 1838, a Greek priest, Panaret, was named metropolitan of Trnovo, a protest movement rose among the Bulgarian clergy, led by a monk, Neofit Bozveli, who sought redress in Constantinople. Imprisoned on Mt. Athos in 1841 for his actions, he escaped in 1844 and returned to Constantinople where he and another young monk, Hilarion Makariopolski, now became the leaders of this religious protest movement.[56]

Czajkowski met Hilarion in Constantinople in 1843 and quickly immersed himself in Bulgarian ecclesiastical affairs. He viewed Hilarion as a "man of the future."[57] Czajkowski also believed that he could use Bulgarian conditions to gain support for the Catholic church, which would then benefit the Polish position *vis-à-vis* Rome. With Neofit's arrival in 1844, Czajkowski recommended that he present his case to the Porte and seek its protection.

Czajkowski felt that the ecclesiastical issue made it possible to cooperate with the Lazarists, especially with Leleu.[58] Their common base was the view that they could exert sufficient influence over Neofit and Hilarion to lead the Bulgarians into a union with the Catholic church. At that moment, as they saw it, the Greek clergy, supported by Russia, controlled the Bulgarian church. If the Poles and the Lazarists, through their support of Neofit and Hilarion, could help establish an independent Bulgarian church, it was possible that the Bulgarians would unite with the Catholic church for their own protection.

In his role as coordinator, Czajkowski brought the Bulgarians into a closer relationship with the Lazarists. He also took the opportunity to acquaint them with the Hotel Lambert's views regarding the Slavic peoples in the Balkans.[59] Neofit and Hilarion also took up residency with the Lazarists. The effect of these actions soon seemed to promise success in the effort to convert the Bulgarians to Rome. At least the Lazarists believed so, as Leleu later demonstrated in a letter to the head of the order in France, written in March 1845: "We already have among us the future Patriarch, who is three quarters Catholic."[60]

Shortly after Neofit's arrival, Czajkowski, in cooperation with the Lazarists, took steps to ensure a sympathetic hearing for the Bulgarians. By arranging a conference between Neofit and Emin Effendi, Czajkowski hoped that he could benefit all parties. He believed that any Bulgarian gains would also convince the Porte of the wisdom of Polish action.[61]

Throughout late 1844 and early 1845, under Polish guidance, Neofit and Hilarion followed a course designed to secure their position with high Ottoman officials before formally requesting autonomy. Conferences with, and memoirs to, Ottoman officials appeared to solidify support for the Bulgarians. Czajkowski himself requested that Mehemet Ali Pasha act as the Bulgarians' protector.[62] In a meeting between Neofit and Mehemet Ali Pasha in February 1845, the latter formally accepted the title of protector of the Bulgarians and gave assurances of Ottoman support for them.[63] At the same time, Neofit presented a request to the Porte for a series of measures which would have effectively given autonomy to the Bulgarian church and which would have recognized the Bulgarians as an entirely separate nationality.[64]

In May, the Patriarch, who totally opposed the Bulgarians' quest for autonomy, struck back. He requested that Neofit move into the Patriarchate rather than live in the city itself. Neofit, fearing for his freedom of action, approached Czajkowski who suggested that he try to leave the capital temporarily.[65] Czajkowski warned the Porte that it must do something to aid the Bulgarians. Moreover, he tied the Patriarch's action to the growing influence of Russia in Bulgaria.[66]

Despite these efforts to force the Ottomans into taking some action, the government did nothing. By late July, Neofit had only vague promises from the Ottomans, though Czajkowski remained confident that the government favored the Bulgarians and that it would honor its assurances.[67]

At the end of July, the Patriarch ordered the arrest of Neofit and Hilarion and their exile to Mt. Athos. Czajkowski immediately protested to the Porte. He suggested it take control of the Bulgarians to judge them, arguing that it was within the Porte's powers to try its subjects for political crimes.[68] Czajkowski discussed the matter with Bourquenay but doubted that the French would provide any support to the two monks. The Patriarch had accused them of holding heretical views (Catholicism), creating a new church (schism), disobeying proper authority, and arousing the Christians against the Porte.[69] Though the accusations were clearly false, the fact that the Patriarch had made this a religious issue effectively meant that the Ottoman government had no legal basis to intervene. Little hope of success remained, but the Hotel Lambert continued its efforts to improve conditions within Bulgaria and to secure the release of the two priests.

The outbreak of revolution in Paris in 1848, and the ministerial changes this engendered, prompted Czajkowski to revive the Bulgarian question. In April 1848, he wrote to the new ambassador, Aupic, portraying the Bulgarian cause as a valiant struggle for religious and cultural independence.[70] This last effort, however, received no positive response from the French.

1848 marked the end of significant Polish involvement in the Balkans. The coming of the revolutions, and their effects within the region, only served to make clear the fact that, whatever their earlier usefulness, programs and policies advocated by the Hotel Lambert no longer seemed especially relevant to the peoples involved. While perhaps grateful for Polish aid, they felt no debt of honor to the Poles. It was time to go in other directions.

Much the same was true for the relations the Hotel Lambert had built with France. This relationship had been almost totally a political one. The factors of tradition, culture, and religion had played a significant role in predisposing the Poles toward seeking French support and had strongly colored the program the Hotel Lambert undertook in its efforts to regain an independent Polish state. Political conditions in Europe after 1840 permitted the Poles to take advantage of French support and to achieve some success. However, the cooperation between the two sides was to last only as long as a great enough degree of similarity in Polish and French interest in the Ottoman Empire permitted. Even with this, the closest ties were always on the local level, in Constantinople and in Belgrade, rather than in Paris. French policy never seriously contemplated the possibility of a restored Polish state. After 1848, French interests moved in other directions and the Hotel Lambert became increasingly isolated, unable to reconcile its interests with the new forces in Europe. The consequences of the Hotel Lambert's orientation toward France, while useful in the short term for the Balkan peoples, later served only to perpetuate the myth, so dearly held by the Poles, that Poland's eventual salvation would be brought about by France.

NOTES

[1]James Edgar Swain, *The Struggle for the Control of the Mediterranean Prior to 1848: A Study in Anglo-French Relations* (Boston, 1933), p. 128.

[2]Czajkowski to Czartoryski, 26 September, 1843, B[iblioteka] Cz[artoryskich] 5486, p. 391.

[3]Sławomir Kalembka, *Wielka Emigracja* (Warszawa, 1971), p. 58.

[4]The most detailed studies of French influence on Polish thought in the nineteenth century are to be found in: Marceli Handelsman, *Les Idées Françaises et la Mentalité Politique en Pologne au XIXe siècle* (Paris, 1927); and Jósef Feldman, *Dzieje polskiej myśli politycznej w okresie porozbiorowym* (Kraków, 1913).

[5]A useful recent work on Lelewel and his ideas is: Joan S. Skurnowicz, *Romantic Nationalism and Liberalism: Joachim Lelewel and the Polish National Idea* (New York, 1981). Her bibliography is especially useful for those wishing to study the Polish Left.

[6]Marceli Handelsman, *Czartoryski, Nicholas I et la Question du Proche Orient* (Paris, 1934), pp. 11-12. See also Hans Henning Hahn, "Possibilities and Limits of Foreign Policy Negotiations in Exile: The Example of Prince Adam Jerzy Czartoryski" (Unpublished MSS).

[7]The most significant works on Czartoryski and his diplomatic activities include: Marceli Handelsman, *Adam Czartoryski* (3 vols., Warszawa, 1948-1950); Handelsman, *Czartoryski, Nicholas I* (see above, note 6); Marian Kukiel, *Czartoryski and European Unity 1770-1861* (Princeton, 1955); Jan Wszołek, *Prawica Wielkiej Emigracji wobec narodowego ruchu włoskiego (przed rewolucją 1848 r.)* (Wrocław-Warszawa-Kraków, 1979); Jerzy Skowronek, *Polityka bałkańska Hotelu Lambert (1833-1856)* (Warszawa, 1976); Barbara Konarska, *W kręgu Hotelu Lambert: Władysław Zamoyski w latach 1832-1847* (Wrocław-Warszawa-Kraków-Gdańsk, 1971); Hans Henning Hahn, *Aussenpolitik in der Emigration: Die Exildiplomatie Adam Jerzy Czartoryskis 1830-1840* (München-Wien, 1978); and Robert Allen Berry, "Czartoryski and the Balkan Policies of the Hotel Lambert 1832-1847" (Unpublished Ph.D. dissertation, Indiana University, 1974).

[8]Quoted in Handelsman, *Idées*, p. 96.

[9]*Ibid.*, pp. 96-106.

[10]Kukiel, *Czartoryski*, pp. 30-31. *Polski Słownik Biograficzny*, IV, p. 258. See also Czartoryski's *Memoirs*, I, p. 44 and pp. 55-56.

[11]Adam Czartoryski, *Essai sur la diplomatie, par un Philhelléne* (Marseilles, 1830; Paris, 1864).

[12]A very complete study of Czartoryski's Balkan plans in this period can be found in Jerzy Skowronek, *Antynapoleońskie koncepcje Czartoryskiego* (Warszawa, 1969). See also Jerzy Skowronek, "Le programme Européen du prince Adam Jerzy Czartoryski en 1803-1805," *Acta Polonica Historiae*, XVII (1968), pp. 137-159.

[13]Later, as Curator of Wilno University, he attempted to lay a foundation for a Polish Slavic Studies, located in either Warsaw or Cracow, to tie together culturally the Poles, Czechs, and South Slavs. Henryk Batowski, *Podstawy sojuszu bałkańskiego 1912 r.* (Kraków, 1939), p. 15; and Handelsman, *Adam Czartoryski*, I, p. 129.

[14]In the period 1835-1840, close relations with the Foreign Office were maintained through its under-Secretary, William Fox Strangways. As with Sir Stratford Canning, the relationship developed into close friendship. Kukiel, *Czartoryski*, pp. 230-231.

[15]Konarska, *W kręgu*, p. 119.

[16]Kalembka, *Wielka Emigracja*, devotes several chapters to the early experiences of the Polish emigrés in France.

[17]Kukiel, *Czartoryski*, p. 231.

[18]Konarska, *W kręgu*, p. 154. A detailed study of Chrzanowski's missions to the Ottoman Empire will be found in Henryk Graniewski, "The Mission of General Chrzanowski to Turkey (1836-1840)," *Antemurale*, XII (1968), pp. 115-264.

[19]Woronicz' reports on Cîmpineanu, Ghica, and on the political situation of the Principalities are located in the manuscript holdings of the Czartoryski Library, BCz, 5408.

[20]Władysław Zamoyski, *Jenerał Zamoyski* (6 vols., Poznan, 1910-1930), IV, p. 88.

[21]This section is based on M. S. Anderson, *The Eastern Question* (New York, 1966), pp. 95-104.

[22]Graniewski, "Chrzanowski," p. 258.

[23]A bifurcated policy seems to have developed. Czartoryski continued to maintain his relationship with the British government, but now tended to look to it more in terms of legal support for the Polish cause, stressing questions related to international law and the Polish question. The French policy became more attuned to a general level of activism, whether in Paris, Constantinople or elsewhere. It is possible that Czartoryski himself was not totally cognizant of the path his diplomacy was taking. Hahn's work on Czartoryski (see note 7) tends to support this view.

[24]See Wszołek, *Prawica*, for a detailed study of this aspect of Czartoryski's foreign policy.

[25]BCz 5325, pp. 107-112, "Project d'une Société slave."

[26]Feldman, *Dzieje*, I, p. 198.

[27]Czajkowski to Czartoryski [October 1841], BCz 5410, p. 503.

[28]For more detail, see Berry, "Czartoryski," pp. 185-205.

[29]Kukiel, *Czartoryski*, p. 247; Nicholae Iorga, *Histoire des états balcaniques à l'epoque moderne* (Bucharest, 1914), pp. 252-253.

[30]Czajkowski arrived in Belgrade on 22 May 1843. After meeting with Petronijević, he presented a plan to resolve the question of a new election by calling a national assembly to re-elect Alexander. His idea was accepted, but Czajkowski was forced to leave Serbia before the assembly met. The election was not able to prevent the expulsion of Vučić and Petronijević. Czajkowski to Czartoryski, 17 June 1843, BCz 5486, p. 156.

[31]For details on the internal developments of Serbia see Zach's early reports, BCz 5390.

[32]See Berry, "Czartoryski," pp. 205-223 for a fuller discussion.

[33]Czajkowski to Czartoryski, 7 August 1843, BCz 5486, pp. 271-272.

[34]Marceli Handelsman, *La question d'Orient et la politique yougoslave du Prince Czartoryski après 1840* (Paris, 1929), pp. 38-39; Petronijević to Zamoyski, 18 August 1843, BCz 5404; Czajkowski to Czartoryski, 17 September 1843, BCz 5486, pp. 381-382; Czajkowski to Czartoryski, 26 September 1843, BCz 5486, p. 391.

[35]Czajkowski to Czartoryski, 16 October 1843, BCz 5486, pp. 363-364.

[36]Czajkowski to Czartoryski, 17 March 1844, BCz 5487, pp. 111-112. He also noted that Bourquenay had received a note from Ilija Garašanin and had already prepared a note to be communicated to the Reis Effendi concerning the Serbian question.

[37]Czajkowski to Czartoryski, 7 April 1844, BCz 5487, pp. 148, 154-157.

[38]Zach to Czajkowski, 20 April 1844, BCz 5390, pp. 513-514.

[39]Czajkowski to Czartoryski, 16 August 1844, BCz 5487, p. 456. Earlier that summer, Bourquenay had ordered Cor to inform the Porte of the need for the return of Vučić and Petronijević. Czajkowski to Czartoryski, 5 July 1844, BCz 5487, p. 341.

[40]Berry, "Czartoryski," pp. 248-268 gives greater details on the situation.

[41]Czajkowski to Czartoryski, 26 August 1845, BCz 5489, p. 213.

[42]Vladimir Dedijer, *et al*, *History of Yugoslavia* (New York, 1974), p. 289.

[43]For a more detailed summary see Berry, "Czartoryski," pp. 352-382.

[44]Czajkowski to Czartoryski, 6 November 1844, BCz 5487, pp. 659-660.

[45]Władza to Czajkowski, 7 January 1845, BCz 5395, pp. 7-8; BCz 5414, pp. 17-20.

[46]Czajkowski to Emin Effendi, March 1845, BCz 5414, pp. 440-442.

[47]Czajkowski to Bourquenay, 5 May 1845, BCz 5415, pp. 61-66.

[48]Czajkowski to Bourquenay, 25 August 1845, BCz 5416, pp. 211-218.

[49]Czajkowski to Czartoryski, 6 September 1845, BCz 5489, pp. 255-257.

[50]Czajkowski to Czartoryski, 27 December 1845, BCz 5489, pp. 559-560; Czajkowski to Czartoryski, 7 January 1846, BCz 5490, p. 37.

[51]Czajkowski to Czartoryski, 7 July 1842, BCz 5486, p. 171.

[52]Czajkowski to Czartoryski, 27 April 1844, BCz 5487, p. 202.

[53]Czajkowski to Czartoryski, 26 June 1844, BCz 5487, p. 348.

[54]*Ibid.*

[55]Czajkowski to Czartoryski, 6 September 1844, BCz 5487, p. 511.

[56]Mercia Macdermott, *A History of Bulgaria, 1393-1885* (London, 1962), pp. 144-145. See also Berry, "Czartoryski," pp. 327-352 for further details.

[57]Czajkowski to Czartoryski, 26 June 1844, BCz 5487, p. 330.

[58]Czajkowski to Czartoryski, 17 March 1844, BCz 5487, p. 114.

[59]Ludwik Widerszal, *Bułgarski ruch narodowy 1856-1872* (Warszawa, 1937), p. 26.

[60]*Ibid.*, p. 27. Widerszal quoted a letter in the Lazarist archives, Leleu to Etienne, 27 March 1845.

[61]Czajkowski to Czartoryski, 6 September 1844, BCz 5487, pp. 508-510.

[62]Czajkowski to Czartoryski, 16 January 1845, BCz 5488, pp. 113-114; Czajkowski to Czartoryski, 26 January 1845, BCz 5488, pp. 182-184.

[63]Czajkowski to Czartoryski, 6 February 1845, BCz 5488, pp. 215-219.

[64]Czajkowski to Czartoryski, 16 February 1845, BCz 5395, p. 51; BCz 5414, pp. 308-309. The text of the Bulgarian request is in French translation, BCz 5414, pp. 347-354, appended to the report.

[65]Czajkowski to Czartoryski, 16 May 1845, BCz 5488, pp. 494-499. He noted "Shekib Effendi favors the Bulgarians and their affair and he accepts coldly the proceedings of the Russians in this measure."

[66]Czajkowski to the Porte, 18 May 1845, BCz 5415, pp. 187-194.

[67]Czajkowski to Czartoryski, 26 July 1845, BCz 5489, pp. 95-96.

[68]Czajkowski to Riza Pasha and Shekib Effendi, 31 July 1845, BCz 5416, pp. 51-52; Czajkowski to the Porte, 3 August 1845, BCz 5416, pp. 55-57.

[69]Czajkowski to Czartoryski, 16 August 1845, BCz 5395, p. 179.

[70]Czajkowski to Aupic, 30 April 1848, BCz 5432, pp. 32-34.

THE ROMANIAN DILEMMA: RUSSIA AND THE DOUBLE ELECTION OF CUZA

Richard Frucht
Northwest Missouri State University

For the Russian government, the double election of Alexandru Ioan Cuza by the United Principalities of Moldavia and Wallachia in 1859 would prove to be little more than a Pyrrhic diplomatic victory. The state that had once sponsored the concept of a Holy Alliance among nations, served as the principal defender of the idea of legitimacy in Europe, and helped put down nationalist movements in East Central Europe in 1848-49, since 1856 had found itself in the curious position of supporting nationalist demands for union in the Principalities, a policy heretofore seemingly antithetical to Russia's own best interests. The reasons for this sudden reversal in both policy and principle were, in light of the humiliations of 1854-56, to a degree justifiable (at least in the short term) but the net effects of St. Petersburg's support for union in the Principalities proved costly in the long run. Once again, the diplomatic quagmire of the Eastern Question contained no easy solutions.

As with many other changes initiated under Alexander II, the impetus behind Russia's diplomatic maneuvers in support of Moldavia and Wallachia in 1856 and the election of the native prince Cuza in 1859 stemmed not so much from a desire to promote Romanian nationalism as a positive good, but rather reflected a policy borne out of necessity, a reaction to events.[1] For Russian policymakers to rally behind Romanian nationalism represented a 180° change in its foreign policy. It was based not on altruism but rather an attempt at direct retaliation against Austria for the latter's failure to come to Russia's aid during the Crimean War, and a calculated gamble that St. Petersburg could drive a wedge in the wartime alliance between France and Great Britain. In so doing, however, Russia chose to abandon its longstanding support of conservative interests in the Principalities for a nationalist cause that posed inherent dangers should similar yearnings arise in places like Poland. In the end, Russia's role in, and reaction to, the events surrounding the election of Cuza left St. Petersburg with very little.

Russian influence in the affairs of the Principalities dated to the eighteenth century. However, it was not until the Treaties of Ackermann in 1826 and, more importantly, Adrianople in 1829 that St. Petersburg came to hold a dominant position in the Romanian lands. Not only did tsarist troops occupy Moldavia and Wallachia for five years, but the governing structure of the two fell under the control of Count Pavel Dmitrievich Kiselev, who headed the two ruling divans until 1834. Kiselev also authored the Organic Statutes, a series of administrative edicts which regulated the region's political and economic life in a manner certainly more enlightened than the Principalities had experienced during the previous century of Phanariot rule, but also in a fashion harmonious with Russia's own regional designs.[2] Not surprisingly, the system devised relied heavily upon the boiar class. The Statutes designated the boiars as the hereditary owners of the land, thus ensuring their domination over life within the Principalities, while at the same time serving, as St. Petersburg hoped, as potential surrogates for Russian interests. After the Convention of St. Petersburg was signed in 1834 and its troops withdrawn, Russia continued to watch events in the Principalities closely, primarily through its consulates in Bucharest and Iaşi. At the same time, the princes, mindful of the presence and importance of the tsar's representatives, naturally had to pay close attention to Russia's wishes.

For Russia and the Romanian boiars, the Organic Statutes provided a valuable symbiotic relationship. The boiars recognized the importance of the protectorate.[3] That does not necessarily mean that they were singularly pro-Russian; the very nature of Romanian politics, plagued by intrigue and self-interest, precluded that. Moreover, there was direct interference in Romanian affairs by all the great powers through their own consulates, thereby enabling the boiars to look to others, notably the British and French, as intermediaries.[4] However, the protectorate generally served as a bulwark for boiar interests, and the Russian consuls became one of three centers of power in the Principalities along with the hospodars and the assemblies.[5] By the same token, Russia's principal objectives had been gained without any real, direct costs, that is, a friendly, conservative state on its border, dominated by St. Petersburg politically through its consulates and economically by its control of the Danube grain trade. If the reign of Nicholas I represented the height of conservative Russian influence in Europe, nowhere was this more apparent than in Moldavia and Wallachia.

But the dreams of Nicholas to preserve the status quo in Europe proved to be as chimerical and timeless as the legacy of Ozymandius. Russia became the defender of pre-1789 Europe in a world rife with nationalism. And, although it was able to suppress nationalist revolts in Moldavia and Wallachia, among others, in 1848-49,[6] and to reassert its authority in the Principalities, Russian troops could not quell the fever of nationalism. Balta Liman may have provided for Russia's naming of the hospodars, but the generation of 1848 was to become the real leaders of Romanian political life. Their revolutionary program had as its central goal union under a foreign prince. For them, the major obstacle to the fulfillment of that dream was not the Ottoman Empire. Instead, for the young generation of Romanian nationalists only one nation stood in the path of their own state: Russia.

Russia's policy prior to Crimea, therefore, was a difficult one: blunt nationalist sentiments, preserve the Concert of Europe, and ally itself with conservative elements against liberal/national movements inimical to its own perceived *raison d'être* as a great power. Its "Protectorate" could only be maintained as long as principal power in Moldavia and Wallachia "remained the monopoly of a few great (boiar) families" backed by Russian troops.[7] As long as Russia preserved the aura attached to it since its victory over Napoleon in 1812, the domination of the Principalities, although despised by Romanian nationalists, was secure.

The debacle of 1854-56 not only shattered illusions regarding Russia's military prowess, it also forced the new tsar to move in directions heretofore not considered with great favor. Given the scope of Russia's defeat, the reasons were obvious. The blow to the country's pride was immeasurable. Grand Duke Konstantin's lament that "we cannot deceive ourselves any longer...we are both weaker and poorer than the first-class powers"[8] pertained to far more than administrative and economic failures. Russia had little choice but to reevaluate its policies, including those directed toward the Principalities.

The decisions reached at the Paris conference were punishing, the most important forcing Russia to agree to the neutralization of the Black Sea and the loss of southern Bessarabia (thus ending Russia's domination of maritime Danube commerce). As for the Principalities themselves, the new Foreign Minister, Alexander Mikhailovich Gorchakov, faced a situation wherein Russia had become merely one of seven guarantors; its days of primacy passed. For the moment at least, Paris "marked a striking decline of the Russian position in southeastern Europe...."[9] Were these liabilities to be overcome, Russia would need time to re-group, re-seek influence in the Balkans, and most importantly, break the British-French wartime coalition. Were Russia to remove the stain of Crimea, satisfaction would have to be achieved, primarily in the form of retaliation against Vienna for not only failing to come to Russia's assistance during the war but also for seeking to profit from St. Petersburg's military withdrawal from the Principalities in 1854.[10] In short, the Principalities became an important diplomatic battleground for Gorchakov and his attempt to reverse Russian fortunes. As such, Russia, which had once "acted to suppress liberal and national agitation," would now turn to France "in support of a nationalist program" in the Principalities.[11]

Napoleon III, who emerged from the Crimean conflict as the "political arbiter" of Europe, not only "presented a variety of options which the Romanians astutely seized,"[12] he also handed Russia the opportunity it needed to break the Crimean System.[13] Taking advantage of the clash between the French emperor's perceived role as defender of nationalism in Europe generally, and the Principalities specifically, as well as Great Britain's determination to use the Porte as a shield for London's interests in the Eastern Mediterranean,[14] Russia found its needed opening. Using the question of the Principalities, St. Petersburg would enter into a curious relationship with France that would last until the Polish uprising in 1863. The threads binding the two were little more than opposition to the general treaty structure in Europe.[15] Although some historians have dismissed Russia's motive as simply one in which it "is always wise for the defeated party to court the least vindictive of its enemies,"[16] in point of fact, it was a very real attempt to use the Principalities as a vehicle to overcome its own isolation.[17] Whereas Kiselev had once pondered the annexation of Moldavia and Wallachia,[18] now, without any formal agreement with the French, Russia threw its weight behind the Romanian nationalist movement.[19]

At Paris, the plenipotentiaries placed the Romanians under a European guarantee but could not resolve the most important issue, union or separation, preferring to leave the matter of determining the administration to the Romanians themselves without defining the limits of that decision. The powers instead created an international commission to oversee events and make final recommendations to a follow-up conference to be held in Paris, thereby deferring any resolution of their differences to a future date. Such a *denouement* would not be easily attained, however. Britain, Austria, and the Ottoman Empire firmly opposed any notion of unification, while France and Russia favored a political union under (at least initially) a foreign prince.[20] Once Gorchakov announced his support of the French position, Russia, fully cognizant of the fact that Paris would be the beneficiary of Romanian nationalists' gratitude, and that a united state would be more difficult to control than a divided one,[21] made union an important part of its foreign policy.

The electoral process in the Principalities left little chance (if any, in fact, existed at all) that the question of government in Moldavia and Wallachia could be resolved to the satisfaction of all. First, the Romanians themselves realized that the divisions among the great powers gave them extra latitude in pursuing their national demands. Second, each of the powers attempted to direct Romanian political affairs, with the principal antagonists being the Austrian representative, Gödel de Lannoy, and his French counterpart, Victor Place. For the time being, Russia kept a low profile. Kiselev, now ambassador to Paris, continued to support French calls for the creation of a central commission in the Principalities, something which would obviously serve as a steppingstone to union. Napoleon III and Alexander II also met in Stuttgart in September 1857 but reached no formal understanding, save to agree to consult on the Balkans in the future.[22] In the Principalities themselves, Russia joined France in condemning the chaotic electoral process in Moldavia and the apparent attempt by Austria to create a separatist movement in Iaşi. The Russian Commissioner to the International Commission, Constantine Mikhailovich Basily, and the consul in Iaşi, Sergei Ivanovich Popov, were adamant in their opposition to the Austrian-backed caimacam, Nicholas Vogorides.[23] Basily set the tone for Russian policy when he declared:

> The essential factor for us, even more, the only object that we have...is the free expression of the wishes of the country. The question of union...is for the moment outside of the sphere of our preoccupations. But if anyone uses any means whatever to influence the expression of the wishes of the country in one sense or another...we should watch out for it....[24]

But again, was Russia's a voice to promote genuine union as a positive good or rather one that reflected merely a policy of expedience? Gorchakov, in a letter to Kiselev, may have supported "complete freedom for the expression of the wishes of the populations"[25] but it is questionable whether he foresaw what would transpire when those "wishes" were freely expressed.

When the electoral lists in Moldavia threatened to produce an obviously engineered election, Russia joined with France, Prussia, and Sardinia in breaking relations with Porte. Although this succeeded in forcing Constantinople to retreat from its support of Vogorides, Kiselev had begun to warn Gorchakov that France was never going to sever its ties with Britain.[26] In fact, the meeting at Osborne in August 1857 between Napoleon III and Victoria not only kept alive the Crimean Alliance, it was also kept secret from France's erstwhile ally at Stuttgart. France, in at least formally abandoning its public demand for union at Osborne, had left Russia in the dark.[27]

By 1858, Russia began to have second thoughts about developments within Romanian circles that appeared both unfriendly and unstable. But concerns about the rise of the liberals in the Principalities were tempered by the alternative of separation. In Moldavia, for example, such an act might lead to Austrian domination. Moreover, were Russia to change now, it would mean moving against France and voiding previous pronouncements in support of the "wishes" of the Romanian population. The only feasible course of action therefore was to continue quiet support for union, but now under a native prince.[28] The reason for the subtle change in strategy was logical. There was little chance that a foreign prince would be Orthodox. More importantly, if a native was to lead the Principalities there would be a greater likelihood that he might reflect conservative interests friendly toward Russia. Russia would also gain valuable time until it might again assert its authority in Moldavia and Wallachia without jeopardizing its relationship with France. Thus, as the powers reconvened in Paris, Kiselev continued to support Count Walewski, the French minister, "with even more vehemence" than before.[29]

The August Convention that created the so-called "United Principalities of Moldavia and Wallachia" has perhaps best been described as an "awkward halfway house"[30] which was easily manipulated by the Romanians to the benefit of Romanian nationalism[31] and to the detriment of Russia's long-term interests. While Gorchakov's instructions to his consuls (Nicholas Karlovich Giers in Bucharest and Popov in Iaşi) called for strict adherence to the rules of the Convention, Russia quickly saw its plans for reasserting its influence in the Principalities begin to unravel. Like the other great powers, Russia found itself a prisoner of the actions taken by Romanian nationalists. Making matters worse, Gorchakov, often prone to delivering imprecise instructions, failed to make known to either Giers or Popov his exact wishes. "Our mission" he wrote, "will be to make sure that the agreements...are respected, because they dedicate to the profit of the Christian peoples the fruits of our preserving efforts, even though they stem from a way of thinking hostile to us...they must be respected...."[32] He ordered Giers and Popov "to enlighten public opinion and the influential in the Principalities of their true interests," remain neutral, but not "passive and sterile," and gain the Romanians' "respect and confidence."[33] Beyond that lofty language though, four different interests were at stake besides support for Romania's "true" wishes, whatever Gorchakov thought those might entail: maintain the August Convention, cooperate with France, block Austrian designs south of the Iron Gates, and prevent Ottoman interference in any results.

Giers read his Foreign Minister's directives to mean little more than continued support of conservative interests in Wallachia. Toward that end, Giers, who would look back upon his tenure in the future Romanian capital with less than enthusiasm, did not show favoritism toward any one candidate (although he was never loathe to offer advice). Giers simply looked to fulfill the dictates of the August Convention.[34] Popov, on the other hand, was genuinely supportive of the Romanian nationalists. Despite instructions to avoid open espousal of any faction,[35] Popov was a steadfast ally of Place and therefore the liberals in Iaşi. In a letter to his friend Giers, Popov revealed that his interpretation of Gorchakov's missives was to cooperate with France and thwart the Austrians. He (and therefore Russia) were obliged:

> to defend legality and the rights of the country just as energetically as our friends the French. I agree that we should avoid complications; but if the Turko-Austrians all want them--and that is evident--what can we do? We must accept the situation on a day-to-day basis. While waiting let us try to disrupt their intrigues by the firmness of our attitude and the invariability of our principles.[36]

Despite the obvious differences between the consuls as to Russia's correct course of action, both continued to express (at the minimum at least) tacit support for union (although in the case of Giers, not with great zeal). However, whether the motive for backing was at its origin pro-French, pro-Orthodox, or directed against the "pernicious activity" of the Austrians,[37] Russian support for the results of the elections in 1859 would prove to be critical.

The dual election of Alexandru Ioan Cuza in Moldavia on the 5th of January and in Wallachia on the 22nd (both dates Old Style) therefore represented a victory of sorts for Russia's post-Crimean foreign policy. The essential aims of St. Petersburg had been fulfilled. Although admittedly Russia had doubts about the efficacy of violating the August Convention, which the elections seemed to do, the naming of a native prince was preferable to that of a foreigner. However, the crucial question for Russia was whether this was merely an act of will or the beginning of a revolution.[38] The ultimate test rested with the actions of Cuza himself.[39]

The outcome of the elections caught St. Petersburg by surprise. Both Giers and Popov (neither of whom had supported Cuza and, like most other foreign observers, were caught off-guard by his election) were left without instructions for weeks,[40] not surprising given the defensive nature of Gorchakov's policies to that point. Giers asked "What is to be done? Is all lost? If in effect a sudden change in our policy in the east has occurred, it would be well if we were furnished with clear and positive instructions."[41] Giers, who had backed conservative interests in Wallachia, was uncomfortable with a liberal/national tidal wave that seemed to violate the spirit, if not the letter, of the August Convention. Despite the opposition of Austria and the Porte, and his own doubts about the Convention's intentions, Giers pressured Cuza to begin acting as if everything was already finalized and that his "position was already assured."[42] That seemed to be the only practical policy. In contrast to Giers' awkward feelings, Popov, long an advocate of Romanian nationalism, had few doubts as to the correct course of action. Although he admitted he did not know Cuza prior to the election, Popov found himself "captured" by a man whose election represented "discomfiture" for the Austrians.[43] As he told Giers, "I am for Cuza frankly and openly, even at the risk of compromising myself."[44] Having written that prior to the election in Wallachia, Popov was nothing short of overjoyed when Wallachia followed the lead of Moldavia. Like his French counterpart Place, he believed that the move toward union was irreversible and that Russia's only recourse was to support Romanian nationalism openly and energetically.[45]

The different reactions of Giers and Popov were understandable given the absence of firm direction from St. Petersburg. This allowed them to interpret the situation in the manner in which they were the most comfortable. Even though the double election had, in effect, handed Russia and all of the great powers a virtual *fait accompli*, not until early February did the often cautious Gorchakov advise his minister in Constantinople, Alexei Borisovich Lobanov-

Rostovskii, that Russia stood behind the elections and would work with the French against all opposition.[46] Whether the August Convention had been violated was not critical; the overriding necessity was the maintenance of the *démarche* with France and keeping "Austria and Turkey off balance."[47] Since overturning the Black Sea clauses was still the first priority, "aligning themselves with a French emperor who preached the principle of nationalities seemed (to be) a small price to pay for such gains."[48] As a result, Kiselev, still in Paris, vigorously opposed any notion of Ottoman intervention aimed at overturning the results of the elections.[49]

Again, fate seemed to step in on the side of the Romanians. Cuza cleverly used the international crisis between France and Austria in the Spring of 1859 to win time and to move the idea of union as far as his principal supporters, France and Russia, would allow. His apparent willingness to heed the advice of the Russian consuls had a mollifying effect on Giers. The latter wrote:

> Cuza has displayed great activity for the maintenance of order and public tranquility....His attitude inspires much confidence and one can hope that he will know how to resist the influence of (those)...who wish to see him enter upon the road of dangerous reforms incompatible with the political situation of the country.[50]

For Giers, the notion of order and stability was always paramount; for the moment at least he was satisfied. The intentions of the August Convention were indeed flaunted in his opinion but the meaning of the Treaty of Paris, which stipulated that the wishes of the Romanian people be considered, was not. Moreover, he believed that the vote in Wallachia merely signified a desire for personal union under Cuza rather than a permanent merger.[51] It was essential, therefore, for the maintenance of order that the elections be recognized and not dealt with by a "foreign armed force."[52] There was also a fear that France and Austria might strike a deal as a means of ending their conflict, or that revolutionary activity might spread into Hungary or Poland if the Romanian question continued to fester. Russia thus had to watch events in the Principalities closely, supporting Cuza, but, at the same time, pressuring him to avoid any revolutionary activities. In May, Giers informed the new prince as a "friend who wishes well for the country" that "in rushing into adventures one risks compromising the advantages already acquired...."[53] Beyond that Russia could do very little.

In September 1859, the powers, perhaps out of a desire simply to close the door on an issue that had divided them for three years, agreed to a complicated settlement that allowed the double election to stand. If Britain and Austria were afraid that the Principalities would prove to be little more than a pliant tool of Russia, their fears were hardly well-founded.[54] If Russia thought that the September resolutions would close the issue of union, St. Petersburg was gravely mistaken. Giers, in fact, would quickly despair that Russia would ever have Romania's confidence.[55] Such disillusionment was not merely the property of the often pessimistic Giers; Popov too would grow less and less fond of the new prince.[56] For the next two years, Russia pursued a futile policy of trying to keep Cuza on a moderate course favorable to its own conservative interests. In 1861, when Cuza declared complete union, Russia, although opposed, could do little since it was again reluctant to jeopardize its tenuous relationship with France. In 1866, Cuza's overthrow and the subsequent invitation to Charles of Hohenzollern-Sigmaringen would complete the process of unification which M.S. Anderson called "the one great constructive result of the Crimean War."[57] Again, only Russia voiced opposition, but by now its stiffened attitude toward Romanian nationalism was but of minor consequence. A liberal, national state, tied to a France that was no longer viewed with favor by St. Petersburg, sat on Russia's southwestern border. Only the fact that, as Gorchakov said, this "might invalidate existing treaties or disturb existing territorial and international arrangements in the East"[58] offered Russia even a hint of a silver lining, a pretext for 1870.

In 1823, Great Britain received little benefit from its attempt to take the lead in defending the revolutions in South America; the United States instead received all the credit with the pronouncement of the Monroe Doctrine. Likewise, Russia too would gain little from its support of the double election of Alexandru Ioan Cuza. It failed to win the trust of Romanian nationalists who instead continued to look to Paris for inspiration. Once its traditional conservative supporters failed to preserve their control over Romanian politics, Russia had to face a now united state governed by a generation unlikely to forgive or forget past actions. No longer would Russia have easy access to the Danube. More importantly, Russia's support of union and the election of Cuza was predicated on obtaining two primary objectives that by 1866 were but fleeting memories: revenge against Austria and the forging of an alliance with France. With regard to Austria, it is questionable how much Vienna was punished for her perceived duplicity during the Crimean War. Austria's attempt to dominate Romanian economic life (especially Danube trade) was blunted to be sure, but, beyond that, Austria had more important things to worry about in 1859 (and throughout the 1860s) than the matter of the Principalities. Secondly, cooperation with the French held little real chance for any longstanding benefits, and indeed, with the Polish revolt of 1863, the question of nationalism, so vital in the case of the United Principalities, now ironically came to divide St. Petersburg and Paris again. Even though Russia did gain the precedent for overturning the provisions of the Paris accords, a fact not lost upon policymakers in St. Petersburg who would renounce the clauses demilitarizing the Black Sea in 1870, that was the only tangible benefit Russia seemed to obtain. As Gorchakov would succinctly remark in looking back on the Romanian episode "those people there forget altogether what they are and from where they come...."[59]

NOTES

[1]Pan-Slavism was emerging in Russia in the 1850s, often with an emphasis on protection of the Orthodox peoples. But there is a question as to its effect on policy. It seems to have had little, if any, effect on the Romanian Question. See, for example, Michael Boro Petrovich, *The Emergence of Russian Pan-Slavism 1856-1870* (Westport, 1956).

[2]Numerous historians have argued that the Organic Statutes in fact paved the way for later unification by creating common codes. See, for example, W.G. East, *The Union of Moldavia and Wallachia 1859: An Episode in Diplomatic History* (Cambridge, 1929), pp. 22-28.

[3]Some historians like East have questioned the use of the term "protectorate" as being too strong. However, East admits that the influence of the Russian consuls was "considerable." *Ibid.*, pp. 17-18.

[4]See Charles and Barbara Jelavich, eds., *The Education of a Russian Statesman: The Memoirs of Nicholas Karlovich Giers* (Berkeley, 1962).

[5]*Ibid.*, p. 123.

[6]Cuza, in fact, was present in Iaşi in 1848 at an important gathering of leading Romanian nationalists. Gerald Bobango, *The Emergence of the Romanian National State* (Boulder, 1979), pp. 54-58.

[7]Jelavich and Jelavich, *Giers*, p. 126.

[8]Paul Kennedy, *The Rise and Fall of the Great Powers: Economic Change and Military Conflict from 1500 to 2000* (New York, 1987), p. 177.

[9]Nicholas Riasanovsky, *A History of Russia*, 4th ed. (New York, 1984), p. 339.

[10]Buol and Orlov did not even bow to each other at Paris. T.W. Riker, *The Making of Roumania: A Study of an International Problem, 1856-1866* (London, 1931), p. 37.

[11]Barbara Jelavich, *History of the Balkans: The Eighteenth and Nineteenth Centuries* (Cambridge, 1983), p. 290.

[12]Paul Michelson, *Conflict and Crisis: Romanian Political Development 1861-1871* (New York, 1987), p. 32.

[13]See W.E. Mosse, *The Rise and Fall of the Crimean System 1855-1871* (London, 1963).

[14]The "still powerful" British minister Stratford de Redcliffe had a strong influence on Great Britain's policies. M.S. Anderson, *The Eastern Question 1774-1923: A Study in International Relations* (New York, 1966), p. 151.

[15]Napoleon III reported to Clarendon that the "great fault" of the Congress of Vienna was listening to sovereigns and not the interests of their subjects. Riker, *Roumania*, pp. 42-43.

[16]*Ibid.*, p. 41.

[17]Anderson, *Eastern Question*, p. 150.

[18]It should be noted, however, that the Romanian Question was never the central focus of Russian policy.

[19]According to Count Walewski, when asked by Napoleon III what attitude Russia would take, he was told: "Sire, we shall vote with you for or against union, according to your desires." Riker, *Roumania*, p. 41.

[20]Riker contended that the French-British alliance "seemed to be shattered." *Ibid.*, p. 128.

[21]Barbara Jelavich, *Russia and the Formation of the Romanian National State 1821-1878* (Cambridge, 1984), p. 68.

[22]Anderson, *Eastern Question*, p. 152.

[23]For a look at Russia's diplomats during the era, see V. Vinogradov, "Cu privire la rolul diplomaţiei ruse în unirea ţărilor române," *Studii: Revista de Istorie* (vol. 12, nr. 2), 1959.

[24]Basily to Popov, quoted in Jelavich, *Formation*, p. 78.

[25]Gorchakov to Kiselev, quoted in *ibid.*, p. 306, note 10.

[26]Vinogradov, "Cu privire la rolul diplomaţie ruse," pp. 44-47.

[27]Jelavich, *Formation*, p. 52. Russia got word of Osborne through the rumor mill.

[28]*Ibid.*, p. 85.

[29]Riker, *Roumania*, p. 159.

[30]Anderson, *Eastern Question*, p. 152.

[31]For Romanian actions during this period, see, for example, N. Corivan, "Lupta diplomatică pentru reconoasterea dublei alegeri a lui Al. I. Cuza," in: Andrei Oţetea, *Studii privînd unirea principatelor* (Bucureşti, 1960), pp. 386-412. Documents on Romanian activities are contained in a number of sources including D.A. Sturdza, *Acte şi documente relative la istoria renascerei României* (Bucureşti, 1900-1909).

[32]Popov to Giers, quoted in Barbara Jelavich, *Russia and the Rumanian National Cause 1858-1859* (Bloomington, 1959), p. 39.

[33]*Ibid.*, pp. 39-40.

[34]Jelavich, *Formation*, p. 91.

[35]Bobango, *Emergence*, p. 78.

[36]Popov to Giers, quoted in Barbara Jelavich, "Russia and the Double Election of Alexander Cuza, 1858-1859: The Letters of S.I. Popov to N.K. Giers," *Sudost-Forschungen* 24 (1965), p. 124.

[37]Popov to Giers, quoted in Jelavich, *Rumanian National Cause*, p. 40.

[38]Riker, *Roumania*, p. 213.

[39]For internal Romanian affairs, see, for example, Bobango, *Emergence*; and Vlad Georgescu, *The Romanians: A History* (Columbus, 1991), ch. 4.

[40]Jelavich, *Rumanian National Cause*, p. 61.

[41]Popov to Giers, quoted in *ibid.*, p. 63.

[42]Riker, *Roumania*, p. 222.

[43]Popov to Giers, quoted in Jelavich, "Russia and the Double Election," p. 132; Popov to Giers, quoted in Jelavich, *Rumanian National Cause*, p. 50.

[44]Jelavich, *Rumanian National Cause*, p. 50.

[45]Lobanov did write Giers to tell Popov to cool his ardor. *Ibid.*, pp. 64-65.

[46]Bobango, *Emergence*, p. 71. Corivan, "Lupta diplomatică," pp. 398-404.

[47]Bobango, *Emergence*, p. 81.

[48]*Ibid.*

[49]Russia also put strong pressure on the Porte not to intervene. Corivan, "Lupta diplomatică," pp. 392-393.

[50]Giers to Lobanov, quoted in Jelavich, *Formation*, p. 106.

[51]Riker, *Roumania*, p. 225. Barbara Jelavich, "Russia and the Double Election," p. 120.

[52]Giers to Gorchakov, quoted in Jelavich, *Formation*, p. 106.

[53]Gorchakov to Giers, quoted in Jelavich, *Rumanian National Cause*, p. 75.

[54]*Ibid.*, p. 77.

[55]*Ibid.*, p. 76. Russian-Romanian relations, especially by 1866, would remain poor.

[56]*Ibid.*, p. 91.

[57]Anderson, *Eastern Question*, p. 146.

[58]Mosse, *Crimean System*, p. 146.

[59]Quoted in Jelavich, *Rumanian National Cause*, pp. 123-124.

A PERILOUS LIAISON: RUSSO-ROMANIAN RELATIONS IN 1877

Frederick Kellogg
University of Arizona

Romanian statesmen frequently sought the advice of the great powers during the Balkan Crisis of 1875. Danubian Romanians believed their goal of independence could solely be won via a victorious war against the Turks, with the aid of the great powers. The powers, however, no longer cooperated as they had immediately after the Crimean War. The alliance between Great Britain, France, and Italy had ceased to exist. Only the British had an immediate interest in maintaining the status quo in Turkey, especially after their purchase of the Suez Canal shares in 1875. France, shattered by its war with Germany, thought more about Alsace and Lorraine than about Southeastern Europe. Italian leaders concentrated on making their state viable and lasting. Likewise, Germany focused on national consolidation; it needed peace to fulfill the task of political unification. Conditions in the Habsburg Empire in 1876 and 1877 had changed dramatically; after being defeated by Prussia in 1866, the newly-constituted Austria-Hungary was distracted by its many nationalities. It lacked a militant foreign policy, was not prepared for war, and would remain neutral throughout the crisis. Nor was Russia ready for war in 1875 or 1876; but it became absorbed by events nonetheless.

Russia's interest in the Balkans was partly emotional. Many Russians identified with the South Slavs, who were also Orthodox Christians. Some were eager to break the Turkish grip on the South Slavs. Others went further, hoping to erect a new South Slav state dependent on Russia. Russia also wanted to rectify boundaries. From 1812 to 1856, Russia had held all of Bessarabia. One of the humiliating results of its defeat in the Crimean War was the loss of the southern portion of Bessarabia to Moldavia. Finally, some Russians dreamed of extending their empire's borders to the Bosporus and the Dardanelles, something opposed by Britain and Austria-Hungary. A Russian attack in the Balkans, however, had to have not only Austria-Hungary's approval, or at least neutrality, so that Russia's western flank would not be exposed. It also had to take into account Romania.

Romanians had several alternatives to an alliance with Russia. They could remain neutral and rely on Austria-Hungary to protect them. But, according to the Budapest Conventions of 1877, Austria-Hungary was itself to be neutral in case of a Russo-Turkish war. Austria-Hungary was not willing to employ its resources defending Romania's neutrality, notwithstanding its need for an autonomous or independent state on the Lower Danube River that might prevent Russia's hegemony in the Balkans. Romanians also had the option of staying in the Ottoman Empire. Some Romanians wished indeed to retain their country's autonomy, for the Russians were deemed a greater menace than Turks. Under Turkish suzerainty, Romania had its own constitution, conducted its own foreign policy, and raised its own army and taxes. Tribute to the Ottoman sultan was, nonetheless, the badge of vassalage, and Romanians had little likelihood of winning independence in league with the suzerain power. A third alternative was to do nothing, that is, to join no power or powers and to await the outcome of the anticipated war. Few Romanians favored this policy, for it meant full reliance on the great powers to determine Romania's future, quite possibly without reference to Romania's aspirations. Hence, Romania's goals appeared obtainable, primarily in cooperation and alliance with Russia.

Russians and Romanians had no formal alliance since 1711 and subsequent Russo-Turkish wars were fought without the aid of the Danubian principalities. Even after the fall of the Phanariot regime in 1821 and the restoration of native princes in Moldavia and Wallachia, Russia did not negotiate directly with Danubian Romania. Instead, Russia exercised a protectorate of its own over the principalities from 1829 to 1856. Its failure in the Crimean War and the unification of the Danubian principalities, however, created a new situation. No longer might Russia ignore the possibility of military opposition by other great powers when invading Romania; it needed to negotiate.

With war in the offing by early 1877, Romanians both feared and favored a treaty with Russia. They worried that a concert with the Russians might result in the forfeiture of territory or even autonomy. No Romanian wished to return to the pre-Crimean War days of a Russian protectorate. As already noted, one of Russia's humiliations following the Crimean War had been the retrocession of Southern Bessarabia to Moldavia. Romanians, to be sure, still considered all of Bessarabia to be part of Moldavia. Romania had demonstrated a degree of independence in making commercial conventions, and many Romanians thought a political-military treaty with one of the great powers, such as Russia, would confirm their country's political independence. Romanian statesmen were fully aware of their inability to withstand an invasion by either Russia or Turkey. Hence, Romania chose to deal with the probable victor, that is, Russia. For Danubian Romanians, everything depended in 1877 on what the Russians decided and did.

The constant aim of Russia's policy was to preserve its league with Austria-Hungary and Germany, but Russian statesmen did not always agree on what to do regarding Romania. Their ambassador at Constantinople, Nikolai P. Ignat'ev, deemed that Russia ought to occupy Romania during the Balkan Crisis so as to bring pressure on the Ottoman Empire to make reforms.[1] The assistant minister of foreign affairs, Nikolai K. Giers, believed Romania should have an "attitude of abstention" with only moral support for Balkan Christians; Romania should be a refuge for Bulgarians and a purchaser of military supplies for the insurgents.[2]

When fighting broke out between Serbs and Turks in 1875, Romania's neutrality posed problems for Russians wishing to aid the South Slav rebels. Despite Russia's official stance, Gorchakov advised the Danubian Romanians to "close their eyes" to border infractions and to avoid favoring Muslims over Christians.[3] After the defeat of the Serbs at Aleksinac in 1876, about 5,000 Russian volunteers left Serbia. Russian statesmen now asked what Romania would do if Russia intervened militarily in the Balkan Peninsula. The Romanian minister of foreign affairs, Nicolae Ionescu, replied cautiously that he could not predict Romania's plans.[4]

Not all Romanians wanted to deal with Russia. The Junimist leader, Petre Carp, thought Russia sought solely to ruin Romania; he would rather see his country ally with Austria-Hungary, the Ottoman Empire, and Great Britain.[5] The vice-president of the Senate, Ion Ghica, went to Vienna and London, and the prime minister, Ion C. Brătianu, visited the Habsburg Emperor, Franz Josef, at Sibiu in Transylvania. But the main bargaining was at

Livadia, the tsar's vacation residence in the Crimea. Members of the Romanian delegation included Brătianu and the minister of war, Gheorghe Slăniceanu; they saw, among others, Aleksandr II, Gorchakov, and Ignat'ev.[6] According to Brătianu, the tsar announced that he had already resolved on war against the Turks, and so Russia needed an agreement with Romania for the passage of Russian troops. Brătianu inquired "and in case we refuse?" Gorchakov responded "you will be crushed."[7] Brătianu retorted that Russia could hardly begin a campaign to free Christians from Muslims by destroying a Christian army. But, at the same time, he recognized that the Romanian army should be prepared to serve as Russia's advance guard.[8] Gorchakov, for his part, temporized: "If it comes to war, we shall understand one another."[9]

A key concern for the Romanians was their country's territorial integrity. Brătianu expressed his fear that Russia wanted to regain Southern Bessarabia; to this, Gorchakov rejoined cryptically, "What an idea."[10] Aleksandr I. Nelidov, who was at first entrusted with Russo-Romanian parleys for a convention, later recalled that Brătianu knew that the tsar coveted the retrocession of Southern Bessarabia.[11] The chief issue was, however, the passage of Russian troops through Romania, not Romanian military cooperation or land. Gorchakov favored, according to Prince Carol, a military pact without political ramifications, for Russia was not yet set on recognizing an independent Romania.[12]

Serbia's collapse, Russia's support of the Bulgarians, and the prospect of Russia's interference in the Balkans increased the importance of Romania for Russia. A Russian crown council at Livadia during October 1876 met to discuss alternatives to war against the Ottoman Empire. Aleksandr II listened to appeals for moderation from his minister of finance, Mikhail Kh. Reitern, and his minister of war, Dmitrii A. Miliutin. More militant declarations came from Gorchakov and Ignat'ev. Russia's financial instability and military unpreparedness were the arguments against a conflict; working for war, were Russia's frustration at Serbia's being vanquished and Russia's historic role as protector of Orthodox Christians. The tsar first decided to negotiate. He hoped that by participating in the conference of ambassadors at Constantinople Russia would acquire a European mandate for its unilateral military action. If the conference did not back Russia's policy, including the creation of a Bulgarian state, then Russia should mobilize for war. Such a mobilization was not, of course, a proclamation of war; the army was only to deploy on the Turkish frontier during December 1876 and to stand ready for as "rapid as possible" a campaign. To ensure the "rapid" movement of Russian troops, a convention was to be concluded with Romania.[13]

Although Russia and Romania signed no military accord at Livadia, negotiations for one commenced. Russian experts studied Romanian railroads, ferries, and national credit. A member of the Russian general staff, Vasilii G. Zoltarev, inspected Romania's military preparations and offered advice.[14] Hence, the Livadia talks provided the basis for a future Russo-Romanian entente and gave some Romanians added confidence that their political aspirations might be realized. Miliutin proceeded, furthermore, to draft plans that envisioned Romania's military cooperation.[15]

After the Romanian delegation returned from Livadia, Carol announced to the legislature: "Our relations with foreign states are the best...all the guaranteeing powers encourage us to maintain our neutral attitude...now perhaps the Ottoman Empire will be disposed to recognize the justice of our demands."[16] Since the Livadia discussions had been secret, the deputies were aware only of a formal exchange of greetings. Carol, of course, knew about the projected convention with Russia, and so his remark about Romania's "neutral attitude" was hypocritical. The deputies responded by affirming that "strict neutrality" corresponded to the "desires of the whole country" and conformed to "our national interests."[17] Brătianu, for his part, worried that Romanian politics had become "most entangled."[18] Romanian neutrality was certainly incompatible with a Russo-Romanian military alliance.

Negotiations began in utmost secrecy between Brătianu and Nelidov at Bucharest, without the cognizance even of Ionescu. While Miliutin encouraged the deliberations, Gorchakov showed little regard for Romanian affairs.[19] Ignat'ev called on Brătianu to agree on "anticipated eventualities" and to "conclude a military convention" that had already been "accepted in principle by both sides" at Livadia.[20] Brătianu questioned the propriety of dealing with Nelidov, since the latter was not empowered to make a treaty and had what Brătianu considered to be merely a letter of introduction from Ignat'ev. He consented nonetheless to discuss a draft pact that would be signed immediately before the outbreak of war.[21]

During these deliberations, the vital problem of Bessarabia arose. Nelidov was not entrusted to pledge that Russia would not reclaim Southern Bessarabia after the war. He argued that the treaty ought not have a political flavor and should cover only the Russian army's presence in Romania. He promised nevertheless that Russia would protect the security of Romania "if it should be menaced by the passage of Russian troops."[22] Regarding the probable loss of Southern Bessarabia, Brătianu remarked: "I understand this, I had the feeling at Livadia that this is a question of honor for the emperor...(but) we will seek compensation and I will be able to prepare our public opinion." Nelidov responded that Russia could not dispose of regions it did not possess; to this, Brătianu replied rhetorically: "And if the war is disastrous, how will you defend us?"[23] The first Russian draft convention stipulated that Romania's wholeness would be maintained for the "duration of the war."[24] Brătianu opposed this clause, and it was replaced by a vague assurance that Russia would safeguard the "actual integrity" of the country.[25] Throughout the negotiations, Brătianu was reluctant to commit himself or his government to an agreement that contravened Romania's neutrality. Russia was also not eager to compromise its position vis-à-vis the other great powers. Hence, both Russia and Romania would await the outcome of the conference of ambassadors at Constantinople and the forging of a firm deal between Russia and Austria-Hungary before proceeding with their own treaty.

Simultaneous with the Brătianu-Nelidov discussions at Bucharest, other talks took place at Constantinople between Stephen B. Lakeman and the Turkish minister of foreign affairs, Savfet Pasha. Lakeman, also known as Mazar Pasha, had served in the Turkish army during the Crimean War. He had married a daughter of Gheorghe Slăniceanu; and it was in Lakeman's house that the so-called Mazar Pasha coalition formed in 1875 to plan the ouster of the conservative Romanian cabinet. Brătianu was a member of this coalition, but we do not know if he or Slăniceanu asked Lakeman to speak on behalf of the country. Lakeman apparently expressed Romania's willingness to resist militarily a Russian invasion if the Ottoman Empire would recognize the name "Romania" instead of the "United Principalities of Moldavia and Wallachia."[26] Lakeman espoused Romania's neutral policy and an increase in the size of the army; but, at the same time, he warned that the Romanian army could not withstand a Russian onslaught. Thus, Turkish aid was required. Secret negotiations for Turco-Romanian cooperation were to be conducted in Bucharest because the Romanian diplomatic agent at Constantinople, Ion G. Ghica, was pro-Russian.[27] A Romanian newspaper leaked a story about Lakeman's presence in Constantinople and about a solid "understanding" that had been reached with Savfet and the grand vezir Midhat Pasha. This "understanding" included the Ottoman Empire's recognition of Romanian passports, regulation of the frontier on Danubian islands, approval of Romania's claim to make commercial treaties, and the dispatch of a Turkish agent to Bucharest to represent the Empire.[28] Whatever was considered at Constantinople, the Turkish governor of Tulcea, Ali Bey, visited Bucharest to promise thirty battalions of Turkish troops for Romania's defense; Turkish arms and munitions would, moreover, be available to the Romanians in case of war.[29]

The great powers, in general, favored Turco-Romanian military cooperation. Representatives of Great Britain, France, and Italy argued that Romania's only ally could be the Ottoman Empire.[30] Since deliberations were already underway at Bucharest for a Russo-Romanian pact, the talks at Constantinople and with Ali Bey were a convenient cover masking Romania's intentions. Owing to Romania's neutral posture, Brătianu recommended that Carol see neither Nelidov nor Ali Bey.[31] Savfet Pasha, for his part, declared that the proper line of Turkish defense was the Danube River; the Ottoman army would not enter Romania to stop a Russian attack.[32] The Turks evidently expected the Romanians would militarily assist them, or at least act as a buffer for the Empire by a continued program of neutrality.

Advice from Germany and Austria-Hungary differed from that of the Western powers. The German chancellor, Otto von Bismarck, suggested that a convention for the passage of Russian troops would be more desirable than no agreement at all; but, he cautioned that a contract signed before Russia was ready would offer the Turks a pretext to invade.[33] Meanwhile, the Austro-Hungarian minister of foreign affairs, Gyula Andrássy, counseled Romania to preserve its neutrality by withdrawing its army and by avoiding contact with Russian forces.[34] He gave the impression, on the one hand, that a Russo-Romanian treaty might be a pretext for an Austro-Hungarian march into their country;[35] but, on the other hand, Austria-Hungary would not back Romania in an anti-Russian challenge.[36] Vienna aimed first at securing Russia's support for the Habsburg Empire's pretensions to Bosnia and Hercegovina before any alliance between Russia and Romania.

Negotiations at Bucharest went on during the ambassadorial conference at Constantinople.[37] Neither Brătianu nor Gorchakov was willing, of course, to finish the business while the ambassadors were working for a peaceful solution to the Balkan Crisis.[38] Russian military leaders, however, impatiently insisted on a firm deal with Romania. Miliutin feared that Brătianu's neutral attitude would damage, or at least retard, the discussions. He therefore advocated an immediate accord.[39] Grand Duke Nikolai Nikolaevich and the chief of the Russian general staff, Artur A. Nepokoichitskii, at Kishinev in Russian Bessarabia, also feared danger in delay. By a draft provision, Carol was to ratify the treaty twenty-four hours before Russia's declaration of war. Nepokoichitskii assumed Carol's hesitation to be a refusal to unite militarily with Russia unless forced to do so by a Turkish invasion of Romanian territory.[40] He nonetheless anticipated the involvement of Romanian troops with the Russian army during the war and even recognized the possibility of Carol taking supreme command over the armies of both countries.[41] Brătianu indeed asked for fifty thousand Peabody guns plus a loan of twenty million francs, some of which was to be used to prepare militarily.[42] Grand Duke Nikolai was apparently more skeptical than was his chief of staff concerning Romania's eventual participation, and he foresaw Carol maintaining neutrality by repudiating battle.[43]

The evident difference of opinion between Nikolai Nikolaevich and Nepokoichitskii owed much to the dynastic nature of Russia's aims. Aleksandr II sought to regain the dynasty's honor by defeating the Turks without outside aid, and by retaking Southern Bessarabia. The tsar's younger brother, Grand Duke Nikolai, shared Aleksandr's hope, in contrast to Nepokoichitskii's more pragmatic approach. Russians agreed nevertheless on strategy in Romania. Miliutin, Gorchakov, and Aleksandr concurred on the necessity of occupying the ports and former fortresses of Galaţi, Brăila, and Ismail.[44] This meant Russian control of the most important ports on the Danube River, Southern Bessarabia, and the eastern parts of Moldavia and Wallachia. Nikolai explained, however, that Russia intended no military conquest but wished only to defend Balkan Christians. Russia would respect Romania's "independence, authority, and welfare" by means of a practical entente of a "purely military" and nonpolitical character.[45]

Carol had another idea. He wanted a "political" act to regulate Russo-Romanian relations, one to be signed on the eve of hostilities.[46] Although Nikolai favored a pact, he feared that its ratification immediately before the outbreak of war would render it worthless; the Russian army would be forced to forage for food and supplies as if in enemy territory.[47] Romania would relinquish its neutrality if it concluded an anti-Turkish alliance with Russia, and would, to be sure, assure Russia's troops a secure passage to the Danube. But what would Romania gain by assisting Russia? Brătianu asked Russia to supply his country with money, guns, horses, and torpedoes.[48] Miliutin consented, in effect, to Brătianu's demands.[49] Carol, who hoped to see Romania's independence won on the field of battle, promised the Russian army a "sympathetic and fraternal reception."[50] He was indeed disappointed, however, that Russia's plans excluded Romania's military participation; Romanian forces were not even to guard the vital railway bridge across the Siret River at Barboşi--the only rail link between Moldavia and Wallachia.[51] For the moment, however, Russian troops continued to mobilize in Bessarabia, and Turkish soldiers concentrated on the Danube at Silistria and Vidin; Romania strengthened defenses at Calafat on the Danube and at the Barboşi bridge.[52] Although the drift toward war persisted, by January 1877 neither Russia nor the Ottoman Empire had decided irrevocably on conflict. As such, a Russo-Romanian convention remained on hold.

Romania's repeated declarations of neutrality stemmed from lacking a political or military convention and from not knowing precisely Russia's intentions. Romania's army was, nonetheless, partially mobilized, and the legislature approved funds to pay for munitions from an Austro-Hungarian firm.[53] In Russia, Romania's neutrality was understood to be merely a "necessity of the moment."[54] The apostle of neutrality, Nicolae Ionescu, wishfully suggested that Russia craved peace and would not start a war.[55] He had earlier indicated that Romania would not "cooperate actively" with Russia even if the latter received a European mandate for intervention.[56] Romanian popular opinion, as expressed in newspapers and brochures, backed Ionescu's stand. The opposition journal *Timpul* reiterated Austria-Hungary's advice: in case of a Russian invasion, Romania's soldiers were to withdraw, protect Romania's soil, and await the outcome. The Turcophil, Ion Ghica--not to be confused with the Russophil diplomat at Constantinople, Ion G. Ghica--anonymously published in February 1877 a pamphlet, *Uă cugetare politica* (A Political Thought), in which he argued for the maintenance of Romania's neutrality. Romania was not to associate militarily with either Russia or the Ottoman Empire and was not to resist the entry of any foreign army. Brătianu's friend, Constantin A. Rosetti, in his influential newspaper *Românul*, rejected this view but recognized the impossibility of stopping the passage of Russian troops--with or without Romania's consent.[57]

As war increasingly appeared inevitable, Gorchakov called for the expeditious conclusion of a Russo-Romanian military pact.[58] He had evidently overcome his former reluctance to talk to Romania, owing to his inability to gain Europe's approval for unilateral Russian action in Southeastern Europe. Carol and Brătianu now posed conditions. Payment for supplies consumed by the Russian army was to be in gold rather than in Russian paper currency; the agreement was furthermore to be adopted by Romania's legislature on the first day of the war.[59] Aleksandr II noted that the fulfillment of these prerequisites would be "difficult" for "even we ourselves do not know" when the war will begin.[60] Russia rejected remuneration in coin instead of paper; to use gold would have considerably raised the cost of the Russian march through Romania. Brătianu also requested large caliber guns and one thousand horses in return for lumber to build pontoon bridges across the Danube. Miliutin thought the projected military convention provided for these things.[61] All that was needed to cement Russo-Romanian relations was the signing of the convention.

Romanian statesmen continued to seek Austria-Hungary's advice as contacts with Russia became increasingly intimate. Some Romanians feared, as noted above, that their involvement with Russia would lead to Romania's absorption into the Russian Empire. Andrássy, who had signed a Budapest Convention with Gorchakov in January 1877,[62] did not, of course, oppose the passage of the Russian army through Romania, but he would not accept a Russian occupation or annexation of Romania.[63] Andrássy's posture was not frank due to his prior approval of Southern Bessarabia reverting to Russia. His apparent guarantee was moreover valueless because Austria-Hungary's own neutrality precluded intervention on behalf of Romania. Then, Ionescu resigned in protest against deeds that he felt compromised Romania's neutrality; he was replaced by Ion Cîmpineanu as ad interim minister of foreign affairs.[64] Cîmpineanu informed Andrássy that Romania would remain neutral yet would be compelled to yield to the overwhelming might of the Russian army. He asked that Austria-Hungary help Romania by sending gunboats to safeguard Danubian commerce at Brăila and Galaţi.[65] Without Austro-Hungarian aid on the Danube, and with the "inevitable" and "imminent" outbreak of war, Cîmpineanu recognized the need to regulate the traversing of Russian troops. Although he hoped to avoid any alliance or cooperation with either Russia or the Ottoman Empire,[66] as Carol observed, "theoretical neutrality" was already a stand "long since abandoned."[67]

Russia meanwhile decided irrevocably on war. A council on 11 April 1877 established a timetable for operations. The Russian army was to be fully mobilized by 15 April, war was to be declared on 24 April, and, on the same day, Southern Bessarabia and the Caucasus were to be invaded.[68] The Ottoman Empire had already mobilized along the Danube; a large concentration of Turkish forces was at Vidin, the nearest Danubian fortress to the Serbian frontier.[69] The Turks undoubtedly anticipated that the Serbs would join in the fray. Romania's troops were, nonetheless, more threatening to the Turks. Cîmpineanu assured Istanbul that Romania's army was only prepared to "tranquilize spirits" and to halt the exodus of Danubian residents whose lives had been endangered by Turkish troops across the river.[70] Romania's defensive measures against the Ottoman Empire notwithstanding, Carol rejected Russia's invitation to participate directly with the Russian army. He followed Austria-Hungary's recommendation in announcing that he would withdraw the Romanian army into Oltenia.[71] Carol earnestly wanted to win glory on the battlefield and, by doing so, to achieve Romania's independence. He did not, however, have the complete support of his cabinet for military action, nor did he wish a subordinate role in the Russian high command.

A crown council met at Bucharest to discuss neutrality and what should be done in case of a Russo-Turkish war. The government had not, of course, been neutral in the negotiations for a military treaty with Russia; but, since those dealings were secret, Romanian leaders could retain an outward posture of neutrality. The majority in the council considered it best to yield to overpowering might. The Turcophil Ion Ghica warned that Romania could not repulse a Turkish invasion; if the Turks destroyed Danubian towns, however, Romania should then fight back. He advocated neutrality vis-à-vis both Russia and Turkey. A prominent jurist, Constantin Bosianu, understood Romania's neutrality as implying free and equal transit across the country for both Russia and Turkey. Manolache Costache Epureanu, who had headed the Mazar Pasha coalition in 1875-76, did not insist on neutrality, but recognized the need to agree with Russia on the passage of its army; hence, a Russo-Romanian alliance was required. A conservative party chief, Dimitrie Ghica, saw no point in neutrality and envisioned a European mandate going to Austria-Hungary to occupy Romania in order to prevent an invasion by either Russia or the Ottoman Empire. The diplomat Alexandru G. Golescu proposed that Romania safeguard itself with Turkish help; otherwise, he argued, Romania would forfeit the collective guarantee of its privileges by the great powers. If the powers were not willing to protect Romania, then conventions regulating troop travel ought to be made with Russia and Turkey. The liberal publisher, Constantin A. Rosetti, opposed Turkish troops entering Romania and supported a pact with Russia that would preserve Romania's territorial integrity. Mihail Kogălniceanu feared the loss of Southern Bessarabia and the creation of a large Slavic state south of the Danube after a victorious Russian campaign. He felt Romania would not benefit by associating itself with Russia; instead, aid should be sought from Austria-Hungary to block Turkish incursions. For Kogălniceanu, Romania's first concerns were to defend its borders and to maintain its neutrality.[72] Cîmpineanu, for his part, thought an accord with Russia ought to cover purely administrative matters but not cooperation.[73]

Those present at the council reached no decision. They were undoubtedly motivated by their national interests; but the great powers, and now especially Russia, dictated Romania's stance. The strongest champion of a Russo-Romanian alliance was, of course, Brătianu. He apparently won Kogălniceanu to his side, and the latter replaced Cîmpineanu as minister of foreign affairs. Although Kogălniceanu notified Romanian diplomats that his appointment ensured a "prudent policy," that is, neutrality within the limits of practicality, he signed a military convention with the Russian representative at Bucharest, Dmitrii F. Stuart. He did so, he said, so that Romania would not become a battleground for Russia and Turkey.[74]

Kogălniceanu and Stuart really signed two conventions at Bucharest on 16 April 1877--one political and the other technical. The preamble to the political pact recognized a duty "to ameliorate the conditions" of Balkan Christians. Russia was "to respect the inviolability of the territory" of Romania, "to maintain and defend the actual integrity of Romania," and "to respect the political rights" of the Romanian state as to "internal laws and existing treaties." The Russian army, in return, was to have free passage across Romania and was to remunerate the latter for its needs.[75] The technical convention, which had been discussed by Brătianu and Nelidov, covered details of troop transit. By this accord,

Russia obtained the use of Romania's railroads, roads, rivers, post and telegraph systems, and supplies. The rail tariff was reduced by forty percent and a committee representing the railway companies, led by the minister of public works and assisted by a Russian military attaché, was to direct rail traffic and improve the lines. A Romanian commissioner was assigned to Russian headquarters to procure munitions and to support setting up camps, hospitals, ambulance services, and pharmacies. No Russian soldiers were to enter Bucharest; the sick and wounded were to be treated in Russian hospitals established along the army's route, but not in Bucharest or other large towns so as to obviate or at least restrict Russia's influence in Romania's affairs. Romania was to support the building of bridges and the turning back of Russian deserters. The cost of transit was to be paid in French or Romanian currency or in short-term bonds, but not in gold or silver.[76]

Despite this formal agreement, Russia and Romania would be at odds over what constituted Romania's territorial integrity, the price of Russia's march through Romania, and the acquisition of local supplies.[77] Yet, although points of friction emerge, to be sure, from contracts involving national interests, the conventions represented a distinct gain for the Danubian Romanians. They had, as already noted, been unable to ally themselves with any foreign power for well over one hundred years. The 1877 entente did not provide perforce for military action by Romania; but it admitted Romania's importance to Russia's war effort and acknowledged Romania's prerogative to conclude political treaties.

Romania mobilized its permanent and territorial army, along with its militia and town guards, after the making of the conventions but before the outbreak of war.[78] Romanian statesmen nonetheless reasserted their country's neutrality and warned of the undesirable consequences of war. Kogălniceanu feared that Russian troops entering Romania would create a "troublesome situation" before the Romanian legislature had approved the accord.[79] Romania would thereby become a theater for military operations; hence, he reaffirmed Romania's neutrality.[80] Romanians indeed had cause for concern; Savfet Pasha had withdrawn his assurance that Turkish soldiers would not overrun Romania.[81] Between twenty and thirty thousand Turkish irregular troops--the başıbozuks--were ready, Kogălniceanu thought, to invade as soon as Russia crossed the frontier. Although Savfet was unaware of the Russo-Romanian pact and so had no concrete reason to suspect the Romanians of duplicity, he would not tie the hands of the Turkish army should it defeat Russia's forces. To have clung to the Danube River as the perimeter of the Ottoman Empire's defense in Europe would have been to renounce pursuit after a Turkish victory.

The Turkish grand vezir, Edhem Pasha, advised that the concentration of Russian troops on the border dictated that Romania take "military measures in common" with the Ottoman Empire "to assure the defense" of Romania.[82] This counsel stemmed from Romania's obligations as a vassal and was in harmony with international treaties. Both the 1856 Paris treaty and the 1858 Paris convention stipulated that Romania's army was to secure the country's interior and frontier; the army was to take "extraordinary measures of defense" in concert with the Turks "to repel all foreign aggression." The Turks, however, might not intervene militarily in Romania without the prior approval of the great powers.[83] Kogălniceanu therefore justified his reply that a "grave measure" of security required consideration by the Romanian legislature.[84] To the great powers, Kogălniceanu equivocated that Romania had no alliance with Russia, but he also asserted that his country would retain its "national administration" by regulating the passage of Russian troops through the country in such a way as to preserve Romania's ancient rights and privileges.[85] The transit of these troops would, after all, be with the "more or less tacit" consent of the powers.[86] Romania was moreover set to rebuff a Turkish invasion.[87] Kogălniceanu saw the imperative need to yield to possible Russian demands despite the Russo-Romanian conventions. This was a question of power and survival. He and his colleagues wanted to choose the most propitious moment to break with the Turks, and they also hoped to gain the fruits of military triumph.

Romanians turned to Russia for help in financing their country's protection. Kogălniceanu thought the "alpha and omega" of Russo-Romanian relations lay in obtaining a Russian loan of five million rubles.[88] Aleksandr seemingly favored such a concession, and, during the campaign, Romania got most of what it sought. Before Russia's declaration of war, however, Russia provided Romania with 300,000 silver rubles (919,702 francs) to avoid a fiscal crisis.[89] This money came from income on monastic lands in Russian Bessarabia. In a sense, the Orthodox Christian church paid for the Orthodox Christian crusade against the Muslim Turks. Carol announced an additional extraordinary credit of more than one million francs for general supplies and the military payroll. The Chamber of Deputies approved this decree.[90] This subvention was apparently based on the Russian grant. Russia was certainly interested in a solvent Romania, prepared to aid the passage of Russian troops and equipped to perform military service if need be.

Still, Romania was not ready. After the rupture of Russo-Turkish relations, Carol requested Russia postpone going to war for a few days. He and his ministers hoped, on the one hand, that during such a delay the Russo-Romanian conventions could be discussed and endorsed by the Romanian legislature. Brătianu admitted, on the other hand, that the Russian high command could not be tied to Romania's desires. Nikolai, Miliutin, and Ignat'ev decided that the campaign could not be put off to satisfy Romania's constitutional obligations.[91] Nikolai reminded Romanians that Russia came as an old friend; its forces would pass rapidly and peacefully through the land, respecting the laws, customs, and property of the people. To the Russian army, Nikolai proclaimed the holy cause of the tsar liberator who had no goal of conquest.[92] As Russian troops crossed the frontier into Southern Bessarabia, a Romanian crown council, in order not to prejudice future deliberations of the legislature, resolved to maintain neutrality. Prefects of police were instructed not to interfere with the transit of soldiers but were to represent--at Russian headquarters--along with town mayors, the interests of those residing in occupied areas. Persons living near the Danube were advised to move themselves and their possessions to the interior of the country to avoid the dangers of a Turkish attack.[93]

Clashes of opinion occurred almost immediately between Russian and Romanian leaders. Kogălniceanu discovered a "patent contradiction" in the conventions and Nikolai's proclamation. The latter mentioned nothing about Romania's "rights" nor did it "safeguard the dignity" of the country or the prince; rather, it appealed over the government to the people.[94] To salve Romania's injured pride, Aleksandr II sent the governor of Moscow, Vladimir A. Dolgorukov, to Bucharest to explain Russia's deeds. Russian troops arrived as "sincere friends" of the Bulgarians because the Ottoman Empire had refused to conciliate. Romania could "count on the traditional interest" and "constant support" of Russia.[95] Nikolai wrote Carol that restraint had been impossible; "strategic necessities" dictated that the tsar--"forced by circumstances"--declare war and begin the offensive. He undertook to keep Carol informed of Russian troop movements and suggested a joint "understanding" about operations.[96] Carol responded that he grasped the plans and promised to defend the Barboşi bridge between Galaţi and Brăila until Russians replaced his soldiers. After that, the Romanian army would divide: part of it would protect Bucharest on the Sabar-Argeş line, and the bulk of it, about nineteen thousand men, would remain encamped in Oltenia. Carol thought that by the time Nikolai received his letter, the conventions would have been adopted by the legislature, and so he wished him the "most glorious success" in fulfilling a "grand and noble mission."[97]

Edham Pasha demanded Romania's cooperation after Russia's declaration of war.[98] Kogălniceanu disingenuously answered that Romania's neutrality might be changed only by the legislature that was to meet in a day or so.[99] As Russian troops entered the Turkish province of Armenia and the Turkish principality of Romania, Safvet Pasha reconfirmed his view that the Ottoman Empire need not attack open towns on the left bank of the Danube River; although he could not restrain the Turkish army, no aggressive action was contemplated against Romania.[100] The Turks held strongly fortified positions at Vidin, Ruse, and Silistria on the Danube; the river was still the Turks' first "line of defense,"[101] anticipating that the powers would intervene to save the Empire from territorial loss and political collapse. The Empire and Romania were not yet at war, and, therefore, Romanian citizens continued to receive civil protection wherever they lived or traveled in Turkey.

The Ottoman Empire nonetheless broke telegraph connections to Bucharest.[102] The Turks were fully within their rights in doing so, according to the international telegraph convention that both sides had signed. By this pact, each signatory had the prerogative of halting dispatches that endangered the state's security.[103] The rupture of Turco-Romanian telegraphic relations indicated how little the Empire trusted a Romania that had evidently been written off as a possible ally against Russia.

A joint session of the Romanian Senate and Chamber of Deputies convened with a speech by Carol two days after the outbreak of war. He pointed out that, because no one recognized the country's neutrality, Romania had to assure "at all costs and at any sacrifice" that the country would not become a battlefield, that Romanians not be "massacred," and that Romania's wealth and property not be destroyed. Since the great powers had not stopped the entry of Russian troops, Carol requested that the legislature give his government the "necessary means" to "defend the rights and interests" of the country. From the moment he had arrived in Bucharest, Carol had contemplated the "revival of Romania, the fulfillment of its mission at the mouths of the Danube, and above all the preservation of its rights *ab antiquo*."[104] Romania's "revival" and its "mission" were vague expressions of national policy. Romanians had, of course, already experienced a cultural and political "revival;" but their "mission" focused on national survival and independence, not on leading Christian Slavs of Southeastern Europe against Muslim Turks. The Russo-Romanian conventions provided a basis for both survival and independence.

Opposition legislators expressed many of the fears Romanians held about dealing with Russia. The publicist Nicolae Blaremberg characterized the conventions as a program of gravediggers.[105] He would rather submit his country to fire and ruin than accept Russia's sympathy and divorce from Turkey. Would the Russo-Romanian conventions replace the collective guarantee by the great powers for a unilateral one by Russia? Would this not be a return to the Russian protectorate over Danubian Romanians? While he acknowledged the presence of Russian troops in Romania, he hoped his country would not violate international treaties by participating militarily south of the Danube. Nicolae Ionescu and

Dimitrie Sturdza agreed with Blaremberg in not wishing to abandon the powers' guarantee. Manolache Costache Epureanu, while also objecting to the pact, did not think Russia aimed at annexing Romania, for Austria-Hungary would block such a step.[106] Vasile Boerescu asked for a vote on neutrality before addressing the conventions.[107] Petre Carp argued that any vote on neutrality at the point of three hundred thousand Russian bayonets would be that of a "stillborn child." He saw an obvious dichotomy between "strictest neutrality" and unilateral Russian assurances that would lead to an "abyss between crown and country." The accord was based on inequality owing to the differences in strength of the two sides. The conventions entailed "enormous sacrifice." Romania was "neither rich enough nor happy enough" to forfeit the protection of the great powers. Thus, the conventions had no "material or moral use."[108]

Members of the government, of course, supported the conventions. Kogălniceanu noted that they ensured the territorial status quo; the country's "integrity," with its rights, customs, and frontier, would be preserved. The conventions were needed, he said, to avert a Turkish invasion.[109] Brătianu reminded the legislators that the war was between Russia and the Ottoman Empire and did not include Romania. He had worked to maintain neutrality but had learned from the powers that neutrality did not conform to reality. Had he continued to assert neutrality, in the face of the Russian advance, he would have become a ridiculous "Don Quixote of Turkey." He called for "devotion, prudence, and courage," and, assured Romanians that the conventions protected Romania's political privileges, institutions, and wholeness. They had, after all, been approved by Aleksandr II in a "solemn act."[110] Brătianu explained moreover that the government had taken emergency measures in establishing a fund to finance the mobilization of the army and in requisitioning war materials. These moves had indeed transgressed the constitutional prerogatives of the executive branch; but the Senate voted to absolve the administration in view of the crisis.[111] Two days after debate began (four days after the outbreak of hostilities), the Chamber of Deputies adopted the conventions by a margin of 79 to 25. The next day, the Senate approved them by a vote of 41 to 10. A few days later, Carol endorsed them.[112]

Romanians debated the conventions in newspapers, salons, the legislature, and the corridors of power. Austria-Hungary was obviously neither ready nor interested in intervening militarily to prevent a Russian or Turkish occupation of the country. Habsburg statesmen saw no reason to waste their empire's resources in defending Romania's neutrality. If the Russian campaign were successful and the Turks defeated, Romania expected to gain more in the peace settlement by aiding rather than hindering Russia. Romania's national aspirations could certainly not be won in league with the suzerain Ottoman Empire. Perhaps the accord with Russia would end the collective guarantee of the great powers that Romania had enjoyed since 1856, but many Romanians thought the chance worth taking. Only then might Romania's economic independence, as expressed in the earlier commercial treaties with Austria-Hungary in 1875 and with Russia in 1876, be expanded to political independence.

NOTES

[1]The Romanian diplomatic agent at Constantinople told Carol about his conversation with the Russian ambassador Nikolai P. Ignat'ev. *Aus dem Leben König Karls von Rumänien: Aufzeichnungen eines Augenzeugen* (Stuttgart, 1894), II, p. 483; hereafter cited *ALKK*.

[2]Emil Ghica (St. Petersburg) to Ministerul Afacerilor Străine, 12/24 May 1876; *Charles Ier, Roi de Roumanie: Chronique, Actes, Documents*, ed. Démètre A. Sturdza (Bucarest, 1904), II, p. 44.

[3]Ion Cantacuzino (St. Petersburg) to Ministerul Afacerilor Străine, 16/28 August 1876; *Documente privind istoria Romîniei: Războiul pentru independenţă*, ed. Mihail Roller (Bucureşti, 1954), I pt. 2, p. 323.

[4]Emil Ghica (St. Petersburg) to Ministerul Afacerilor Străine, 16/28 September 1876; *ibid.*, I pt. 2, p. 359; Nicolae Ionescu to E. Ghica, 19 September/1 October 1876, *ibid.*, p. 361.

[5]Petre Carp (Iaşi) to Titu-Liviu Maiorescu, 9/21 October 1876, Fond Petre Carp, S18(29)/XII, nr. 3289, Biblioteca Academiei Republicii Socialiste România, Secţia de Corespondenţă; Carp to

Maiorescu, 11/23 November 1876, Fond Petre Carp, S18(31)/XII, nr. 3291, *ibid.*

[6]Nicolae Ionescu's circular, 24 August/5 September 1876, *Documente privind istoria Romîniei*, I pt. 2, p. 331.

[7]Alexandru D. Xenopol, *Resboaele d'intre Ruşi şi Turci şi inriurirea lor asupra ţerilor române* (Jassy, 1880), II, pp. 329-330.

[8]See note dated 29 September 1876 in: *Dnevnik D.A. Miliutina*, ed. Pëtr A. Zaionchkovskii (Moscow, 1949), II, p. 92.

[9]*ALKK*, III, p. 63.

[10]Xenopol, II, p. 331; see Ion Brătianu's speeches in the Senate, 13/25 February and 28 September/10 November 1878 in *Ion C. Brătianu: Acte şi cuvântări*, ed. Constantin C. Giurescu (Bucureşti, 1930), III, p. 192; *ibid.*, IV, p. 104.

[11]Alexandre de Nelidov, "Souvenirs d'avant et d'après la guerre de 1877-1878," *Revue des Deux Mondes*, XXVIII (15 July 1915), p. 245.

[12]*ALKK*, III, pp. 62-63.

[13]See note dated 4/16 October 1876 at Livadia in: Zaionchkovskii, *Dnevnik D.A. Miliutina*, II, pp. 93-95.

[14]Nikolai Ignat'ev (Buyudéré) to Ion Brătianu, 17/29 October 1876, Fond I.C. Brătianu, LVI/1a, Biblioteca Centrală de Stat, Secţia Manuscriselor; hereafter cited BCS,SM; Feodor Geiden (St. Petersburg) to Ignat'ev, 7/19 October 1876; *Osvobozhdenie Bolgarii ot turetskogo iga*, ed. Sergei A. Nikitin (Moscow, 1961), I, p. 443.

[15]Miliutin to Geiden, 5/17 October 1876, Nikitin, *Osvobozhdenie Bolgarii*, I, p. 439.

[16]For Carol's speech opening the Romanian legislature, 21 October/2 November 1876, see *Documente privind istoria Romîniei*, I pt. 2, p. 394.

[17]For the reply from the Chamber of Deputies, 1/13 November 1876, see *ibid.*, p. 411.

[18]Brătianu (Bucharest) to his wife Pia, 22 October/3 November 1876; *Din corespondenţă familiei Ion C. Brătianu*, 2nd ed. (Bucureşti, 1936), I, pp. 160-161.

[19]See note dated 21 October/2 November 1876 (Chetnerg) in: Zaionchkovskii, *Dnevnik D.A. Miliutina*, II, p. 104.

[20]Ignat'ev (Pera) to Brătianu, 5/17 November 1876, Fond I.C. Brătianu, LVI/1a, BCS,SM.

[21]Nelidov, p. 249.

[22]*Ibid.*, p. 250.

[23]*Ibid.*, pp. 250-251.

[24]Xenopol, II, p. 332; cf. Nelidov, pp. 253-254.

[25]Nicolae Iorga, *Istoria Românilor* (Bucureşti, 1939), X, p. 168.

[26]Ion G. Ghica (Pera) to Nicolae Ionescu (Bucureşti), 30 October/11 November 1876, nr. 463, Fond Războiul pentru independenţă, vol. 21, p. 260; Arhiva Ministerului Afacerilor Externe (Romania); hereafter cited AMAE.

[27]Ibrahim Halil Sedes, *1875-1878 Osmanli ordusu savaşlari: 1877-1878: Osmanli-Rus ve Roman savaşi* (Istanbul, 1935), I, p. 38.

[28]Iorga, *Istoria*, X, pp. 169-170; Iorga cites the newspaper *Pressa* for 29 September 1877 [1876].

[29]Sedes, I, pp. 37-38; cf., Iorga, *Istoria*, X, p. 170.

[30]Ion Ghica (Paris) to Ministerul Afacerilor Străine, 20 November/2 December 1876, *Documente privind istoria Romîniei*, I pt. 2, pp. 462-463.

[31]See note dated 16/28 November 1876, *ALKK*, III, p. 76.

[32]Ion G. Ghica (Pera) to Ministerul Afacerilor Străine, 7/19 November 1876, *Documente privind istoria Romîniei*, I pt. 2, p. 440.

[33]Otto von Bismarck (Berlin) to Friedrich Johann von Alvensleben (Bucharest), 28 December 1876, nr. 19; Hauptarchiv des Auswärtigen Amtes (Prussia), Politischer Schriftwechsel: Türkei 24, vol. 55; hereafter cited HAA,PS.

[34]Gyula Andrássy to Bosizio (Bucharest), 17 December 1876; Haus-, Hof-, und Staatsarchiv (Austria), Politisches Archiv--XXXVIII Konsulate: Bukarest, Karton 211; hereafter cited HHS,PA.

[35]Alvensleben to Bernhard von Bülow (Berlin), 11 January 1877, nr. 6, HAA,PS: Türkei 24, vol. 55.

[36]Andrássy to Bosizio, 21 February 1877, HHS,PA--XXXVIII Konsulate: Bukarest, Karton 217.

[37]See note dated 12/24 December 1876 in: *ALKK*, III, p. 85; Dmitrii F. Stuart (Bucharest) to Aleksandr M. Gorchakov, 16/28 December 1876, Nikitin, *Osvobozhdenie Bolgarii*, I, p. 567.

[38]Stuart to Gorchakov, 16/28 December 1876, *ibid.*, I, p. 567; Nelidov, p. 253.

[39]See notes at St. Petersburg, dated 16, 20, 23 November /28 November, 2, 5 December 1876 in Zaionchkovskii, *Dnevnik D.A. Miliutina*, II, pp. 112-114.

[40]Artur A. Nepokoichitskii (Kishinev) to Miliutin, 23 December 1876/4 January 1877; Nikitin, *Osvobozhdenie Bolgarii*, I, p. 571; see also note at St. Petersburg dated 14/26 December 1876 in: Zaionchkovskii, *Dnevnik D.A. Miliutina*, II, p. 123.

[41]See Nepokoichitskii's report (Kishinev), 23 December 1876/4 January 1877, *Documente privind istoria Romîniei*, I pt. 2, pp. 542-543.

[42]Stuart to Nikolai K. Girs, 6/18 December 1876; *Rossiia i natsional'no-osvoboditel'naia bor'ba na Balkanakh, 1875-1878*, ed. Aleksei V. Narochintskii (Moscow, 1978), p. 206.

[43]Nikolai Nikolaevich (Kishinev) to Aleksandr II, 26 December 1876/7 January 1877, *Documente privind istoria Romîniei*, I pt. 2, p. 548.

[44]See note at St. Petersburg dated 2/14 January 1877 in: Zaionchkovskii, *Dnevnik D.A. Miliutina*, II, p. 129.

[45]Nikolai (Kishinev) to Carol, 12/24 January 1877; *Independenţa României: Documente*, ed. Ştefan Hurmuzache (Bucureşti, 1977), I, pp. 27-28.

[46]Carol to Nikolai, 21 January/2 February 1877, *Charles Ier, Roi de Roumanie*, II, pp. 490-491.

[47]Nikolai to Aleksandr II, 28 December 1876/9 January 1877, *Documente privind istoria Romîniei*, I pt. 2, p. 548.

[48]Nepokoichitskii (Kishinev) to Miliutin, 7 and 8 January 1877, Narochintskii, *Rossiia i natsional'no-osvoboditel'naia bor'ba na Balkanakh*, pp. 216, 217; see note at St. Petersburg dated 6/18 January 1877 in: Zaionchkovskii, *Dnevnik D.A. Miliutina*, II, p. 132.

[49]Miliutin to Nepokoichitskii, 8 January 1877, Narochintskii, *Rossiia i natsional'no-osvoboditel'naia bor'ba na Balkanakh*, p. 217.

[50]Carol to Nikolai, 21 January/2 February 1877, Fond Brătianu LIX/6, BCS,SM.

[51]Alvensleben to Bülow, 11 January 1877 nr. 6, HAA,PS: Türkei 24, vol. 55.

[52]See a report from St. Petersburg dated 3 December 1876 and an administrative note of 18 January 1877 in Nicolae Iorga,

Correspondance diplomatique roumaine sous le roi Charles Ier (1866-1880) (Paris, 1923), pp. 176, 180-181.

[53]Gheorghe Slăniceanu to Ionescu, 26 January/7 February 1877, *Documente privind istoria Romîniei*, II, pp. 43-44; Ionescu to Ion Bălăceanu (Vienna), 5/17 February 1877, *ibid.*, 54; Bălăceanu to Ionescu, 11/23 March 1877, *ibid.*, pp. 78-79.

[54]Emil Ghica (St. Petersburg) to Ministerul Afacerilor Străine, 3/15 November 1877, *ibid.*, I pt. 2, p. 419.

[55]Ionescu to Bălăceanu, 15/27 February 1877, Iorga, *Correspondance diplomatique roumaine*, p. 182.

[56]Alvensleben to Bülow, 4 November 1876 nr. 163, HAA,PS: Türkei 24, vol. 55.

[57]Titu Maiorescu, *Istoria contimporană a României (1866-1900)* (Bucureşti, 1925), pp. 113-114; see notes for 12, 15, 17/24, 27, 29 February in Ion C. Brătianu, *Discursuri, scrieri, acte şi documente* (Bucureşti, 1912), II pt. 2, 461, 464, 469.

[58]Summary of Gorchakov's dispatch to Stuart, 14/29 March 1877, Nikitin, *Osvobozhdenie Bolgarii*, I, p. 629.

[59]Stuart to Gorchakov, 18/30 March 1877, *ibid.*, I, p. 623.

[60]See Aleksandr II's marginal note on Stuart's report to Gorchakov, 18/30 March 1877, *ibid.*, I, p. 623.

[61]Nepokoichitskii to Miliutin, 25 March/6 April 1877, *ibid.*, I, pp. 626-627; Miliutin to Nepokoichitskii, 31 March/12 April 1877, *ibid.*, I, p. 629.

[62]Austria-Hungary was to remain neutral in case of war and then take the provinces of Bosnia and Hercegovina, but not the *sancak* (provincial subdivision) of Novi Pazar between Serbia and Montenegro. Russia was to enter Bulgaria and obtain Southern Bessarabia. No large South Slavic state was to be set up in the Balkans, and Russia was not to occupy Serbia. Austro-Hungarian influence, in effect, was to predominate in Serbia, while Russia was to be confined to operations in Romania and Bulgaria.

[63]See note dated 20 March/1 April 1877 in Brătianu, *Discursuri*, II pt. 2, 558; and note dated 29 March/10 April 1877, *ibid.*, 567.

[64]Carol to Karl Anton, 28 March/9 April 1877, *ALKK*, III, p. 115.

[65]Ion Cîmpineanu to Bălăceanu, 29 March/ 10 April 1877, in Brătianu, *Discursuri*, II pt. 2, 566. Austria-Hungary, which had a seat on the European Danube Commission, would have violated its own neutrality had it complied.

[66]Ion Cîmpineanu's circular of 1/13 April 1877, Iorga, *Correspondance diplomatique roumaine*, p. 187.

[67]Carol to Karl Anton, 28 March/9 April 1877, *ALKK*, III, p. 112.

[68]The council met at St. Petersburg 30 March/11 April 1877, Zaionchkovskii, *Dnevnik D.A. Miliutina*, II, p. 153.

[69]See notes for 15/27 and 17/29 March 1877 in Brătianu, *Discursuri*, II pt. 2, 537, 548.

[70]Cîmpineanu to Grigore Ghica (Constantinople), 2/14 April 1877, *Corespondenţa generalului Iancu Ghica: 2 aprilie 1877-8 aprilie 1878*, ed. Radu R. Rosetti (Bucureşti, 1930), p. 27.

[71]See Carol's comment to Grand Duke Nikolai's adjutant Georgii I. Bobrikov, 2/14 April 1877, *ALKK*, III, p. 117.

[72]See excerpts from the crown council 1/13 April 1877 in Brătianu, *Discursuri*, II pt. 2, 569-571.

[73]Cîmpineanu to Vienna, 1/13 April 1877, *Charles Ier, Roi de Roumanie*, II, pp. 545-546.

[74]Mihail Kogălniceanu's circular, 4/16 April 1877, Iorga, *Correspondance diplomatique*, p. 192. For the convention of 4/16 April 1877, consult *Charles Ier, Roi de Roumanie*, II, pp. 550-558. Alexandru Cernat became minister of war and Ion G. Ghica went on an "extraordinary mission" to report Romanian interests to the tsar. Kogălniceanu to Gorchakov, 4/16 April 1877, *Documente privind istoria Romîniei*, II, p. 108.

[75]For the political convention of 4/16 April 1877, see *Charles Ier, Roi de Roumanie*, II, pp. 550-551.

[76]For the technical convention of 4/16 April 1877, see *ibid.*, II, pp. 551-558.

[77]Georgii I. Bobrikov, "V Rumynii pered voinoi 1877 g.," *Russkaia Starina*, CL (May, 1912), p. 292.

[78]See Carol's decree of 6/18 April 1877 in *Războiul pentru independenţă naţională, 1877-1878*, eds. Dan Berindei *et al* (Bucureşti, 1971), pp. 105-106.

[79]Kogălniceanu to Ion G. Ghica (Kishinev), 11/23 April 1877, *Independența României: Documente*, IV, 231.

[80]See Kogălniceanu's circular, 5/17 April 1877 in *ibid.*, 221-222.

[81]Savfet Pasha to Mussurus Pasha (London), 4/16 April 1877, *Charles Ier, Roi de Roumanie*, II, p. 559.

[82]Edhem Pasha to Carol, 10/22 April 1877, *ibid.*, p. 577.

[83]See articles 26 and 27 of the Paris treaty of 30 March 1856; *Archives diplomatiques: Recueil de diplomatie et d'histoire*, VI pt. 2 (avril, mai, juin 1866), p. 31; see also article 8 of the Paris convention of 19 August 1858, *ibid.*, XIII pt. 3 (juillet, août, septembre 1873), p. 118.

[84]Kogălniceanu to Edhem Pasha, 11/23 April 1877, *Charles Ier, Roi de Roumanie*, II, pp. 580-581.

[85]Kogălniceanu to Edhem Pasha, 7/19 April 1877, *ibid.*, pp. 563-564.

[86]Kogălniceanu's circular, 5/17 April 1877, *Independența României: Documente*, IV, pp. 221-222.

[87]Carol to Karl Anton, 7/19 April 1877, *ALKK*, III, p. 127.

[88]Kogălniceanu to Ion G. Ghica (Cernauți), 9/21 April 1877, *Documente privind istoria Romîniei*, II, p. 155; Ion G. Ghica (Kishinev) to Kogălniceanu, 10/22 April 1877, *Corespondența generalului Iancu Ghica*, p. 33.

[89]Stuart to Brătianu, 7/19 April 1877, *Charles Ier, Roi de Roumanie*, II, p. 563; Brătianu to minister of finance Gheorghe Cantacuzino, 7/19 April 1877, *Documente privind istoria Romîniei*, II, p. 142. The Chamber of Deputies accepted the funds, 14/26 April 1877, *ibid.*, pp. 228-229.

[90]See decree of 8/20 April 1877, *ibid.*, pp. 148-150.

[91]See notes for 12/24 April 1877 (Kishinev) in: Zaionchkovskii, *Dnevnik D.A. Miliutina*, II, p. 130. The tsar's declaration on 24 April expressed concern for Balkan Christians, *Charles Ier, Roi de Roumanie*, II, pp. 585-587.

[92]For Nikolai's declaration of 12/24 April 1877 (Bucharest), see Narochintskii, *Rossiia i natsional'no-osvoboditel'naia bor'ba na Balkanakh*, pp. 235-236; for Nikolai's announcement of the same date (Kishinev), see *ibid.*, pp. 234-235.

[93]See a decree by council of ministers, 12/24 April 1877 in Brătianu, *Discursuri*, II pt. 2, 593.

[94]Kogălniceanu to Ion G. Ghica, 12/24 April 1877, *Corespondenţa generalului Iancu Ghica*, pp. 37-38.

[95]See note for 13/25 April 1877 in: Zaionchkovskii, *Dnevnik D.A. Miliutina*, II, pp. 158-59; Ion G. Ghica (Kishinev) to Kogălniceanu, 12/24 April 1877, *Independenţa României: Documente*, IV, pp. 233-34; Aleksandr II (Kishinev) to Carol, 13/25 April 1877, *ibid.*, I, p. 59.

[96]Nikolai (Kishinev) to Carol, 14/26 April 1877, *ibid.*, p. 60.

[97]Carol to Nikolai, 17/29 April 1877, *Charles Ier, Roi de Roumanie*, II, pp. 673-674.

[98]Edhem Pasha to Carol, 13/25 April 1877, *ibid.*, p. 602.

[99]Kogălniceanu to Edhem Pasha, 11/23 April 1877, *Independenţa României: Documente*, IV, p. 230.

[100]Savfet Pasha's circular, 13/25 April 1877, *Charles Ier, Roi de Roumanie*, II, p. 601.

[101]Edhem Pasha to Abdul Kerim Pasha, 17/29 April 1877, *ibid.*, pp. 675-676.

[102]Notice from the director-general of post and telegraph to Kogălniceanu, 12/24 April 1877, *Documente privind istoria Romîniei*, II, p. 215.

[103]See section V of the treaty of 21 July 1868 signed at Vienna, *Collectiune de Tratatele şi Conventiunile României cu Puterile Străine*, ed. Mihail Mitilineu (Bucureşti, 1874), p. 138.

[104]See Carol's speech of 14/26 April 1877, *Independenţa României: Documente*, I, p. 62.

[105]See note for 16/28 April 1877 in Brătianu, *Discursuri*, II pt. 2, 608.

[106]Mikhail M. Zalyshkin, *Vneshniaia politika Rumynii i rumyno-russkie otnosheniia, 1875-1878* (Moscow, 1974), pp. 230-232; *Neue Freie Presse* (Vienna), 23 April 1877.

[107]See notes in Brătianu, *Discursuri*, II pt. 2, 619.

[108]For speeches of 17/29 April and 23 April/5 May 1877, see Petre P. Carp, *Discursuri, 1866-1888* (Bucureşti, 1907), I, pp. 129-132, 133-136.

[109]See speech of 16/28 April 1877 in Mihail Kogălniceanu, *Opere*, ed. Dan Simonescu (Bucureşti, 1978), vol. 4, *Oratorie II, 1864-1878*, pt. 4 (1874-1878), ed. Georgeta Penelea, pp. 404, 406, 410, 411-413.

[110]For speeches of 16/28 and 17/29 April 1877, see Brătianu, *Discursuri*, II pt. 2, 616, 619, 622.

[111]For the speech of 20 April/2 May 1877 and the Senate vote (25 to 11), see *ibid.*, 601-606.

[112]Chamber vote of 16/28 April 1877; Senate vote of 17/29 April 1877. Carol approved them on 21 April/3 May 1877. Gorchakov did likewise on 24 April/6 May 1877. The ratifications were exchanged at Bucharest 16/28 May 1877. AMAE(R), Fond Convenţii, dosar 9, pp. 3-100.

THE ENDING OF HOSTILITIES ON THE ROMANIAN FRONT: THE ARMISTICE NEGOTIATIONS AT FOCŞANI, DECEMBER 7-9, 1917

Glenn E. Torrey
Emporia State University

The Bolshevik Revolution of November 1917 was the culminating disaster for Romania's participation in the First World War. Her defeat by the Central Powers in the autumn of 1916 had led to the evacuation of Wallachia and Dobrudja, with the government and what remained of the Romanian army taking refuge in Moldavia under the protective umbrella of almost one million Russian troops. The February Revolution had gradually transformed these allies from an indispensable asset into a pacifist (and even hostile) liability. Nevertheless, the Romanian army, reorganized under the leadership of a French military mission headed by General Henri Berthelot, had fought brilliantly and successfully in the summer of 1917. All this appeared for naught, however, as Lenin called for peace negotiations in November and ordered Russian troops to seek an armistice with the Central Powers.[1]

A direct result of Lenin's orders to seek peace was the decision of the Romanian cabinet on December 4, 1917, to seek an armistice with the Central Powers as well. Although Lenin's authority was not recognized by General D.G. Shcherbachev, the commander of Russian forces on the Romanian front, revolutionary and pacifist currents among his troops forced him on December 3 to ask for independent negotiations with the Central Powers. With the Russian army not only withdrawing from the war, but actually a serious threat to Romanian security through disorder and violence, the government in Iaşi had no feasible alternative but to ask for an armistice.[2] The Central Powers welcomed Romania's willingness to begin the peace process for the same reasons that made Lenin's offer attractive: Austria's internal problems and Germany's desire to liquidate the eastern front in preparation for the upcoming offensive in the west.[3]

While arrangements were being worked out for the formal armistice discussions at Focşani, local truces were arranged along the front. On the Russian sectors, contacts with the enemy were spontaneous, accompanied by much fraternization and even revelry.[4] But the Romanian contacts, for the most part, were limited and restrained, conducted under strict supervision of the Romanian High Command (M.C.G.).[5] Nevertheless, there was evidence of polite, if not friendly, relations, and the reports of Romanian parliamentarians, who crossed the lines at five locations on December 5, are full of warm, human insight into the enemy.

For the Romanian visitors, who had endured privation for most of the war, the strength and comfort of the German positions were impressive. The enemy officers had decorated their rooms with gaily-colored Romanian rugs and they ate to the accompaniment of a small orchestra. They were solicitous of their Romanian guests, offering them food, drink, and pro-German newspapers, all of which were refused. They were extremely generous in their praise of the fighting ability of the Romanian army.[6]

The Romanians observed numerous indications that both men and officers among the enemy welcomed the armistice. At one point, 150 German soldiers cheered the Romanian delegate and one advised him to see that the armistice be of long duration "otherwise we will go to the western front."[7] A Romanian brigade commander visiting the enemy positions found many other indications that the enemy welcomed peace: "One soldier said that they were hungry....A colonel wept before me saying that he had lost two sons in battle....Another colonel complained about the heavy German losses at Mărăşeşti." Nevertheless, the Romanian observer reported that German discipline was strong and the men under the control of their officers.[8]

The Romanian military leaders took extensive measures to minimize the negative effect that the negotiations (and even restricted contact) might have on the discipline and fighting spirit of their own armies. Well acquainted with the example of the Russian army, they forbade Romanian soldiers to discuss the armistice or to gather even in small groups. Officers down to platoon level were ordered to make continual inspections of the trenches to see that the men were in their posts. Any kind of intercourse across the lines with the enemy was to be prevented "at any price." Newspapers thrown over by the enemy were to be burned. Positively, the officers were to explain to their men that the armistice might end at any minute and to appeal to their patriotism to maintain a responsible attitude. Measures of counter-propaganda were set up.[9] Although these orders seemed to have been enforced generally, there were numerous instances of fraternization of a minor nature.[10] The Romanians, who were generally suspicious of the Germans, warmed up to Austrians like the young lieutenant who criticized the Kaiser: "We love the young Emperor Karl, but the wolf of Berlin, who perseveres in continuing the war, we would wring his neck."[11]

The Central Powers, anxious to get the negotiations underway, began to assemble their delegation at Focşani on December 4. The Germans were led by General Curt von Morgen, an army corps commander on the Romanian front, and the Austrians by General Oskar Hranilovici, onetime Austro-Hungarian military attaché in Bucharest.[12] For the Germans, the most important aim was to secure the freedom to transfer troops westward. For the Austrians, it was peace and opening the Danube to food imports.

The Russo-Romanian delegation, numbering about 25, was headed by Russian 9th Army commander, General Anatoli Keltchevskii, and the Romanian vice-chief of staff, General Alexandru Lupescu. They assembled at Tecuci, traveled to Mărăşeşti by special train, then met the Germans on the road to Focşani. Their German hosts were hospitable, even friendly, offering them a "nice lunch" and attempting to turn the meal into an elaborate ceremony. Although their guests reluctantly accepted the lunch, and insisted negotiations begin immediately thereafter, there were the customary toasts. General Lupescu utilized his to emphasize the independence of the Romanian delegation. The Russians' chief objective was to achieve an armistice quickly while the Romanians' desire to end hostilities promptly was tempered by a commitment to aid their western allies by preventing Austro-German troop transfers to the west. General Berthelot, chief of the French military mission, had made it clear that he would consider the latter "a stab in the back" for France.[13]

The dynamics of the sessions were extremely interesting. The Russian delegation, as at Brest-Litovsk, was the chief focus of attention. Its political diversity was reflected in the seating arrangements. General Keltchevskii and his chief of staff, Colonel

Baumgarten, occupied the center position, flanked by the majority socialists, while the Bolsheviks and left socialists were banished to another wing of the table, separated by the Romanians from the other Russians. Although careful to support publicly the Constituent Assembly to which Shcherbachev professed loyalty, Keltchevskii and Baumgarten privately confessed their hope for the return of the monarchy. The representatives of the extreme left were not taken seriously by anyone present. When, on the first day, the Bolshevik delegate tried to speak, Colonel Baumgarten repeatedly cut him off sharply. On the second day, the Bolshevik was "as good as silenced." The dominating Russian personality, according to Austro-German eyewitnesses, was Baron Emanuel von Tizenhausen, a longtime social revolutionary who had experienced Siberian exile several times. They marveled at this mere captain who, by virtue of his position as the provisional government's commissar of the Romanian front, repeatedly contradicted Keltchevskii and forced the general to accept his views "unconditionally."[14] Although Tizenhausen's position was sometimes more favorable to the Central Powers than his superiors', the Austro-Germans had much personal sympathy for the plight of Keltchevskii and Baumgarten. As conservative officers, they understood the latter when he confided that only "the most pressing necessity could have led him to appear in such company."[15] Although the Russians' overriding aim was to achieve peace, on most issues they supported the Romanians and resisted enemy attempts to divide their delegations.[16]

The Austro-Germans also evinced interest in the personnel of the Romanian delegation. In addition to General Lupescu, who was praised as a "modest...simple soldier," it included Colonel Vasile Răşcanu, one-time Romanian military attache in Berlin. They had been expressly instructed to negotiate strictly on military issues and were extremely reserved at first. On the second day, they "warmed up somewhat," as specifically Romanian issues came up. They expressed much bitterness over the "robbery, plundering of every kind" of the Russian "marauders," which was forcing the withdrawal of Romanian regiments from the front to keep order. In commenting on the radical influence of the Russians, Răşcanu remarked, "We still have our own people in hand but only because we blockade ourselves on all sides against the Russians as against the enemy."[17]

The Central Powers also sought to use the Romanian delegation to further their future plans for Romania. Since the Romanian defeat of 1916, they had been seeking to unite the opposition politicians remaining in Bucharest into a coalition which would carry out a *Staatsstreich* (deposing the dynasty, proclaiming a new constitution, and reorienting Romania once again toward Germany and Austria) under German aegis. This policy had floundered on a variety of problems including political and personal incompatibility among the Romanians, rivalry between Austria and Germany, and, most importantly, the failure of the Central Powers to conquer Moldavia. Now, the imminence of peace negotiations made it imperative that the Central Powers consider other options. One, advocated by Alexandru Marghiloman, was to negotiate peace with the present King, a policy bitterly opposed by Petru Carp, who insisted on the King's abdication. In order to assess the attitude of the army toward these solutions, two Romanians, Constantin and Virgil Arion, representing the political camps of Marghiloman and Carp respectively, were sent from Bucharest to Focşani to make contact with the Romanian delegates.[18]

General Lupescu, whom Constantin Arion described as having "the air of a wounded wild animal seeking a hole in which to hide," was reserved, insisting that he could speak only with official enemy delegates.[19] Răşcanu, however, acting "more civilized," spoke with Arion. He emphasized that the King was popular and the Queen "very beloved" and that the army had made it "a point of honor" to defend the dynasty. Arion, reflecting his Romanian patriotism more than his German sympathies, reportedly told Răşcanu "maintain the army and, if you can, occupy Bessarabia."[20]

The Austro-Germans, who had been told in Bucharest that the dynasty was unpopular and the army might be induced to join a *Staatsstreich*, were surprised at what they learned at Focşani. Even Colonel Hentsch, head of the German occupation administration and chief advocate of a *Staatsstreich*, returned to Bucharest admitting that "the generals hold the army in hand" and that it was "loyal to the King."[21] The resolute attitude of the Romanians marks an important step in the evolution of a more realistic attitude on the part of the Germans. It also gave impetus to the Austrians who soon began to support Marghiloman's policy of a reconciliation with Iaşi, a move made easier by a belief that Hentsch's *Staatsstreich* was tied up with his Austrophobia. Hranilovici bragged to the AOK that the Austrian delegation had "paralyzed" Hentsch's influence at Focşani.[22]

By the end of the negotiations, a good deal of rapport had been established among the leaders of the opposing delegations, especially between the Russians and Germans. As Baumgarten bid goodbye to Morgen, he gripped his hand and remarked "I wish for your Excellency that you do not experience in your country and in your army the same conditions that now exist with us."[23] The Germans readily responded to a Russian request for a group photograph involving all the delegations, developing and autographing it on the spot. This photograph proved to be an embarrassment to the Romanian delegates when it became known in Iaşi. The French military mission, which was very sensitive about any Romanian accommodation with the enemy, was "highly disgusted," while some Romanian leaders were indignant and ashamed. It became such a *cause célèbre* that it was discussed in a cabinet meeting and an investigation called for to punish the "guilty ones." However, the minister of war, General Constantin Iancovescu, who if he had been there would have probably posed himself, did not treat the issue so seriously.[24]

The atmosphere of good will that prevailed, plus the fundamental desire of all parties to achieve an armistice, expedited the discussions (although there were several key points of disagreement). The Central Powers, who were in the process of imposing terms favorable for themselves on the hapless Bolsheviks at Brest-Litovsk, first sought to get that agreement recognized on the Russo-Romanian front. But Shcherbachev and the Romanians insisted that they did not recognize the authority of Lenin's government and could have no part in agreements it might sign.[25]

Failing to get their enemies to adhere to conditions agreed on at Brest-Litovsk, the Austro-Germans sought to incorporate a number of its terms into the Focşani agreement. For the Germans, this included a formula allowing considerable freedom to transfer troops to the western front. The Romanians, on the other hand, desirous of protecting their allies, had expressly instructed their delegation to obtain "at any price" a clause prohibiting troop transfers from the Romanian to the French front. Preventing or limiting such transfers was a point of personal and national honor. The Austro-Germans complained among themselves that the Romanians were obstinate, serving exclusively Entente interests. On this and other issues, they attempted to divide the Russians from the Romanians but with little success.[26]

Another point the Germans tried to carry over from the Brest-Litovsk agreement was "freedom of commerce and commercial shipping" on the Black Sea and the Danube. This was of special concern to the Austrians whose need to tap the reputedly rich grain reserves of the Ukraine made this point "pressingly desirable." Whereas the Romanians would have been willing to open up the Danube as far as Galaţi (which they controlled), they were opposed to extending this neutralization to Brăila which would have opened this artery to the Central Powers.[27]

A third provision of Brest-Litovsk that engendered discussion at Focşani was the question of free movement in the neutral zone between the lines. On the basis of their previous success in demoralizing the Russian army through fraternization and propaganda, the Germans had made provision in the armistice with the Russians for such activity to continue and saw an "unconditional necessity" for creating a similar opportunity at Focşani. The Romanians, on the other hand, wanted strict prohibitions on both issues, although their Russian colleagues, having long since lost control over their troops, made no analogous demands. Hranilovici summed up the differing intentions of the negotiators:

> The Russians wish to export socialist ideas into the armies of the Central Powers while the Romanians fear the enlightenment of their men who are kept in complete ignorance of the actual state of affairs. On the one hand, we must strictly supervise the movement of our troops, on the other it is necessary to promote energetically with all means, propaganda among the Romanian troops.[28]

By the evening of December 7, after only a half-day of negotiation, disagreement on the first of these items alone remained. The Germans held to their demand for a liberal wording of the clause on troop transfers, but secretly the Austrian delegation was under orders not to let the negotiations fail on this issue. General Lupescu made a slight move toward a compromise by conceding that up to two divisions could be transferred if they had been so ordered before the suspension of hostilities on December 5. That evening, the negotiations were suspended while General Morgen sought instructions on the issue from his superiors. The Russians returned to their special train at Mărăşeşti, while the Romanians remained at Focşani.[29] No official sessions were held on December 8, but, late that night, Morgen sent Keltchevskii a letter stating that he had received authorization to accept the December 5 cut-off as long as it included up to ten percent of all forces found on the eastern front. In reporting this to the Romanian High Command, Lupescu recommended against the ten percent figure, but suggested raising the permissible transfers from two to four divisions. He pointed out that the Russians were determined to get an armistice at any price. If the enemy did not accept this compromise, he proposed to seek a suspension of hostilities for ten days.[30]

The next day, December 9, the Austro-Germans capitulated on their demand that either the total number be increased or the cut-off date for transfers be extended. They accepted an agreement based on the transfer of troops already under transit orders when hostilities were suspended December 5 and not at the time the agreement was signed (as at Brest-Litovsk). As Hranilovici explained to AOK, "Again it was the Romanians who opposed with such determination [our position]...that it had to be changed to our disfavor." Anyway, he continued, December 5 was acceptable because the German High Command had told Morgen that orders had already gone out for the entire eastern front.[31] The Romanian High Command, which had stood firm against troop transfers, rationalized their concession by arguing that the troops already under orders could be considered no longer existing on the front anyway.[32] Although the Romanians drove a harder bargain than the Russians did at Brest-Litovsk, the restrictions placed on troop transfers were dependent upon self-enforcement and both parties appear to have interpreted them loosely.[33]

In the area of fraternization and propaganda, the Romanians also got their way, essentially. Articles 10-13 established a neutral zone into which entry was forbidden and the sale and consumption of alcohol was banned. They warned the Central Powers that they would not only forbid entry into the neutral zone, but would absolutely prevent it, although in the armistice they promised to make violators prisoners rather than shoot them.[34]

On the third disputed issue, freedom for commerce and commercial shipping on the Black Sea and Danube, both parties agreed to refer the matter to a special commission for continuing negotiation. This commission met in Brăila in January.

In conclusion, it is important to point out the political significance of what was primarily a military agreement. First, the cessation of hostilities freed up the Romanian army to occupy Bessarabia in January 1918. But this was an incidental consequence and not a motive for the armistice as some have maintained.[35] In December, the Romanians were concerned about survival, not expansion.

Second, the experience of the Central Powers at Focşani contributed to a shift in their policy regarding the future of Romania. The Germans, especially, had gone to Focşani with hopes of persuading all or part of the Romanian army to join the Germanophiles, headed by Carp, in a *Staatsstreich*: overturning the dynasty and re-aligning Romania with the Central Powers. They came away from Focşani aware of the popularity of the dynasty and began to consider an accommodation which would leave it on the throne, a policy advocated by Carp's rival, Alexandru Marghiloman. Focşani marks the beginning of a *rapprochement* between Marghiloman and the regime in Iaşi, which led to the former's call to power in March 1918 with a mandate to negotiate peace.[36]

Thirdly, the negotiations at Focşani document the deepening differences and feelings of mistrust that existed between the Austrians and the Germans. The Austrians feared, with good reason, that the Germans intended to demand a Romanian settlement which would slight Austro-Hungarian interests and possibly prolong the war. These differences would be exploited by the Romanians in subsequent peace negotiations.

Finally, Focşani marked the beginning of the estrangement of Romania from her allies. Although Premier Ion Brătianu loudly proclaimed that the negotiations were merely a move to gain time and that he intended to continue the war, Romania marched steadily toward a separate peace. Berthelot, once automatically included in the highest councils, was now ignored. Although the allies temporarily reversed their earlier opposition to the armistice and accepted the *fait accompli* at Focşani, their commitment to support Romania's war aims was seriously weakened.

The negotiations at Focşani, therefore, were not only a chapter in Romania's military operations but also a crucial event in the creation of a greater Romania.

NOTES

[1]On the condition of the Russian army and the impact of Lenin's decision, see Alan Wildman, *The End of the Russian Imperial Army*, Vol. II (Princeton, 1987), especially pp. 350-405.

[2]See Glenn E. Torrey, "Romania Leaves the War: The Decision to Sign an Armistice, December 1917," *East European Quarterly*, XXIII, No. 3 (September 1989), pp. 283-292.

[3]Ingeborg Meckling, *Die Aussenpolitik des Grafen Czernin* (Munich, 1969), pp. 250-254; Andre Scherer and Jacques Grunewald, eds., *L'Allemagne et les problems de la paix*, Vol. III (Paris, 1976), pp. 28, 76.

[4]Kriegsarchiv (Vienna), A.O.K. Fasz. 6283; Wildman, *End of the Russian Imperial Army*, pp. 382-386.

[5]Arhiva Marele Cartier General [M.C.G.] (Bucharest), General Moşoiu to Division 12a, December 5-6, 1917. Kriegsarchiv (Vienna), 1st Armee Kmdo, Fasz. 124, December 2, 4, 5.

[6]Arhiva M.C.G., Report of Captain Dumitrescu, December 5; General Grigorescu to M.C.G., December 6; Report of Captain Andreescu, December 5.

[7]*Ibid.*, Report of Captain Culin, December 5-6.

[8]*Ibid.*, Report of Colonel Vladescu, December 6; Report of Major Trincu, December 11.

[9]*Ibid.*, M.C.G. to Armata II, December 4; Circular Orders of Armata II and Division 12a, December 4, 5, 6, 7.

[10]Kriegsarchiv (Vienna), 1st Armee Kmdo Fasz. 124, December 4, 6, 11, 12.

[11]Arhiva M.C.G., Armata I, Buletin de Informaţie, December 6.

[12]Kriegsarchiv (Vienna), A.O.K., Fasz. 6275 "Verhandlungen in Focşani...Tagebuch."

[13]Arhiva M.C.G., Dosar 34, General Viranovskii to General Prezan, December 14; General Keltchevskii to Shcherbachev, December 7; Ion Gheorghe Duca, *Amintiri politice*, Vol. III (Munich, 1982), p. 19. The Romanian government was simultaneously involved in assuaging Clemenceau's anger on the decision to begin armistice negotiations. See note 2 above.

[14]Kriegsarchiv (Vienna), A.O.K. Ops. Nr. 670/34, Nachrichten offizier (O.K.M.) to A.O.K., December 13.

[15]*Ibid.*, Ops. Nr. 28.

[16]Rudolf Kiszling, "Unterlagen über die österreich Mitwirkung bei den Frieden Verhandlungen mit Rumänien." Manuscript in Kriegsarchiv (Vienna).

[17]Kriegsarchiv (Vienna), A.O.K., Ops. Nr. 28.

[18]Victor Anastasiu, *et al*, *România în primul război mondial* (Bucharest, 1979), pp. 368-374; Alexandru Marghiloman, *Note politice 1897-1924*, Vol. III (Bucharest, 1927), pp. 101, 105, 205, 207-214, 223, 243-244; Kriegsarchiv (Vienna), A.O.K. Ops. Geh. Nr. 525, Hranilovici to A.O.K., December 6.

[19]Marghiloman, *Note politice*, III, pp. 251-252; Kriegsarchiv (Vienna), A.O.K. Ops. Nr. 28, "Gang der Verhandlungen in Focşani, December 7."

[20]*Ibid.*, A.O.K. Ops. Geh. Nr. 531, Hranilovici to A.O.K., December 7; Marghiloman, *Note politice*, III, pp. 251-252.

[21]Kriegsarchiv (Vienna), Ops. Nr. 28; Marghiloman, *Note politice*, III, p. 252.

[22]Kriegsarchiv (Vienna), A.O.K. Fasz. 6275.

[23]Curt von Morgen, *Meiner Truppen Heldenkämpfe* (Berlin, 1920), p. 129.

[24]Duca, *Amintiri politice*, Vol. III, p. 19.

[25]Morgen, *Meiner Truppen Heldenkämpfe*, p. 128; Kriegsarchiv (Vienna), A.O.K. Ops. Geh. Nr. 531, 543; Hranilovici to A.O.K., December 7. Ludendorff at first appears to have thought of getting Shcherbachev to recognize the agreement at Brest-Litovsk and then negotiate a separate agreement with the isolated Romanians. Confusion on this issue continued for some time. *Ibid.*, Ops. Nr. 437, 440, 508; Ludendorff to A.O.K., November 22, 24, December 12. Texts of agreements reached at Brest-Litovsk and at Focşani can be found in: Austria, Kriegsarchiv, *Oesterreich-Ungarns Letzter Krieg 1914-1918*, Vol. VI (Vienna, 1936), pp. 762-769.

[26]Paul Oprescu, "Interuperea operaţiilor militare pe frontul românesc (noiembrie 1917-martie 1918) şi relaţiile României cu aliaţii," *Studii şi Materiale de Istorie Modernă*, Vol. VI, pp. 159-180. Kriegsarchiv (Vienna), A.O.K., Ops. Nr. 28.

[27]*Ibid.*, A.O.K. Fasz. 6275. Hranilovici to A.O.K., no date; *Ibid.*, A.O.K. to Mackensen, December 12.

[28]The Austro-Germans wanted freedom to allow propaganda officers, not their troops, to cross the lines. *Ibid.*, Foerster to A.O.K., December 8; Hranilovici to A.O.K., no date. On the previous success the Germans had experienced with the Russian army, see Gerhard Wettig, "Die Rolle der russischen Armee in revolutionaeren Machtkampf," *Forschungen zur Ostereuropäischen Geschichte*, Vol. XII [1967], pp. 264ff. and Alan Wildman, *The End of the Russian Imperial Army*, Vol. I (Princeton, 1980), pp. 346-362, Vol. II (1987), pp. 383ff.

[29]Apparently this lull in the negotiations gave opportunity for the unofficial conversations between the Romanian delegates and the emissaries from Bucharest mentioned above. See Vasile Liveanu, "Armistiţiul de la Focşani" (1917), *Studii: Revista de Istorie*, Vol. VII (4), October-December 1954, p. 130, note 6.

[30]Arhiva M.C.G., Dosar 34, Lupescu to M.C.G., December 8, 9. Kriegsarchiv (Vienna), A.O.K. Ops. Geh. Nr. 531, 543; Hranilovici to A.O.K., December 7, 9; *Ibid.*, A.O.K. Fasz. 6275; A.O.K. to Hranilovici, December 8.

[31]*Ibid.*, Hranilovici to A.O.K., December 9; *Ibid.*, Hranilovici to A.O.K., no date; Kiszling, "Friedens Verhandlungen mit Rumänien."

[32]Arhiva M.C.G., Dosar 34, Prezan to Lupescu, December 9; Antonescu to Lupescu, December 9.

[33]Kriegsarchiv (Vienna), Fasz. 6275, Hranilovici to A.O.K., no date. This point is made forcefully by Liveanu, "Armistiţiul de la Focşani," p. 137. However, Liveanu is wrong in portraying the Brest-Litovsk wording on troop transfers as more restrictive than the Focşani formula.

[34]Kriegsarchiv (Vienna), Fasz. 6275, Hranilovici to A.O.K., no date.

[35]Vasile Liveanu, *1918. Din istoria luptelor revoluţionare din România* (Bucharest, 1960), p. 163.

[36]See Glenn Torrey, "Alexandru Marghiloman of Romania: A War Leader" in Béla K. Király, ed., *East Central European War Leaders: Civilian and Military* (New York, 1988), pp. 100ff.

EVOLVING SOVIET VIEWS OF THE NAZI-SOVIET PACT

Teddy J. Uldricks
University of North Carolina at Asheville

The Nazi-Soviet Pact has sparked intense controversy ever since it was signed on 23 August 1939. Since 1934, the USSR had championed the cause of collective security against fascist aggression. The Nazi-Soviet Pact signaled not only the failure of this effort, but also the abandonment of the anti-German course which the USSR had pursued for six years.[1] Although not entirely unforeshadowed, the pact came as a shock to most observers.

This dramatic reversal in foreign policy transformed the USSR from the champion of anti-fascism into a virtual ally of Nazi Germany. Accompanied by unpublished secret protocols which divided all of eastern Europe into Soviet and German spheres of interest, the pact freed Hitler to destroy Poland without fear of provoking a disastrous two-front war. Moreover, a series of Russo-German economic accords largely insulated the Third Reich from the most powerful weapon which the western Allies brought to bear against Germany--economic blockade. When Soviet troops breached Poland's eastern border on 17 September, the USSR, in effect, joined the Nazi attack. Ultimately, the USSR became so intertwined with Nazi aggression that Stalin considered joining the Axis, while the western Allies planned to attack the Soviet Union.

Stalin was anxious, however, to mask his cooperation with Hitler. Given the Marxist, internationalist pretensions of the USSR and its recent leadership of the anti-fascist campaign, revelation of the degree to which Nazi-Soviet collaboration had developed would have been highly embarrassing. Although the economic, non-aggression, and border treaties were published, the various sets of supplementary protocols were kept strictly secret. The outside world, the Soviet public, and even much of the Kremlin elite remained ignorant about the extent of the collusion between Stalin and Hitler. The details of this quasi-alliance were worked out personally by Stalin and Molotov, without the participation of either the Politburo or the Commissariat of Defense. Moreover, the protocols were never submitted to the Politburo for approval or to the Soviet government for ratification. Also, unlike the non-aggression treaty itself, which was processed in the normal way, the secret protocols were neither registered in the International Treaties and Agreements Section of the Commissariat of Foreign Affairs nor deposited in its archives. Instead, the original and copies of the protocols were apparently kept in Molotov's office safe.[2] While there may have been hushed Kremlin rumors about a Russo-German arrangement more elaborate than the published treaties, no one in the USSR could quote, cite, or even acknowledge the existence of the secret protocols. This unwritten rule continued in effect long after Stalin's death. The Germans, too, kept the various protocols secret. The entire diplomatic staff of the German embassy in Moscow was required to sign a pledge never to mention the protocols.[3]

Stalin still defended the political correctness of having signed the Nazi-Soviet Pact, even after Hitler betrayed him by attacking the Soviet Union on 22 June 1941: "What did we gain by concluding the non-aggression pact with Germany? We secured our country peace for a year and a half, and the opportunity of preparing its forces to repulse Fascist Germany should she risk an attack on our country despite the pact."[4] Although he still justified the pact, Stalin now had more reason than ever to suppress the secret protocols. With the USSR fighting alongside the western democracies as part of the Grande Alliance against Axis tyranny, the existence of a cynical, territorial deal with Hitler was an inconvenient fact best left hidden. Of course, Soviet occupation of parts of Finland, the Baltic states, eastern Poland and parts of Romania--unopposed and uncondemned by Berlin--was a strong indication that the two dictators had worked out some sort of territorial division of eastern Europe. Yet, with both Moscow and Berlin hiding the existence of their former collaboration, Stalin could still deny that an unsavory deal had ever been struck.

While the war lasted, the western powers were not disposed to seek incriminating evidence against their Soviet ally. Instead, the governments and most of the press in the democratic states strove to project a positive image of the USSR. The breakdown of the Grande Alliance after the defeat of Germany and the onset of the Cold War changed all that. In the western campaign to transform the image of the USSR from valiant ally to dastardly foe, identification with the hated Nazi enemy proved the most effective technique. The theory of totalitarianism, suddenly popular among politicians, the press, and the academic community, served that function well. It seemed to demonstrate that German fascism and Soviet communism, far from being polar opposites, were essentially the same detestable phenomenon.[5] Nazi-Soviet cooperation became an important element in western Cold War propaganda.

It was in this context that one of Molotov's assistants destroyed the original Russian language version of the secret protocols in 1946. The original German language version of the secret protocols held by the Auswärtiges Amt had been destroyed at Ribbentrop's order shortly before the end of the war. Accompanying maps, with the signatures of Stalin and Ribbentrop on them, survived, however. Copies of the protocols were preserved in safe, remote, underground storage. There they were uncovered by American and British troops advancing through Germany in 1945. The first public mention of the secret protocols came in 1946 at the Nuremberg trials of Nazi war criminals. The German copies which had fallen into western hands were leaked to the defense. The attorney for Rudolf Hess introduced the protocols, over vigorous Soviet objection, in an attempt to disrupt the trials by provoking a conflict among the Allied prosecutors and justices. Although this tactic did not succeed in wrecking the Nuremberg trials, the disclosure led the following day (22 May 1946) to publication of the full text of the secret protocols in the *St. Louis Post Dispatch*.[6]

In 1948, as part of its on-going effort to discredit the USSR, the United States government published a full volume of documents, *Nazi-Soviet Relations, 1939-1941*, which contained English translations of the German versions of all the various sets of secret protocols, as well as much other incriminating material on Russo-German collaboration.[7] The editors opened the collection with the record of a meeting between the Soviet ambassador in Berlin, Aleksei Merekalov, and German State Secretary, Baron von Weizsäcker on 17 April 1939. This memorandum seemed to suggest that the Nazi-Soviet Pact was not a regrettable second choice for which Stalin opted after years of rebuff by the West, but rather a deal which the Soviets initiated and pursued aggressively.

The publication of *Nazi-Soviet Relations* was a bombshell in the Cold War. The Kremlin's angry retort testified to how deeply it had been wounded. That response took the form of a highly polemical, alternative interpretation of the roles played by the western powers and the Soviet Union in the origins of World War II. This 61 page pamphlet, entitled *Falsificators of History*, established an official Kremlin version of international affairs in the 1930s.[8] Hundreds of subsequent Soviet works would expand upon and embellish it, but they would not depart from it.

The official version of pre-war diplomacy drew its inspiration from the previously expressed views of the Kremlin leaders. Stalin, addressing the 18th Congress of the Communist Party in March of 1939, had advanced the theory that the policy of appeasement, pursued by Britain and France and supported by the United States, was in fact an anti-Soviet conspiracy designed to embroil the USSR and the Third Reich in a mutually debilitating war, while the western powers remained unscathed.[9] Similarly, in presenting the treaty to the Supreme Soviet on 31 August 1939, Molotov and A. S. Shcherbakov accused the western powers of merely having feigned interest in cooperating with the USSR to prevent aggression, while, behind the scenes, they really sought to provoke a Russo-German war.[10]

According to *Falsificators of History*, from 1933 to 1939 the Soviet Union attempted to build a European-wide framework of collective security against the threat of German aggression. It pursued that policy with single-minded determination, without deviation or exception. Pursuit of this objective was a matter not merely of Russian national interest, but of the highest moral principle. In contrast, Great Britain, France, and the United States fostered the rise of Hitler, facilitated the rearmament of the Third Reich, and colluded in the launching of Nazi aggression. In this view, "...Anglo-French policy was aimed not at mustering the forces of the peace-loving states for a common struggle against aggression, but at isolating the USSR and directing the Hitlerite aggression toward the East, against the Soviet Union, at using Hitler as a tool for their own ends."[11]

Thus, the real goal of western appeasement was to deflect German expansion toward the homeland of socialism. The Munich deal, whereby the western imperialists sacrificed Czechoslovakia to Nazi rapacity in order to channel the tide of war toward the Soviet

Union, exposed this cynical policy in its most brutal form. While the western powers subsequently made a show of negotiating with Moscow for an anti-German defensive alliance, they were never sincere in this endeavor. They only wanted to prolong talks with Moscow in order to pressure Hitler into another agreement like the one signed at Munich. The authors of *Falsificators of History* recounted with particular indignation the secret Anglo-German negotiations which were going on while the Anglo-French delegation was stalling the military talks in Moscow. Soviet leaders were under great pressure to find some means to enhance Soviet security, since it was clear that war would soon erupt in Europe and there was also some danger of a Japanese attack on Soviet territory in the Far East. Therefore, given the duplicitous western policy of conniving at German aggression, the Soviet Union had no choice but to sign a non-aggression pact with the Third Reich. This step prevented the formation of a coalition uniting all the major imperialist powers against the USSR, it avoided the immediate outbreak of a war in which Soviet Russia would have to fight Nazi Germany single-handedly, and it provided a breathing space for the further improvement of Soviet defenses.[12]

Missing from *Falsificators of History* is any reference to surreptitious Soviet contacts with Germany during the collective security campaign. At various times, Soviet emissaries Karl Radek, David Kandelaki, and Sergei Bessonov secretly explored the possibilities of a *rapprochement* with Berlin. There was no room, however, for such troubling details in an account which stressed the unilinear and "principled" nature of the Kremlin's foreign policy. Similarly, there was no analysis of factors which made the USSR a less attractive alliance partner for the West. The effect of the recent purge of the Red Army officer corps on western evaluations of Soviet military potential was ignored, as was the impact of Soviet irredentist claims on Polish and Romanian territory. There was also no discussion, or even any mention, of the secret protocols to the non-aggression pact. Scattered throughout the text, however, were references to "forgers," "documents which are one-sided and tendentious, giving an account of events from the Hitler Government," and "all sorts of memoranda and German drafts of some sort of 'protocols' and other similar 'documents.'"[13] However, it is certainly significant that at no point in the pamphlet is the existence of the secret protocols explicitly denied; they are simply ignored and their existence denied only by inference and circumlocution. This treatment set the precedent for all subsequent Soviet publications up to 1988. Most Soviet discussions of the diplomacy of the 1930s completely ignore the issue of the secret protocols. A few of them cast doubt on the validity of the protocols published by the United States, stating that no such documents have ever been found in Soviet archives.

Publication of *Falsificators of History* was supplemented by the appearance of the two-volume collection, *Documents and Materials Relating to the Eve of the Second World War*.[14] In contrast to *Nazi-Soviet Relations*, published by the United States, this collection focused on German relations with Britain and France, especially highlighting the Munich agreement. The documents obviously were selected to demonstrate that it was the western powers, not the USSR, which had contributed materially to the launching of German aggression. The volumes were composed entirely of captured German documents; they contained no material from Soviet archives.

Besides bringing an end to the pervasive Stalinist Terror, the Khrushchev era also brought higher standards of scholarship, and the partial opening of some previously closed historical subjects. Those years also saw the reemergence, albeit still in a tight Marxist-Leninist framework, of the serious, academic study of contemporary international relations and diplomatic history.[15] In his well-known "secret speech" to the 20th Party Congress in 1956, the new Soviet leader exposed Stalin's crimes against the party in the Great Purges and also his deficiencies as a wartime leader.[16] Yet, while the dictator's domestic policy in the 1930s was pilloried, his foreign policy remained immune to critical examination, and the practice of pretending the secret protocols never existed continued as before. This reflected Khrushchev's intent that the "destalinization" campaign be kept in very strict bounds to avoid any harm to the image of the Soviet state and the Communist Party. It also indicated Khrushchev's personal acceptance of the official line.[17] Khrushchev apparently had some private doubts about the propriety and prudence of seizing territory from Finland, the Baltic states,

Poland, and Romania while in quasi-alliance with the Third Reich, but he never voiced these misgivings while in power. The following remarks were even deleted from the memoirs sent to the West for publication. They were published only after the advent of *glasnost'*:

> Hitler had lured Stalin into a trap, enticing him to seize the land of others while Hitler prepared for his major goal: to attack the Soviet Union and annihilate the Slavs. Many historical factors, today evaluated in different ways, came together to cause the Soviet Union to make its pact with Hitler. It was not a pact made out of logic or good sense, but rather out of necessity.[18]

At one point, Khrushchev apparently planned to sponsor a somewhat more thorough examination of Soviet foreign policy in the 1930s. Evgenii Gnedin, who had been First Secretary at the Soviet embassy in Berlin and subsequently a press officer at the Commissariat of Foreign Affairs in the 1930s, was commissioned in 1962 to prepare a report for the Central Committee on relations between the USSR and the Third Reich. This politically motivated report was to focus on the "miscalculations and mistakes" of Viacheslav Molotov. But, the project was soon aborted and Gnedin's mandate to reassess the collective security policy was canceled.[19] Gnedin continued the investigation on his own, though without access to Soviet archives. He concluded that Stalin actually ran two foreign policies simultaneously. Through Litvinov and the Foreign Commissariat, he sought to recreate a Triple Alliance with Britain and France in the well-advertised collective security campaign. At the same time, operating through Molotov and using several non-diplomatic operatives (Radek, Kandelaki, and Bessonov), he tried secretly to build a partnership with the Third Reich. This second approach was kept hidden even from Litvinov and most of the Soviet elite. Gnedin suggested that Stalin was an "opportunist" who saw little distinction between the fascist states and the Anglo-French "bandits." In this view, collective security was not the only, and perhaps not even the primary, foreign policy of the USSR. Unfortunately, Gnedin's reconstruction of Stalin's policies is as conjectural as it is fascinating.[20]

Gnedin raised two vitally important issues which are largely ignored in the official Soviet historiography--foreign policy factionalism and the policy-making process. There is no hint in any Soviet accounts of the collective security policy that there may well have been contradictory views among the Soviet elite about the policy itself as well as about its implementation. Moreover, the process of foreign policy formulation is not discussed in Soviet works. Instead, inevitably correct policies simply seem to emerge automatically from a monolithic party-state structure so in tune with the march of history that trial and error, misperception, and human eccentricity never intrude on the process.

In contrast to Gnedin's dissident voice, the first volume of the official, six-volume Soviet history of the Second World War, which appeared in 1960, was typical of Khrushchev-era historiography. Its editors attempted to repair the political damage to the image of the USSR done by the *Nazi-Soviet Relations* revelations by claiming the idea of secret protocols had been purely a German initiative which was rejected out-of-hand by Moscow. In this version, Ribbentrop suggested to Georgi Astakhov, Soviet Chargé in Berlin, on 3 August 1939 a "secret Soviet-German protocol which would delineate the interests of both powers along the entire area from the Black Sea to the Baltic." According to the editors, this unprincipled offer was rebuffed.[21]

Soviet historians were seriously handicapped by lack of access to Soviet archives and the absence of a published Soviet diplomatic document series. Such a series, *Dokumenty vneshnei politiki SSSR*, was begun in 1957. Its editors declared in the first volume that they intended to provide material for an accurate and objective assessment of Soviet diplomacy because "the foreign policy of the Soviet state has become the subject of countless falsifications in bourgeois countries...."[22] However, documents which the authorities feared would not depict the USSR in a properly heroic light were omitted from the collection or appeared in censored form.[23] The series, which began with documents from the time of the Bolshevik revolution in 1917, never reached the 1930s during Khrushchev's tenure in power.

One significant set of documents was published in Khrushchev's time. In 1959, Soviet records of the August 1939 British-French-Soviet military negotiations appeared in the journal *Mezhdunarodnaia zhizn'*. British records of these same talks had been available since 1954. The Soviet editors discounted the British documents as "abridged and tendentious." The introduction to these Soviet records advanced the view that the Soviet delegation worked sincerely to cement a mighty East-West alliance which would have stopped Hitler, while the Anglo-French representatives merely sought to drag out the talks and avoid any concrete commitments.[24]

The fall of Khrushchev in 1964 and the consolidation of the Brezhnev regime marked a retreat from the previous emphasis on reform and destalinization. Yet the trend toward elaborating a more sophisticated historiography of the origins of World War II and the publication of more archival material continued unabated.[25] The official interpretation of the collective security policy and the Nazi-Soviet Pact did not change at all. According to the authoritative *History of Soviet Foreign Policy*, co-authored by then Foreign Minister Andrei Gromyko:

> When the nazis seized power in Germany, the threat of another world war became very real in Europe. However, at the time it was still possible to avert fascist aggression through the concerted efforts of countries desiring peace. Had the Soviet proposals for collective security been put into effect it would have been possible to erect a powerful barrier to any aggressor....But this project was wrecked by the joint efforts of the fascist states and Poland with British encouragement....In this atmosphere the Soviet Union never for a moment relinquished its efforts to create a system of collective security.[26]

The monographic literature added details but did not alter the basic line laid down in this textbook, namely that the Nazi-Soviet Pact was necessitated by the grim threat of a two-front war against both Germany and Japan and by the preference of the western powers to cooperate with Hitler rather than the USSR. The secret protocols are ignored or denied in each of these works.[27] Soviet historians even argued that the Nazi-Soviet Pact was good for the world communist movement in that it ensured the preservation of the movement's one secure bastion, the USSR.[28] Aleksandr Nekrich, who with V.M. Khvostov, wrote *Kak voznikla vtoraia mirovaia voina* [How the Second World War Occurred], which followed the official line exactly, later emigrated and admitted the constraints under which he and his colleagues operated:

> Although the book was devoted to the origins of the Second World War, we avoided a discussion of one of the most important questions: the role of the Soviet-German Pact of 1939 in unleashing the war. This question was and is the most delicate point of Soviet historiography. None of the Soviet historians dared at that time to transgress the boundary of what was allowed....Had we tried to do so our manuscript would never have been published.[29]

Although the overall interpretation of the origins of the Second World War did not change significantly after Brezhnev rose to power, the official line was elaborated with greater refinement and its documentary basis was substantially augmented. For example, Soviet scholars began to notice some difference between the French and British positions at the Moscow military negotiations in August of 1939. They also examined western proposals for a new Triple Alliance in greater detail to uncover the inequitable burden the USSR would have borne in such an arrangement.

The *Dokumenty vneshnei politiki SSSR* series finally reached the 1930s, providing a large number of important, but previously unavailable, items from Soviet archives. The documents published supported the official interpretation of Soviet collective security policy and of the western powers' failure to cooperate with the USSR against aggression. Unfortunately, the editors omitted any documents pertaining to the covert Nazi-Soviet contacts involving Kandelaki, Radek, or Bessonov. Moreover, after publishing a volume every year from 1957 to 1977, the series suddenly stopped with volume XXI (1938) without explanation. The volume for the pivotal year of 1939 has never appeared.[30] This defect was partially remedied by the publication of *SSSR v bor'be za mir nakanune vtori mirovoi voiny (sentiabr' 1938g.--avgust 1939g.): Dokumenty i materialy*.[31] This collection contained many new and useful documents, but they too were selected in order to expose the western powers' collusion with Hitler and their failure to cooperate with the USSR. The evolution of Nazi-Soviet relations in 1939 is largely missing from these volumes. A second edition of *Dokumenty i materialy kanuna vtoroi mirovoi voiny* was even more disappointing.[32] It contained no new Soviet documents.

The Brezhnev years also saw the publication of several memoirs by Soviet diplomats. Best known is the work of Soviet ambassador in London, Ivan Maiskii. In his view, "the stubborn sabotage by the Governments of Chamberlain and Daladier prevented the conclusion on the eve of the war of a triple pact of mutual assistance by the USSR, Britain, and France--the only measure which could have hindered Hitlerite aggression and prevented Germany's attack on Poland."[33] Of course, none of the Soviet memoirists discussed, or even mentioned, the secret protocols to the Nazi-Soviet Pact, though Maiskii made one carefully veiled reference to them.[34]

Soviet historians in research institutes and universities have been constrained to support the official interpretation of the Nazi-Soviet Pact and the broader Russo-German relationship. Two other groups of Soviet writers--defectors and dissidents--have largely escaped these constraints. Some defectors have claimed that Stalin never intended to ally with the western democracies against Hitler. In this view, the whole collective security campaign was nothing more than an attempt to frighten Hitler with the prospect of an anti-German East-West alliance and thereby gain some leverage in negotiating with Berlin. Stalin's real goals were to gain territory in eastern Europe and to undermine the capitalist societies by pitting the fascist powers and the democracies against each other in a highly destructive war. Abdurakhman Avtorkhanov, a party bureaucrat who defected in 1943, believes that the dictator's speech to the 18th party congress in March of 1939 "reveals Stalin's own hidden intention of provoking a war between Germany and democratic powers, allowing them to become exhausted in a mutually destructive war so that he himself could march in when it was all over...and impose on them his peace conditions."[35] The defector literature is not united in this interpretation, however. Other defectors, though equally hostile to the Stalin regime, express no doubts about the sincerity of the collective security and Popular Front strategies.[36]

Roy Medvedev, the leading dissident historian in the Brezhnev era, justified the pact as unavoidable:

> The nonaggression pact between Germany and the Soviet Union was not the best solution for either the Soviet Union or the forces favoring peace in the world. A collective-security treaty among all the antifascist powers would have been far preferable, but the United States was keeping its distance from European affairs, while England and France were playing an insecure and dangerous political game. They dragged out the negotiations with the Soviet Union while holding secret talks with Germany, still hoping that Germany would direct its aggression eastward....I do not intend to justify Stalin's entire policy. I have already shown how he obstructed a united front in Germany, decimated the comintern, dissolved the Polish Communist Party, killed the best Red Army commanders. All this greatly facilitated Hitler's drive to war. But the nonaggression pact should not be added to this list of Stalin's errors and crimes.[37]

Medvedev does mention the secret Russo-German contacts prior to 1939, which he characterizes as "reconnaissance," and he readily admits the existence of the secret protocols. These he defends as "a natural extension of that pact."[38]

Mikhail Gorbachev came to power in 1985 determined to pick up the mantle of reform wrenched from Khrushchev's hands two decades earlier. He did not initially intend to destroy the whole framework of the Marxist-Leninist polity. Yet, once the door to reform was thrown wide open and the muzzle of repression taken off the Soviet people, not even Gorbachev could control the explosive process of transformation loosed in the USSR.

As part of his attempt to end the Cold War, Gorbachev introduced a doctrinal revision which had great potential impact on specialists in international affairs and diplomatic history:

> ...with the emergence of the weapons of mass, that is, universal destruction, there appeared an objective limit for class confrontation in the international arena: the threat of universal destruction. For the first time there appeared a real, not speculative and remote, common human interest--to save humanity from disaster...we deemed it no longer possible to retain in [the Communist Party Program] the definition of peaceful coexistence of states with different social systems as a "specific form of class struggle."[39]

The implication is clear. If there are universal human interests which supersede class interests, then there can also be a level of analysis (of foreign affairs, for example) which transcends a narrower class-based viewpoint.

Gorbachev did not intend, however, to dredge up episodes from the 1930s which would embarrass the USSR. When challenged by British Prime Minister Margaret Thatcher about the Soviet Union's role in opposing Nazism before 1941, he:

> objected, reminding her that the Soviet Union had fought against fascism politically from 1933 and, from 1936, with arms too. As for the non-aggression pact with Germany (whose meaning is constantly being distorted by our opponents), it could have been avoided, as could many other things, if the ruling circles of Britain and France had agreed to cooperate with the Soviet Union against the aggressor at that time.[40]

The official line of *Falsificators of History* was still in place and the secret protocols still lay deeply buried. That continuity was reflected in the new edition of the official *Istoriia vneshnei politiki SSSR* which appeared in 1986 without a substantial revision of its account of the origins of the war or mention of the protocols.[41]

History has always been a political weapon in the Soviet Union. It was inevitable, then, that such sensitive moments in the Soviet past as the Nazi-Soviet pact should become issues in the struggle for and against reform in the 1980s.[42] Reformist historian Iurii Afanas'ev warned in 1985 that the myth-laden official historiography was a powerful barrier to *perestroika*, while the poet Evgenii Evtushenko decried all of the "blank spots" in Soviet history.[43] Gorbachev, after some initial reticence, joined the call to fill in some of those blank spots. A ferocious debate developed in 1987 and 1988 between traditionalist and reform-minded historians, mainly over such domestic issues as the ideas of Nikolai Bukharin and the collectivization of the peasantry.

In contrast, *glasnost'* seemed to have little initial effect on the writing of diplomatic history. In a book on Soviet foreign policy from 1936 to 1939, published in 1987, Vilnis Sipols, a leading Soviet diplomatic historian, departed only a short way from the orthodoxy of *Falsificators of History*. Sipols blamed the failure of East-West cooperation entirely on the western powers whose overriding goal, he claimed, was "the annihilation of Soviet independence itself."[44] He did admit that the weakening of the Soviet officer corps by the purges (which he euphemistically called "removal from their posts"!) hindered collaboration between Moscow and the West. However, even this was the fault of western anti-communists whose "class hatred" caused them to exaggerate the importance of the "removals."[45] The Nazi-Soviet Pact was forced on the USSR by western duplicity and, of course, there was no mention of the secret protocols. Thus, while specialists in Soviet political history were debating openly such controversial issues as the rehabilitation of Bukharin and even Trotskii, foreign affairs writers still clung passively to the old line.

Finally, the resurgence of nationalism in the Baltic republics of the USSR accomplished what traditionalist senior historians had been unwilling to do--provoke an open and frank discussion of

Soviet foreign policy in the 1930s, including the Nazi-Soviet Pact and even the heretofore unmentionable secret protocols. Nationalist forces in Lithuania, Latvia and Estonia saw the secret protocols of August and September 1939 as the key to their forcible absorption into the USSR and therefore demanded that those protocols be exposed and "repealed." These demands first surfaced in all three Baltic capitals on 23 August 1987, the forty-eighth anniversary of the infamous pact.[46] Subsequently, on 9 October 1987, the Polish journal, *Zycie Literackim*, published the protocols for the first time ever within the Soviet bloc. There was speculation that Gorbachev would open the subject for public discussion by disclosing the protocols at the seventieth anniversary celebrations of the Bolshevik revolution, but his speech contained only the standard defense of the Nazi-Soviet Pact and no mention of the protocols.

Almost a year later, on 20 August 1988, the protocols were finally published in the Soviet Union by the Lithuanian writers' union weekly, *Literatura ir menas*. Then they were reprinted by the Vilnius-based Russian language journal, *Vestnik litovskogo dvizheniia za perestroiku*. On August 23, the protocols were a focal point of massive demonstrations in the three Baltic capitals. In Tallinn, Soviet historian Iurii Afanas'ev declared the protocols to be authentic and readily admitted that they had been instrumental in the subversion of Estonia's independence. "In no other country," he proclaimed, "has history been falsified to such a degree as in the Soviet Union. Every school child in the West knows about these protocols, but we still deny them...."[47] At an even larger rally in Vilnius, Lithuanian historian, Liudas Truska, told the audience: "Enough of acting as if the [protocols] did not exist!...As a historian, I am ashamed that for so long we did not tell the public the entire truth, at times less than half, and that is the biggest lie."[48] If the secret protocols and the evil effects of Russo-German collaboration were now front page news in the Baltic republics, the commotion was virtually ignored by the state-controlled press in the rest of the USSR.

Much of the scholarly community in the Baltic republics was soon busy demolishing the official line. For example, historian Heino Arumäe of the Academy of Sciences of the Estonian SSR, writing in a mass circulation newspaper in 1988, denied that the Nazi-Soviet Pact was signed only because the western powers failed to cooperate with Moscow to check German aggression. In striking contrast to a staple theme of the official interpretation, he contended that "there is no way to claim that London and Paris wanted to provoke war by directing Germany against Poland and then against the USSR."[49] Instead, Arumäe argued strongly that Stalin preferred to ally with Hitler and provoke war in 1939 in order to pursue aggressive territorial ambitions in the Baltic and throughout eastern Europe.[50]

Despite attempts by the regime to prevent the spread of this heresy, the controversy soon swept throughout the Soviet intelligentsia. Revisionist and traditionalist views vied with each other not just in specialist journals, but also on the pages of such widely read periodicals as *Literaturnaia gazeta*. Viacheslav Dashichev attacked the official line, arguing that Soviet foreign policy in the 1930s was fundamentally deformed by Stalin's expansionist ambitions.[51] Mikhail Semiriaga targeted the core of the traditional interpretation that the USSR had no choice but to sign the Nazi-Soviet Pact because the West refused to negotiate in good faith. Semiriaga countered:

> It is true that the talks proceeded with difficulty in a zigzag fashion, but they nonetheless did proceed, and this flickering flame had to be maintained come what may. It was at this complex moment that the Soviet leaders lost their sense of realism and restraint. They ostentatiously signed the fatal pact with Germany, which essentially meant the rejection of further talks with Britain and France. In the spring and summer of 1939 the Soviet leadership acted sensibly, maintaining contact with the western powers and with Germany, and keeping both doors open. But unfortunately it shut the wrong door....That Hitler was in such a hurry to sign the pact meant that the other side should have, conversely, taken time to think about the motives for this haste and should have displayed the utmost caution....[52]

Three weeks later Semiriaga's view was counterattacked on the pages of the same journal. Aleksandr Orlov and Stephan Tiushkevich, both of the Institute of Military History of the USSR Ministry of Defense, denied that there was a realistic alternative to signing the pact with Germany. If the USSR had held back from that course as Semiriaga suggested, the western states still would not have come to terms with Moscow and Nazi aggression would not have been checked.[53] A.S. Iakushevskii also defended the pact on the traditional grounds of western failure to cooperate, arguing that the pact therefore kept the USSR out of a two-front war in 1939, prevented the formation of a German-British-French alliance directed against the Soviet Union, gave the country two more years to further shore up its defenses, and created a basis for the Grande Alliance which had not existed in 1939.[54] (The last point strains the credulity of even the most sympathetic reader!)

In sharp contrast, two historians at the Academy of Sciences, Institute of the USA and Canada condemned the whole approach to the study of Soviet diplomacy which undergirded the official line. "We are working," they proclaimed, "to do away with the sad legacy of simplistic ideologized approaches, excessive secrecy, propagandistic self-admiration and self-deception."[55] Historian Vitaly Kulish published an important examination of foreign policy disagreements during the early 1930s within the Kremlin elite in *Komsomolskaia pravda*.[56] Stalin, Molotov, Voroshilov, and Malenkov feared a general "capitalist encirclement" and viewed the Nazis as only one element of this larger threat, while Bukharin, Litvinov, and Tukhachevskii saw Nazism as especially dangerous and therefore advocated an alliance with the West. Munich, Kulish suggested, undermined the credibility of this second line of analysis. Dmitrii Volkogonov, the author of the first serious, non-hagiographic Soviet biography of Stalin, defended the pact as an unavoidable necessity, but criticized Stalin for letting the secret protocols drag the USSR into complicity with Hitler.[57] Moreover, such hitherto banned dissidents as Roy Medvedev were now allowed to publish their critical views of Stalin's diplomacy in major historical journals.[58] The debate over the Soviet role in the origins of the war continued to swirl. In a round table discussion published by *Voprosy istorii*, one of the participants actually introduced the text of the secret protocols, and thus made them public, in Russian, for all Soviet readers.[59]

A recent volume, *1939: Lessons of History*, gives some indications of the extent and the limits of the "new thinking" among mainstream, senior Soviet historians.[60] Published in 1989, it consists of articles by a number of leading specialists from the Institute of World History of the Soviet Academy of Sciences and the Institute of Military History of the USSR Ministry of Defense. This book would have been a great step forward if it had appeared in 1984, but it does not fully reflect the tide of sweeping historical reassessment unleashed in subsequent years. In the introduction and most of the chapters, the analysis of the rise of Nazism and the general causes of the Second World War strictly follows the Leninist model of politics in the era of imperialism. These sections could just as well have been written under Brezhnev or even under Stalin. However, most of the authors are willing to admit that Stalin's "crimes" (especially the Great Purges) "undermined confidence in the USSR, in its foreign policy."[61] Aleksandr Chubarian calls for a balanced revision of the old interpretation, admitting that Stalin erred in rejecting anti-fascist cooperation with the western Social Democrats before 1934 and that western policy was considerably more complex than the typical Soviet caricature of appeasement, but, at the same time, rejecting the more radical criticisms of Semiriaga and Medvedev.[62] Oleg Rzheshevskii concedes various errors and miscalculations on Stalin's part, but these seem to play little role in his analysis of why collective security failed. "The reality of the maturing German-British alliance" meant that "the USSR took the only correct decision" in signing the Nazi-Soviet Pact.[63]

Not surprisingly, the recently published memoirs of former Foreign Minister Andrei Gromyko present an entirely unreconstructed view of the events of 1939. For Gromyko, the Nazi-Soviet Pact "was the result of the policy of a number of Western powers which did not wish to join the USSR in blocking Hitler's path to aggression and the unleashing of war."[64]

Given the political ramifications of this historical revisionism, for the cohesion of the union as well as for the moral authority of the party, the authorities quickly entered the debate. Both the party and the Congress of People's Deputies established special commissions to study the problem. The legislative commission was headed by reformist Politburo member, Aleksandr Iakovlev. His report, submitted on 23 December 1989, condemned the previous policy of silence about the secret protocols, for which, he said, the country had "paid a high political and moral price...."[65] The commission's report was critical of the western powers for their unwillingness to cooperate with the USSR and their desire to deflect war to the East. Yet, it conceded that "all parties lacked a sense of responsibility, to say nothing of wisdom," and that Stalin's foreign policy was not well grounded in "serious strategic considerations."[66] The report further contended that the Nazi-Soviet Pact was a German initiative, that Stalin still held open the option for an alliance with Britain and France until well into August 1939, and it speculated that he mistakenly hoped that signing the pact would make the western powers willing to cooperate with the USSR. Stalin was castigated for his inability to distinguish between the very different levels of threat posed to the Soviet Union by the Nazis and the western leaders. Most importantly, the commission affirmed the existence of the secret protocols and the authenticity of the copies long available in the West.

The Iakovlev commission was badly split concerning the propriety of the Nazi-Soviet Pact. Some of its members believed that the pact was politically justified under the circumstances, because the USSR had "no other alternative," and that it did "at least delay the beginning of the war."[67] Others on the commission charged that:

> ...Stalin agreed to conclude a non-aggression pact for entirely different reasons. His chief motivation was not the agreement itself, but what became the subject matter of the secret protocols--the possibility of bringing troops into the Baltic republics, Poland, Bessarabia and...Finland. In other words, imperial ambitions were the driving force behind the Treaty.[68]

Responding to this report, a formal resolution of the Congress of People's Deputies, dated 24 December 1989, declared the Nazi-Soviet Pact to have been lawful and proper, but the secret protocols were condemned as "deviations from the Leninist principles of foreign policy," and therefore "illegal and invalid."[69] Subsequently, the Soviet Foreign Ministry printed photocopies of the protocols in its magazine, *Vestnik*.[70]

These developments finally broke the barrier which for over twenty years had stalled the publication of Soviet diplomatic documents for 1939. A special two volume collection, *God krizisa*, appeared in 1990 which included a large number of previously unpublished documents from Soviet archives.[71] The most interesting item in the collection is Aleksei Merekalov's memorandum of his meeting with Ernst Weizsäcker on 17 April 1939. This apparently pivotal meeting, known previously only through the German report of it, had led many western scholars to identify this as the point when the Soviet government took the initiative in pursuing an agreement with Germany.[72] However, Merekalov's report does not show any Soviet initiative for an improvement of political relations between Moscow and Berlin and it indicates that it was the Germans who took the role of the pursuer in this courtship.[73] Clearly, interpretations of the triangular relationship among the USSR, Nazi Germany, and the western powers in 1939 will have to be revised to take into account this newly available documentation.

By 1990, the majority of Soviet researchers seemed to be moving toward a substantially revised interpretation of the origins of the Second World War and the role of the USSR in that process. In this view, the fundamental cause of the rise of Hitler to power and the onset of the war is still seen as the crisis of capitalism in its imperialist phase. Stalin's initially mistaken assessment of the nature of fascism and his hostility to western social democrats facilitated the Nazi seizure of power in Germany. Although Hitler deliberately launched the war, Britain and France must bear some degree of responsibility for tolerating, even fostering, Nazi aggression. Appeasement was designed to safeguard the western capitalist states from German assault and deflect that aggression eastward, ultimately against the USSR. Collective security was the genuine policy of the USSR, not a tactic to pressure the Germans into a deal. Alliance with the West, so long as the obligations were truly reciprocal and thoroughly spelled out, remained the preferred objective of Soviet policy until the third week of August 1939. The purges made the USSR a less attractive ally for the western powers and the Soviet government might have continued to pursue an alliance with the West even more assiduously in August and beyond. Nonetheless, responsibility for the breakdown of negotiations for a new Triple Entente belongs to the western powers, especially Britain, because London only wanted to go through the motions of talks with the USSR (in order to influence Hitler), not to weld a binding alliance with Soviet Russia. Given western unwillingness to cooperate, the certainty that war would break out soon in eastern Europe, and the serious possibility of a Japanese attack on the USSR, the Soviet Union had no choice but to sign a non-aggression pact with Germany. The initiative for the pact came from Berlin, not Moscow. That pact kept the USSR out of war for almost two years and thereby provided valuable time to augment the nation's defenses. Unfortunately, Stalin did not use that time as wisely as he should have, while Nazi strength grew enormously. The secret protocols published earlier in the West were indeed part of the Russo-German agreement. There is still no consensus about the propriety of those protocols. The Nazi-Soviet Pact, the occupation of eastern Poland, and the Border and Friendship Treaty confused and thereby weakened communists, anti-fascists, and progressive forces generally throughout the world.

Moreover, many recent Soviet studies of these issues are much less shrill, considerably less polemical and more carefully nuanced than their predecessors. They are also more thoroughly grounded in Soviet archival sources. A spirit of freer inquiry and a willingness to debate controversial issues is developing among Soviet international relations specialists.

Yet, by the end of 1990, there were still some aspects of Moscow's pre-war policy which had not yet been properly addressed by Soviet historians. Most importantly, Soviet approaches to Nazi Germany before 1939 had not been carefully explored and integrated into a coherent explanation of Soviet foreign policy. The whole process of decision-making in regard to the inception, execution, and abandonment of the collective security line still required detailed analysis. Finally, many Soviet scholars had not fully shed the old Manichean perspective and achieved a more balanced view of the considerations motivating western decision makers. Some of them still did not realize that foreign policy decisions in western countries are sometimes made for reasons which have little to do with the USSR.

The propositions outlined above represent a considerable departure from the orthodoxy of *Falsificators of History*, although some of its tenants are retained. A number of them are also considerably closer to the views of such western scholars as Jonathan Haslam, Geoffrey Roberts, and the present author. In contrast, other Soviet researchers--Semiriaga and some of the Baltic historians, for example--have begun to argue along the lines suggested by Gerhard Weinberg, Robert Tucker, and Jiri Hochman, that Stalin may have actually preferred an alliance with Germany to facilitate his expansionist ambitions.[74] Soviet historians are now entering a controversy (as serious, scholarly participants, not mere regime propagandists) that has raged hotly in the West for some time.

Since 1990, a combination of factors (including the continuing process of democratizing Soviet society, the further growth of independence--that is, the decline of *partiinost*--among Soviet scholars, and, most dramatically, the failure of the right-wing coup in August 1991) seems to have opened the floodgates of scholarly inquiry and historical revisionism. The subsequent abolition of the USSR removed what little rationale may have remained for protecting the historical image of the Soviet regime.

At a conference of Soviet and Western scholars held in Moscow in February 1992, Aleksandr Chubarian condemned the Nazi-Soviet Pact as illegal and immoral.[75] Moreover, Chubarian and several of his colleagues criticized the dogmatic thinking which underlay much of Soviet foreign policy and the ideologically based "class approach" which frequently led to misperception of developments in the western states. At the same conference, Lev Bezymenskii criticized the KGB and conservative forces in the former Soviet government for preventing the publication of the secret protocols until December 1989.[76] His exposé of the workings and tribulations of the Iakovlev Committee also appeared in the mass circulation magazine, *Sovershenno sekretno*.[77]

Still more startling, the taboo issue of Soviet approaches to Nazi Germany during the Collective Security era has finally been addressed in public. An article dealing with David Kandelaki's contacts with German leaders, based in part on previously unused archival documents, appeared in the May/June 1991 issue of *Voproy istorii*.[78] Its authors, Lev Bezymenskii and Nikolai Abramov, readily admit these contacts as well as the desire of the Soviet government to avoid conflict with the Third Reich and to maintain a mutually beneficial economic relationship with Berlin. At the same time, they contest the view, advanced by some western scholars, that Kandelaki's missions amounted to a *sub rosa*, alternative foreign policy run secretly by Stalin. They demonstrate that Litvinov knew about Kandelaki's probes and that they constituted part of a unified, if multifaceted, foreign policy. The authors also suggest that, as Geoffrey Roberts has previously argued, these missions were designed to appeal to German political leaders (especially Schacht and Goering) who were thought to be less bellicose toward the USSR than was Hitler. Certainly, in the absence of open access to Soviet archives, there will continue to be divergent speculation about how the contacts made by Kandelaki and others with German leaders in the 1930s fit into Moscow's overall foreign policy. Now, however, Russian scholars are at last free to join the debate over the nature of the Collective Security policy and its failure.

NOTES

[1]See Geoffrey Roberts, *The Unholy Alliance: Stalin's Pact with Hitler* (London, 1989), chs. 4-7; and Jonathan Haslam, *The Soviet Union and the Struggle for Collective Security in Europe, 1933-39* (New York, 1984).

[2]Felix Kovalev, "Secret Protocols: A Look into the Files," *Vestnik*, March 1990, p. 57.

[3]For a detailed examination of the provenance and fate of the Nazi-Soviet Pact documents, see Helmut König, "Das deutsch-sowjetische Vertragswerk von 1939 und seine Geheimen Zusatzpro-

tokolle: Eine Dokumentation," *Osteuropa*, vol. 39, no. 5 (May 1989), pp. 413-458.

[4]Stalin's speech of 3 July 1941 is reprinted in Joseph Stalin, *The Great Patriotic War of the Soviet Union* (New York, 1945), p. 11.

[5]Les K. Adler and Thomas G. Paterson, "Red Fascism: The Merger of Nazi Germany and Soviet Russia in the American Image of Totalitarianism, 1930's-1950's," *The American Historical Review*, vol. LXXV, no. 4 (April 1970), pp. 1046-1064.

[6]Vladimir Abarinov, "Lies for Lies' Sake," *The Independent Newspaper from Russia (Nezavisimaya Gazeta)*, vol. I (23 April 1991), pp. 14-15; and Joe J. Heydecker and Johannes Leeb, *The Nuremberg Trial* (Westport, 1975 [1962]), pp. 189-192. Also see Yuri Zorya and Natalia Lebedeva, "The Year 1939 in the Nuremberg Trials," *International Affairs*, 1989, no. 10, pp. 117-128.

[7]Raymond J. Sontag and James S. Beddie, eds., *Nazi-Soviet Relations, 1939-1941: Documents from the Archives of the German Foreign Office as Released by the Department of State* (Washington, D.C., 1948).

[8]Aleksandr Nekrich, a Soviet historian who emigrated to the West in 1976, has identified the authors as G.A. Deborin, B.E. Shtein and V.M. Khvostov. See Nekrich, *Otreshis' ot strakha: vospominaniia istorika* (London, 1979), p. 66. Veteran Soviet diplomat and international relations specialist Viktor Israelian suggested in an interview with the author (16 December 1991) that Deborin was not one of the document's authors; rather, Khvostov and Shtein had prepared the pamphlet under the direct supervision of Stalin. Vyshinskii apparently carried drafts to the Kremlin where Stalin personally edited and amended them. A virtually identical edition was published in London by "Soviet News" in 1948 and a slightly revised version was issued in Moscow by the Foreign Languages Publishing House in 1951, both under the title, *Falsifiers of History*.

[9]*XVIII s'ezd vsesoiuznoi kommunisticheskoi partii (b), 10-21 marta 1939g., stenograficheskii otchet* (Moscow, 1939), p. 13.

[10]Alexander Werth, *Russia at War, 1941-1945* (New York, 1964), pp. 73-75.

[11]*Falsificators of History (An Historical Note)* (Moscow, 1949), p. 16.

[12]*Ibid.*, pp. 40-41.

[13]*Ibid.*, pp. 5, 40, 54.

[14]Vol. I, *November 1937-1939*, and vol. II, *The Dirksen Papers (1938-1939)* (Moscow, 1948).

[15]See William Zimmerman, *Soviet Perspectives on International Relations, 1956-1967* (Princeton, 1969); Allen Lynch, *The Soviet Study of International Relations* (Cambridge, 1987); and Oded Eran, *The Mezhdunarodniki: An Assessment of Professional Expertise in the Making of Soviet Foreign Policy* (Ramat Gan, 1979).

[16]Nikita S. Khrushchev, *The Crimes of the Stalin Era* (New York, 1962).

[17]Nikita S. Khrushchev, *Khrushchev Remembers*, (Boston, 1970), pp. 131-132. Also see N.S. Khrushchev, *Khrushchev Remembers: The Glasnost Tapes* (Boston, 1990), p. 81.

[18]*Ibid.*, p. 108.

[19]E. Gnedin, *Iz istorii otnoshenii mezhdu SSSR i fashistskoi Germanei: Dokumenty i sovremennye kommentarii* (New York, 1977), pp. 7-8. Also see *Katastrofa i vtoroe rozhdenie: memuarnye zapiski* (Amsterdam, 1977); and *Vykhod iz labirinta* (New York, 1982).

[20]See Teddy J. Uldricks, "A.J.P. Taylor and the Russians," in: Gordon Martel, ed., *The Origins of the Second World War Reconsidered* (London, 1986) pp. 178-179 for an examination of the weaknesses of Gnedin's work.

[21]*Istoriia velikoi otechestvennoi voiny sovetskogo soiuza, 1941-1945*, 6 vols., (Moscow, 1960-1985), vol. I, p. 174.

[22]*Dokumenty vneshnei politiki SSSR* (Moscow, 1957), vol. I, p. 5.

[23]Nekrich, *Otreshis' ot strakha*, pp. 139-140.

[24]M. Andreyeva and K. Dmitriyeva, "The Military Negotiations Between the Soviet Union, Britain and France in 1939," *International Affairs*, 1959, no. 2, pp. 107-110.

[25]See Margot Light, "The Soviet View," in: Roy Douglas, ed., *1939: A Retrospect Forty Years After* (Hamden, 1983), pp. 74-89.

[26]*History of Soviet Foreign Policy, 1917-1945* (Moscow, 1969), pp. 337-338.

[27]See, for example, I.F. Maksimychev, *Diplomatii mira protiv diplomatii voiny* (Moscow, 1981); A.L. Narochitskii, ed., *SSSR v bor'be protiv fashistskoi agressi, 1933-1941* (Moscow, 1976); I.K.

Kobliakov, *USSR For Peace, Against Aggression, 1933-1941* (Moscow, 1976); and Pavel Sevostyanov, *Before the Nazi Invasion* (Moscow, 1984), p. 67.

[28]V.M. Khvostov, *Problemy istorii vneshnei politiki SSSR i mezhdunarodnykh otnoshenii* (Moscow, 1976), p. 412. Contrary to Khvostov, the real effect of the Nazi-Soviet Pact was to disorient and discredit the world communist movement. See Wolfgang Leonhard, *Betrayal: The Hitler-Stalin Pact of 1939* (New York, 1989), especially ch. 4; and Fernando Claudin, *The Communist Movement* (New York, 1975), ch. 4.

[29]Nekrich, *Otreshis' ot strakha*, p. 157.

[30]For a discussion of all Soviet diplomatic document collections published through the early Gorbachev years, see Robert H. Johnson, ed., *Soviet Foreign Policy, 1918-1945: A Guide to Research and Research Materials* (Wilmington, 1991), pp. 89-101.

[31]2 vols. (Moscow, 1971); English edition: *Soviet Peace Efforts on the Eve of World War II*, 2 parts (Moscow, 1973). This collection is evaluated by John Herman, "Soviet Peace Efforts on the Eve of World War Two: A Review of the Soviet Documents," *Journal of Contemporary History*, vol. 15, no. 3 (July 1980), pp. 577-602.

[32]Moscow, 1981.

[33]Ivan Maisky, *Memoirs of a Soviet Ambassador: The War, 1939-43* (New York, 1968), p. 4. A fully developed indictment of western policy is found in Ivan Maisky, *Who Helped Hitler?* (London, 1964).

[34]Maisky, *Who Helped Hitler?*, p. 201.

[35]Abdurakhman Avtorkhanov, "Behind the Scenes of the Molotov-Ribbentrop Pact," in *Kontinent 2* (Garden City, 1977), p. 86. Similar views are expressed by W.G. Krivitsky, *I Was Stalin's Agent* (London, 1939), pp. 18-34, 37-40; and Vladimir Petrov, "The Nazi-Soviet Pact: A Missing Page in Soviet Historiography," *Problems of Communism*, vol. 17 (January 1968), pp. 42-50.

[36]For example, Alexander Barmine, *One Who Survived* (New York, 1945). Barmine, a Soviet diplomat who helped to carry out the collective security policy before his defection, gives no indication of a *sub rosa*, pro-German policy different from the official line.

[37]Roy Medvedev, *Let History Judge* (New York, 1989), pp. 727-728.

[38]*Ibid.*, pp. 725, 729.

[39]Mikhail Gorbachev, *Perestroika: New Thinking for Our Country and the World* (New York, 1988), p. 133.

[40]*Ibid.*, pp. 177-178.

[41]*Istoriia vneshnei politiki SSSR* (Moscow, 1986), pp. 296-388.

[42]See Thomas Sherlock, "Politics and History under Gorbachev," *Problems of Communism*, vol. XXXVII, no. 3-4 (May-August 1988), pp. 16-42; R. W. Davies, *Soviet History in the Gorbachev Revolution* (Bloomington, 1989); and Donald J. Raleigh, ed., *Soviet Historians and Perestroika: The First Phase* (Armonk, 1989).

[43]Iu. Afanas'ev, "Proshloe i my, " *Kommunist*, 1985, no. 14, pp. 105-116; *The New York Times*, 19 December 1985, p. A-10.

[44]Vilnis Sipols, *Vneshniaia politika sovetskogo soiuza, 1936-1939 gg.* (Moscow, 1987), pp. 4-5. Also see Hugh Phillips, "*Glasnost'* and the History of Soviet Foreign Policy," *Problems of Communism*, vol. XL, no. 4 (July-August 1991), pp. 63-68.

[45]*Ibid.*, p. 154.

[46]For details on events in the Baltic republics, see Alfred Erich Senn, "Perestroika in Lithuanian Historiography: The Molotov-Ribbentrop Pact," *The Russian Review*, vol. 49, no. 1 (January 1990), pp. 43-56; Izidors Vizulis, *The Molotov-Ribbentrop Pact of 1939: The Baltic Case* (New York, 1990); *Lituanus*, vol. 35, nos. 1 & 2 (Spring and Summer 1989); and Leonhard, *Betrayal*, pp. x-xviii.

[47]Quoted in Leonhard, *Betrayal*, p. xiv.

[48]Quoted in Senn, "Perestroika in Lithuanian Historiography," p. 50.

[49]H. Arumäe, "Esce raz o sovetsko-germanskom pakte o nenapadenii," *Sovetskaia estoniia*, 17-18 August 1988.

[50]Heino Arumäe, "Noch einman zum sowjetisch-deutschen Nichtangriffspakt," in Erwin Oberländer, ed., *Hitler-Stalin-Pakt 1939: Das Ende Ostmitteleuropas?* (Frankfurt a.M., 1989), pp. 114-124. The pact and its protocols continue to fuel the fires of ethnic separatism. The new Republic of Moldova held the first-ever international conference on "The Molotov-Ribbentrop Pact and Its Consequences for Bessarabia" in June 1991. The non-Russian

majority of that republic can use the same historical evidence as that employed by the Baltic peoples to buttress their case for independence or possible reannexation by Romania. See Paul E. Michelson and Dennis Deletant, "Moscow 1939--Kishinev 1991: The Ribbentrop-Molotov Pact Conference in Moldavia," *Report on the USSR*, vol. III, no. 34 (23 August 1991), pp. 16-18.

[51]Viacheslav Dashichev, "Vostok-zapad: poisk novykh otnoshenii: O prioritetakh vneshnei politiki sovetskogo gosudarstva," *Literaturnaia gazeta*, 1988, no. 20 (May 18), p. 14.

[52]Mikhail Semiriaga, "23 avgust 1939 goda: Sovetsko-germanskii dogovor o nenapadenii: Byla li alternativa?," *Literaturnaia gazeta*, 5 October 1988, p. 14.

[53]A. Orlov and S. Tiushkevich, "Pakt 1939 goda: alternativy ne bylo," *Literaturnaia gazeta*, 26 October 1988, p. 14.

[54]A.S. Iakushevskii, "Sovetsko-germanskii dogovor o nenapadenii: vzgliad cherez gody," *Istoriia KPSS*, 1988, no. 8, pp. 82-96. Also see "K istorii zakliucheniia sovetsko-germanskogo dogovora o nenapadenii 23 avgusta 1939 goda (dokumentalny obzor)," *Novaia i noveishaia istoriia*, 1989, no. 6, pp. 3-21.

[55]Vladislav Zubok and Andrei Kokoshin, "Opportunities Missed in 1932?," *International Affairs*, 1989, no. 2 (February), p. 112.

[56]V.M. Kulish, "U poroga voiny," *Komsomolskaia pravda*, 24 August 1988, p. 3.

[57]Dmitrii Volkogonov, *Triumf i tragediia: Politicheskii portret I.V. Stalina* (Moscow, 1989), book II, part I, pp. 11-49.

[58]R.A. Medvedev, "Diplomaticheskie i voennye proschety stalina v 1939-1941 gg.," *Novaia i noveishaia istoriia*, 1989, no. 4 (July-August), pp. 140-163.

[59]"'Kruglyi stol': vtoraia mirovaia voina--istoki i prichiny," *Voprosy istorii*, 1989, no. 6, p. 20. Also see "Sovetskii soiuz v 30-e gody: kruglyi stol, " *Voprosy istorii*, 1988, no. 12, pp. 3-46; and "The Road to World War II: Soviet Historians on Hitler's Pact with Stalin, the Soviet-Finnish War and Other Controversial Issues," *Moscow News*, 1988, no. 36, pp. 8-9.

[60]*1939: Lessons of History (Fifty Years of the Beginning of the Second World War)* (Moscow, 1989).

[61]*Ibid.*, p. 7.

[62]*Ibid.*, pp. 9-25.

[63]*Ibid.*, pp. 131-132. A more detailed exposition of Rzheshevskii's views is available in his book, *Europe 1939: Was War Inevitable?* (Moscow, 1989).

[64]Andrei Gromyko, *Memoirs* (New York, 1989), p. 38.

[65]*On the Political and Legal Assessment of the Soviet-German Non-Aggression Treaty of 1939* (Moscow, 1990), p. 5.

[66]*Ibid.*, p. 15.

[67]*Ibid.*, p. 23.

[68]*Ibid.*

[69]*Ibid.*, pp. 28-30. This condemnation also encompassed the secret protocols to subsequent Nazi-Soviet agreements between 1939 and 1941. The commission's conclusions reflect Iakovlev's own views (and probably those of Gorbachev as well), as expressed previously in a *Pravda* interview. See Alexander Yakovlev, *The Events of 1939: Looking Back After Fifty Years* (Moscow, 1989).

[70]"Secret Protocols," pp. 60-63.

[71]*Ministerstvo inostrannykh del SSSR, God krizisa, 1938-1939: Dokumenty i materialy*, vol. I, *29 sentiabria 1938 g.--31 maia 1939 g.*, and vol. II, *2 iiunia 1939 g.--4 sentiabria 1939 g.* (Moscow, 1990).

[72]*God krizisa*, vol. I, p. 389. The German version is in *Nazi-Soviet Relations*, pp. 1-2. See D.C. Watt, "The Initiation of the Negotiations Leading to the Nazi-Soviet Pact: A Historical Problem," in: C. Abramsky and Beryl J. Williams, eds., *Essays in Honour of E.H. Carr* (Hamden, 1974), pp. 152-170, for an example of an interpretation which sees this meeting as evidence of an about-face in Soviet policy.

[73]The impact of this newly available document is discussed by Geoffrey Roberts, "Infamous Encounter? The Merekalov-Weizsäcker Meeting of 17 April 1939," *The Historical Journal*, forthcoming.

[74]Jiri Hochman, *The Soviet Union and the Failure of Collective Security* (Ithaca, 1984); Gerhard Weinberg, *The Foreign Policy of Hitler's Germany*, vol. II, *Starting World War II, 1937-1939* (Chicago, 1980); and Robert Tucker, *Stalin in Power* (New York, 1990), chs. 10-21.

[75]Aleksandr Chubarian, "Politics and Ethics in Soviet Foreign Policy." Paper presented at a special conference on "Soviet Foreign Policy, 1917-1991: A Retrospective," co-sponsored by the

Institute of General History of the Russian Academy of Sciences and the Cummings Institute of Soviet Studies of Tel Aviv University. The proceedings will be published by Frank Cass, London, under the tentative title of *The Soviet Union and the West, 1917-1922.*

[76]Lev Bezymenskii, "Sekretnye protokoly 1939 goda kak problema sovietskoi istoriografii."

[77]Lev Bezymenskii, "Tainy pakta: kak rabotal komissiia iakovleva," *Sovershenno sekretno*, 1991, no. 12, pp. 4-8.

[78]N.A. Abramov and L.A. Bezymenskii, "Osobaia missiia Davida Kandelaki," *Voprosy istorii*, 1991, no. 4-5, pp. 144-156.

LESSONS OF THE EAST EUROPEAN REVOLUTIONS OF 1989[1]

Gale Stokes
Rice University

At the beginning of 1989, most specialists recognized the political and economic dangers facing the communist regimes of Eastern Europe. Foreign debt, loss of legitimacy, weakening of support from the Soviet Union, and economic malorganization were only the most obvious and well-known deficiencies of the region. At the same time, these weaknesses did not seem to be significantly undermining the ability of Eastern Europe regimes to maintain control over their societies, with perhaps the exception of Hungary, where significant movement was under way. Even in Poland, where roundtable discussions led to the stunning elections of June 1989, those discussions had been stalled for four months and faced serious opposition among the rank and file of party leaders. The other countries of Eastern Europe seemed no closer to real reform than they had been in 1970 or 1980. In the GDR, Erich Honecker was trying to avoid perestroika by ignoring it. A smooth transition of power from Gustav Husák to Miloš Jakeš in Czechoslovakia had produced no change in the strict social controls in force since 1968. Romania's dictator, Nicolae Ceauşescu, despite having ruined the country's already weak economy, had little trouble crushing the few brave but isolated incidents of dissidence. And, in Bulgaria, Todor Zhivkov continued to propagate purposefully ineffective reform proposals.

One year later, the situation was unrecognizably different. Not only was Honecker replaced, but the Berlin Wall was down and what had been called East Germany was on a headlong path toward becoming eastern Germany. Hitherto illegal Solidarity had formed a government in Poland and begun shock therapy for its moribund economy. Václav Havel, almost straight from prison, was President of Czechoslovakia and Czechs were greeting historical videos of their former leaders with a devastating response: laughter. Ceauşescu was dead, and Zhivkov was gone. If one believes that a widespread change in government personnel, coupled with a total rejection of the philosophy of the previous system, dynamic efforts to utterly transform an economic system, and creation of a new social basis for rule constitute a revolution, whatever the level of violence might be, then 1989 was a revolutionary year, or at least a year in which the necessary beginnings of a revolutionary transformation took place.

Now, only a few years later, the revolutions of 1989 are already slipping into a fund of conventional wisdoms about the fate of communism, the failures of centralized planning, the virtues of western policy, and the efforts of the East Europeans to right themselves, so to speak, increasingly are greeted with yawns. Before the thrilling moments of 1989 lose all their freshness, therefore, it seems appropriate to attempt a sketch of what lessons those dramatic and unanticipated events might hold for students of Eastern Europe.

There is little doubt what the greatest lesson of 1989 is: communism failed. This failure was not a parochial event limited in its significance to Eastern Europe, to the resolution of the Cold War, or to western policy initiatives, but rather a moment of global importance in the most important family of events of the last few hundred years. These events do not have a satisfactory name, even though we all know how fundamental they are. We can call them the industrial revolution, modernization, the great transformation, the single transition, the emergence of capitalism, or the energy revolution, but whatever name they go by, the unprecedented economic and social changes they have brought about in just a few generations have forced every human society to find new ways of organizing itself. In my view, three basic kinds of solutions to the fundamental challenges of the past few hundred years, all first broached in the eighteenth century, have characterized the twentieth century. I call them the anti-rationalist genre, the hyper-rationalist genre, and the pluralist genre.

By the first of these I mean, of course, those movements of rage and rejection from the first half of the twentieth century that craved the power of the great transformation--the technology, the military strength, and the standard of living--but rejected the economic calculus of market capitalism and the political calculus of parliamentary democracy. Instead, they espoused what Thomas Mann called "a highly technical romanticism," adopting Schelling's view that the universe contains "a primal, non-rational force that can be grasped only by the intuitive power of men of imaginative genius."[2] Nazism and fascism repudiated the eighteenth century bases of middle class culture for what they believed were the superior principles of mass culture, rejecting reason for power, individuality for *sacro egoismo*, virtue for vainglory, transparency for obscurantism, constitutions for the *Führerprinzip*, humanitarianism for racial fanaticism, objectivity for prejudice, and, in the end, the guillotine for the gas chamber.

The hyper-rational genre, on the other hand, moved in the opposite direction by routinizing the application of reason into a rigid political formula. Stalinism is the *reductio ad absurdum* of Descartes' assertion that we humans can "render ourselves the masters and possessors of nature," a dream that found a confident echo as late as 1961 in the statement of the Hungarian author who wrote that socialism was on the verge of "the *final* maneuvers...for the *ultimate* conquest of the material world."[3] In the twentieth century the agent for accomplishing this end was first the vanguard party sustained by its scientific (i.e. rational) understanding of human history, then the vanguard of the vanguard, and finally the great leader, who imposed himself as the ultimate source of human rationality that could transform the world.

The third genre is pluralism, which, in contrast to the other two genres, is not so much a system as it is an indeterminate set of political devices for structuring process. Because pluralist institutions are based on the prosaic observation that human beings are fallible and liable to contention, they are designed to prevent any "primal non-rational force" or "vanguard scientific party" from directing the affairs of society for very long. This does not mean they will not err, but it does mean that they will change--not immediately, not easily, and often with a great deal of pain and political struggle, not to mention cant and humbug. Pluralism's balanced and multilayered political configurations and processes, variety of ownership forms, diversity of associational possibilities, and openness of public discourse have proven flexible enough to match the protean developmental surge of the energy revolution.

Without going into any detail, it seems to me that the experience of the twentieth century has taught us something about political organization that we did not know when the century began, namely that both the anti-rationalist and the hyper-rationalist genres are incapable of successfully solving the problems posed by rapid social and economic change. 1945 showed the bankruptcy of the anti-rationalist genre, and 1989 demonstrated the bankruptcy of the hyper-rationalist genre. The message of the twentieth century is not, as some observers would have us believe, that pluralism is the final answer to the energy revolution and that history is over. Indeed, the paradox of Fukuyama's notorious claim is that the end of history has occurred because of the victory of the only genre within which history can occur. Both the anti-rational and hyper-rational systems sought final solutions and found stasis instead. The ease with which pluralism incorporated the information revolution of the past fifteen years, compared to the difficulties socialist systems had with that revolution, is a recent instance of pluralism's ability to respond to the unexpected challenges of the energy revolution poses.

But that does not mean that pluralism has adequately solved the modern problematic. When we observe the misery in which not just most people in the third world, but a large number of people in the first world, live, we understand that many issues remain on the agenda, not the least of which is the problem of finding a plausible framework for opposition to injustice in societies that are suffused with self-satisfaction. The great message of the twentieth century is not the positive accomplishments of pluralism, although there are many, but the negative message of the other two genres: we have not learned what works as surely as we have learned what does not work. Pluralism has its problems, but the other two genres are dead ends. History is not over, just the twentieth century.

The most important lesson of 1989, therefore, the reason that year can be added to the short list of dates that students will learn as the landmarks of the modern era (the others are 1789, 1848, and 1945), is that the second of the twentieth century's two great experiments in coping with the energy revolution failed. "We have made one important contribution," Soviet reformer Yuri Afanasyev said, "We have taught the world what *not* to do."[4] Unfortunately, however, that failure does not present the same kind of unique opportunity for positive reconstruction that the failure of the anti-rationalist genre in 1945 did. In 1945, Europe was devastated not only physically, but psychically as well. The optimism of the nineteenth century was not only long gone, but the entire civilization that had spawned the disasters of two great wars seemed spent. This was a calamity, but a calamity with a positive side. Moments like 1945 are rarely seen in history--a wiping of the slate, if not clean, then close to it. Of course the wiping was done with blood--not something we would choose, but it was precisely the grotesque and bloody futility of the great thirty years war from 1914 to 1945 that convinced men like Alcide de Gaspari, Konrad Adenauer, Henri Spaak, Robert Schuman, and Jean Monnet--in a way that conferences, speeches, articles, and diplomacy never could have--that the old obsessions could not form the basis of a stable Europe. They built their new community not on *sacro egoismo*, but on voluntary association and a politics of accommodation.

Surprisingly, given all the ink that has been spilled about the failure of the early dreams of creating a European political union, in a little more than thirty years this new community has become not just a strong economic unit, but also a vertical structure for containing the passions that burst the traditional European system of empires apart. Today, if you live in Florence, for example, you can be a booster of your neighborhood and city, a Tuscan patriot, a citizen of Italy, and an advocate for Europe, all at the same time, or singly on the appropriate occasions. One may fear that the increasingly inward looking preoccupations of the Community will eventually turn Europeans into multi-national nationalists, but the absurdity today of Germans shooting Frenchmen, or Italians bombing Spaniards, both commonplaces of our fathers' time, is obvious.

One of the greatest costs of Stalinism in Eastern Europe was that it excluded the East Europeans from the unique cesura that made new solutions possible in the West. Eastern Europe had no *stunde null*. In 1989, many East Europeans emerged from their own devastating era of grotesque obsessions with no sense of despair over the collapse of civilization, but rather harboring both enthusiastic expectations and a host of ideas from the past that had been suppressed for forty years. Francois Furet has said that the most striking thing about 1989 was the absence of new ideas.[5]

East Europeans are exuberant at their release from lies, but some of them appear anxious to create their own deceptions; other East Europeans are convinced that their particular people has been unjustly treated for forty years, but stand ready to do the same to others; East European elites are frustrated by a long generation of humiliating compromises, but for that very reason find it difficult to practice a politics of compromise. Some authors have suggested that these data show that the East Europeans have reverted to the mentality of the twenties and thirties, to that moment at which they left off from Europe sixty years ago. It would be more accurate to say that, having missed the unique window of opportunity that the bitter tonic of 1945 offered to others, they have not yet had the chance to learn first hand the futility of some of the old ideas. This does not mean they will find it impossible to create the structures that will contain their passions, because, unlike 1918, the existence of the European Community will exert a constant pressure on them to democratize and to marketize. But, feeling that their predicament is not their fault, but rather something imposed on them from outside, socialized to the ethic of a paternalistic state, and retaining a sense that some of the bad old ideas are not really all that bad, they will find it more difficult to take advantage of their particular cesura.

A third thought on the revolutions of 1989 came to me when I saw those first pictures of Soviet tanks being loaded on trains in Hungary for their journey east. For the past forty years, Western governments have quite naturally focussed on the military and economic strengths of the Soviet Union and Eastern Europe. Enormous bureaucracies are devoted to understanding and countering every military threat, especially at the technological level, to evaluating relative strengths in the leadership elites, and to analyzing the details of trade, finance, and investment. In the world of power relationships that civil servants and politicians inhabit, only data of that sort carried the conviction of being realistic. The hard-nosed analyst was preoccupied with studying the implications of the Nth Party Congress, charting CMEA statistics to estimate the none-too-good prospects for the next five year plan, assessing the meaning, or even the existence, of the Sonnenfeldt Doctrine, or analyzing the disposition of Warsaw Pact forces.

The academic community was preoccupied with similar concerns.[6] Studies in conflict resolution, security issues, economic analysis, policy options, and various kinds of modeling focussed attention on those areas of public life that are quantifiable, that are consistent with social science theorizing, or that have policy implications. Fearing, with good reason, that they might be considered soft or unscientific, academics too gravitated toward "realistic" assessments of East European affairs.

The events of 1989 clearly show how limited a view this was, how, if you like, unrealistic. If anything is clear about the sudden swoon of the hollow East European regimes in November and December 1989, it is that those collapses were the result of moral rot at least as much as economic or political failure. After the Soviet invasion of Czechoslovakia convinced East European intellectuals that it would be impossible to create socialism with a human face, they turned from debating how to reform the system to a much more devastating device--total rejection of the regimes' thoroughgoing falsity. What is the basis of hope in a hopeless situation? Living an ethical life, Leszek Kolakowski answered in 1971. Hope is not a prognostication about the future, Václav Havel said, but the conviction that something has meaning, which is what permits the undertaking of the hopeless enterprise of living in truth. "Even if people never speak of it," Havel said in his open letter to Gustáv Husák in 1975, "they have a very acute appreciation of the price they have paid for outward peace and quiet: the permanent humiliation of their human dignity."[7] This desire, necessity even, to live in truth is what lay behind the creation of KOR, Charter 77, and even Solidarity. "What all of us had in mind were not only...bread, butter, and sausage," said the Solidarity program of October 1981, "but also justice, democracy, truth, legality, human dignity, freedom of convictions, and the repair of the republic," which is why Andrzej Gwiazda characterized Solidarity as a "moral revolution."[8] It was not economic deprivation that brought the people onto the streets in Eastern Europe in November and December 1989. They had suffered economic hardship for a long time, and in countries like Czechoslovakia and Bulgaria times were not even that hard. It was their humiliation, their disgust with the falsity of their regimes, their desire for freedom. That is why when the fall took place it was the uncompromised advocates of living in truth, the musicians, historians, philosophers, sociologists, and playwrights--the cultural leaders--who came to power. All the studies of strategic balances proved inappropriate and useless. The Soviet troops simply got on their trains and went home.

The events of 1989 have not only shown that strategic studies do not adequately take into account such intangibles as ethical values, religion, and national sentiment, but they have greatly changed the character of the kind of analysis we need in the future. At least when we faced a competitor with massive nuclear forces who was competing with us in many parts of the world using an ideology that claimed ultimate victory there were excellent justifications for concentrating on the strategic balance. After 1989, however, the situation has changed. Without question we must continue our study of policy options, to analyze the economic strengths and weaknesses of our competitors, and to monitor the status of military forces in the world. I do not propose giving up such vitally important work. But as the surprising outcome of the Iraq war, which unleashed the unexpected outpouring of Kurdish fears, confirms, we need to spend a bit more time on the intangibles.

For example, it was quite clear in 1975 what we meant by human rights. We meant that oppressive regimes, but particularly communist ones, should permit more freedom of speech, more free travel, and so forth. We purposefully avoided the obvious fact that human rights also means minority rights, since minority issues occur typically within already established states rather than among them and imply that established borders might have to change. Today minority rights, which in the Wilsonian era went under the name "self-determination of peoples," are a central issue of East European politics that threaten the stability of the region, and even the existence of two of the states. How are we to deal with the apparent incompatibility of our advocacy of self-determination (minority rights) and stable borders? At this point we do not know. But strategic studies alone will not provide a fully adequate answer, because the issues involved are cultural, religious, ethical, and emotional as well as strategic.

Michael Howard has put this point well in his recent book *The Lessons of History*. The real lessons of history, he says, are not so much about pride, folly, and stupidity, as about "people, often of masterful intelligence, trained usually in law of economics or perhaps political science who have led their governments into disastrous miscalculations because they have no awareness whatever of the historical background, the cultural universe of the foreign societies with which they have to deal. It is an awareness for which no amount of strategic or economic analysis, no techniques of crisis management or conflict resolution...can provide a substitute."[9] Professor Howard wrote those words in 1980, but they constitute an elegant way of saying that 1989 made a good case for soft-nosed analysis.

My fourth suggestion is closely connected with this third point. The events of the past two years have shown how important leadership is.[10] For a historian like myself, there is little question that we all operate within a historically determined and relatively limited range of creative possibilities. But 1989 has shown once again, if it needed showing, and apparently sometimes it does, how important and unpredictable is the ability of individual leaders to stretch that range. Whatever the final assessment will be on Gorbachev, whether he is the Alexander II of our day, beginning a reformer and ending a conservative, or the Kemal Ataturk who completely changes his nation's direction, there seems little doubt that his decision to let Eastern Europe go was original, unexpected (probably even by him), and difficult. If there was one thing we knew for certain about the Soviet relationship with Eastern Europe, it was that whatever else might happen, the Soviet Union would never relinquish its special relationship with the region. To have done so was not a socio-economic imperative or a structural necessity, although arguments in that vein are being made. The loss of Eastern Europe was the outcome of a policy conceived and introduced by a particular individual, representing a significant strain of Soviet thought, who saw, perhaps briefly, a possibility to revivify socialism while at the same time creating a constructive place in Europe for the Soviet Union that it had never had in the past. If we compare Gorbachev's rhetoric about autonomy of choice and his actions about arms reduction and withdrawal from

Afghanistan with what we reasonably might have expected from his Brezhnevian rival from 1985, Viktor Grishin, we can grasp the power and originality of Gorbachev's leadership.

And Gorbachev was not the only original leader of 1989. It was not written that a German Chancellor should have moved as single-mindedly as Helmut Kohl did toward unification, nor that he should have done so in such a relatively restrained and un-nationalistic way.

For the next few years I think leadership will be a key factor in determining whether the individual countries of Eastern Europe will be able to make rapid transitions in the aftermath of 1989. One of the striking differences between East Central Europe and Southeast Europe lies precisely in this sphere. Moderate men with great prestige now lead Poland and Czechoslovakia, and even in Hungary Jozsef Antall at least understands parliamentary democracy. Unlike many of the politically inexperienced members of their societies, both among the public and among elites, these men recognize the fragility of their current position, know that it takes time to create the institutions of interest representation, and understand that democracy is a politics of accommodation. This is true even of Lech Walesa. Despite the fears many Poles express about the possibilities of a Pilsudskian resolution in Poland, one of the basic characteristics of Walesa's career has been his ability to seek out solutions rather than confrontations. During the Solidarity period, he probably spent as much time advising the workers not to strike as in any other single activity.

In Southeast Europe, by contrast, we have at least one and probably more inward-looking and radically selfish leaders in Yugoslavia, a self-appointed and none too legitimate government in Romania, and a scramble that has not produced any clear leadership in Bulgaria. This contrast can only have a differential impact on the future development of these two regions. Unfortunately, we can only dream of the benefits for Yugoslavia if Serbia and Croatia had leaders of the stature of a Walesa or a Havel. Structural analysis is useful and important, particularly when it is turned to past events. But 1989 has reminded us that leaders can make original decisions and that they can shape forces. We hardly notice, however, because these decisions quickly enter the structure of our presuppositions, changing them radically but almost imperceptibly as we go along. The dramatic reversals in our perceptions of Soviet possibilities based on our assessment of Gorbachev's actions--in 1987 still skeptical, by the Congress of People's Deputies in 1989 enthusiastic, by the bloody intervention in Lithuania early 1991 gloomy, in mid-1991 after an apparent agreement with Yeltsin and the republics more optimistic, and so forth--illustrate the point.

I stress leadership because it goes against the grain of most current social science theorizing, but, in doing so, I do not want to give the impression that it was leadership alone that brought 1989 about, or that Gorbachev simply called a tune and the East Europeans jumped. Centralized planning failed, regimes lost their moral underpinnings, and Soviet policy changed, but unless internal developments in Poland and Hungary had created a strong independent society in the first case, and a strong communist reform faction in the second, Gorbachev's initiatives might have had far less effect. When we marvel at Poland and Hungary's primary role in getting the avalanche of 1989 started, we tend to forget that Honecker, Jakeš, Ceauşescu, and Zhivkov rejected *perestroika*. Had Jaruzelski turned out to be a Honecker, and Kádár a Husák, or, put another way, had the internal developments in Poland and Hungary been less pluralistic in the eighties, then 1989 would most likely not have been 1989 at all.

This point is linked with a much larger theme, the last one I want to raise. Many people understood the weaknesses of centrally planned systems very well. But the actual drama of 1989 was foreseen by no one. The final lesson of 1989 is to remind us of something that in an intellectual sense we already know: the near-term future is unpredictable. And yet laymen and specialists alike seem to harbor a touching hope that we will find just that knowledgeable person who can tell us what the future holds. Anyone who has given a public talk about Eastern Europe or the Soviet Union recently can attest that the first question posed after the talk is certain to be "What is going to happen next?" One of the things that sustains that hope, I think, is that historians find it possible to trace causal strings though past events. We feel that the same kind of linear logic should permit us to extrapolate events into the future. But linearality only works backwards. Forwards, we live in a non-linear world where surprises lurk. The historian's ability to trace causal strings is an illusion, a slight of hand granted us by the fact that we already know, in a certain sense at least, what happened.

The future, by contrast, is subject to what chaos theory calls the butterfly effect, which is the modern version of that old tale of how the empire was lost for want of a nail. Its point is simply that no matter how large the amount of data we accumulate about complex systems, there always exist uncertainties that radically transform outcomes.[11] Václav Havel has a more personal way of putting the point: "We never know when some inconspicuous spark of knowledge, struck within range of the few brain cells, as it were, specially adapted for the organism's self-awareness, may suddenly light up the road for the whole of society, without society ever realizing, perhaps, how it came to see the road."[12] 1989 has turned the post-World War II era from current events into history, so that we now can talk about post-war Eastern Europe with a confidence that we did not have in 1985, let alone 1975 or 1960. We know what happened. But we must resist the temptation of turning our new-found confidence that we understand 1989 into a new-found memory that we understood it, because that will only continue to sustain our already overdeveloped hunger to predict the unpredictable.

The basic lesson of 1989, then, is that the twentieth century is over, with both the anti-rationalist and the hyper-rationalist genres of solutions to the energy revolution having proven to be political, economic, and moral dead ends. This has not provided humanity with any magic solutions for the future, but it has lessened the likelihood that we will repeat the grossest of errors. Unfortunately, however, the East Europeans will probably not profit as much from their deliverance from hyper-rationalism in 1989 as western Europe did from its deliverance from anti-rationalism in 1945, although the goal of entering Europe does provide them with powerful positive incentives. Another strength that East Europeans bring to their efforts to find a pathway back to Europe is that their revolutions of 1989 were moral events as well as political and economic ones. Insufficiently accounted for in strategic assessments during the cold war period, moral and cultural factors will have to be taken into account to a greater extent in the post-communist era. The quality of leadership in individual countries also will be an important ingredient in the differential development that appears to be the destiny of East Central Europe and Southeast Europe. Finally, 1989 offers a trenchant reminder that human affairs remain non-linear. However persuasively we are able to trace the causes of events that have already happened, the only prediction about the future we can make with complete confidence is that surprises await us.

NOTES

[1]A modified version of this article appeared in *Problems of Communism*, 20: 5 (September-October 1991), pp. 17-24.

[2]Jeffrey Herf, *Reactionary Modernism: Technology, culture, and politics in Weimar and the Third Reich* (Cambridge, 1984), p. 2; Schelling quoted by Isaiah Berlin, "The Counter-Enlightenment," in: *Against the Current*, Henry Hardy, ed. (New York, 1982), p. 19.

[3]Renés Déscartes, "Discourse on the Method of Rightly Conducting the Reason," in Elizabeth S. Haldane and G. R. T. Ross, trans. and eds., *The Philosophical Works of Descartes* (1955), Vol. 1, p. 119; Mihaly Vaci, quoted by Ivan Berend, *The Hungarian Economic Reforms, 1953-1988* (Cambridge, 1990), p. 148.

[4]Robert G. Kaiser, *Why Gorbachev Happened: His Triumphs and His Failure* (New York, 1991), p. 228.

[5]Ralf Dahrendorf, *Reflections on the Revolution in Europe in a letter intended to have been sent to a gentleman in Warsaw* (New York, 1990), p. 27.

[6]See W.R. Connor, "Why Were We Surprised?" *The American Scholar* (Spring 1991), pp. 175-184.

[7]Václav Havel, *Living in Truth*, Jan Vladislav ed. (London, 1987), p. 31.

[8]Solidarity Program of 1981 in Gale Stokes, ed., *From Stalinism to Pluralism* (New York, 1991), p. 209; Timothy Garton Ash, *The Polish Revolution, Solidarity* (New York, 1984), p. 280.

[9]Michael Howard, *The Lessons of History* (New Haven, 1991). Quotation taken from Ronald H. Spector's review, *Washington Post*, March 3, 1991.

[10]See Stanley Hoffman, "The Case for Leadership," *Foreign Policy*, 81 (1990), pp. 20-38.

[11]See James Gleick, *Chaos: Making a New Science* (New York, 1987).

[12]Václav Havel, "Letter to Dr. Gustáv Husák," *Living in Truth*, pp. 21-22.

LIST OF CONTRIBUTORS

Catherine Albrecht is Assistant Professor of History at the University of Baltimore. She received her doctorate from Indiana University in 1986. Currently she is researching nineteenth century economic thought and policy in the Habsburg Empire.

Gerasimos Augustinos is Professor of History at the University of South Carolina where he teaches courses on the history of Central and Southeastern Europe and nationalism in the modern world and has published three books on those topics. He received his Ph.D. from Indiana in 1971.

Robert A. Berry is Associate Professor of History at Salisbury State University. His teaching and research interests include nineteenth century East European history as well as Russia and the Middle East. He completed his Ph.D. at Indiana in 1974.

James Ermatinger received his Ph.D. from Indiana in 1988 in Roman History. Currently Assistant Professor of History at the University of Nebraska at Kearney, he is working on a monograph about Diocletian's economic reforms.

Lawrence J. Flockerzie is Assistant Professor of European History at the University of Dayton. His research interests focus on small state diplomacy, with special interest on the period 1815-1848. He received his doctorate from Indiana in 1987.

Richard Frucht is Professor of History at Northwest Missouri State University. Most recently he directed the Public Education Project on Teaching Eastern Europe in the Secondary Schools for the American Association for the Advancement of Slavic Studies. He received his doctorate from Indiana in 1980.

Yeshayahu Jelinek received his Ph.D. from Indiana in 1966. Currently a Researcher at Ben-Gurion University of the Negev, Israel, he specializes in general and Jewish history of Central and Southeastern Europe, as well as modern and contemporary Jewish history.

Frederick Kellogg is Associate Professor of History at the University of Arizona. He is currently managing editor of the multidisciplinary journal *Southeastern Europe* and published *A History of Romanian Historical Writing* in 1990. He received his doctorate from Indiana in 1969.

Paul E. Michelson is Distinguished Professor of History at Huntington College. He completed his doctorate at Indiana in 1975. His wife, **Jean T. Michelson**, is a freelance consultant and writer. The Michelsons have worked and done research in Romania and elsewhere under the auspices of three Fulbright and two IREX grants in 1971-1973, 1982-1983, and 1989-1990.

William O. Oldson is Professor and Director of the M.A. Program in Historical Administration and Public History at Florida State University. His recent monograph, *A Providential Anti-Semitism: Nationalism and Polity in Nineteenth Century Romania* won the American Philosophical Society's distinguished book award in 1991. He completed his doctorate at Indiana in 1970.

Thomas Pesek is Associate Professor of History at Washington State University where he has taught since 1966. He received his Ph.D. from Indiana University in 1970.

Thomas Sakmyster received his Ph.D. from Indiana in 1971 and has taught since then at the University of Cincinnati where he is Professor of History. Currently he is working on a biography of Admiral Horthy. From 1986-1990 he was president of the American Association for the Study of Hungarian History.

Gale Stokes is Professor of History at Rice University. Among his numerous publications is *From Stalinism to Pluralism* published by Oxford University Press in 1991. The original version of his paper came from a talk to the Academic Advisory Committee of the East European Program of the Woodrow Wilson Center (chaired at that time by Charles Jelavich). He received his doctorate from Indiana in 1970.

Glenn E. Torrey was introduced to the study of Romania while a student of Charles Jelavich at the University of California. Since receiving his doctorate from the University of Oregon in 1960, he has taught at Emporia State University where he is Professor of History.

Teddy J. Uldricks is Professor of History and Director of the Master of Liberal Arts Program at the University of North Carolina at Asheville. The author of a number of works on Soviet Foreign Policy, he is currently writing a history of Soviet international relations which emphasizes the issues of image and perception. He received his Ph.D. from Indiana in 1971.

Peter Wozniak completed his doctorate at Indiana in 1987. Since then he has been Assistant Professor of Russian and East Central European History at Auburn University at Montgomery.

Edward D. Wynot, Jr. received his Ph.D. from Indiana in 1970. The author of numerous articles and books on modern Polish history, he is currently the editor of the *Encyclopedia of Modern East Europe*, a work currently in progress for Garland Publishing. He is Professor of History at Florida State University.

Other Books From Slavica

Ronelle Alexander: *The Structure of Vasko Popa's Poetry.*

American Contributions to the Tenth International Congress of Slavists, Sofia, September, 1988, Linguistics, ed. **Alexander M. Schenker.**

American Contributions to the Tenth International Congress of Slavists, Sofia, September, 1988, Literature, ed. **Jane Gary Harris.**

American Contributions to the Ninth International Congress of Slavists (Kiev 1983) Vol. 1: Linguistics, ed. **Michael S. Flier.**

American Contributions to the Ninth International Congress of Slavists, (Kiev 1983) Vol. 2: Literature, Poetics, History, ed. **P. Debreczeny.**

American Contributions to the Eighth International Congress of Slavists, Vol 1: Linguistics and Poetics, ed. **Henrik Birnbaum.**

American Contributions to the Eighth International Congress of Slavists Vol. 2: Literature, ed. **Victor Terras.**

Howard I. Aronson: *Georgian: A Reading Grammar.*

Natalya Baranskaya: *Неделя как неделя Just Another Week*, ed. *Lora Paperno, Natalie Roklina,* and *Richard Leed.*

Adele Marie Barker: *The Mother Syndrome in the Russian Folk Imagination.*

R. P. Bartlett, A. G. Cross, and **Karen Rasmussen,** eds.: *Russia and the World of the Eighteenth Century.*

John D. Basil: *The Mensheviks in the Revolution of 1917.*

Christina Y. Bethin: *Polish Syllables The Role of Prosody in Phonology and Morphology.*

Henrik Birnbaum & Thomas Eekman, eds.: *Fiction and Drama in Eastern and Southeastern Europe: Evolution and Experiment in the Postwar Period.*

Henrik Birnbaum and **Peter T. Merrill:** *Recent Advances in the Reconstruction of Common Slavic (1971-1982).*

Marianna D. Birnbaum: *Humanists in a Shattered World: Croatian and Hungarian Latinity in the Sixteenth Century.*

F. J. Bister and **Herbert Kuhner,** eds.: *Carinthian Slovenian Poetry.*

K. L. Black, ed.: *A Biobibliographical Handbook of Bulgarian Authors.*

Other Books From Slavica

Ralph Bogert: *The Writer as Naysayer Miroslav Krleža and the Aesthetic of Interwar Central Europe.*

Marianna Bogojavlensky: *Russian Review Grammar.*

Rodica C. Botoman, Donald E. Corbin, E. Garrison Walters: *Îmi Place Limba Română/A Romanian Reader.*

Ranko Bugarski and **Celia Hawkesworth**, eds.: *Language Planning in Yugoslavia.*

Diana L. Burgin: *Richard Burgin A Life in Verse.*

R. L. Busch: *Humor in the Major Novels of Dostoevsky.*

Terence R. Carlton: *Introduction to the Phonological History of the Slavic Languages.*

Jozef Cíger-Hronský: *Jozef Mak* (a novel), translated from Slovak.

Julian W. Connolly & Sonia I. Ketchian, eds.: *Studies in Honor of Vsevolod Setchkarev.*

Andrew R. Corin: *The New York Missal: A Paleographic and Phonetic Analysis.*

Gary Cox: *Tyrant and Victim in Dostoevsky.*

Anna Lisa Crone and **Catherine V. Chvany**, eds.: *New Studies in Russian Language and Literature.*

Carolina De Maegd-Soëp: *Chekhov and Women: Women in the Life and Work of Chekhov.*

Dorothy Disterheft: *The Syntactic Development of the Infinitive in Indo-European.*

Per Durst-Andersen: *Mental Grammar Russian Aspect and Related Issues.*

Thomas Eekman and **Dean S. Worth**, eds.: *Russian Poetics.*

M. S. Flier and **R. D. Brecht**, eds.: *Issues in Russian Morphosyntax.*

John M. Foley, ed.: *Oral Traditional Literature A Festschrift for Albert Bates Lord.*

John Miles Foley, ed.: *Comparative Research on Oral Traditions: A Memorial for Milman Parry.*

Other Books From Slavica

Zbigniew Gołąb: ***The Origin of the Slavs A Linguist's View.***

Diana Greene: ***Insidious Intent: An Interpretation of Fedor Sologub's*** **The Petty Demon.**

Charles E. Gribble, ed.: ***Medieval Slavic Texts, Vol. 1, Old and Middle Russian Texts.***

Charles E. Gribble: ***Reading Bulgarian Through Russian.***

Charles E. Gribble: ***Russian Root List with a Sketch of Word Formation.***

Charles E. Gribble: ***A Short Dictionary of 18th-Century Russian/ Словарик Русского Языка 18-го Века.***

Charles E. Gribble, ed.: ***Studies Presented to Professor Roman Jakobson by His Students.***

Morris Halle, ed.: ***Roman Jakobson: What He Taught Us.***

Morris Halle, Krystyna Pomorska, Elena Semeka-Pankratov, and **Boris Uspenskij**, eds.: ***Semiotics and the History of Culture In Honor of Jurij Lotman Studies in Russian.***

Charles J. Halperin: ***The Tatar Yoke.***

William S. Hamilton: ***Introduction to Russian Phonology and Word Structure.***

Michael Heim: ***Contemporary Czech.***

Michael Heim, Z. Meyerstein, and **Dean Worth:** ***Readings in Czech.***

Warren H. Held, Jr., William R. Schmalstieg, and **Janet E. Gertz:** ***Beginning Hittite.***

Peter Hill: ***The Dialect of Gorno Kalenik.***

M. Hubenova & others: ***A Course in Modern Bulgarian.***

Martin E. Huld: ***Basic Albanian Etymologies.***

Charles Isenberg: ***Substantial Proofs of Being: Osip Mandelstam's Literary Prose.***

Roman Jakobson: ***Brain and Language***

L. A. Johnson: ***The Experience of Time in*** **Crime and Punishment.**

Other Books From Slavica

S. J. Kirschbaum, ed.: *East European History (Selected Papers from the Third World Congress for Soviet and East European Studies).*

Emily R. Klenin: *Animacy in Russian: A New Interpretation.*

Andrej Kodjak, Krystyna Pomorska, and **Kiril Taranovsky**, eds.: *Alexander Puškin Symposium II.*

Andrej Kodjak, Krystyna Pomorska, Stephen Rudy, eds.: *Myth in Literature.*

Andrej Kodjak, Michael J. Connolly, Krystyna Pomorska, eds.: *Structural Analysis of Narrative Texts.*

Mark Kulikowski: *A Bibliography of Slavic Mythology.*

Konstantin Kustanovich: *The Artist and the Tyrant: Vassily Aksenov's Works in the Brezhnev Era.*

Ronald D. LeBlanc: *The Russianization of Gil Blas: A Study in Literary Appropriation.*

Richard L. Leed, Alexander D. Nakhimovsky, and **Alice S. Nakhimovsky:** *Beginning Russian, Second Revised Edition.*

Richard L. Leed and **Slava Paperno:** *5000 Russian Words With All Their Inflected Forms: A Russian-English Dictionary.*

Edgar H. Lehrman: A *Handbook to Eighty-Six of Chekhov's Stories in Russian.*

Lauren Leighton, ed.: *Studies in Honor of Xenia Gąsiorowska.*

Gail Lenhoff: *The Martyred Princes Boris and Gleb: A Social-Cultural Study of the Cult and the Texts.*

Jules F. Levin and **Peter D. Haikalis**, with **Anatole A. Forostenko:** *Reading Modern Russian.*

Maurice I. Levin: *Russian Declension and Conjugation: A Structural Description with Exercises.*

Alexander Lipson: *A Russian Course.*

Yvonne R. Lockwood: *Text and Context Folksong in a Bosnian Muslim Village.*

Sophia Lubensky and **Donald K. Jarvis**, eds.: *Teaching, Learning, Acquiring Russian.*

Other Books From Slavica

Horace G. Lunt: *Fundamentals of Russian.*

Paul Macura: *Russian-English Botanical Dictionary.*

Robert Mann: *Lances Sing: A Study of the Igor Tale.*

Stephen Marder: *A Supplementary Russian-English Dictionary.*

V. Markov and **D. S. Worth**, eds.: *From Los Angeles to Kiev Papers on the Occasion of the Ninth International Congress of Slavists.*

Cynthia L. Martin, Joanna Robin, and **Donald K. Jarvis:** *The Russian Desk: A Listening and Conversation Course.*

Mateja Matejić and **Dragan Milivojević**: *An Anthology of Medieval Serbian Literature in English.*

Peter J. Mayo: *The Morphology of Aspect in Seventeenth-Century Russian (Based on Texts of the Smutnoe Vremja).*

Arnold McMillin, ed.: *Aspects of Modern Russian and Czech Literature (Selected Papers from the Third World Congress for Soviet and East European Studies).*

Gordon M. Messing: *A Glossary of Greek Romany As Spoken in Agia Varvara (Athens).*

Vasa D. Mihailovich and **Mateja Matejic**: *A Comprehensive Bibliography of Yugoslav Literature in English, 1593-1980.*

Vasa D. Mihailovich: *First Supplement to* A Comprehensive Bibliography of Yugoslav Literature in English *1981-1985.*

Vasa D. Mihailovich: *Second Supplement to* A Comprehensive Bibliography of Yugoslav Literature in English *1981-1985.*

Dragan Milivojević and **Vasa D. Mihailovich**: *A Bibliography of Yugoslav Linguistics in English 1900-1980.*

Edward Możejko, ed.: *Vasiliy Pavlovich Aksënov: A Writer in Quest of Himself.*

Edward Możejko: *Yordan Yovkov.*

Alexander D. Nakhimovsky and Richard L. Leed: *Advanced Russian, Second Edition, Revised.*

T. Pachmuss: *Russian Literature in the Baltic between the World Wars.*

Other Books From Slavica

Lora Paperno: *Getting Around Town in Russian: Situational Dialogs*, English translation and photographs by **Richard D. Sylvester.**

Slava Paperno, Alexander D. Nakhimovsky, Alice S. Nakhimovsky, and **Richard L. Leed:** *Intermediate Russian: The Twelve Chairs.*

Ruth L. Pearce: *Russian For Expository Prose.*

Jan L. Perkowski: *The Darkling A Treatise on Slavic Vampirism.*

Gerald Pirog: *Aleksandr Blok's Итальянские Стихи Confrontation and Disillusionment.*

Leonard A. Polakiewicz: *Supplemental Materials for First Year Polish.*

Stanley J. Rabinowitz: *Sologub's Literary Children: Keys to a Symbolist's Prose.*

Gilbert C. Rappaport: *Grammatical Function and Syntactic Structure: The Adverbial Participle of Russian.*

David F. Robinson: *Lithuanian Reverse Dictionary.*

Don Karl Rowney, ed.: *Imperial Power and Development: Papers on Pre-Revolutionary Russian History (Selected Papers from the Third World Congress for Soviet and East European Studies).*

Don K. Rowney & G. Edward Orchard, eds.: *Russian and Slavic History.*

Catherine Rudin: *Aspects of Bulgarian Syntax: Complementizers and WH Constructions.*

Norma L. Rudinsky: *Incipient Feminists: Women Writers in the Slovak National Revival.*

Barry P. Scherr and **Dean S. Worth,** eds.: *Russian Verse Theory.*

William R. Schmalstieg: *Introduction to Old Church Slavic.*

P. Seyffert: *Soviet Literary Structuralism: Background Debate Issues.*

Kot K. Shangriladze and **Erica W. Townsend,** eds: *Papers for the V. Congress of Southeast European Studies (Belgrade, September 1984).*

J. Thomas Shaw: *Pushkin A Concordance to the Poetry.*

Efraim Sicher: *Style and Structure in the Prose of Isaak Babel'.*

Rimvydas Šilbajoris: *Tolstoy's Aesthetics and His Art.*

Other Books From Slavica

M. S. Simpson: *The Russian Gothic Novel and its British Antecedents.*

Theofanis G. Stavrou and **Peter R. Weisensel:** *Russian Travelers to the Christian East from the Twelfth to the Twentieth Century.*

G. Stone and **D. S. Worth**, eds.: *The Formation of the Slavonic Literary Languages, Proceedings of a Conference Held in Memory of Robert Auty and Anne Pennington at Oxford 6-11 July 1981.*

John W. Strong, ed.: *Essays on Revolutionary Culture and Stalinism (Selected Papers from the Third World Congress for Soviet and East European Studies).*

Roland Sussex and **J. C. Eade**, eds.: *Culture and Nationalism in Nineteenth-Century Eastern Europe.*

Oscar E. Swan and **Sylvia Gálová-Lorinc:** *Beginning Slovak.*

Oscar E. Swan: *First Year Polish.*

Oscar E. Swan: *Intermediate Polish.*

Jane A. Taubman: *A Life Through Poetry Marina Tsvetaeva's Lyric Diary.*

Charles E. Townsend: *Continuing With Russian.*

Charles E. Townsend: *Czech Through Russian.*

Charles E. Townsend: *A Description of Spoken Prague Czech.*

Charles E. Townsend: *The Memoirs of Princess N. B. Dolgorukaja.*

Charles E. Townsend: *Russian Word Formation.*

Janet G. Tucker: *Innokentij Annenskij and the Acmeist Doctrine.*

Essays in Honor of A. A. Zimin, ed. **D. C. Waugh**.

Daniel C. Waugh: *The Great Turkes Defiance On the History of the Apocryphal Correspondence of the Ottoman Sultan in its Muscovite and Russian Variants.*

James B. Woodward: *The Symbolic Art of Gogol: Essays on His Short Fiction.*

Yordan Yovkov: *The Inn at Antimovo* and *Legends of Stara Planina*, translated from Bulgarian by John Burnip.